P9-EMG-721

The History of

Orchestration

by

Adam Carse

DOVER PUBLICATIONS, INC., NEW YORK

781.632
C23h

LIBRARY
ATLANTIC CHRISTIAN COLLEGE
WILSON, N. C.

Published in the United Kingdom by Constable and Company, Limited, 10 Orange Street, London W. C. 2.

This Dover edition, first published in 1964, is an unabridged and corrected republication of the work first published by Kegan Paul, Trench, Trubner and Company, Limited, in 1925.

This edition is published by special arrangement with Routledge, Kegan Paul, Limited.

The publisher wishes to thank the Public Library of the City of Westminster, England, for supplying a copy of this book for reproduction purposes.

International Standard Book Number: 0-486-21258-0

Library of Congress Catalog Card Number: 64-17314

Manufactured in the United States of America

Dover Publications, Inc.
180 Varick Street
New York 14, N. Y.

LIBRARY
ATLANTIC CHRISTIAN COLLEGE
WILSON, N. C.

DEDICATED TO
SIR DAN GODFREY
WHO, BY LETTING THEM HEAR THEIR
ORCHESTRAL WORKS PERFORMED, HAS
GIVEN TO SO MANY BRITISH COMPOSERS
THEIR MOST VALUABLE LESSONS IN
ORCHESTRATION

81- 552

PREFACE

No independent investigation has been made for the purposes of this volume of dates and matters concerning general musical history ; the statements of standard histories and dictionaries of music have been accepted.

For orchestration, purely as such, *only the evidence of the actual full scores has been accepted.* Every care has been taken that the scores consulted should show their orchestration as the composers left it. With this object in view, first editions, contemporary prints, and MSS. have been consulted in preference to reprints. For historical purposes, modern performing editions, arrangements or adaptations of seventeenth and eighteenth century music are obviously useless. Historical reprints, such as the *Denkmäler der Tonkunst* series, those of the *Gesellschaft für Musikforschung* and sundry reprints or quotations in the historical works of such as Goldschmidt, von Winterfeld, Eitner, Röchlitz, Schering, and other German historians have been found to be reliable and historically accurate. The experience of the author has been that, on the whole, the conscientious German historian quotes faithfully. No one would make such elementary blunders as to mistake additional parts to Handel's scores by Mozart for Handel's orchestration, nor in similar cases of Bach-Franz or Gluck-Wagner is there any likelihood that even the most unsophisticated investigator would be misled. But many more carefully concealed pitfalls await the unwary historian who would get at orchestral music as it was really written and played in the seventeenth, and in the first-half of the eighteenth century. From the time of Haydn and Mozart onwards there is no such difficulty.

The particulars relating to musical instruments appearing in these pages have been gleaned at first hand from sources which cannot but be considered reliable. The works of Virdung, Prætorius, and Mersennus in the sixteenth and seventeenth centuries, similar works by Mattheson and Majer in the first half of the eighteenth century, followed by the early text books on orchestration appearing shortly before the close of the eighteenth century, and leading up to Berlioz's well-known work in the nineteenth century, have provided much useful information about instruments such as were used when those books were written. This has been amplified and confirmed by the information given in the instruction books or tutors which began to appear towards the close of the seventeenth century, and which were greatly increased in number and scope during the course of the eighteenth century. Further sources of information concerning instruments have been the earlier musical dictionaries— Walther, Grassineau and Gerber in the eighteenth century, Koch, Busby and Gassner in the early nineteenth century. Finally, collections of old instruments, permanent or otherwise, at Brussels, Paris, Munich, Vienna, London, and other places, together with the various descriptive catalogues appertaining to these collections, have also yielded particulars about old orchestral instruments without which the evolution of orchestration could only have been imperfectly collated. From the pages of various books by such as Mattheson, Quantz, Rousseau, Cramer, Dörfell, Burney, Forkel, Marpurg, and Hanslick have been culled particulars as to the constitution and personnel of orchestras in the past, and from the autobiographies of such as Dittersdorf, Spohr, and Berlioz, interesting facts relating to the conditions under which orchestral music and playing have been cultivated.

Any attempt to supply anything approaching an adequate number of quotations from full scores for the whole period of this survey would obviously prove impracticable and, moreover, would have been unnecessary now that a great abundance of the scores of Bach, Handel, Haydn, all the nineteenth century classical, and many modern, composers are available in miniature form. The examples, therefore, have been confined to excerpts from seventeenth century, and some eighteenth century, scores which are either unprocurable or only accessible with difficulty or inconvenience.

ADAM CARSE.

Winchester.

CONTENTS

LIST OF ILLUSTRATIONS

Also fifty-three musical examples.

INTRODUCTION

THE story of the orchestra and of orchestration may be said to begin when, modal vocal polyphony having reached its culmination in the sixteenth century, educated musicians began to turn their attention to the composition of music designed specifically for stringed, wind, and keyboard instruments in combination, and in particular to the embryonic forms of opera, oratoria, and ballet, which, accompanied by primitive and unorganized orchestras, then began to take shape and to absorb much of the energy which musicians had hitherto expended almost exclusively on the composition of ecclesiastical and secular vocal music—the Mass, Motet, and Madrigal.

The birth of the orchestra is thus connascent with the creation of secular instrumental music as a cultured form of the art, and largely arises out of the transition from modal polyphony to monody. It coincides with the inception of purely instrumental music for bowed string instruments, of dramatic music, and with the beginning of the gradual obsolescence of the viol type rendered inevitable by the greater suitability and practical superiority of the newly invented violins ; also with the beginning of the gradual rejection of plucked string instruments as a medium for the expression of serious music.

The evolution divides itself broadly into two periods, the first ending soon after the middle of the eighteenth century with the death of the two great masters of harmonic polyphony, Bach and Handel ; the second beginning with the rise of modern orchestration in the hands of Haydn and Mozart. The transition is chronologically spanned by the work of Gluck and a group of secondary composers of which perhaps the best remembered are Philipp Emanuel Bach and Hasse.

Intimately and inseparably connected with the history of orchestration are : progress in the art and technique of musical composition ; improvements in the construction of musical instruments, both of which are again associated with the growth of instrumental technique.

Influences not without considerable effect on the subject are those arising out of the circumstances and conditions under which composers carried on their work, also the positions occupied socially and geographically by the men who made musical history. One may instance for example, the small public reached by Bach's music during his lifetime and for long after his death ; the comparative isolation and limited influence of Purcell ; the obscurity of Schubert's life ; or more favourable conditions such as the position and opportunities of Lulli at the court of Louis XIV of France ; the cosmopolitan activities of Handel ; the advantages enjoyed by Haydn as an orchestral composer under princely patronage ; or the quick diffusion of his orchestral music by the socially gifted and much-travelled Mendelssohn.

Other influences are those arising from the political and national histories of European countries and dynasties during the last three centuries ; commercial conditions in so far as they concern the music-printing and publishing trade, and the manufacture of musical instruments ; also from the enterprise of operatic, dramatic, and concert-giving institutions. The tastes and tendencies of society and public in various countries at various times, the patronage of musical art by royalty, nobility, or wealth, and the different systems of musical education which have been in vogue ; all those have reacted directly on general musical history, and not indirectly on the evolution of orchestration.

Rapid and easy communication between countries, and facilities for the quick diffusion of orchestral music by means of printed scores and parts are conditions which did not prevail during the seventeenth and eighteenth centuries ; thus, progress made even by prominent composers in one country did not necessarily spread to other musical centres with the same rapidity as at present, or during the nineteenth century. Indeed, considering the comparative isolation of some composers, and the fact that much of their music remained in manuscript during their lifetimes, the wonder is that progress was so general as it proved to be. Little if any of Bach's, Mozart's or Schubert's orchestral music was published while they lived ; both Bach and Schubert remained to be practically rediscovered by later generations, while others wrote in and for one country, in some cases forming musical backwaters which could not communicate any considerable impetus to the main stream of general progress.

The same applies to orchestral, and in particular to wind instruments and the improvements to their mechanism which have transformed them from crude signals of the chase, the field, or the fair, to the highly organized artistic media of the modern concert-room or theatre. Thus, the clarinet, " invented " *circa* 1690, does not appear as a regular constituent of the orchestra till quite a hundred years later ; trombones, known and used long before orchestration can be said to have begun, do not permanently join the orchestral body till the nineteenth century ; and valves as applied to brass instruments, from their inception early in the same century took quite fifty years to come into anything approaching general use.

The diffusion of orchestral music before the nineteenth century depended largely on the circulation of manuscript copies of scores and parts, or the personal travels of composers carrying with them their manuscripts. A visit to a particular musical centre would result in the composition of some work written and orchestrated to suit the resources of a particular theatre or concert-orchestra ; thus, Mozart wrote " Prague " and " Paris " symphonies, Masses for Salzburg, operas for Milan, Munich, Prague, and Vienna ; similarly, Haydn wrote a large number of works for the orchestra maintained by his employer, Prince Esterházy, six symphonies for Paris, and twelve for London. Lengthy residence in one locality produced works designed for the orchestral combination to which the composer had access ; Lulli and Bach wrote each for their own resources respectively at Paris and Leipzig ; Handel for the opera at Hamburg, Hannover, for Italy or England according to where he settled for the time being ; Gluck wrote for Vienna or Paris, and so on. Parts are even occasionally added to or deleted from scores when a work was transferred from one centre to another where the orchestra differed in constitution. Further, there is abundant evidence that composers often adapted their orchestration to suit even individual players, and would contrive an exceptional part for a conspicuously good player, and allot insignificant matter to inferior players, or would write no part at all for instruments which in particular orchestras were not available or their players incompetent.

All these conditions unite in producing a more or less unstable selection of instruments in the scores of composers who wrote before the time when increased facilities for the wider circulation of orchestral music caused them to orchestrate for the musical world generally, and to score their works for standard combinations of instruments which they could rely on finding at all centres where orchestral music was seriously cultivated. The change takes place about the close of the eighteenth century, before which time composers vary their orchestration to suit particular orchestras, and after which orchestras, when varying at all, are adjusted to suit particular scores.

Easier communication between countries, increased production and circulation of printed scores and parts, the establishment of more numerous and larger orchestras, and changing conditions which encouraged a more free exchange of music, caused during the nineteenth century a gradual decentralization and more rapid spread of influences which make for progress, till, as at the present time, the effect of one successful composer's work may easily make a universal impression in the course of a few years. The innovation of one man now quickly becomes the common property of all, the only essential being that his work should be generally accepted and admired. As soon as Wagner's music became popular his orchestration coloured the work of all but the very conservative, while Berlioz, whose work has never had more than sporadic success, for all his innovations, progressiveness, and specialization in orchestral effect, has exerted little real influence on the art. A single effect can now exercise a world-wide influence in a few years ; it may have to wait on public taste for success, but once having achieved popularity it soon becomes absorbed into the current orchestral language of all composers, whether they are in sympathy with the style of music in which the effect had its origin or not.

For convenience and clearness a survey of progress in orchestration must be divided into periods which, however, should not be conceived as showing clearly defined demarcation of time, nor do they admit of rigid classification. The evolution is always gradual, albeit uneven, but nevertheless continuous and generally progressive.

Going hand in hand, it is impossible to completely separate orchestration *per se* from the advance of musical art, the technique of composition, the mechanical development of orchestral instruments, or the concurrent growth of instrumental technique ; but as far as is possible, the matter will be treated more as concomitant with instrumental technique and construction than with the more generally familiar history of the art and technique of musical composition, and with a leaning to the practical rather than to the æsthetic point of view.

A broad division into two periods has already been made, the first starting with the appearance of the violin type and witnessing the gradual formation of the string orchestra which, well established by the end of the seventeenth century, has remained unaltered ever since.

Conterminous with the first period is the use of keyboard-instruments and lutes in the orchestra in order to supply harmony, and played from the figured-bass part which is found in all scores of the period. This feature is so universal and characteristic of all orchestral writing from the early attempts near the end of the sixteenth century till the advent of Haydn and Mozart that it might appropriately be labelled " the period of *basso-continuo* ". The use and selection of wind-instruments during this period lacks organization, stability, and good balance, and remains unsettled till near the middle of the eighteenth century, when the beginning of what eventually developed into the so-called " classical " orchestra of Haydn and Mozart is seen to be in process of crystallization.

The first period covers the transition from modal polyphony to monody, and culminates in the harmonic polyphony of Bach and Handel ; it sees the creation and establishment of opera and oratorio, the instrumental suite, and other forms ambiguously called overture, symphony, and concerto, and precedes the classical sonata-form, symphony, and solo-concerto. The *aria* with *da capo* is a child of this constructive period which in its early stages also witnesses the popularity of masques, ballets and *intermezzi*. The growth of the string orchestra of violin type hastens the devitalization of music for plucked string instruments —the lute, theorbo, and many kindred varieties—it seals the doom of tablature notation, frets on the fingerboards of bowed string instruments, the five or six-stringed tuning of viols in fourths and a third, and only allows the occasional use of sympathetically stringed instruments such as the *viola d'amore*. This period sees the triumph of the transverse flute over the *flûte-à-bec*, recorder, and flageolet ; the transformation from shawm and *bombard* to oboe and bassoon ; the disappearance of the old wooden *cornetti* and the elevation of the Hunting-horn into the orchestral horn.

The second period is marked by the expulsion from the orchestra of the *basso-continuo* played on a keyboard-instrument. This leaves to the string orchestra the responsibility of supplying the main harmonic structure, of which it had been fully capable for at least three-quarters of a century, and if it deprives the orchestra of one broad change of colour, does away with an incongruity of blend. At the same time an organized and better balanced wood-wind section becomes established, consisting of pairs of flutes, oboes, clarinets, and bassoons, clarinets being the last comers. Melodically and harmonically independent of one another, these two main groups form a two-part body with an additional group of horns, trumpets, and drums, which, however, owing to the imperfections of the instruments are unable to supply independent harmony or melody, and this is the improved but hardly fully-grown orchestra which Haydn and Mozart hand over to their great successor, Beethoven.

The early years of the nineteenth century see an increase in the number of horns and the occasional use of trombones—long in common use for Church music— in symphonic scores, but the most pregnant change which the orchestra is yet to undergo is the result of the invention and application of lengthening-valves to horns and trumpets during the first half of the century, which with the growing use of trombones, transforms the orchestra into a three-part body of string, wood-wind and brass, each group harmonically and melodically independent, self-contained, chromatic in nature, and with the drums constituting the ordinary full orchestra of to-day.

A steady increase in the number of players to each string part disturbs to some extent the accepted principles of balance between the three groups, and from the early days of Wagner and Berlioz, there is an increasing tendency to add wind instruments of allied nature differing principally in dimensions to the already established wind groups, but except for the introduction of bass-tuba and harps, the orchestra of late Beethoven and Weber remains the nucleus of all modern combinations, and has sufficed as a medium of expression for most of the finest conceptions in orchestral language by the great writers of the late nineteenth century.

The greater appreciation of the use of tone-colour, of blend, and of dramatic fitness, is a feature of orchestration which developed and expanded rapidly from the time of Weber onwards, leaving the formality and traditional stiffness of Haydn's, Mozart's and Beethoven's orchestral manner far behind, but which as yet has not rendered the orchestration of those masters too out-of-date and old-fashioned in feeling to give pleasure and satisfaction to present-day audiences.

This second broad division in the evolution of orchestration accompanies the development of musical art through the periods usually dubbed " classical ", " romantic ", and " modern " ; it covers two reforms of opera inaugurated by Gluck and Wagner, the creation and higher development of modern symphony, solo-concerto and concert-overture, the inception of symphonic-poem and programme-music generally, and still follows the art into its present-day ramifications—" atmospheric ", " futuristic ", and what not.

However much the growth of the orchestra has been the toy of circumstances, conditions, or the mechanical or technical development of instruments, the real driving force behind such evolution is after all the insistently growing demand of musical art for fit means of expression. The impelling power of a constantly advancing art has always carried with it the realization of better and more worthy means of expressing itself, and with the demand, the man, the instrument, and the opportunity have always been forthcoming.

CHAPTER I

THE lute and its larger kin, the theorbo and archlute or *chitarrone*, share with the harpsichord, spinet, or organ, the distinction of having served as the backbone of such rudimentary orchestras as were used to accompany the vocal parts of the earliest opera and oratorio dating from the year 1600. It was at that time and for those instruments that the figured-bass part or *basso-continuo* was devised ; and although no specific " parts " for the instruments appear in the scores, there is abundant evidence to show that those chordal and keyboard instruments, playing either together or alternately, supplied a continuous harmonic background for orchestral music, even long after the string orchestra was sufficiently well organized to have undertaken that fundamental duty unassisted. During the greater part of the seventeenth century, *recitative* and vocal solos were provided with no more written accompaniment than a bare bass part on which chords were superimposed by the instrumental players according to the figuring. The system died hard, and, as is well known, lingered even throughout the period of Haydn and Mozart for the accompaniment of *recitative* in sacred or secular dramatic music, though by that time the lutes had become obsolescent, leaving their functions entirely to keyboard-instruments.

It is to that core of merely chordal harmony that a group of bowed string instruments and pairs of wind instruments attached themselves, ever growing in number and volume of tone, till eventually the core itself became superfluous and was discarded as an unnecessary and incongruous appendage.

The principal interest of seventeenth century orchestral instruments, however, centres around the bowed string groups, the viol and violin types which together formed the first string orchestras, and before the end of the century had settled down into a group entirely of violin type, the four-part body of first violins, second violins, tenor violins, and basses, the orchestral string " quartet " employed by Scarlatti, Purcell, Bach, Handel and all their successors.

Viols, the dominating bowed string instruments of the sixteenth century, were made in three main sizes : the treble or discant, the tenor or *viola da braccio* (arm-viol), and the bass or *viola da gamba* (leg-viol), roughly corresponding in size to the ordinary violin, tenor or viola, and violoncello as we know them now. A fourth variety of sixteen-ft. tone, the double-bass or contra-basso, at one time known in Italy as the *violone*, did not undergo complete metamorphosis from viol to violin, and retains to this day some of the principal characteristics of the viol type. Other varieties appeared from time to time, differing in size, tuning, number of strings, and shape, but have never joined the standard string orchestra as permanent members. Amongst these are the viols, which, in addition to the strings played on by the bow, were provided with a set of metal strings passing under the bridge and the finger-board close to the belly, tuned so as to vibrate in sympathy with the gut strungs above the fingerboard ; the *viola d'amore* and *viola bastarda* were respectively tenor and bass instruments of this variety, which also figure under various names such as *barytone* or *viola di bordone*. The *lira grande* and *lira doppia* appear to have been many-stringed varieties of bass-viol which were required to join the lutes and keyboard-instruments in the *basso-continuo* of the earliest opera and oratorio.

The main and essential differences between viol and violin types are : the flat back of the viols as against the moulded or rounded back of the violins which rises towards the centre line and sinks towards the edges where the back joins the ribs : the deeper ribs of the viol : its sloping " shoulders " and less pronounced " corners " : viols were strung with five, six, or more strings tuned according to the lute system in fourths and thirds, but at the time when violins appeared on the scene to challenge their supremacy had settled down to a more or less standardized arrangement of six strings tuned in fourths, but with a third between the two middle strings. The sound-holes of viols,

EXAMPLE 1

infinite in variety but latterly of C shape, differ from the *f* holes of violins, and other differences include the internal strengthening and the non-essential frets on the finger-board which were common to lutes, guitars, and kindred instruments, and were frequent but not invariable in the viol family.   These constructional differences result in a tone which on the viols is described

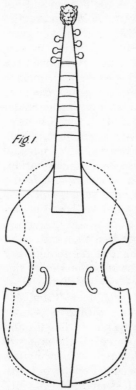

Fig. 1

Outlines of Viol and
Violin types.
Violin in broken line.

as being veiled and nasal but penetrating, and on the violins is fuller, rounder, and brighter.   Charles II preferred a band of violins because they were " more airie and brisk than viols ", and Thomas Mace, an eminent English lute player, writing in 1676[1], refers to " scolding " violins, and recommends that when they are added to a " consort " of viols, a pair of theorbos should be provided as well, so that the violins " may not out-cry the rest of the musick ".

While it will probably never be determined when and by whom the first violin was made[2], and though the word " violin " as distinguished from " viol " occurs before the middle of the sixteenth century, the second half of that century marks the advent of the period during which violins gradually supplanted viols in the orchestra, a process lasting altogether well over a century. Before the year 1600, the notable makers of Brescian and Cremonese schools, Gaspar da Salò and Andrea Amati, had made true violins, tenors, and violoncellos, also double-basses, examples of which are still in existence, and practically established the form of these instruments for all time.   Thus, before Peri, Cavalieri, and Monteverde had made their first rudimentary

[1] *Musick's Monument,* p. 246.

[2] Several historians affirm that Gaspar Duiffopruggar (variously given as Dieffoprukhar, or in German Tieffenbrücker) was the first to make violins at Bologna as early as 1511.

experiments in orchestration, instruments for a complete and well-balanced string orchestra were available, but had to wait nearly a hundred years for proper organization and worthy handling.

The years 1550 to 1750 roughly cover the golden age of violin making and the working lives of that chain of great makers, Gaspar da Salò, Amati, Stradivarius, Guarnerius, and many others who made violins, violas, violoncellos, and double-basses which have never been surpassed in quality, and surrounded the craft with that atmosphere of romance, mystery, and almost worship which clings to what people love to believe is a " lost secret ".

About the end of the eighteenth century advancing technique caused players to have the necks of old violins slightly lengthened, and a higher bridge demanded that the finger-board should be raised. Otherwise the instruments were perfected before the manner of playing on them had progressed beyond the type of part which might almost equally well have been sung, and had none of the characteristics of true violin music based on a four-stringed tuning in perfect fifths over an arched bridge. The double-bass, though subject to much variety of tuning and some vacillation as to numbers of strings[1], has on the whole retained the viol system of tuning in fourths, and has gained some practical benefit in handling by improved peg-mechanism[2].

While the instruments were brought to perfection within such a short space of time, the bow of the sixteenth century was comparatively primitive and clumsy. Short, heavy, inelastic, and without proper mechanism for adjusting the tension of the hair, the bow passes from a form which clearly betrays its origin, through successive stages of improvement to its present state in the time of the great French master Tourte, at the end of the eighteenth century.

It should not be imagined that the production of a practically perfect group of violins before the end of the sixteenth century meant the immediate wholesale adoption of these instruments for orchestral purposes in place of viols. Composers at that time had not yet realized that string-tone was to furnish the foundation

---

[1] Seventeenth century double-basses were provided with five or six strings. Praetorius mentions both. They were still used in the middle of the eighteenth century (Quantz, 1752).

[2] The invention of the metal peg-mechanism has been attributed to Carl Ludwig Bachmann, of Berlin, in 1778 (Gerber, *Lexikon*, 1790).

tone of the orchestra. Early seventeenth century scores rarely specify the instruments for which they were written, and though there can be little doubt that many of the scraps of instrumental part-writing in early operas and oratorios were intended for bowed string instruments, the names of instruments do not appear at the beginning of each part as they do in eighteenth and nineteenth century full scores. For at least half a century from the year 1600 the single *basso-continuo* staff was the slender thread on which were strung such instrumental parts as the composers considered it necessary to write out in score. In a few cases sundry instruments were named in the ample introductory letterpress which prefaces these rudimentary scores, but the instrumental parts of the few scored *sinfonie* and *ritornelli* were left bare of any indication as to which instruments were to play the parts. This may have been quite satisfactory under the conditions prevailing at the time, but is vague and disconcerting to the historian of three hundred years later, when tradition or usage are either hopelessly lost, or the means of reconstructing them difficult and scattered. Such few indications as there are, confirmed by occasional directions in the prefaces and the nature of the parts themselves, show that the treble violin asserted its superiority over the discant viol for the two highest string parts very soon after the new instrument came into being. In France the treble violin was readily adopted, and this probably accounts for the naming of the *duoi violini piccoli alla Francese* in the score of Monteverde's famous opera *Orfeo* (1607).

It is difficult to determine at what period the tenor violin took the place of the tenor or " mean " viol in the orchestra ; and that there was much uniformity in the constitution of orchestras is unlikely at a time when composers obviously scored their works for the varied resources of particular churches or theatres. The two upper parts of the string group in early scores are sometimes headed *violini*, but the tenor parts, though almost invariably written with C clefs, are seldom specified. Even the actual occurrence of the word " Viola " makes no clear distinction between viol and violin type, as the Italian "*viola*" is the generic term which covers the whole family of viols of whatever size.

The bass parts for string instruments in scores up to the last quarter of the seventeenth century are equally indefinite. The one universal figured bass part, the Italian *basso-continuo*, French *basse-continue*, or German *generalbass*, does duty for the lowest part of the harmony played on keyboard-instruments, lutes, bass viols or violins of low pitch. The word *violone* occurs in a few scores, but the large violins, violoncello, or *contrabasso*, are not named till the time of Scarlatti and Purcell, when the violoncello is frequently specified. The words " tener violin " also occur in Purcell's scores, and there is little doubt that the string orchestra was by that time composed entirely of instruments of violin type. That violins, tenor violins, and violoncellos were made before the year 1600 proves nothing, for tenor and bass viols continued to be made for long after that date, and the bass viol or *viola da gamba* remained a favourite instrument both as a melodist and a provider of bass parts for vocal and instrumental forms till even after the time of Handel and Bach. All that can be conclusively stated regarding the type of instrument employed in seventeenth century string orchestras is that the treble violin almost immediately triumphed over the light-toned discant viol, and that the bass viol was the last to give way to the violoncello.

It is very evident that the words, *violini, violons,* or " violins " were used to signify the string orchestra as a body rather than the actual treble instrument. The famous French *vingt-quatre violons* and the twenty-four " violins " of Charles II are said to have been complete string orchestras, and if contemporary scores are any sure guide, the French band was organised in five parts and the English " violins " in four parts. Certain works by Locke and Purcell show indisputably that the word " violins ", as used in these scores, covered the whole family of instruments.

Of the wood-wind instruments destined to be retained as permanent members of the orchestra, flutes, oboes, and bassoons figure fairly frequently in seventeenth century scores.

Two varieties of flutes were then in use : the *flûte-à-bec*, (*flûte douce,* common flute, *flauto dolce, plockflöte, schnabelflöte*) blown through the end as were the flageolet and English recorder, and the transverse flute (*flûte traversière, flauto traverso, querflöte*) which in the following century entirely superseded the former instrument for orchestral use. A distinction in favour of the latter is made in some scores by the terms *traverso, flûte allemande* (or *d'allemagne*), and in England by the designation " German flute ".

Pierced with seven finger-holes and thumb-hole underneath, and commonly made in at least three sizes[1], the upper or medium

---

[1] Prætorius mentions no less than eight sizes of *flûtes-à-bec*.

flûtes-à-bec were generally employed, playing parts which demand a limited compass of rather under two octaves, covering approximately the same range as the two lower octaves of the modern flute. Of the *flûtes-à-bec* illustrated and described in Virdung's

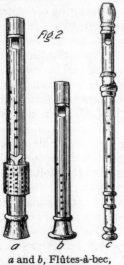

Fig. 2

Musica Getutscht (1511) and in Agricola's *Musica instrumentalis* (1529), the middle member practically corresponds in length to the modern flute, and seems to have 2 ft. C as its fundamental note. The discant flute is pitched a fourth higher (in F) and the lower variety an octave lower than the discant[1]. The compass given by both authors is approximately two octaves. The Hamburg composer, J. Mattheson, writing in 1713[2] mentions a similar set of three *flûtes douces* ; the *discant flöte* in F, the *alt* in C and the *bass* in low F, each having a compass of exactly two octaves above their respective fundamental notes[3].

a and *b*, Flûtes-à-bec, sixteenth century ;

c, Flûte-à-bec, seventeenth century.

Oboes, an improvement on the earlier shawm, like the flutes, appear to have been made in not less than three sizes, of which the two-foot instrument has come to be regarded as the normal type. Oboes constituted the nucleus of wind-bands in the seventeenth century and occupied the same position as clarinets do at present in military bands until they were to a large extent superseded by the latter instruments during the course of the next century. Played with a larger and coarser reed, oboes were evidently used in numbers, certainly more than one to each part. The treble oboe and the middle member of the flutes had a fundamental sounding length of about two feet, and all sizes were bored with six holes for the first three fingers of both hands, and in addition, a seventh hole near the lower extremity which could be covered by the little finger, or even as early as the time

[1] The approximate lengths of these instruments were eighteen inches, two feet and three feet.

[2] *Das Neu-eröffnete Orchester.*

[3] Similar sets of three in F, C, F are described in early eighteenth century books.

of Virdung were, in the case of the larger instruments, fitted with
a key which was at first covered over by a perforated protection.
These early forms of key-mechanism with the cumbrous protecting
box can be seen depicted in the works of Virdung, Prætorius[1],
and Mersennus[2] ; from those are derived many of the illustrations
of early wind instruments in later musical histories. Duplicate
holes for the little finger were bored in early flutes and oboes
so that the player could use either hand for the lower part of the
instrument ; the hole which was not required was then filled up
with wax. When a key was fitted to cover
the lowest hole, it was likewise provided with
two finger-plates, one turning right and the
other towards the left.

Sounding a fundamental note in accordance
with the length of the tube when all finger-
holes are covered, the successive uncovering
of the holes shortens the sounding length of
the instrument and gives the notes of the first
octave ; greater wind pressure and cross-
fingering produces the next octave and some
chromatic notes which served to give the
instruments a wider key-range, till the subsequent addition of holes with keys placed
between the finger-holes converted these
primitive flutes and oboes into the more
useful and more chromatic instruments of the
late eighteenth and nineteenth centuries.
Transverse flutes with the D-sharp key and
oboes with keys for their lowest C and E-flat[3]
were known before the end of the seventeenth century and remained standard types
till towards the end of the eighteenth
century.

Bassoons are occasionally specified in
seventeenth century scores, more particularly
in those of the second half of the century.
The tube being doubled on itself may be

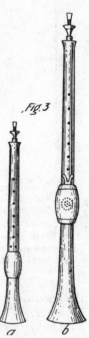

Fig 3

(a) Treble Shawm,
sixteenth century;

(b) Tenor Shawm
or Pommer,
sixteenth century.

[1] Prætorius, *Syntagma Musicum*, 1615–1620.

[2] Mersennus, *Harmonie Universelle*, 1636.

[3] The C key stood open, and the E-flat key stood closed.

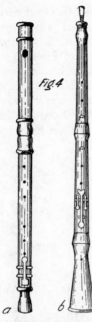

Fig. 4

(*a*) Transverse Flute with D sharp key,

(*b*) Oboe with C and D sharp keys, late seventeenth and eighteenth century.

taken as the most convenient distinction between the bassoon proper and the old bass varieties of oboe, the *pommer* or *bombard*, also between the tenor bassoon and tenor oboe.

Of the many sizes made, the ordinary bass instrument, having a total length of about eight feet of tube and a compass of two-and-a-half octaves, would seem to have been the most suitable instrument for playing the bass parts which are given to bassoons in company with string basses in opera, and a bass-trombone in seventeenth century Church music. Seventeenth century bassoons, according to Prætorius, had two keys covering holes sounding their lowest F and D, and the compass normally descended to 8 ft. C. Before the end of the century the low B-flat key was already known and fixed the downward compass of the bassoon for all time.

Gabrieli (1557-1613) and Schütz (1585-1672) are probably the earliest composers whose bassoon parts have survived, but it is not till after the mid-century that the instrument is frequently demanded in scores.

The *cornetti* or German *zinken* are constantly associated as treble instruments in combination with trombones in seventeenth century Church music, and have nothing in common with the nineteenth century cornet except the name and the cup-shaped mouthpiece by means of which the column of air is set in vibration, just as it is in a brass instrument. Parts for *cornetti* appear only

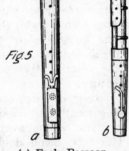

Fig 5

(*a*) Early Bassoon, sixteenth and seventeenth century;

(*b*) Bassoon with three keys, early eighteenth century.

rarely in seventeenth century opera scores ; the instrument lingers during the first half of the eighteenth century in its original capacity for use in ecclesiastical music.

These obsolete instruments represent a class by themselves. Of strictly conical bore, but without a spreading bell, they were made of wood or ivory, and were pierced with a thumb-hole behind and six finger-holes in front, which on being uncovered, shortened the sounding length of the tube in exactly the same way as they do on flutes, oboes or bassoons. The mouthpiece and method of blowing, however, were similar to those of the brass instruments with which they were usually grouped. Two forms were used, one slightly curved and the other straight ; the latter having apparently a gentler tone were called *cornetti muti*, or in German *stille zinken*, and were made with the mouthpiece and the body of the instrument all in one piece. Not less than three sizes were known, and of these the favourite appears to have been the middle member, about two feet in length and corresponding roughly in compass to the range of a soprano voice. The smaller size, according to a *cornetto* part of Monteverde's, could ascend as high as D above the treble staff and was evidently an instrument from which considerable agility of execution was expected. Parts for *cornetti* continued to be written during the first half of the eighteenth century, even as late as Gluck's *Orfeo* (Vienna, 1762), after which time the instrument disappears altogether from the orchestra. A lower-pitched instrument of the same type was the strangely curved serpent[1] which survived longer in the orchestra. The shortening-hole system was applied in turn to its lineal successors the bass-horn and ophicleide, which with the keyed-bugle represent the last of the wind instruments blown through a cup-shaped mouthpiece and pierced with finger or key-holes in the side of the tube.

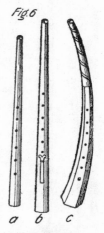

Fig.6

a   b   c

(*a, b*) Cornetti muti
(from Prætorius),

(*c*) Cornetto
(from Mersennus),

sixteenth and
seventeenth
century.

---

[1] According to von Gontershausen (*Neu Eröffnetes Magazin Musikalischer Tonwerkzeuge*, 1855), the serpent was invented (*erfunden*) by Edme Guillaume of Auxerre, France, about 1590.

Like the *cornetti*, trombones appear infrequently in seventeenth century opera scores but were freely used in Church orchestras. Trombone parts dating from the end of the sixteenth century exist in the works of Giovanni Gabrieli, organist of St. Mark's, Venice, at the time, and instances of their use occur in certain operas by Monteverde and Cesti. Legrenzi's orchestra at St. Mark's in 1685 included three trombones. Trombones stand alone

Fig.7

Trombone, seventeenth century.

amongst orchestral wind instruments in that they were mechanically perfect before any sort of organized orchestras were in existence. According to Prætorius four sizes were used : the alto, apparently in F ; the tenor in B-flat, the *quart* in low F (an octave lower than the alto) and the "octave" in B-flat, a fifth lower than the *quart*[1]. Mersennus describes the seven positions of the slide which gave the instruments a complete chromatic scale over all but the very lowest part of their compass. By the end of the seventeenth century the treble trombone (in B-flat), an octave higher than the tenor, had made its appearance and soon after is specified occasionally in scores under various names. Bach's *tromba da tirarsi*[2] could be nothing else but a treble trombone. This instrument should not be confused with the English slide trumpet of the nineteenth century, which was provided with a small slide which was drawn towards the player sufficiently far to lower the pitch of the open notes either a semitone or a tone, whereas on the treble trombone the slide was pushed out, away from the player, far enough to lower the open notes to anything from a semitone to a diminished fifth. If the treble trombone was known to seventeenth century composers, its place as the upper member of the family was consistently usurped by the *cornetti* ; even throughout the first half of the eighteenth century the latter obsolete instruments figure commonly in Church music in association with three trombones. It seems strange that composers should have for so long neglected to make

[1] Galpin, " The Sackbut, its evolution and history ", p. 17. Extract from the *Proceedings of the Musical Association*, 1906-7.

[2] Literally " slide trumpet ".

more use of trombones in their opera orchestras. While constantly struggling with the imperfections of natural horns and trumpets, they only began to include trombones in opera scores with any regularity after the middle of the eighteenth century and kept them out of the concert orchestra till some time after the beginning of the next century.

Opera scores of the seventeenth century frequently include trumpet parts when dramatic situations of warlike or jubilant character demand suitable reflection in the music. The tube of the instruments required to play the parts would be either eight or about seven feet long, thus standing in either C or D[1]. Prætorius states that the normal tonality of the trumpet was D, but that instruments had recently been made long enough to sound the harmonics of (8 ft.) C ; also that the change from D to C might be effected by means of *krumbügel, i.e.*, additional lengths of tubing, in fact none other than the crook or shank of the present day. The parts are non-transposing in seventeenth century scores and are either of " fanfare " type, or of the high-pitched conjunct variety which even then had long been associated with the word *clarino*, but the distinction between them,

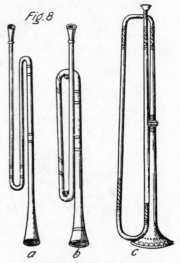

Fig. 8

(*a, b*), Trumpets (from Virdung), sixteenth century ;

(*c*) Trumpet, seventeenth and eighteenth century.

which concerns the portion of the harmonic series used rather than the actual instrument, is not so clearly marked in seventeenth century trumpet parts till the time of Stradella, when the florid *obbligato* parts characteristic of the well-known clarino-style of Handel and Bach begin to make their appearance.

Timpani are associated with trumpets in the scores of Lulli and other French composers. The constant and intimate

[1] Seventeenth and eighteenth century mutes raised the pitch of trumpets a tone higher. (Walther, 1732 ; Majer, 1741 ; and Altenburg, 1795.)

association of trumpets and drums in the sixteenth and seventeenth centuries strongly suggests the view that drums would be used in conjunction with trumpets even though no specific parts were written for the former in the scores. The illustrations in the works of Virdung, Prætorius, and Mersennus show drums practically in their present-day form with tuning-screws all round the rim. The roll is not indicated in seventeenth century scores though repeated semiquavers may be found in some parts.

The orchestral horn, derived by development and refinement from the semi-circular or circular hunting horn, belongs to eighteenth century orchestras in spite of Lulli's parts for *trompes de chasse* in *Princesse d'Élide* (1664) and other isolated

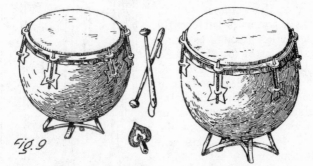

Timpani, sticks and key (from Prætorius), seventeenth century.

or doubtful instances ; likewise the clarinet, but with these exceptions all wind instruments of the modern orchestra are represented in seventeenth century scores, at all events in type.

Flutes, oboes, and trumpets were usually provided with two parts, which, unlike the later custom, were evidently intended to be played by more than one instrument to each part. Bassoons were given only one part and that always the bass part. Trombone parts already foreshadow the now conventional grouping in three.

It is significant that although practically all wind instruments were made and used in three, four, or more sizes, the size that eventually survived for orchestral use is that which was most frequently employed towards the end of the seventeenth century. The two-foot flute and oboe, the eight-foot bassoon and trumpet are commonly demanded and already appear to be the normal size, whereas parts for larger or smaller instruments of the same type appear only exceptionally.

Parts for other and usually obsolete instruments occur sporadically, but already in the seventeenth century the process of " the survival of the fittest " amongst wind-instruments appears to be in operation, and though the wind section is far from being settled in constitution, the end of the century shows flutes, oboes, bassoons, trumpets, and drums well on their way towards being established and indispensable members of the orchestra.

CHAPTER II

THE orchestra, if we understand the word to signify an organized combination of bowed string and wind instruments, can hardly be said to have existed before the seventeenth century. Cultured music, whether ecclesiastical or secular, was almost entirely choral ; it was polyphonic in texture and largely modal.

Apart from that written for keyboard-instruments and lutes, the status of instrumental music can be appraised by the light of such phrases as " apt for voices or viols ", " *buone da cantare et sonare* ", " *zu singen und auf instrumenten zu gebranchen* " or similar descriptions which appear on the title pages of many sixteenth and even seventeenth century musical works. Parts designed to suit the nature and compass of human voices were thus considered equally suitable for instruments capable of sustained tone, and the effect of such parts in combination was naturally found to be satisfactory when instruments were playing in unison with voices of similar range, or even if the voices were silent.

Lists of instruments constituting so-called sixteenth century orchestras are on record, and comprise practically every musical instrument known at the time. Often imposing in number and suggestive of sonority in combination, these lists, however, are misleading, and can hardly be considered even as a starting point in the evolution of the orchestra. Several of these " orchestras " are familiar to students of musical history, for example, Striggio's orchestra of viols, flutes, cornets, trombones, lutes, etc. ; and Elizabethan band of violins, flutes, oboes, cornets, drums, and fifes (1561) ; the violins, viols, lutes, lyres, harps, trombones, and organs in Caccini's *Intermezzo* (1589) ; likewise a " concert " in which were heard cornets, trumpets, violins, bastard violins, double harps, lutes, flutes, harpsichords, and voices[1] (1598). If indeed these and numerous other recorded combinations ever played together, there remains nothing to show

---

[1] Hawkins's *History of Music*, 1776, Vol. iii., p. 225.

how or what they played. Scores and parts, if ever written, have not survived ; but what evidence there is points decidedly to the custom of using the instruments successively in groups, each family by itself, just as is understood by the term " consort " in the musical annals of our own Tudor and Stuart times. Italian *Intermezzi*, French Ballets, and English masques, usually produced for entertainment at Royal weddings or similar festive occasions, have left behind them the mere record of such unorganized orchestras, the instruments of which were often in the hands of the stage players or dancers.

The establishments maintained by Royal or noble houses in nearly all European countries in the sixteenth century include lists of musicians and the instruments they played on. These and the records of German " Town bands " generally show a strong preponderance of wind instruments, and must be considered more as precursors of the military band than of the orchestra, though the grouping of some instruments, such as the consistent association of *cornetti* with trombones, of trumpets with drums, and the alliance of shawms or oboes and bassoons is noteworthy, and constantly crops up in the unstable constitution of the wind sections in seventeenth century orchestras.

The direct line in which progress in orchestration can be definitely traced starts from a more slender basis than these motley collections of sixteenth century instruments and players. It is found in the works of the Italian composers who at the very end of the sixteenth century resolutely broke away from the semi-modal polyphony of the time, and established the monody which completely changed the course of musical art, and through the medium of the newly-invented opera and oratorio forged the first link in the chain of modern tonality and modern music. It is from these desultory scraps of instrumental music, the embryo overtures, the introductory and concluding passages in early opera, variously named *sinfonia, sonata*, or *ritornello*, that the larger orchestral forms, overture and symphony, have been developed. During the course of the seventeenth century these efforts were met by the then growing forms of string music, more chamber than orchestral music, which through the string sonata and *concerto grosso*, in the hands of a long line of violinist-composers, evolved another large orchestral form—the concerto.

Before tracing the more connected story of orchestration which conveniently begins with the first surviving opera and oratorio scores in the year 1600, certain instrumental parts of earlier date claim some attention.

Such sixteenth century instrumental music as has survived on paper is principally for lutes or organs, but some dances printed in part-books may conceivably be considered as having some bearing on the beginnings of orchestration. Perhaps the best of the few available examples are the dances by Tielman Susato (died *circa* 1561), printed at Antwerp in 1551. They are arranged in four parts and are described on the title page as being "suitable for performance on all musical instruments". Viols or any group of wind instruments would no doubt easily negotiate these complacently moving parts of small compass, distinguished from one another simply as Discant, Contratenor, Tenor, and Bass.

An early French ballet provides what is possibly the oldest existing set of band parts. This work, entitled *Balet comique de la Royne*, was produced by Baltasarini de Beaujoyeulx—one of the earliest of known violinists—in 1581, and was printed in Paris in 1582. The dances are printed in the form of five parts for instruments labelled respectively, *Superius*, 2nd *Superius*, *Contra*, *Tenor*, and *Bassus*. In the text describing the Ballet a large number of instruments are mentioned as being in the hands of the dancers. Some music by oboes, *cornetti*, trombones, "*et autres instruments de musique*" provided the unwritten overture to this ballet, and was probably nothing more than the usual preliminary flourish of noisy character which heralded the beginning of dramatic performances in the sixteenth century. Some of the illustrations in this fascinating relic are of interest, and show quite accurate pictures of a bass viol and another viol, also some less happy representations of *cornetti* and a few other wind instruments.

The first dance, put into score, begins thus: (Example 2).

An attractive Gavotte from the same work has often been quoted[1]. Other dances are on the same lines, showing five well-distributed parts for unnamed instruments. The choice of five parts is significant as this proved to be the standard number of parts in music for strings for about a hundred years after the date of this ballet.

[1] *The Oxford History of Music*, Vol. iii, p. 220. Oxford, 1901–5 ; Grove, *Dictionary of Music and Musicians*, Art. " Orchestration ", London, 1878–1889.

EXAMPLE 2

(Balet comique de
  la Royne. 1581)

Le son du premier balet
en 5 parties.

à première entrée

Contra

Tenor

Bassus

The *Sacræ Symphoniæ* of Giovanni Gabrieli, which survive
in the form of printed part-books, show the attitude of this
prominent Church musician towards such instruments as were
deemed worthy of being included in the musical service of the
Church just at the time when the Monodists were making their
first experiments in Music-Drama, and act as a link between the
vocal polyphony of the sixteenth century and the instrumental
part-writing of the seventeenth century. This distinguished
organist of St. Mark's, Venice, was essentially a contrapuntist
and wrote for two, three, or four choirs with independent parts
for *cornetti*, violins, trombones, and bassoons. In this case there
is no ambiguity as to the instruments required ; being issued in
part-books, each book is necessarily named. The parts headed
violini prove to be for the tenor instrument and frequently
descend too low for the treble violin, but there is no attempt to

LIBRARY
ATLANTIC CHRISTIAN COLLEGE
WILSON, N. C.

81- 552

group these instruments as a self-contained string orchestra. Strings and wind are treated alike ; they are simply so many instruments capable of rendering parts which are similar in character and compass to the vocal parts. Balance of tone, tone-colour, or individual technique are hardly taken into account ; all are on an equality and unite with the voices in a rich web of severe and dignified counterpoint. While no distinction is made between the characteristics and capabilities of voices, trombones, violins, or *cornetti*, the latter are perhaps the most active and are always treated as the treble instruments of the combination. The following extract is representative of the bulk of Gabrieli's instrumental parts, and is drawn from a portion marked *sinfonia* :

[In the following and in all subsequent examples, the G or violin clef is substituted for C clefs on the first or second lines, and for the G clef on the first line of the staff, but the original clefs are always shown at the beginning of each extract. The notation is otherwise only modernized where necessary to facilitate reading. For this purpose time and key-signatures are sometimes altered or inserted and bar-lines are occasionally introduced. The grouping of quavers and all shorter notes is carried out in present-day fashion, and the old diamond-shaped notes are replaced by their modern equivalents. The arrangement of the scores, naming of instruments and other features are otherwise represented as faithfully as modern print will allow. Any word or sign in brackets is not in the original.] (Example 3.)

Antiphonal treatment of choirs was a feature of choral music at the time, and this is carried out by Gabrieli to a limited extent with the available instrumental forces, but without any very distinctive grouping of tone-colours ; thus, in the same work the " Alleluia " is antiphonally presented on two groups, the first comprising 1st *Cornetto*, 1st Viola, 3rd Trombone (tenor), tenor and bass voices ; this is answered by 2nd *Cornetto*, 2nd Viola, 1st, 2nd, and bass-trombones and alto voice. Some oddly balanced and poorly contrasted groups are found in other works of Gabrieli, for example—one *cornetto* and three trombones alternating with one viola and three trombones. Better contrasted are the two *cornetti* answered by two violas which occurs in one of the *Sacræ Symphoniæ*, and there are instances of one choir plus all instruments alternating with a second unaccompanied choir ; but on the whole, sharp contrasts of tone-colour are either not understood or not desired.

LIBRARY
ATLANTIC CHRISTIAN COLLEGE
WILSON, N. C.

EXAMPLE 3

EXAMPLE 3 (*Continued*)

Of instrumental accompaniment or figuration there is not a trace in this essentially polyphonic orchestration, and the characteristic technique of individual instruments is not recognized.

Gabrieli's instrumental conbinations vary slightly. Anything from two to six trombones, two or three *cornetti*, one or two violas, and sometimes a bassoon, make up his orchestra. The addition of an extra choir or two does not dismay this inveterate polyphonist, nor does it compel him to resort to the doubling of vocal parts by instrumental voices. His desire is a full and rich volume of tone ; co-operation rather than individualism is his instrumental creed, and an impartial distribution of material his only resource. It is impossible to fix the exact date of these compositions. Some were printed in 1597 and others appeared collectively in 1615, two or three years after Gabrieli's death, so must have been composed at the very end of the sixteenth or in the first decade of the seventeenth century. Gabrieli was probably the first to write independent parts for string and wind instruments in Church music, and soon after his death similarly constructed works by Capella and Leoni were printed in Venice, while his pupil Heinrich Schütz carried the same style and the same instrumental combinations into Germany.

These examples of early instrumental part-writing, drawn from French dramatic and Italian ecclesiastical art, perhaps owe their prominence to the fact that they both achieved the distinction and permanence of print in their own time, and are not necessarily the only works of their sort written at that period.

A " Dialogo Musical ", by Baldassare Donati (1520-1603) entitled *Giudizio d'Amore* and dated 1599 exists in manuscript ; it is interesting in that it shows what may be the earliest known instance of the employment of a particular feature of violin-playing—the quickly-repeated note, an effect which gives vigour and movement to the music without involving constant change of harmony. This thoroughly orchestral idiom, neglected by composers who were much pre-occupied with the polyphonic movement of parts, though discovered so early, hardly became a common feature in orchestral music till the last quarter of the seventeenth century. The *sinfonia* in which this occurs is written in three parts, probably intended for treble violins and a bass string instrument.

EXAMPLE 4 (a) AND (b)

(a) Sinfonia   B.Donati.(Giudizio d'amore. 1599)

(b)

Manuscript music is easily lost, destroyed or forgotten ; other composers whose names are possibly unknown to us may have produced equally significant work which may even yet come to light. As it is, the works just described are the earliest surviving examples of instrumental music which can be considered at all orchestral in style, and are all the more interesting as they just pre-date or overlap the time of the earliest work by the Monodists, and the revolutionary change in the art which was to develop in a direction ever growing more and more favourable to the production of true instrumental and orchestral, as distinguished from vocal music.

The foregoing shows little more than that educated musicians were, at the close of the sixteenth century, beginning to concern themselves with writing for instruments which had for so long been more in the province of the uneducated or itinerant classes, those who learned and played by ear and could not, or at any rate did not, write down what they played.

That instruments could play in parts and blend their tones as well as voices is practically all the foundation and precedent the pioneers of orchestration found ready to hand when they began to devise the little *sinfonie* and *ritornelli* which brighten up the bare vocal scores with *basso-continuo* of the first music-dramas.

CHAPTER III

THE last quarter of the seventeenth century approximately marks the conclusion of the initial stage in the history of orchestration. At that time the standard four-part string orchestra succeeded to the grouping of string instruments in either three or five parts which was hitherto the rule in the orchestral works of Italian, French, and German composers. Alessandro Scarlatti (1659-1725) and Henry Purcell (1659-1695) are the most prominent of those whose scores exemplify the axiom that strings were best handled in four parts, namely, 1st Violins, 2nd Violins, Tenor Violins, Violoncellos, and Double-basses, the last two playing the bass of the harmony in octaves as instruments of eight and sixteen-foot tone.

By the end of the century the string orchestra was finally settled in constitution, and the string-tone produced by instruments entirely of violin type was firmly established as the foundation-tone of the orchestra.

An examination of scores left by composers whose working lives extended from about the end of the sixteenth till near the end of the seventeenth century will demonstrate the state and growth of orchestral art during its first or initial period. Chronologically this will carry the history almost into the time of the two great composers of the first half of the eighteenth century, Bach and Handel, who with Rameau and Gluck in turn touch or overlap the work of the parents of modern orchestration, Haydn and Mozart. But an intermediate period, which may conveniently be labelled Scarlatti-Purcell, must be sandwiched in between the initial and the Bach-Handel periods.

It must be understood that this division into periods is made for the sake of method, clearness, and as an aid to memory, and is based on the work of these composers and their contemporaries rather than on the actual span of their lives.

The initial period embraces the work of the most prominent Italian composers before the time of Scarlatti, namely Cavalieri, Peri, Monteverde, Gagliano, Landi, the two Rossi's, Cavalli,

Cesti, Legrenzi, Carissimi, Stradella, and many others ; Lulli, the famous composer of French Ballet and Opera, and his immediate successors ; contemporary Germans such as Schütz, Albert, Tunder, and Hammerschmidt. In their lives and by their work pre-dating Scarlatti and Purcell, these composers wrote almost invariably for strings in either five or three parts, with an unsystematic and irregular use of such wind instruments as appeared to be at their disposal at different places and on different occasions.

To the present-day musician trained on an educational system of four-part writing, the grouping of voices or instruments in four parts seems natural and almost inevitable. This convention, however, did not exist for the early orchestral composer, to whom it was equally natural to write in five or three parts. Both systems are adopted by practically all composers of this period, the five-part group for introductory movements, *Sinfonie, Ritornelli* Dances, Marches, etc., also to double choral parts, and the three-part group sometimes for entire works, and often for accompanying vocal solos when anything but a figured-bass part was provided ; also for many introductory, intermediate and concluding *Ritornelli*. " Sinfonia a 5 " is a frequent heading for the purely instrumental overtures which occur in nearly all works up to the advent of the French " ouverture ".

The instruments required are not often clearly specified in the earliest scores. Written directions sometimes state that the music is to be played by " all instruments ". Composers were apparently content to write so many parts, and to leave to chance, custom, varying circumstances, or the judgment of others the decision as to how the parts should be distributed amongst the available instruments. The only guidance provided is the clef and compass of each part, which would naturally be made the first consideration when allotting the already written parts to instruments of varying size and pitch. Prætorius, in his *Syntagma Musicum* (1615–20), gives some details of how this process of fitting instruments to parts was carried out. He writes, that if the part was written with the G clef, or with the C clef on the second line, Discant violins or *cornetti* would be given that part to play. In the same way Tenor and Bass instruments were to be given parts with appropriate clefs, in short, whatever part suited their compass best. Composers were clearly not much concerned with balance or tone-colour. The effects of particular combinations of instrumental colour could hardly enter into their calculations when a part was liable to be undertaken by instruments of such differing tone-quality and weight as either violins or *cornetti*, tenor viols, violins, or trombones, bass viols, bassoons, or bass trombones. This seeming indifference to instrumental effect, however, is not so remarkable when it is remembered that under the conditions prevailing in the seventeenth century, the composer as a rule was also the conductor, and would thus prepare the performance of a work himself, allotting the parts and superintending the rendering personally.

Later scores hint that a string orchestra was intended by the occasional appearance of the words *violini* or *violons*, and a few give exact specifications of the instruments. From these one may gather that the most common arrangement of the five-part string orchestra was as follows : 1st violins, 2nd violins, 1st tenors, 2nd tenors, and basses. The G clef, on either the first or the second line of the staff was undoubtedly used for treble violin parts, but the alto and tenor C clefs make no clear distinction between viols and violins of tenor register.

The three-part string orchestra appears to be invariably for two treble instruments and basses ; clefs, compass, and occasional directions indicate that violins were universally in favour for the two upper parts. The *basso-continuo* is, as a rule, the only bass part provided in the scores. When a separate bass part for string instruments is written, the terms *violone* (large violin) or *basses des violons* are sometimes attached, but it is by no means clear whether the eight or the sixteen-foot-tone instruments were intended, or whether both were used together[1]. The word *violoncello* does not occur till towards the end of the century, by which time viols are evidently banished from the orchestra except for occasional solo parts.

Later on in the seventeenth century the first few of a long line of practical violinist-composers, starting with Vitali, Corelli, and Torelli, adopted the same method of writing two violin and a bass part. To them and their successors is due the development of true violin technique which by the end of the century had given a distinctive style to music written for string instruments, and had finally individualized the dull and ambiguous parts which most

---

[1] Warnecke in *Der Kontrabass*, Hamburg, 1909, states that double-basses were first used in opera at Naples in 1700, and from the same date at Vienna.

of the earlier operatic composers impartially distributed between instruments of totally different capacity and tone-colour. Masses of Sonatas for two violins and a figure-bass were poured out from that time onwards, and a similar handling of the string orchestra in three parts remained a strong influence throughout the eighteenth century in spite of the available fourth part for tenor instruments. Much of the work of Handel, Haydn, Mozart, and their contemporaries is actually in three parts, the violas usually following the course of the bass part an octave higher.

In many cases the three-part group is employed throughout whole works, and this, with an unstable selection of wind instruments, points to the probability that composers often wrote for the combination of instruments available in particular orchestras. A MS. copy of Cesti's *La Dori* (1663) is scored entirely in three parts, whereas his *Il Pomo d'Oro* (1667), written to signalize a festive occasion and produced with all the lavish resources of the Vienna Opera House, is scored for a five-part string orchestra, and contains, in addition, parts for flutes, trumpets, *cornetti*, trombones, and bassoon in certain movements.

Cases also occur in which the same work has evidently been rearranged to suit a particular orchestra. The MS. copy of *La Dori* in the British Museum is the three-part version referred to above, but a score of the same work in the Royal Library at Vienna contains an entirely different overture scored for a five-part orchestra, and several other *Sinfonie* are similarly arranged ; there are also signs in the Vienna version that trumpets were used. Another MS. volume in the British Museum contains no less than eight of Lulli's operas arranged for two violins and basses, whereas the same operas in the printed scores published during the composer's lifetime show all the most important instrumental movements in the usual five-part form.

Full scores, such as they are, written during the first quarter of the seventeenth century show little actual scoring for instruments apart from the introductory *Sinfonie, Ritornelli,* and occasional dances. As they stand, the orchestra appears to be used only when the voices are silent ; but the perfunctory methods of the time by no means required that every part played should be written out in the score. The earliest examples often give only vocal parts and the *basso-continuo*, with written directions to the effect that certain instruments are to play in particular movements. It is quite probable that string instruments were meant to double the choral parts, and it is very improbable that composers would take the trouble to write out such duplicated parts in their scanty full scores, nor incur the unnecessary expense of having the doubled parts printed out in full when a work was published. The *Ritornelli* usually precede and follow the vocal parts on the same staff, and the only distinguishing sign is that there are no words to the instrumental music, or that the word *Ritornelli*, or sometimes *violini*, occurs at the point where the instrumental portions begin. Many specific cases of the doubling of chorus parts by instruments could be quoted. It occurs in Monteverde's *Orfeo* (1607) and in Gagliano's *Daphne* (1608). The preface to the latter opera includes a direction to the effect that an introductory *Sinfonia* is to be played by " various instruments, which also serve to *accompany the choruses* and to play the *Ritornelli* ". In neither case do any instrumental parts, except the *basso-continuo*, appear in the score of these choruses. A later instance is in Matthew Locke's *Psyche* (1673); such headings as " Chorus and violins ", " Song and Dance accompanied in the chorus with kettledrums, wind instruments, violins, etc." appear frequently where only vocal parts are provided in the score. Lulli's full scores were printed with no regard for either expense or economy of space ; in these the string parts invariably double the chorus parts and are printed out in full ; but few composers had their scores so lavishly printed as Lulli. The combination of evidence is quite in favour of the assumption that strings as a rule played in unison with choral parts of corresponding range during the greater part of the seventeenth century, and *that it was not considered necessary to write out duplicate parts in the full scores*.

Emilio del Cavalieri's oratorio *Rappresentazione di Anima e di Corpo*, and the two operas entitled *Euridice* by Peri and Caccini, are the earliest surviving examples of their kind, and in that they all date from the year 1600, constitute unique and definite starting points in the history of these two important musico-dramatic forms.

They may equally well be utilized to represent the babyhood of orchestration, an almost imperceptible beginning of a distinctive appurtenance to musical art, the conception of which can hardly have been suspected by its unconscious parents. These scores consist of vocal parts and *basso-continuo*, the latter being rendered by " *una Chitarrina alla Spagnola* " and " *un Cimbaletto con Sonaglino* " in Cavalieri's work.   This composer also directs that his two five-part *Sinfonie* and the few scored *Ritornelli* are to be played by a " large number of instruments "—*gran quantita di stromenti*.   That instrumental colour and effect had hardly begun to be appreciated at that time seems evident from the remark in the preface to this oratorio that a good effect—*buonissima effetto*—would result if a violin was played in unison with the " soprano " throughout the work.   A " sonata " for two flutes, two *Sinfonie* and a few *Ritornelli* are the only bits of specifically instrumental writing in the whole oratorio.   The un-named parts have no characteristics through which they could be identified with particular instruments, and are in style and compass similar to the vocal parts, although in the first *Sinfonia*, after a few bars of introduction, the uppermost part breaks into a rhythm which certainly shows some slight appreciation of instrumental style:

EXAMPLE 5

Cavalieri (Anima e di Corpo, 1600)

Peri's *Euridice* shows even less actual scoring for instruments, in fact nothing but a *Sinfonia* for three flutes appears in the score, and then only to represent the music supposed to be played on a triple flute by one of the characters on the stage. These parts, written close together and of very limited compass, can be seen in Grove's *Dictionary*[1], also in Burney's *History of Music*[2].

With these rudimentary efforts the art of orchestration made a formal though hardly recognizable début in the first year of the seventeenth century, and started the composition of music designed for orchestral instruments on its path towards emancipation from the shackles of a purely vocal style.

The art had not long to wait for a foster-parent whose enterprise and invention gave a more definite standing to this new adjunct to musical composition.

Claudio Monteverde (1567–1643) stands out as the first creator of orchestral effect, as an innovator whose daring though unsystematic handling of the embryo orchestra proved almost too bold for immediate absorption into the current language of instrumental music. Plunging headlong into the heart of a virgin art, Monteverde was the first to attempt to exploit the individual character and technique of instruments in order to intensify dramatic feeling, and in doing so hit on effects which at that time were no doubt startling as they were novel.

The great needs of the orchestra in these early days were organization and the development of individual styles which should be peculiar to and inseparable from the music allotted to each type of instrument. Towards a properly balanced organization of the orchestra as a whole Monteverde contributed little, but as regards variety of tone-colour and the individualization of instrumental parts he broke the ice and set an example which his more timid successors were slow in following.

His opera *Orfeo* (1607) stands out as the first prominent landmark in the path of an infant art, and has all the irresponsibility and precocity of unguided but enterprising effort at the threshold of unknown and limitless possibilities.

The following instruments took part in the first performance at Mantua, and are given in a list on the second page of the printed score[3] :

[1] Article, " Opera ".
[2] Vol. iv., p. 31.
[3] Two editions : Venice, 1609 and 1615.

(a) Duoi Gravicembani.
(b) Duoi Contrabassi de Viola.
(c) Dieci Viole da Brazzo.
(d) Un Arpa doppia.
(e) Duoi Violini piccoli alla Francese.
(f) Duoi Chitaroni.
(g) Duoi organi di legno.
(h) Tre Bassi da gamba.
(i) Quattro Tromboni.
(j) Un Regale.
(k) Duoi Cornetti.
(l) Un Flautino alla vigesima seconda.
(m) Un Clarino con tre Trombe sordine.

These may be explained as follows :

(a) Two keyboard-instruments with the quill or jack-mechanism, *i.e.*, Harpsichord, Spinet (more usually spelt *Clavicembali*).
(b) Two string double-basses.
(c) Ten arm-viols, *i.e.*, Discant or Tenor Viols, most probably both.
(d) One harp, double-strung.
(e) Two ordinary treble violins.
(f) Two bass or Archlutes.
(g) Two organs with wooden pipes,
(h) Three bass viols, *Viole da gamba.*
(i) Four trombones.
(j) One small (portable) organ.
(k) Two *Cornetti*, the old instrument with cup-shaped mouthpiece and finger-holes.
(l) One small flute " at the twenty-second ". The interval of a 22nd is equivalent to three octaves. The most plausible explanation of a " flute at the 22nd " is that offered by Dr. Kopfermann, of Berlin, in Goldschmidt's *Studien zur Geschichte der italienischen Oper im 17 Jahrhundert*[1]. He suggests that 8-ft. C. was the standard from which the 22nd was measured. An instrument with a fundamental tone three octaves higher than 8-ft. C. would thus be one foot in length, practically an octave higher in pitch than the ordinary two-foot flute. (Two parts for *Flautini* appear only once in the score, but the instruments necessary to

---

[1] Leipzig, Breitkopf and Härtel, 1901, p. 134.

play the parts at the pitch represented would have to be not smaller than the normal two-foot instrument.)

(*m*) One trumpet, the 8-ft. instrument in C, with (and) three muted trumpets.

A list of " personaggi " appears on the left-hand side of the same page as the list of instruments, and from the fact that the name of each character stands opposite to the name of an instrument, Hawkins[1] conceived the odd notion that the music sung by each character was to be accompanied by a particular instrument or group of instruments. Examination of the score and the given directions provide no support for this extraordinary idea[2].

It would be very misleading to imply that the above list represents the standard constitution of orchestras at the beginning of the seventeenth century. At that time there was no standard, unless a *Clavicembalo* and a few Lutes can be called an orchestra. Nor would it be correct to state that this combination is the basis on which subsequent orchestras were modelled. It is nothing but a collection of instruments assembled for the first production of the opera, a private performance got up to celebrate some wedding festivities under the auspices of Monteverde's employer, the Duke of Mantua. Any theory based on a mere examination of this list gives a wrong impression which will only be corrected when the score of the music and the written directions for its performance are considered and co-related. Those show clearly that, except on the few occasions when " all instruments " are directed to play together, they are used in well-defined groups, of which the following are actual and representative examples :

(*a*) Two Violins with *Clavicembali* and *Chitarroni*.

(*b*) Two Violins and a Bass Viol with ditto.

(*c*) Two *Flautini* with ditto.

(*d*) Five viols and a Double-bass with ditto.

(*e*) Three viols and a Double-bass with ditto.

(*f*) Viols, Bass Viols, Double-bass, and Organ.

(*g*) *Cornetti*, Trombones, and Organs.

(*h*) Trombones, Bass Viols, and Double-basses.

It should be noticed that Viols and Violins are not combined to form a complete string orchestra.

[1] *History of Music*, Orig. Ed., Vol. iii, p. 430.

[2] Many writers have adopted (or merely copied ?) Hawkins's idea.

All instruments—*tutti gli stromenti*—are required to play the Toccata (overture), in one five-part chorus, and in two or three *Sinfonie*; for these five or eight staves of music are provided, but particular instruments are not identified with each staff excepting the trumpet in the Toccata.

These *tutti* are more akin to the "*gran quantita di stromenti*" of Cavalieri's oratorio than to any modern conception of an orchestral *tutti* in which each set of instruments is provided with a part. The distribution of parts would no doubt be carried out according to the principles explained in Prætorius' *Syntagma Musicum*. Some of the five-part *Ritornelli* and the concluding dance—a Moresca— were possibly dealt with in the same way, but the three-part *Ritornelli* are clearly marked for either two violins, two *cornetti*, or two flutes and some string bass and accompanying chordal instruments, while others in five parts are definitely allotted to nothing but viols with one or more of the keyboard-instruments and lutes. It will be seen from the above that while there is plenty of vague instrumentation, the more clearly specified groups of instruments supply some considerable variety of tone-colour, but that as each group is used fixedly throughout a whole movement or scene, the contrasts are very broadly spaced and in this way inaugurate a principle of orchestration which remained in force for rather more than half a century.

The following may be regarded as a typical example of Monteverde's manner of handling a group of viols. This *Ritornello* was to be played by viols, probably discant and tenor, by one double-bass, *Clavicembalo* and *Chitarroni:* (Example 6).

The *Ritornelli* for violins are rather brisker and more characteristic : (Example 7) but in a dramatic scene in Act IV the violins really come into their own and seem to wrench themselves free from the fetters of the colourless style associated with viol-playing. Imitative scale passages and brilliant runs in thirds are interspersed amongst the dramatic utterances of two singers. This activity is then handed on to a couple of remarkably agile *cornetti*, and even the bass-viols have to take an active part in the general outburst of energetic movement : (Example 8).

Monteverde literally sets a new pace for violins, a pace which must have been staggering to players at that time, and sets an example by which neither the contemporary nor the succeeding generation of composers seems to have profited.

EXAMPLE 6

Monteverde (Orfeo 1607)

Fu Sonato questo Ritornello di dentro da cinque Viole da
braccia, un Contrabasso, duoi Clavincembani & tre Chitarroni

EXAMPLE 7

Monteverde (Orfeo)

EXAMPLE 8

(a) Monteverde (Orfeo)

(b)

The idea of a voice singing to a soft, sustained, harmonic background of string-tone has long been a commonplace, but was a novelty in the early days of Monody. The next example must be accounted to Monteverde as an innovation. It is for three viols and one double-bass played " *pian-piano*," and apparently without the aid of the ubiquitous *Clavicembali* or *Chitarroni:* (Example 9).

The stirring overture of *Orfeo* probably owes its character to the prevailing custom of heralding a dramatic performance by three fanfares of trumpets. Monteverde is not satisfied with anything the trumpeters may care to play, and like a true artist, writes his own fanfare. This is quoted in the *Oxford History of Music*[1], and is in five parts of which the upper part is headed " *Clarino* ". A " *Clarino* " is often described as a small trumpet,

EXAMPLE 9

Monteverde (Orfeo)   *Furno Sonate le altre parti da tre viole da braccio, & un Contrabasso de Viola rocchi pian piano*

[1] Vol. iii, p. 51.

probably because the parts are always high in pitch. Clarino-
playing even at that time was a specially cultivated art and could
only be carried out on long instruments. Nothing but an 8-ft.
trumpet[1] could play the consecutive notes of Monteverde's part
without the use of valves or slides, and trumpets at that time had
neither. That the bore of the " Clarino " was narrow and the
cup of the mouthpiece shallow is generally accepted, but otherwise Clarino-playing is simply the use of the higher open notes
of an ordinary long trumpet acquired by practice with a suitable
mouthpiece. It is only from the eighth open note upwards that
adjacent notes can be obtained on any brass instrument without
either valves or slides, and the C and D trumpets alone were
long enough to enable players in the seventeenth century to reach
that portion of the harmonic series lying between the eighth and
sixteenth open notes. The remaining parts of the fanfare
are marked " Quinta ", " Alto e Basso ", "Vulgano[2] ", and
" Basso " ; they are all obviously designed for the open notes

[1] The modern C Trumpet is a 4-ft. instrument.

[2] The term " vulgano " has baffled many historians. Some light is
thrown on the matter in a work written by Girolamo Fantini and published

of trumpets, in fact every part including the *Vulgano* and *Basso* could be played on an 8-ft. trumpet, nevertheless the directions are that *all instruments* are to take part in this, the earliest operatic overture extant.

In the *Ballo delle Ingrate*, another work of Monteverde's performed about the same time, the prelude—according to Winterfeld[1]—took the form of a "thunderous" noise produced by muffled drums playing underneath the stage.

Winterfeld gives the following particulars of the use of instruments in some church pieces by Monteverde grouped together under the title *Sanctissimæ Virgini*, and printed in 1610. Two *cornetti* and two violins in turn rush about in thirds or in rapid imitative phrases above a slow-moving bass and vocal parts. The passages are similar to those already quoted from *Orfeo*, but the violinists on this occasion are required to play as high as the fifth position on the E string ; this at a time when the third position was considered a dangerous and giddy height ! Later on in the same work " *Piffari*[2]", violins, *cornetti*, trombones, and flutes play in succession above a steady bass part, and provide plenty of varied tone-colour. More logical and artistic is the successive use of the well-balanced and contrasted groups : first a group of two violins, tenors and basses, then two *cornetti* and a trombone, which eventually unite with the choral voices in building up a rich and sonorous ensemble. In another piece two *cornetti* and three trombones alternate with a body of string instruments, almost the identical instruments used in groups of mixed tone-colour by Gabrieli just about the same time.

---

in 1636 at Frankfort under the title *Modo per imparar a sonare di Tromba*. According to Fantini the lower open notes on the trumpet were named as follows :

Fundamental note	C	—	*sotto basso.*
2nd open note	C	—	*basso.*
3rd ,, ,,	G	—	*vurgano.*
4th ,, ,,	C	—	*striano.*
5th ,, ,,	E	—	*toccata.*
6th ,, ,,	G	—	*quinta.*

Fantini's " *vurgano* " and Monteverde's "*vulgano*" are evidently the same thing, but it is not quite clear whether these terms were applied to the actual notes or to the parts. Monteverde's "*vulgano*" part is confined to one note, namely the same G which Fantini names " *vurgano* " ; on the other hand Monteverde's *Quinta* part embraces the four open notes : Middle C, and E, G, C, above it.

[1] Von Winterfeld, *Johannes Gabrieli und sein Zeitalter* (Berlin, 1834).

[2] " pipes "=shawms, oboes, or flutes.

Perhaps the most remarkable of the few surviving works by Monteverde is his *Combattimento di Tancredi e Clorinda*, produced in 1624 but not printed till 1638.   In this piece the composer presents two new and genuinely orchestral effects. Both are now the common property of the meanest orchestral composer and arranger, but early in the seventeenth century cannot have been other than startling or even bewildering novelties to ears unaccustomed to anything but a polyphonic movement of parts. Even at that time everybody must have heard string players twang the strings of their instruments with the fingers, but only Monteverde thought of using this as an orchestral effect.   While the fight between Tancredi and Clorinda is in progress he directs the players to discard their bows and to strike the strings with *two* fingers, in short, he creates the *pizzicato* effect. If his notation is not quite logical, the effect is there all the same :

EXAMPLE 10

Monteverde (Il combattimento 1624)
qui si lascia l'arco, e si strappano le corde con duoi diti

EXAMPLE 10 (*continued*)

The *pizzicato* is cancelled by " *Qui si ripiglia l'arco* ".   The above passage follows one which contains what is no doubt the germ of the modern *tremolo*.   The power to reiterate any note at almost unlimited speed is a feature of bowed-string-instrument playing which is shared by neither wind nor keyboard-instruments. The extract, dated 1599, by Donati[1] shows that this feature of string playing was not absolutely unknown before the time of " *Combattimento* ", but Monteverde was undoubtedly the first to make full use of the effect of continuous reiteration of notes as an accompaniment.   His *tremolo*, however, is a measured repetition of semi-quavers, and in effect very different from the continuous buzz of the modern bow *tremolo*.   It was nevertheless a novel and essentially orchestral device, one which could only have been discovered by a string player :

EXAMPLE 11

Monteverde (Il combattimento)

Sti_mol no.vo s'aggiungea pia_ga

[1] See Ex. No. 4.

no_va   d'orain or più si_mos_se e più ris-

When the music was printed in 1638 Monteverde took the opportunity of relating how the players received the innovation. It seems that they hardly took it seriously and could not understand why they should move their bows up and down sixteen times in a bar only to produce repetitions of the same note ! At first they played one long note instead of sixteen short ones, and apparently required some persuasion before they could be induced to play the passage exactly as Monteverde had written it.

Quite as significant as the invention of these effects is the fact that in using them the composer necessarily broke away from the vocal style of writing for instruments. He produces music which is only possible on string instruments played with a bow, music in which the interest is that of harmony, texture, and tone-colour, and is completely independent of any polyphonic or imitative movement of parts. If composers had only exploited and carried on such beginnings of true orchestration as those so boldly inaugurated by Monteverde, the dreary progress through a wilderness of imitative part-writing in the seventeenth century might have been cut out of the story of orchestral evolution. As it transpired, Monteverde's devices remained

to be practically re-discovered by later generations, and did not
become conventions till when, in the eighteenth century,
orchestral writing began to show signs of breaking away from a
style of part writing which was only a further growth of the
vocal polyphony of the sixteenth century. The choice of four
parts for his string orchestra instead of the usual five is equally
typical of Monteverde's independence, and had to wait over
fifty years for general confirmation by the generation of composers immediately preceding Bach and Handel.

Of Monteverde's many operas only one more authenticated
example survives, namely *L'Incoronazione di Poppea* (1642).
This opera and the *Scherzi Musicale* (1628) contain " *Sinfonie* "
and " *Ritornelli* " scored for two violins and " *basso-continuo* ".
The parts are often decidedly rhythmical and instrumental in
style, but there is no sign of the colour-contrasts of *Orfeo*, or the
string effects of *Combattimento*. If *L'Incoronazione* represents
Monteverde's maturity, it would seem that he had lost the enterprising spirit exhibited in the orchestration of his earlier works, and
was content to score in the colourless style of his contemporaries.

The large orchestra of *Orfeo* remains for the present an
isolated example. Only the recovery of several lost scores
composed by Monteverde could reveal whether he ever repeated
or further exploited his discoveries in a virgin field so full of
possibilities and so strangely neglected by composers whose work
covers the first half of the seventeenth century.

After Monteverde's *Orfeo* quite a number of Italian musicians
turned their attention to this form of composition, and the records
of performances in Florence, Rome, and Bologna bring to light
several new names. A few of those works were printed, and
together with those surviving in MS., suggest that the composers
were content with small orchestras in which the " *Clavicembali* "
and lutes do the main work while a few viols or violins partici-
pate as mere accessories. The scores as a rule show two upper
parts, probably intended for violins, and the usual *basso-continuo*,
with occasional indications that some wind instruments were used
to double the string and choral parts. Of such are Gagliano's
Daphne (Florence, 1608) containing a few *Ritornelli* in three parts ;
Quagliati's *Carro di Fedeltà d'Amore* (Rome, 1611) in which the
instrumental portions are written on two staves marked respectively "*Violino ō altro soprano*" and "*Cembalo, Leuto, Tiorba,
e altri instromenti*" ; Landi's *Le Morte d'Orfeo* (Venice, 1619)

is scored in three parts for unnamed instruments. These scores are thin and featureless, only a few " *Ritornelli* " are scored, and then without any attempt at orchestral or dramatic effect.   Boschetti's *Strali d'Amore* (Venice, 1618) has no instrumental parts beyond the " *basso-continuo* ", but Francesca Caccini's Ballet *La Liberazione di Ruggiero dall Isola d'Alcina* (Florence, 1625) shows a few " *Ritornelli* " apparently for three violins and basses, one for three flutes, and another for four viols with four trombones and keyboard-instruments doubling the string parts, also a five part chorus played by five viols, lutes, etc., these instruments presumably doubling the vocal parts.

Two " *Ritornelli* " from Mazzocchi's opera *La Catena d'Adone* (Venice, 1626) will serve as typical examples of the unenterprising orchestration of Monteverde's contemporaries. No instruments are specified, but a distinction is made in the second example between the part which is evidently intended for bass string instruments and the *basso-continuo* part : (Example 12).

Gagliano's *La Flora* (1628) and Giacinto Cornachioli's *Diana Schernita* (1629) are works of similar type produced in Italy at this period.

The evidence of these various scores shows that although the higher viols were still in use, composers were decided in their preference for violins as the upper instruments of the string group. Tenor string instruments are ignored more often than not, just at this period, and though there are instances of three or even four treble violin parts above the " *basso-continuo* " line, the three-part string orchestra is, on the whole, the favourite combination. More important, however, than the slightly varying constitution of the string orchestra is the fact that composers did write principally for strings.   It was probably all to the good that they should learn to handle the strings first, and that this most suitable and elastic medium of expression was selected for their instrumental movements rather than the more unmanageable wind-combinations.   Their very lack of enterprise may have proved to be, after all, progress in the right direction.

1634 is the date of publication of another opera by Landi, named *Il S'Alessio*. In this work the composer handles his orchestra with much more confidence and with quite a good idea of instrument effect.   Players on tenor string instruments seem to have been either scarce or incompetent in Rome during the first half of the century ; whatever the reason, Landi scores his

EXAMPLE 12 (a) AND (b)

Mazzocki (La Catena d'Adone 1626)

opera for 1st, 2nd, and 3rd violins with a bass part for harps, lutes, theorbos, and " *Violoni*[1]" in addition to a figured bass part marked "*Gravicembalo*". The instrumental movements are longer and more important than in the same composer's *Morte d'Orfeo*, and if the music is sometimes light and rather trivial, Landi seems to know exactly what he wants and how to get it. He also knows how to write a score clearly so as to leave nothing to chance. The contrast between loud and soft in one of the longer " *Sinfonie* " is an unusual feature in music of that date:

[1] Large violins, *i.e.*, double-bass or 'cello.

Landi (Il S'Alessio, 1634)   EXAMPLE 13

Landi's frequent use of repeated notes is quite a legitimate feature of string technique, and points more in the direction of progress in orchestration than the imitative polyphony of so much instrumental music produced at that time :

EXAMPLE 14

Landi (Il S'Alessio)

A big six-part chorus at the end of the first act is provided with independent parts for violins, an unusual if not quite novel procedure in opera up to that date, while another "*finale*" is for eight-part chorus with well-timed entries by the strings in a body, thus providing welcome changes of tone-colour in a manner which only became common at a much later date. After Monteverde, Landi certainly merits next place amongst those who mothered the infant art of orchestration. His decided sense for instrumental style, added to the welcome precision with which the music is put down on paper make his *Il S'Alessio* quite a bright spot in a period of annoyingly vague scores and apparent indifference to orchestral effect.

The shortage of tenor string players in Rome again seems apparent in 1637, the date of Michael Angelo Rossi's *Erminia sul Giordano*. This work is scored for treble violins and basses. In this case the composer does not abandon the five-part grouping; he scores his opera for 1st, 2nd, 3rd, 4th violins, "*violone*", and "*basso-continuo per tutti gli stromenti*". The first "*Sinfonia[1]*", with its fugal entries by all four violin parts in turn, is brisk and decidedly instrumental in style. Another "*Sinfonia*", several "*Ritornelli*" and a group of dances unite in giving considerable prominence to the orchestral music in this opera.

The names of Vittoria Loretto and Luigi Rossi should be included amongst the early Italian composers of opera whose work belongs to the first-half of the century and precedes that of the mid-century group—Cavalli, Cesti, etc. The prologue to Luigi Rossi's *Il Palazzo Incantato* (1642) is scored for an unusually constituted string orchestra. Two violin parts are written in addition to a complete five-part group of viols. The viols actually accompany the voice part, and in between the vocal phrases the two violin parts are super-imposed.

Occupying an important position amongst the composers whose work served to develop and establish the new harmonic style of choral music, Carissimi (1604-74) contributed comparatively little towards the growth of a corresponding instrumental style. His many sacred vocal works contain short *Sinfonie* for a three-part orchestra, presumably two violins and basses, and to the choruses and vocal solos two violin parts are often added in a semi-independent manner. These two upper parts, which are written close together and have a faintly instrumental character, give a little variety of colour by occasionally interrupting the flow of the vocal phrases.

From the above survey, covering the work of Italians between 1600 and 1650, it will be seen that the colour contrasts and string effects of Monteverde's *Orfeo* and his *Combattimento* stand almost alone as achievements in orchestral effect which, as far as we know,

---

[1] See *The Oxford History of Music*, Vol. iii, p. 149 ; also Botstiber's *Geschichte der Ouvertüre*, p. 234.

were carried no further even by that composer himself. The true gain to the orchestra so far, was the gradual emergence of a more or less organized string orchestra. Independent writing for wind instruments was yet to come, the grouping of wind in families of wood-wind and brass was hardly even suggested, and little advantage was taken of the effect of sharply contrasting string and wind-instrument tone by alternation. String music had gained in activity of movement but had hardly touched anything like passage-work, figuration or bow effects, in spite of Monteverde's suggestive lead.

In the meantime a few Italian Church composers had carried on Gabrieli's style of writing independent parts for wind instruments, and his pupil Heinrich Schütz (1585-1672), who had attained a foremost position amongst the composers of his own country, supplies some of the earliest examples of instrumental part-writing in association with the sacred vocal music then being cultivated in Germany.

Schütz revisited Italy after Gabrieli's death with the intention of keeping in touch with musical progress in that country, but on the whole remained faithful to the teaching of his master and followed Gabrieli's style both in the selection and handling of his instruments. *Cornetti*, trombones, and bassoons are used much as in Gabrieli's works, with perhaps a special fondness for bassoons ; some of his vocal numbers are accompanied by nothing but three bassoons which, in the *Sinfonie*, solemnly chase one another up and down in scale and arpeggio passages. The *Sinfonia a* 5 for unnamed instruments figures in several of his scores, while trumpets and drums make an occasional appearance by themselves.

When not writing for wind-instruments, Schütz employs a three-part group of strings, two violins and basses, which, in conjunction with the organ, carry out the instrumental portions of his large collections of sacred vocal works called *Symphoniæ Sacræ* or *Deutche Concerte*. The following extracts from Book II of the above illustrate, (*a*) his usual way of treating the two violins in imitation and (*b*) a quite exceptional passage in which he shows himself alive to the fact that instrumental parts need not necessarily be modelled on the style of vocal or organ music. In his anxiety to produce something stirring Schütz stumbles on a passage of trumpet-like character :

EXAMPLE 15 (*a*) AND (*b*)

Some odd instrumental combinations from a work on the subject of John the Baptist by a little known German named Daniel Bollius, and dating from not later than 1628, will help to show what a primitive conception of blend and balance was current at that time amongst the church composers who were pioneers in that very sphere of musical art which paved the way for, and culminated in, the work of Bach :

An introduction for two *cornetti* and one bassoon.

A *Sinfonia* for two violins, *viola bastarda* and organ.

A *Sinfonia* for three flutes.

A *Sinfonia* for one *cornetto*, one violin, flute and bass.

Albert (1604–51), Hammerschmidt (1612–75) and Tunder (1614-67) were amongst the German church composers and organists who followed and carried the instrumental lead of Schütz just over the mid-century, forming links in the chain which, through Buxtehude and others, connected the work of Schütz with that of Bach.

Some of the *Arien* by Albert—a nephew of Schütz—are scored for 1st and 2nd violins, 1st and 2nd tenors, basses and bassoons, a well-blended group much more suitable for his purpose than the odd and rather clumsy combinations of his more famous uncle.

Andreas Hammerschmidt largely favoured the three-part string group, and gave his violins some added briskness, but confined these instruments to either a polyphonic and imitative motion or a simultaneous progress in thirds or sixths.

Franz Tunder employed both three and five-part string groups with much better effect. Patterns based on rhythmical figures and reiterated notes often give his violin figures a more thoroughly orchestral character : (Example 16).

EXAMPLE 16

Tunder (Dominus illuminatio meo)

and some colour-contrasts between violins and tenors, added to a good idea of how to bring in the whole body of strings with good effect at the right moment, reveals a stronger sense for instrumental fitness than was shown by his German contemporaries.

CHAPTER IV

AMONGST the Italian composers who followed Monteverde and his contemporaries, Cavalli (1602–76), Cesti (1623–69) and Legrenzi (1626–90) contribute most to the development and urgently required steadying of the orchestral body. All of them voluminous composers of opera, it is only by the medium of odd surviving scores of their works that we are able to follow the course of orchestration till the time when Lulli became the most prominent figure in an ever-increasing stream of dramatic composers.

Increased reliance on the string orchestra is a most satisfactory feature in the work of this generation. The five-part string orchestra is standard, although three parts generally suffice for accompanying vocal solos, and sometimes for entire works. The *basso-continuo* part still remains the backbone of these scores and never ceases from beginning to end. Strings play all *sinfonie* and *ritornelli*, sometimes accompany the choruses, and only occasionally the solos.

An improving violin technique, which on the whole takes the form of increased activity and brightness, is reflected in the string parts of these mid-century Italian composers. Cesti in particular makes his violins bustle about, and though the instruments are not named in a MS. copy of his *La Dori* (1663), there is no mistaking them for anything but violin parts: (Example 17).

As alternatives to this imitative style composers of the period have little to offer but a solid harmonic structure or the easy device of writing two violin parts in consecutive thirds.

Cavalli's *Giasone* (1655) opens with a *sinfonia* for a five-part orchestra. The instruments are not named in the score, and the parts, written in solid harmony, have no particular instrumental character. The remaining *sinfonie* and several *ritornelli* are scored in three parts, while a few of the vocal solos have similar accompaniments which could hardly be intended for anything but violins and basses. An example of Cavalli's violin parts in thirds can be seen in Grove's *Dictionary* under the article "opera," and

EXAMPLE 17

Cesti (La Dori 1663)

a few from the same composer's *Erismena* are given in Burney's
History of Music[1]. Several examples of three and five-part string
music by Cavalli, Cesti, and Legrenzi are quoted in the *Oxford
History of Music*[2], and are representative of what these composers
did with string instruments.

Parry also quotes a passage[3] from Cesti's *Il Pomo d'Oro* (1667)
which he maintains is a " shuddering " chorus.   It is by no means

[1] Vol. iv, p. 69.

[2] Vol. iii, chap. 4.

[3] *The Oxford History of Music*, Vol. iii, p. 176, Ex. 145b.

clear that these parts were intended for voices ; the evidence of
the clefs points strongly to the conclusion that they are string
parts over which a mysterious wavy line  is drawn and which
may indicate some sort of *vibrato* or *tremolo* effect. The choral
parts throughout the work are written in four or eight parts with
the Soprano, Alto, Tenor, and Bass clefs, whereas the five-part
string orchestra is almost invariably furnished with G (or violin)
clefs for 1st and 2nd violins, soprano clef for 1st tenors, alto
clef for 2nd tenors, and bass clef for basses and *continuo*. The
clefs in the alleged " shuddering " chorus parts correspond
exactly to the clefs used for the string orchestra, moreover the
five-part grouping adds weight to the evidence that these parts

EXAMPLE 18

Cesti (La Dori)

were intended for strings. A similar wavy line occurs over repeated notes for strings in a few scores of the late seventeenth century, and is fairly frequent in eighteenth century scores, but no quite satisfactory explanation of its meaning can be offered [1] [2].

In addition to the string parts, scores of this period occasionally include parts for wind instruments. In operatic scores trumpets are the most favoured, flutes and bassoons occur less frequently, and *cornetti* and trombones very rarely. Drums were probably used in connection with trumpets, but specific parts for drums rarely appear in scores. These wind instruments are sometimes clearly specified, as in the score of Cesti's *Il Pomo d'Oro*, but too often only vague hints suggest that other than string instruments are intended. For example, in Cavalli's early opera *Le Nozze di Teti e Peleo* (1639) when a chorus of soldiers

[1] See Forsyth's *Orchestration* (London, 1914), p. 350.
[2] See Ex. No. 41.

sing the words " *corni e tamburi* ", and later " *e trombe, e trombe* ",
some parts are provided which may be meant for trumpets, and
some quickly repeated notes of lower pitch on another line of the
score are conceivably to be played by hunting horns.   The same
work includes a short movement headed " Chiamata alla Caccia "
in which five parts are provided.   The upper four parts are
repeated triplets on the notes of the common chord of C, and
strongly suggest the use of horns.   Another suggestive case is the
preceding from Cesti's *La Dori* as shown in the Vienna MS.   If
the composer did not introduce trumpets and drums at this
point he certainly missed an opportunity !   (Example 18.)

Il Pomo d'Oro is more fully orchestrated than most operas at
that period.   The five-part string orchestra is freely used for
sinfonie, ritornelli, and occasionally with solos or choral voices,
either in solid vertically planned harmony or in a manner which
derives its character from the contrapuntal movement of parts,
as in the following extracts :

EXAMPLE 19 (*a*) AND (*b*)

(a)   Cesti (Pomo d'oro. 1667)

Variety of colour in the string music is secured, not by varying the treatment, but by replacing the ordinary string orchestra by a group of nothing but viols, and in one scene what appear to be two similarly constituted string orchestras are used antiphonally. The violin parts freely cross one another in imitation and frequently ascend high enough on the E string to require the use of the third position.

The standard group of Ecclesiastical wind instruments, two *cornetti*, three trombones, and a bassoon, alone undertake the entire instrumental parts in one long vocal solo, and are responsible for two *ritornelli*, one of which is harmonically, and the other contrapuntally, planned. For a martial flavouring Cesti turns to trumpets ; the parts are in C and in semi-clarino style : (Example 20) but in one scene with chorus the trumpets are alternated with strings in a manner which only became common towards the end of the seventeenth and at the beginning of the eighteenth centuries : (Example 21).

It is interesting to note that in the trumpet parts in this scene, the 11th open note is used both as F and as F sharp ; also that the

EXAMPLE 20

two trumpeters are on an equal footing, and play the upper part
in turn.

Two flutes, playing mostly in their lower octave, replace the
violins in one *ritornello* and complete the catalogue of Cesti's use
of his orchestral resources on an occasion when he appears to have
had a free hand in the choice of instruments.

The scene from which the last quotation is drawn is one of
few in which distinct tone-colours are combined or contrasted.
Otherwise the general principle of colour distribution follows the
plan of Monteverde's *Orfeo* almost in detail. The use of one
tone-colour for each scene, the separation of viols and violins,
the combination of *cornetti* and trombones, all these coincide

strangely with Monteverde's example of just sixty years earlier. The gains of the orchestra in that period were, a more complete and better balanced group of strings and a more precise method of indicating in the score the parts allotted to particular instruments. Other gains, such as the improved part-writing and more modern harmony, are the result of general progress in musical art and in the technique of composition rather than of any increased sense for orchestral colour and effect. But the parallel of *Orfeo* and *Il Pomo d'Oro* fails in one significant aspect, namely, that, whereas *Orfeo* was a solitary example, a pioneer work, a work of experiment and innovation, Cesti's opera exemplifies the same principles as conventions or common property.

EXAMPLE 21

Cesti (Pomo d'oro)
(Chorus parts double the String parts)

Although shawms or oboes were used in open-air bands before and during the seventeenth century, it is not till after the middle of that century that they begin to be regularly associated with string instruments in the works of the better class of composers. The French in particular had developed the use of oboe bands for military purposes, and Lulli, who undertook the organisation of French military bands in his time, composed or arranged numerous marches for oboes of different sizes. This, with an abundant supply of players, no doubt accounts for the regular appearance of those instruments in his operatic scores, and his prominence and example for the fact that from this time onwards oboe parts are rarely absent from any score in which parts for wind-instruments are included. From about the last quarter of the seventeenth and throughout the first half of the eighteenth centuries they absorb more attention than is given to either flutes or bassoons, and share with trumpets the most important position amongst the wind instruments of the orchestra.

An Italian by birth, Jean Baptiste Lulli (1633-87) by his life and work belongs to the succession of French operatic composers which, from the second half of the seventeenth century and onwards, took an important part in the development of orchestral art. The period of Lulli's activity begins with his early Ballet *Alcidiane* in 1658 and extends till the year of his death in 1687.

By nature ambitious, a courtier, schemer, and successful organizer, Lulli attained the position of musical dictator at the court of Louis XIV of France, and between 1670 and 1687 composed and produced a series of some twenty operas. These were printed in full score during the composer's lifetime or soon after his death, and afford ample means of assessing the value of his contribution to the art of orchestration.

As example and precedent he had before him the work of Cambert and the earlier ballet composers ; he had been associated with Cavalli in some operas which that composer had brought with him from Italy for production in Paris. His early musical experience was that of a practical violinist and director of the " *petits violons* " of the king.

More consistent than progressive, Lulli uses his orchestra methodically and with an almost routine regularity of style[1] throughout the whole of his career. His merits are those of one who establishes or confirms rather than of one who discovers or invents.

To the standard five-part string orchestra he entrusts all his overtures, dances, marches, and purely instrumental movements, also the duty of duplicating chorus parts, and only occasionally of providing accompaniment to vocal solos. The latter are as a rule furnished with nothing but a bare bass part, and when instrumental parts are written they are more often than not for only two violins, or even for two flutes or oboes, and *basse-continue*. *Ritornelli* are likewise generally scored for a three-part orchestra.

Flutes and oboes are given parts in all Lulli's operas, but only play on an average in about six or seven scenes in each

[1] According to Halévy, Lulli wrote only the vocal and bass parts of his operas, leaving the orchestral parts to be filled in by his pupils, Lalouette and Colasse.

opera. They are used in dances, marches, and sometimes in *ritornelli*, but there is as a rule no written part for them in the fuller *ensemble* of the *finale* to each act.

Trumpets and drums are drawn on for special scenes only. Bassoons appear irregularly in the scores, and some unusual[1] or obsolete instruments are specified here and there in particular operas but are not part of Lulli's regular instrumental stock-in-trade.

On many pages of the scores the word *violons* is printed just underneath the 1st violin line ; this is the signboard of the string orchestra, and it is taken for granted that the lower staves are for the remaining string parts, although bass instruments normally share a line of the score with the *basse-continue*. The 1st violin staff is written, according to French custom, with the G clef on the first line, and the inside parts are noted respectively in the soprano, mezzo-soprano, and alto clefs[2] ; when a separate staff is provided for string basses it is marked *basse des violons* and the bass clef is used.

In spite of the different clefs, the two upper parts could be for nothing but treble violins ; the fourth part is clearly for tenor violins or viols ; the third part (mezzo-soprano clef) might be another violin part as far as the usual compass of the part is concerned, however, a few solitary notes of lower pitch than the G string of the violin mark the instrument as a tenor. The words *basse des violons* seem to imply that the instruments were 'cellos and not bass viols, though the latter were not yet obsolete in orchestras at the time when Lulli flourished. There is nothing in the scores to show whether double-basses were included in the combination or not.

A representative example of Lulli's scoring for strings would be assured by taking at random almost any page of full score from amongst hundreds on which string parts occur. Except for occasional entries in fugal manner, all the instruments play continuously together. The part-writing is neither a wholly horizontal polyphony nor a merely vertically planned harmonic

---

[1] Some parts for *trompes de chasse* in *Princesse d'Élide* (1664) were probably for hunting horns.

[2] Mersennus's group of five string parts (*Fantaisse à 5*) are *Dessus* (G clef on first line), *Haute-contre* (C clef on second line), *Tailli* (C clef on third line), *Cinquiesme* (C clef on first line) and *Basse-contre* (F clef on fourth line).

structure, and shows hardly anything that could be called passage-work, nor any figuration based on set patterns.   The parts are well distributed, blend and balance could hardly be anything but satisfactory, but they lack variety and could only prove some-what monotonous in effect.   The following are the beginning and the start of the fugal section of the overture to *Proserpine* (1680) : (Example 22).

A few scenes in certain operas are to be played by muted strings, and for this Lulli may possibly register a claim to be regarded as an innovator.

Lulli's wind parts are likewise stereotyped in style and in the manner in which they are disposed.   When they appear in the score, the two flute or two oboe parts, or both together, either duplicate or replace for a time the 1st and 2nd violin parts.   More rarely they alternate in short phrases with the string orchestra. Of these three possibilities the first is the most frequent and

EXAMPLE 22 (*a*) AND (*b*)

(*a*)   Lulli (Proserpine. 1680)

Ouverture

(b)

EXAMPLE 22 *(continued)*

involves nothing but the addition of some written directions to the violin parts in the score, such as : "*Flûtes et violons*" or "*Hautbois, flûtes, et violons*". This always shows quite clearly when the wood-wind join the violins in unison, and one can only presume that they continue playing in unison till the end of the movement or till cancelled by some further direction such as : "*Violons*" or "*Violons seuls*". At other times a movement is given a general heading, for example : "*pour les violons et les flûtes*"; in either case the intention seems to be that 1st flutes are to play in unison with the 1st violins, and 2nd flutes with the 2nd violins, for it is Lulli's invariable custom to have his wind instruments playing in two parts, whether with or without strings.   The perfunctory directions in these scores can often be read in two ways, *i.e.*, that the wind instruments are added to, or that they replace the strings ; which is intended is by no means always clear.   On the other hand, directions or headings occur which indicate quite clearly that flutes or oboes, or both together are to play alone.   They are then given two parts for which the *basse-continue* invariably supplies the bass and such harmony as is not completed by the two upper parts.

These flute and oboe parts show no characteristics by which they can be distinguished fron string parts, and were it not for the written directions it would be impossible to tell one from the other: (Example 23).

Occasionally *flûtes d'allemagne* are specified, from which it may be assumed that *flûtes-à-bec* are normally employed.

Lulli's violinists are rarely required to play on the G string, or in any but the 1st position.   This limited compass of rather less than two octaves is likewise imposed on flutes and oboes, whether playing alone or in unison with violins.   While that range covers the best part of the oboe, it hardly touches the more brilliant part of the flute.   The third octave seems to be denied to players on these simple flutes ; the idea that a flute part should be higher in pitch or more florid than an oboe part is not discernable in the scores of either Lulli or his contemporaries.

Lulli is apparently just conscious of the variety obtainable by contrasting string and wood-wind tone at close quarters. He uses this device rarely and timidly ; nevertheless, the principle is there, though owing to his custom of writing for wind instruments in not more than two parts, that body lacks fulness and impressiveness when alternated with the string orchestra: (Ex. 24).

EXAMPLE 23 (*a*) AND (*b*)

(a)　　　　Lulli (Thésée — 1675)

Hautbois

Basse-continue

(b)

Flûte d'Allemagne

Basse-continue

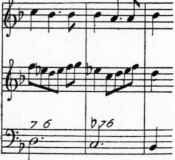

Trumpets, like flutes and oboes, are generally used in pairs, and appear in the scores when the stage situation is concerned with soldiers. Again, they either double or replace the violin parts for short selections, and in order to do that the trumpet parts have to be written high enough to get a few consecutive notes, or the violins have to be restricted to the few open notes of a trumpet fanfare. The instruments are in the key of C and play mainly between the 4th and 13th open notes.

Drums generally join in when trumpets are playing and are given suitably rhythmical parts: (Example 25).

Bassoons, when specified, are given little prominence and no independence. In *Le Triomphe de l'amour* (1681) there is some three part work for two oboes and bassoon not unlike that which frequently occurs in scores by Scarlatti, Purcell, and Handel. In the same opera a flute quartet is employed to play a placid

EXAMPLE 24

" Prélude pour l'amour ".   The specification in the score is
as follows :

Tailles ou Flûtes d'Allemagne (G clef on the 2nd line)
Quinte de Flûtes (C clef on the 1st line)
Petite basse de Flûtes (C clef on the 2nd line)
Grande basse de Flûtes et B. cont. (Bass clef)

A march in *Isis* (1677) introduces " *Musettes* " in unison
with oboes and violins, but these and other instruments, such as
the *trompes de chasse* in *La princesse d'Élide,* are features which do
not recur in other scores, and must be regarded as exceptional.

In view of the opportunities enjoyed by Lulli his orchestration
seems unenterprising and more a matter of routine than of artistic
impulse ; but as an example to others that very quality no doubt
had its value in helping to stabilize and conventionalize some
principles which were necessary for the further development
of orchestration.

The organization of the orchestra in groups of strings, wood-
wind and brass instruments has a tentative beginning in these
scores of Lulli, and in that the wood-wind and trumpets are used

EXAMPLE 25

Lulli (Isis—1677)

EXAMPLE 25 (*continued*)

EXAMPLE 25 (*continued*)

in conjunction with a foundation of strings, and not, as in so many earlier scores, instead of the strings for whole scenes or movements, his methods show an advance on those described in connection with Cesti's *Il Pomo d'Oro*.

The alliance of flutes, oboes, and bassoons in family relationship is clearly foreshadowed in Lulli's scores. He employs his embryo wind-group exactly as he does his three part string orchestra, but has not grasped the seemingly elementary principle of modern orchestration, namely, that wood-wind should be doing one thing while strings are doing another. They either play the same thing together, or the same sort of thing separately. But in that the two groups are used together and separately in the course of the same movements, and in that he carries out this treatment as a fixed formula, regularly and habitually, Lulli's handling of strings and wood-wind points forward rather than backward.

Trumpets and drums are subject to the same treatment ; their colour is added to or substituted for that of strings during the progress of one scene ; eight-bar sections of melody for flutes or oboes are introduced in contrast to louder sections by strings and trumpets. This manner of varying the tone-colour by melodic sections, though stiff and square, has more in common with the manner of Handel than with that of Lulli's predecessors. The formula of a later generation is thus anticipated, and to Lulli must be given the credit of having done much to bring the colours of the orchestra closer together, of having, by consistent example, so largely helped to overthrow the fundamental principles of the earlier Italian composers, namely, that one tone-colour should serve without any variation for an entire scene or movement.

Lulli's work stood firm as a model for his immediate successors in France. Both Colasse (a pupil of Lulli) and Charpentier remained true to the five-part string orchestra while Scarlatti, Purcell, and others had decided for the four-part organization. Colasse has nothing to offer which is not standard in Lulli's scores, but in his *Médée*, Charpentier carries the idea of an orchestral *tutti* a little further by directing not only violins, but flutes and oboes to double some of the upper chorus parts, and string basses and bassoons the lowest part. Another chorus is joined by trumpets and drums in addition to strings and oboes, but there is no independence in the movement of these instrumental parts. Bassoons are given more attention in this score, although they play nothing but bass parts. Trumpets in D are used, and are not written as transposing instruments. Though the score of *Médée* is more specific and the *tutti* rather better handled, the whole is clearly modelled on Lulli's manner, and seems the work of a good improver of a successful example rather than that of an originator.

From amongst many less known contemporaries of Lulli, Antonio Draghi (1635-1700), who wrote numerous operas for Vienna, may be singled out as a composer who had a good idea of writing effectively for strings. His overture to *L'albero del ramo d'oro* (1681) has a vigour which is lacking in Lulli and is often missed by the more profound musicians who were much concerned with the contrapuntal movement of their parts, and thought less of the effects gained by suitable string passages based on a broad and simple harmonic plan. This overture is also interesting as an early example of an operatic programme-overture ; the music is supposed to represent the rush of wind through the trees in a wood.

Stradella (c. 1645-81) and Pallavicino (1630-88) were also important composers of opera during the time of Lulli. From the few examples of their work which survive, it would seem that they were pioneers amongst the Italians who broke with the five-part organization of the string orchestra and wrote only one tenor part. Both also claim some attention for their share in carrying on the development of the true *Clarino* style of trumpet part. In doing so they paved the way for further efforts in this direction by Scarlatti, Purcell, and others who, by the end of the seventeenth century, had established this manner of writing the high florid trumpet parts which culminated in the well-known *obbligato* parts of Bach, Handel, and their contemporaries. In fostering this peculiar and somewhat short-lived feature of orchestration, these early sponsors of the *Clarino* part may conceivably be accounted guilty of having forced the pace of progress in a direction which eventually proved to be unsatisfactory. A proper understanding of the individual styles of parts suited to wind instruments was never thoroughly acquired till the second half of the eighteenth century, and these early writers of *Clarino* parts were only doing with trumpets what they were doing with all other wind instruments, that was, trying to make them play parts as much like violin parts as possible. The trumpet parts of Stradella, Pallavicino, and their followers, figure sometimes as soloists, sometimes as pairs of screaming duetists, each forever imitating the phrases and crossing the melodic path of the other.

The time of Lulli's activity also coincides with the period in which it becomes possible to trace the beginnings of orchestration in the works of a few English composers.

Charles the Second's establishment of " four and twenty fiddlers ", a string orchestra organized in imitation of Louis' " Vingt-Quatre violons ", would provide the stimulus required by composers who had hitherto probably little experience in handling larger instrumental forces than the " chest of viols " or such instruments in " consort " as took part in the earlier masques.

Of the few printed works which survive, the scores of Matthew Locke's *Psyche* (1673), called " The English opera ", and his music to *The Tempest* were both published in 1675, though the latter appears to have been composed as early as 1667. The instrumental music in both works is scored for a four-part orchestra. The two upper staves are furnished with the G clef on the second line, and the tenor part, like the viola parts in Purcell's scores, is written with the C clef on the second line. The use of four parts is noteworthy at a time when all foreign composers still wrote in five parts. Headings such as " Retornello with violins ", " Chorus and violins ", indicate that a string orchestra was used, and wind instruments and drums are directed to play in some of the choruses in *Psyche*. When the orchestra is used in conjunction with the chorus no instrumental parts are provided in the score ; presumably both strings and wind doubled the chorus parts in unison. The specifically instrumental music is colourless and devoid of characteristic string passages or effects except in one chorus where the instruments are allowed a rhythmical presentation of the harmony for two brief moments : (Example 26).

A feature of these scores is the occasional appearance of directions concerning dynamics, speed and manner. The following are from a " curtain tune " in *The Tempest* : " soft "; " Lowder by degrees "; " Violent " ; " soft and slow by degrees ".

A later work by an English composer is John Blow's *Venus and Adonis* (1681-8). The music of this masque shows the four-part string orchestra handled in a much more enlightened manner, and includes an overture which is not at all unworthy of comparison with the best of contemporary foreign work. A pair of flutes are treated very much as if they were violins, and apparently replace the upper string parts for some time.

The initial period in the history of orchestration has thus already overflowed into the time of Purcell, Scarlatti, and the composers who were to form further links in the chain of progress connecting the early Monodists with the musical giants of the eighteenth century.

From the uncertainty and chaos of " all instruments ", a string orchestra, the basis of a wood-wind band and the merest shadow of a brass band have emerged, all still strung together by the incongruous medium of lutes and keyboard-instruments.

EXAMPLE 26

Instrumental part-writing has achieved an independent existence and no longer echoes the characteristics of purely vocal music, while appreciation of instrumental tone-colour has made a tentative appearance.

So far the use of the orchestra has been confined almost entirely to Church and stage works, but some early suites and concertos, even if they did not clearly differentiate between an orchestral and a chamber style, had just presaged a new home for the orchestra, namely, in the Concert-room.

CHAPTER V

PURCELL—SCARLATTI : THE FOUR-PART STRING ORCHESTRA

BEFORE Lulli had completed his last few operas the five-part string orchestra was already doomed. Composers of a new generation were practically unanimous in their decision that one of the two tenor parts almost invariably provided in scores up to that time was redundant. The transition roughly covers the last twenty-five years of the seventeenth century, and the process shows the same overlapping of old and new which is inevitable in all matters relating to musical progress.

Amongst Italians, Stradella, who died about 1681, seems to have been amongst the first to decide in favour of the four-part group, and Alessandro Scarlatti (1659-1725), though at least one of his early operas is for five-part strings, uses the now standard string orchestra of 1st violins, 2nd violins, tenor violins, and basses (violoncellos and double basses[1]) for practically the whole of his enormous operatic output.

French composers, taking Lulli as their exemplar, imitated him in this as in every other respect and clung to the five-part organization until long after the beginning of the eighteenth century.

Steffani (1654-1728), a busy composer of opera in Germany during the last quarter of the seventeenth century, scores all his operatic music excepting one or two of the earlier overtures for four-part strings, but Buxtehude (1637-1707) the famous organist at Lübeck, whose performances of sacred works for voices and orchestra attracted Bach thither in 1705, has left many works scored in five parts for violins, tenor viols and basses.

English composers of the Restoration period favoured the four-part group, and Henry Purcell (1658-95), though his overture to *King Arthur* (1691) has two tenor parts, thoroughly endorses the choice of the majority of composers whose work touches Lulli on the one hand and Handel on the other, by scoring all his Church and stage music for the standard four-part string orchestra.

It is also in the last quarter of the seventeenth century that the lower viols, both tenor and bass, finally give way to tenor

[1] See footnote, p. 34.

violins and violoncellos in the orchestra, though solo parts for *viola da gamba*, *viola d'amore*, and similar obsolescent string instruments continue to appear sporadically in the scores of eighteenth century composers. The violoncello is frequently specified in the scores of Purcell, Scarlatti, and Steffani, and the word " viola ", hitherto a collective name for all instruments of viol type, begins to be identified with the tenor violin only. It is not safe to assume that double basses were in general use at that time to play the lowest of the string parts in company with violoncellos ; contemporary scores shed little light on the matter, and the instrument is rarely named in full scores, although the term *violone* appears fairly frequently.

Thus, the experience of about a hundred years at last sees a foundation of homophonic string-tone firmly established in the orchestra. Well-blended, balanced, and organized in the most convenient number of parts, the constitution of the string orchestra is settled for all time in the last quarter of the seventeenth century.

The newly achieved stability of the strings, coinciding with a further growth of violin technique, marks the last two decades of the seventeenth century as a period of significance in the history of the orchestra. Vitali, Corelli, and Torelli amongst Italians, Biber and Walther amongst Germans, and many others of less permanent renown are of the generation of violinist-composers whose work directly influences the texture of orchestral string music written just before the great masters of the eighteenth century began their working lives. These men were the leaders of orchestras, leaders in a very literal sense and not merely principal 1st violins. While the " conductor " at the *cembalo* was responsible for supporting and shepherding the vocalists, the violinist-leader was in charge of the instrumentalists, a species of dual control which apparently worked better than might have been expected. Themselves composers of consequence, solo-players, conductors and orchestral players all in one, by their example and skill, the solo and even virtuoso element in violin-playing reacts in the form of a higher standard of technique demanded of violinists generally. The expressive and the florid aspects of violin-playing begin to be exploited and appreciated in the period of the rapidly developing string sonata and concerto. New types of passage and figuration appear in the scores, giving birth to new effects, and with a better understanding of what is

suitable to the instruments, hasten the more thorough individualization of the string part.

In considering the state of violin-technique at that time it
should be borne in mind that the shift or change of position had
been little used. The third position was obviously expected
of orchestral players, but rarely anything higher, and the left-hand
work must have been very much hampered by the prevailing
custom of holding the violin with the chin on the *right-hand* side
of the tail-piece. A heavy and inelastic bow precluded the possibility of light bowing and its shortness limited slurring and sustained bowing. The passages which show the advancing technique are mainly those which depend on the power of the bow
to reiterate the same note quickly, to alternate rapidly between
two notes on adjacent strings, or to skip over a string in leaps of
wide intervals. These features are hardly recognized in the
violin parts of Lulli and the earlier Italians. Monteverde's
repeated semiquavers,[1] like other of his innovations, proved to be
like the one swallow which did not make a summer.

Torelli (d. 1708) is sometimes credited with the invention of
the string concerto, a form which partially involved a re-grouping
of the string instruments into solo and *ripieno* sections, or, as they
were called, *concertino* and *concerto grosso*. This feature of string
organization crops up persistently from the time of Stradella—
himself a violinist—to Haydn, and only disappears with the rise
of the later solo-concerto. Under this arrangement the solo
group consisted of either two violins or two violins and violoncello, with a *ripieno* orchestra of two violin, viola, and bass parts.
Stradella, Scarlatti, Bach, and even Haydn in some of his earlier
symphonies, often employ this dual grouping of the string
orchestra for works ambiguously called Concerto or Symphony,
works designed for concert performance, and unassociated with
opera or oratorio. This was a new use for the orchestra, which
hitherto had only been used for Church or operatic music in a
capacity more or less secondary to that of the voices. The early
concerto and symphony are in fact one and the same thing ;
neither form established its individuality till further development
of violin and piano technique evolved the modern or Mozartian
solo-concerto, a form in which the virtuoso element in the solo
part predominates and is distinguished from the classical
symphony in that the latter has no solo part.

[1] See p. 49.

THE FOUR-PART STRING ORCHESTRA

The sponsors of the four-part string orchestra employed that organization principally for their overtures, dances, choruses, and more important instrumental movements, but like their predecessors, were often content to accompany vocal solos by two violin parts and a bass part. Even a single violin part and *basso-continuo* suffice for many of the *arias* in opera and dramatic works by Purcell, Scarlatti and Steffani, a thin method of scoring which often satisfied Handel and his contemporaries.

The wind instruments of Lulli's orchestra on the whole hold good for the period now under survey. Purcell died in 1695, so did not live to see horns adopted in the orchestra, but Scarlatti, who lived for fourteen years after Handel had started his London operatic career with *Rinaldo* in 1711, was amongst the first to include parts for two horns in his scores, beginning with *Tigrane* in 1715. Flutes, oboes, bassoons (one part), trumpets, and drums thus remain the standard orchestral wind and percussion instruments till horns were added early in the eighteenth century.

It should not be understood that parts for all these instruments occur in every work, much less in every movement. Entire works were often scored for nothing but strings, and almost any combination of the above wind instruments may be found, though it is unusual to find all of them in the same work, and still more unusual to find them all playing in the same movement. Oboes and trumpets are rarely absent from scores which include any wind instruments. Flutes and bassoons occur frequently, and drums irregularly. It is obvious that no fixed combination of wind instruments was available in all orchestras at the time. Composers wrote for what they could get rather than for what they wanted ; circumstance rather than choice is evidently the governing factor. Thus, Scarlatti's *La Rosaura* (1690) has no wind parts ; *Il Prigionier Fortunato* (1698) has parts for four trumpets in the overture, and flute, oboe, and bassoon parts occur at other times in the opera ; *Il Trionfo dell'Onore* (1718) has parts for strings and oboes. In Purcell's *Dido and Æneas* (1680) strings only are required, while his *Dioclesian* (1690) demands strings, flutes, oboes, a " tener oboe " (in the *Second Musick*), bassoon, trumpets, and of these flutes are given no part in the otherwise fully scored *Second Musick*, nor do any wind instruments take part in the overture.

It would be impracticable to give anything like sufficient examples from the works of Purcell and Scarlatti adequately to

illustrate their methods. Fortunately the works of the former are
available in the excellent issues of the Purcell Society, but no
such printed collection of Scarlatti's music exists. His manuscripts are scattered far and wide in English and continental
libraries. Probably the most convenient and representative
selection of orchestral extracts is that in Dent's *Alessandro
Scarlatti*[1], a work all the more valuable to English readers in view
of the inaccessibility of the manuscript scores. Isolated examples
may also be found in the *Oxford History of Music*[2], in Grove's
Dictionary[3], and in sundry publications by German musical
historians. All that will be attempted here is to give a few extracts
which will show the more progressive tendencies of orchestration
just prior to the time when a succession of German composers
took over the most important share in shaping the course of
musical history.

A direct link between Lulli and Purcell is the short-lived
Pelham Humfrey (1647-74) who was sent to France to imbibe the
style of musical art so much admired by Charles II. By his own
admission Purcell owns to the benefit he derived from the study
of Italian models. The arrival in England[4] of the violinist Baltzar,
just before the Restoration, and his later appointment as leader
of Charles's "four-and-twenty fiddlers", had no doubt contributed much to the advancement of violin-playing in England, and
Purcell readily incorporated the improved violin technique
in the texture of his string music. His parts are more rhythmical
and figurated, more expressive and more true to the nature of the
instrument than the complacent and rather aimless parts of
Lulli and the mid-century Italians. With his strong feeling for
dramatic effect and the advantage of a better organized string
orchestra, he produced string music which was in style well
abreast of the best of his contemporaries and able to bear comparison with that of his eighteenth century successors. The
vigorous skips over large intervals, the conjunct figures lying well
under the fingers of the player, the quickly reiterated note, in
fact most of the familiar patterns of Handel's string parts are to
be found in the scores of Purcell. He shows some invention and
independence in devising purely instrumental effects which owe
nothing to the contrapuntal movement of parts:

[1] London, 1901–1905.   [2] Vol. iii.   [3] Art. " Overture ".

[4] Variously given as 1655, 1656, and 1658.

EXAMPLE 27

Purcell (Dido & Aeneas _ 1680)

Scarlatti's longer working life and his closer contact with the then rising Italian virtuoso school of violin-playing were advantages which no doubt account for the fact that his string parts are even richer in figuration and more brilliant than Purcell's. The following are types of figure which occur in quick movements:

EXAMPLE 28

A. Scarlatti

The conjunct motion of (a), the arpeggio nature of (b), and the reiterated character of (c) are features which combined to give a greater vigour and life to string music in the last decades of the seventeenth century and brought about orchestral effects which served as patterns for the next generation of composers. Purcell's and Scarlatti's string parts move as with a definite purpose ; always according to some particular harmonic or melodic pattern which is set for each movement, but never aimlessly or insipidly. The imitative style of the music, also the free crossing of parts, are but remains of early Italian vocal polyphony, features which prevailed in instrumental music till long after their time. The parts are well and evenly distributed when the treatment is contrapuntal, but are placed rather close together and more in a position suited to keyboard-instruments when the treatment is harmonical.

Just occasionally Scarlatti looks ahead by making a distinction between violoncello and bass parts. In some cases the difference is simply that between a bass of eight-foot-tone and one of sixteen-foot-tone, but instances occur in *Il Prigionier Fortunato* and in *L'amor Generoso* (1714) when violoncellos are given parts independent of the double basses. Although these 'cello parts are only elaborated or figurated versions of the real bass part, the idea shows appreciation of the individuality of violoncello tone and was no doubt a novelty at that time.

The real gain to the wind section of the orchestra in this period is not so much in organization as in independence of treatment, and to some extent in logical grouping. Lulli either duplicated or replaced his violin parts by wind parts, but both Purcell and Scarlatti freely wrote independent parts for wind in conjunction with the string instruments. Both composers, however, frequently adopt a system of wholesale duplication which is in its way little better than the "*tutti l'instromenti*" of the early Italian pioneers. This process involves nothing more than the addition of a word or two to the specification of instruments at the beginning of a score ; thus, an upper part may be headed *Violini I e Oboe I*, and the next *Violini II e Oboe II*, or a bass part *con fagotto*, and no attempt is made to differentiate between the style of a string and a wind part. Directions of this sort occur in hundreds of scores from the end of the seventeenth to the middle of the eighteenth centuries, and no one availed himself more readily of this thought and labour-saving device than Handel. Haste, indifference, or mere habit may account for this

rough-and-ready way of working ; it also helps to account for the
enormous output of the composers and the extraordinary short
time in which some of their works are said to have been completed.

The writing of independent wind parts was in itself an
important step forwards. A fresh means of securing variety was
added to the resources of the orchestrator and the new possibilities thus opened out were infinite, but the idea that instrumental parts must be contrapuntal, imitative, or fugal in design,
when viewed from a later-day standpoint, seems to have been
almost an obsession with seventeenth century and early
eighteenth century composers. Their wind parts are as near an
imitation of string parts as the technique of the instruments
would allow. This was the bar to progress that threatened to
bring orchestration to a standstill in the first half of the eighteenth
century. Though it was certainly to the good that wind instruments were being treated independently, the resulting contrapuntal orchestration, in which strings and wind were treated alike,
proved to be something like progress along a blind alley. It is to
the early classical composers that the art of writing for the
orchestra owes its release from the obstruction of polyphony.

While making the best use of increasing varieties of excellent
passages and figures for violins, both Purcell and Scarlatti are
prone to cast their wind parts in the same mould. That flutes
escaped much of this second-hand figuration is probably due to the
quiet tone of the *flute-à-bec*, and because flute parts were always
written low, where the tone is weak ; but the burden of imitating violin figures falls heavily on oboes and trumpets, both
of which were better able to cope with and balance the bright
full tone of violins. These instruments were consequently saddled
with florid parts quite unsuited to their character, even if not to
their technique. By their natural limitations forced to play in
their highest register, trumpets suffered most acutely under the
domination of the violin figure, and paid the price of prominence
in the further development of the *clarino* style of playing, a style
which was carried almost to the length of impracticability
by Bach and Handel. Figures such as those in group (a)
Ex. 28, were indiscriminately handed on to oboes and trumpets
without much regard for practicability, balance or effect. In
this respect also the pattern was set for succeeding generations,
but not with satisfactory results. If the string parts are active
and florid, then wind parts must be active and florid, seemed to

be the creed of all composers till the early " classical " school reversed the dictum and discovered that the best backing for florid string parts was a more sustained harmonic background by the constitutionally less active wind instruments. The imitative process was sometimes carried out by means of figurated passages, and sometimes in the course of fugal exposition and development, as, for example, in the quick movements of the overture to Purcell's *Ode on St. Cecilia's Day* (1692).

It was only when the quickly reiterated note—the exclusive property of the bowed-string instrument—came into play, that composers were forced to abandon the florid imitative wind part, and were obliged to devise parts which were broader, simpler, and more in keeping with the true nature of the wind instruments. It is in that very solution of the problem that they at times came nearest to the principles of modern orchestration and made real progress along a road which was not beset with the distractions of imitative polyphony. A few bars of music, respectively from the overtures to *Il Prigionier Fortunato* and *Griselda* (1721) will suffice to show how Scarlatti touched a new sort of independence between strings and wind, the independence which, freed from imitation, became the basic principle of modern orchestration[1]: (Example 29).

The futile exchange of notes in the wind parts of these examples —effects more on paper than in sound—harks back to the vocal polyphony of the sixteenth century, but the employment of chords for wind instruments, even though thinly disposed, while the strings are active, looks forward to the second half of the eighteenth century. Thus old and new principles are mixed. Apart from the context, the one feature marks these last examples as belonging to the seventeenth century, while but for that brand they might almost have been written late in the eighteenth century.

Scarlatti may have been the discoverer of another orchestral device, simple and obvious to the harmonic thinker but quite foreign to the mind which could only conceive music as a combined progress of so many melodic parts. Detached chords by the string orchestra accompanying and reinforcing the accents of music played by one or more wind instruments was at that time quite as novel as the harmonic wind parts quoted in the last example. This is quite a new function for the strings; a sort of independence which owes nothing to the polyphony of the past,

[1] See also Ex. 34.

EXAMPLE 29, (*a*) AND (*b*)

EXAMPLE 29 (*continued*)

EXAMPLE 29 (*Continued*)

one which is impossible on voices, an effect of harmonic and dynamic colour which is sheer invention showing more true understanding of the possibilities of differentiation between the two main orchestral groups than any amount of independent part-writing which has its root in mutual imitation[1].

Much better than the style of their individual wind parts is the way in which Purcell and Scarlatti employ wind instruments grouped together as a foil to string-tone. This feature of orchestration had been only timidly carried out by Lulli and the earlier Italians, but became almost a commonplace by the end of the seventeenth century. The alternation of string and wind-tone is perhaps the broadest contrast available in the orchestra, and offers greater scope of variety of colouring than the combination of the two bodies, more especially so at a time when composers hardly yet understood how to combine strings and wind except by uniting them in a common polyphony. Flutes, oboes and bassoons, oboes and trumpets, trumpets alone or with drums, are the favourite wind groups used at that time in alternation with strings, and of these the most homogeneous is the alliance of oboes and bassoon which, disposed in three parts, figures so largely in the scores of Purcell, Scarlatti, Steffani, and later on, of Handel and his contemporaries. In these groups and in the fact that they were freely used as independent groups, is found a further development of the grouping of orchestral instruments in three sections, namely : strings, wood-wind, and brass. To the above combination Scarlatti added horns, thereby securing still greater variety of colour, but this was not till about twenty years after Purcell's death.

The traditional method of writing wind parts in pairs over a common bass—the *basso-continuo*—prevails throughout this period. Even when more instruments of the same sort are available, as in the overture to *Il Prigionier Fortunato*, it does not occur to the composer to use them as other than two pairs of duettists answering and echoing one another. The two-part writing therefore leaves the wind-groups always deficient in body ; even though there were several instruments playing each part, this thinness is in evidence and is accentuated by the custom of always placing the two wind parts close together, leaving a large gap between them and the bass part. The arrangement of two

[1] See quotation in Dent's *Alessandro Scarlatti*, p. 160.

oboes, a tenor oboe and a bassoon in four-part harmony which occurs in Purcell's *Dioclesian* is exceptional, and only serves to prove the rule.

In the antiphonal use of string and wind-tone, Purcell is quite on a level with his longer-lived Italian contemporary. A typical example of this procedure is the following from the *Ode on St. Cecilia's Day* :

EXAMPLE 30

EXAMPLE 31 Purcell (Dioclesian.—1690)

EXAMPLE 31 (*Continued*)

This feature is quite common in both Purcell's and in Steffani's scores. However many instruments represent the wind group, the composers are always content to write for them in at most three parts. There is no attempt to secure the richer tone-quality procurable by multiplying the number of notes sounded at the same time. Probably a solitary exception to the three-part rule is the four-part group in Purcell's *Dioclesian* (1690): (Example 31).

Here is a homogeneous group of double-reed instruments answering the heavier *tutti* of trumpets and strings, an excellent contrast in tone-colour, carefully thought out and probably unique in orchestration up to that time.

To Purcell and Scarlatti belong the credit of having been amongst the first to break with the tradition that wind instruments should always sound in pairs. Though only one part was provided for bassoons, that part is always the bass of the harmony, and cannot be regarded as a melodic solo for a wind instrument, but solo trumpet parts of the florid *clarino* type are common in the scores of both composers, and Scarlatti's

EXAMPLE 32

A Scarlatti (Il Prigionier fortunato)

EXAMPLE 32 (*Continued*)

occasional solo parts for flute or oboe, or for single string instruments, break new ground and are agreeable and novel features in orchestration at a time when wind instruments were persistently used in pairs. The introduction to an *aria* in *Il Prigionier Fortunato* is extraordinarily unlike contemporary work ; it might belong to the second half of the eighteenth century but for the bareness of the score and the tell-tale specification of instruments at the beginning. The excellent flute solo and the rhythmical comment by the violins (*unisono*) are splendidly contrasted and thoroughly characteristic. The parts seem to belong to the instruments ; there is no ambiguity about them, no borrowing or imitation in this happy bit of orchestration : (Example 32).

The period of Purcell-Scarlatti also introduced the first sign of purely accompanying patterns into the texture of the orchestral music. The technique of composition before that time hardly admitted any such thing as sustained, repetitional, or figurated accompaniments. Instrumental parts were conceived contrapuntally rather than harmonically, and though block-harmonization had been employed in the orchestra ever since the rise of monody, accompanying patterns of rhythmical or figurated type had not yet become conventions. Instrumental accompaniments which might be varied in pattern, texture, rhythm, and tone-colour, opened out more possibilities for the discovery of orchestral effects than a style of music based largely on the melodic movement of parts. The real break with the old style of orchestration based on an impartial distribution of parts from a common fund of polyphony did not come till near the middle of the eighteenth century, but the first signs of the coming change are to be found in the set patterns of accompaniment, and in the few scattered attempts to write purely harmonic parts, features which occasionally peep out from amongst a mass of contrapuntal part-writing in the last quarter of the seventeenth century.

The horn parts in Scarlatti's later scores are for the instruments in F, and are noted an octave higher than the actual sounds. Like other wind-instruments, the horns were treated as melodists within the limitations imposed by the few available open notes ; the two parts are thus necessarily written high in order to get a few adjacent notes, and cross one another freely in imitation :

EXAMPLE 33

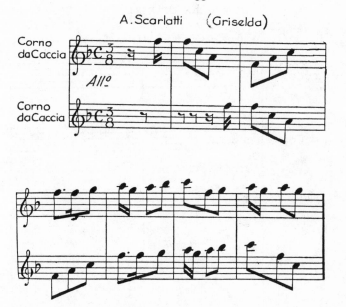

A. Scarlatti   (Griselda)

Later in the same work the horns are used harmonically, and
assist the oboes in providing a harmonic background of wind-
tone for the more effective display of the livelier motion of the
violins.   This clear distinction between the functions of strings
and wind show Scarlatti just beginning to tread the path which
led to modern orchestration : (Example 34).

The name of Agostino Steffani is well worthy of being coupled
with that of Purcell and Scarlatti, even if only on account of his
orchestration.   Famous in Germany as a composer of opera,
statesman, ambassador and Church dignitary, Steffani's operatic
works written for Munich, Hanover and Dusseldorf show him in
a favourable light amongst those who set up a standard of
orchestration for the coming eighteenth century composers.

Although at least two of his overtures are for five-part strings,
Steffani writes almost entirely for four-part strings.   The
Munich operas cover the years 1681 to 1688, and are followed by
a series composed for Hanover, where he was appointed *Kapellmeister* in 1689.   At Hanover Steffani found an orchestra of

EXAMPLE 34

EXAMPLE 34 (*Continued*)

French musicians[1], and, no doubt, to suit them, adopted the French system of clefs, with the G clef on the first line of the staff for 1st violins.   In one score the string parts are named *violons*, *hautecontre*, *taille* and *basses*.   His string music is as vigorous as that of Scarlatti, if a little less brilliant, and shows the same tendency every now and then to abandon polyphony in favour of set patterns of accompaniment based on rhythmical or harmonic figures.   Reiterated chords in quavers or semiquavers occur frequently, and further variety of treatment includes the alternation of solo and *ripieno* groups, also the use of mutes.

Amply supplied with wind instruments, Steffani used his oboes and bassoons much as Handel used them, the former in unison with 1st and 2nd violins, the latter doubling the bass part.   A trio of two oboes and a bassoon often replaces or alternates with the string orchestra, and a similar treatment of flutes, written for in their lower register, gives further variety of colour.   Trumpets in two, three, or four parts, and drums are freely employed in the more spectacular scenes, sometimes in the form of marches or fanfares, at other times in conjunction with the full *tutti* of choral voices, strings and wood-wind.   A march skilfully contrived out of the open notes of four C trumpets occurs in *I Trionfi del Fato* (Hanover, 1695), and shows the practical musician who knew his instruments well : (Example 35).

A somewhat novel feature in some of Steffani's scores are the *obbligato* parts for bassoon solo in conjunction with a solo voice. This form of elaborated duet for solo voice and instrument, supported only by the *basso-continuo*, is quite common just towards the close of the seventeenth century, and suggests that composers wrote the parts especially for particularly skilled individuals in their orchestras.   The violin, 'cello or *viola da gamba*, oboe or trumpet are usually the favoured instruments ; it would seem that Steffani's orchestra enjoyed the services of a conspicuously good bassoon player.

Steffani employs all the best devices of orchestration which were current at the time with ease and frequency.   He handles his forces with confidence and seems to know how to make the most of what was evidently a well furnished and competent body of players.

While this Italian-born Roman Catholic composer was busy writing opera for German audiences, Dietrich Buxtehude

[1] Chrysander's *Life of Handel*.

EXAMPLE 35

Steffani (I Trionfi del Fato _ 1695)

stood for the continuity of the German Protestant Church style of instrumental music which had its beginning in Schütz, and through such as Tunder, Hammerschmidt, and Buxtehude was to reach into the next century and culminate in the work of Bach.

Buxtehude clung to the old organization of strings in either three or five parts, and still allowed the use of viols for the two tenor and the bass parts of his string group.   The bass parts are often specified *violon ò viola da gamba,* and the *continuo* is for *organo.* He was also true to the traditions of the Gabrieli-Schütz school in writing much for *cornetti,* trombones, trumpets and bassoons, and gave less attention to flutes and oboes.   In his polyphonic string music Buxtehude offers little variety of treatment except the alternation of violins with tenor and bass instruments ; this, however, occurs very frequently and seems designed in order to display the difference between violin and viol tone-quality.   At other times each string instrument is made to go into fixed partnership with some wind instrument of like compass, continuing thus for the course of whole movements. In this way *cornetti* often join the violins, trombones the tenor strings, and bass trombone or bassoon the bass string instruments.

The best and most striking feature of Buxtehude's management of instruments is when he divides them into groups for alternative use in the same movement. Handled in a simply conceived and dignified style, those broad effects of instrumental antiphony must have been impressive when carried out in suitable and spacious surroundings. The instrumental parts in a chorus " *Ihr lieben Christen, freuet Euch nun* ", from one of the *Abendmusiken*, will supply a typical illustration of how the instruments were grouped : two trumpets form one group ; another consists of three violin parts in unison with three *cornetti* ; while a third group is made up of three trombones each playing in unison with a tenor or bass string instrument. In another chorus two treble trombones (*trombette*) replace the trumpets. Trumpets are never used as the upper voices in actual combination with trombones, but the old alliance of *cornetti* and trombones occurs. Both trumpets and trombones are frequently marked " *in sordini.*"

Buxtehude's scores show little concern for the individual characteristics or technique of particular instruments. They hark back to the beginning of the century in that the instruments seem to be grouped on a system based on similarity of compass rather than on blend or contrast of tone-colour. His is a choral style adapted to instruments ; dignified and broadly simple, Buxtehude's very orchestration seems to reflect the spirit of the Lutheran church, and remained apparently quite oblivious to all outside influences which even then were faintly pointing out the path to modern orchestration.

———

Such was orchestration at the junction of the seventeenth and eighteenth centuries.

The main stream of progress, passing from the channel of Italian opera, was already turning towards the north. Centres such as Hamburg, Berlin, Dresden, and Vienna, with outposts at Paris and London, were about to replace Florence, Rome, Naples, and Venice as strongholds of orchestral art.

The dying century had given the string orchestra individuality and stability ; the wood-wind had gained a measure of independence without individuality, while the brass was yet hardly a self-contained group. The keyboard-instrument still retained its central position as the conning tower of orchestral organization, and, though not yet threatened with extinction, was already approaching a state of sinecurism.

The scene of activity and progress in orchestration was henceforward to be shared by the theatre and the concert-room, while in that capacity the Church lost ground.

Polyphony, with its adjuncts, imitation and fugal design, still held orchestral music in a firm grip, but was destined gradually to relax its hold under the pressure of a style based more on harmony and rhythm, with an added element founded on the claim of instrumental tone-colour for fuller recognition.

CHAPTER VI

THE PERIOD OF BACH AND HANDEL

THE addition of a pair of horns and the final choice of transverse flutes in place of the old *flûtes-à-bec* are the most important changes to be recorded in the constitution of the orchestra during the first half of the eighteenth century. A second bassoon part is an innovation in some of the scores. Thus, apart from an occasional demand for certain extra, unusual, or obsolescent instruments, the normal full score for operatic or concert purposes during the period of Bach and Handel comprised two flute, two oboe, one or two bassoon, two horn, two trumpet and drum parts, with four string parts, of which the bass was usually figured and was common to violoncellos, double-basses, keyboard-instruments, and the lutes which were still included in the *personnel* of well-found orchestras.

The above specification by no means applies to every score of the period, nor should it be understood that all these wind-instruments were used together in each movement or work. The string group was almost constantly at work, but the number of parts provided for the wind, and the selection of wind-instruments, was subject to considerable variation, showing clearly that orchestras were far from being uniform in constitution. Nevertheless, the above-named instruments may be fairly said to represent the full orchestra of the time, the orchestra of Bach, Handel, Rameau, Hasse, and a host of other composers renowned in their time but now little more than half-forgotten names. Of the various aspirants which failed to gain a permanent place in the orchestra, the larger oboes came nearest to success. *Cornetti*, although gradually going out of use, and trombones were still used in Church orchestras and for sacred choral works, but gained no footing in the opera or concert orchestra.

In spite of such doubtful or solitary instances as those already noted in the works of Cavalli and Lulli, the hunting horn had no place in seventeenth century orchestras. The period of probation for horns was roughly the first quarter of the eighteenth century, after which time they were almost regularly employed.

The following dates are no doubt far from being exhaustive, but show clearly enough the gradual entry of the instrument into the sphere of cultured music. Records show that horns were added to the orchestras of the opera houses at Dresden and Vienna respectively in 1711 and 1712. A pair of horn parts in the score of Keiser's *Octavia* (Hamburg 1705) and Mattheson's remarks in his *Neu-eröffnete Orchester* (1713) bear witness to the fact that the instrument was then beginning to be used in North German orchestras. Scarlatti's parts in *Tigrane* (Naples 1715), those of Handel in his *Water Music* (1715) and *Radamisto* (London 1720), also in Bononcini's *Astarte* (London 1720) serve to mark the entry of the horn into Italian and English orchestras. The parts in Rameau's *Hippolyte et Aricie* and in most of his succeeding operas supply sufficient evidence that the opera orchestra at Paris was provided with horns as early as 1733, and that the credit given to Gossec for having introduced horns into French orchestras in 1757, as stated by several writers, is unmerited.

Keiser's horn parts in *Octavia* are for the instruments in C, Scarlatti's are for F, and Handel's parts are for D horns, while Mattheson apparently knew only F and G horns. Nearly all parts appearing in scores up till about 1740 are for one or other of these four—C, D, F, or G—of which the D and F instruments appear to have been the favourites. Before the mid-century parts for E flat, E and A horns occur, and soon after both high and low B flat crooks are demanded, thus completing the set of nine, namely, low B flat, C, D, E flat, E, F, G, A, and high B flat[1] which occur commonly in scores composed during the second half of the century. No very precise information is available as to when changeable crooks were first applied to horns. The very earliest parts suggest that composers had to deal with only one instrument of fixed length ; no change of crook is required, and the notation is not strictly speaking on the " transposing " system. The very keys of the few movements in which horns were employed seem to be dictated by the key in which the available instrument was pitched. Yet very soon after the first few parts had appeared the system of " transposing " parts began to creep in, which together with the fact that horns in more than one key were occasionally demanded in the course of the same work,

---

[1] Horns with crooks for all nine keys were made in 1755 by Wernern of Dresden (Gerber, *Lexikon*, 1790). An English tutor (*The Muses Delight*, 1754) mentions horns only in G, F, E, D, and C.

implies that players were then using crooks to alter the fundamental pitch of their instruments.

Although the very earliest horn parts appear in the scores
written an octave higher than the actual sounds, the system of
notation in C for all horns very soon became fairly general, but
by no means universal. Usage obviously varied to some extent.
Various clefs were employed by some composers with the object
of accommodating both player of the instrument and reader of the
score at the same time. This device was apparently much in
favour with many composers who wrote opera for London before

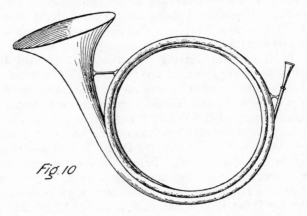

Fig. 10

Hunting Horn, seventeenth and eighteenth century.

and after the middle of the eighteenth century, and was so contrived that the player always read his part in the treble clef,
whereas the part in the score was provided with a clef which gave
the actual sounds. For example, a horn part in Veracini's *Adriano*
(London 1735) is for F horn and is written (with key signature)
in the mezzo-soprano clef, each note appearing exactly as it
sounds. A moment's thought will show that the player had only
to read the same part by means of the treble clef in order to get
the transposed version necessary for the F instrument. The
following examples showing the working of this system of notation
are drawn from the scores of operas produced in London between
1735 and 1763.

EXAMPLE 36

The tonality of D major seems to have been associated with the transverse flute throughout its entire history in the orchestra. Mersennus gives D as the fundamental tone of the instrument in the sixteenth century, and through its period of probation in the latter half of the seventeenth century up to the early nineteenth century, the orchestral flute was built on the basis of the natural scale of D major.   The earlier form was a simple tube of cylindrical bore with six finger-holes, but by the beginning of the eighteenth century a conical bore tapering towards the foot was favoured, and the consequent easier production of the notes of the second and third octaves is reflected in the rather high-pitched flute parts of eighteenth century composers.   At first composers were shy of taking the instrument higher than was customary for the gentle-toned *flûte-à-bec*, but a steadily increasing tendency to write high-pitched parts is easily discernible, and by the mid-century a register roughly an octave higher than that of the oboe was regarded as the proper region for flute parts.   The instrument had gained the D sharp key at the foot end before the end of the seventeenth century[1][2], and other improvements included an adjustable screw-plug at the head-end by means of which the unstable pitch of the period was to some extent accommodated. This later improvement was due to Quantz (1697-1773) the famous flute virtuoso and teacher of Frederick the Great, to whom flute-playing generally owes much of its advancement in the middle of the eighteenth century.   The construction of transverse flutes

[1] See Figure 4.

[2] Hotteterre (*Principes de la Flûte traversière*, 1710) gives the flute a compass from D to G, including all semi-tones except high F natural. *The Modern Music Master* (1731) agrees with this.

in three or more pieces dates from about the same time. Other means of altering the pitch were the use of alternative middle pieces of varying length, or the contrivance of sliding joints which could be pulled out or pushed in according to requirement.

Just as Virdung and Agricola in the sixteenth century and Prætorius and Mersennus in the seventeenth century have left useful accounts of such musical instruments as came under their observation, so Johann Mattheson (1681–1764), the versatile North German composer, provides similar enlightenment covering the early years of the eighteenth century. His book *Das neu-eröffnete Orchester*, published in 1713, is the miniature " Berlioz " of the time and treats of such instruments as were used, at all events, in German orchestras, in his time. A brief summary of the portion of Mattheson's book dealing with orchestral instruments will not be out of place here, and will be found interesting as a preliminary to the further study of eighteenth century orchestration.

The violin is described as the " most difficult " instrument. The compass given is from the open G string for two-and-a-half octaves upwards, with exceptional extension up to high G. The third position was expected of orchestral players and the sixth position was regarded as the extreme limit.

The viola, also named *Violetta, viola da braccio*, or *Brazzo*, is well described as being similar to a violin but larger, and a fifth lower in pitch. Its function is to play middle parts.

The violoncello, *Bassa viola, viola di spala* (shoulder viol) is called a " small bass-fiddle ", the word violoncello being the diminutive of *violone*. The latter instrument is the double-bass, also named *basse de violon* or *grosse bass-geige*. It is said to be of 16 ft. tone and useful for *recitative* in theatres.[1]

The *viola da gamba* was evidently obsolescent in Germany at the time, and seems less familiar to Mattheson, who quotes Rousseau[2] for his description and the tuning of the instrument. The latter corresponds exactly to that given in Example I, Chapter I. He allows the *gamba* a compass of three octaves from its lowest D string.

[1] Eighteenth century double-basses were provided with either five or six strings. Quantz, writing in 1752, recommends that these should be abandoned in favour of the four-stringed instrument.

[2] Evidently Jean Rousseau, a French *gamba* player, born in the seventeenth century ; not the more famous Jean-Jacques Rousseau.

The viola d'amore is said to have five strings tuned to the common chord of C major, with liberty to tune the middle E string to E flat. This differs from the tuning of the instrument with seven strings on the chord of D major, as given by Berlioz and all later writers.

Mattheson catalogues the three sizes of flûtes-à-bec or flûtes douces in F, C, and F exactly as described in Chapter I, and allows each instrument a compass of two octaves from its fundamental note, but insists that the flûte allemande, traversière, " teutche oder Quer-flöte " is the better instrument. The compass of the latter is said to be " as on the oboe ", but without the low C. This instrument is obviously in D, and evidently not usually used higher than its second octave. The favourite keys for the transverse flute are said to be G, A, D major, and E minor. Oboes are given a compass of two octaves from middle C, with a possible high D. Bassoons are allowed a range of two-and-a-half octaves from 8-ft. C, with the possibility of low B-flat and even A, but these two notes are apparently not obtainable on all instruments.

Of the horn (waldhorn) Mattheson says that it "has lately come into use for theatre and chamber music ", that it is most useful in the key of F, and is pitched a fifth lower than the trumpet in C. He also mentions a horn in G.

For trumpets Mattheson gives the open notes of an 8-ft. C instrument, and says that for " Kammer thon "[1] the trumpet in D is the most suitable. " Mund-stücke " (mouth-pieces) which lower the pitch " a good semitone " are presumably lengthening shanks or crooks.

Four trombones are specified, a small alto, a large alto, a tenor or " grosse-quart " and a bass trombone. Presuming the bass trombone to have been in F, the "grosse-quart" would refer to the B flat tenor instrument[2]. Trombones, according to Mattheson, were seldom used except in churches and for solemn occasions.

The cornetto, " the most difficult to blow ", is described as sounding from afar like a rough unpolished human voice, and is said to be going out of use, though still used in churches.   Timpani, tuned a fourth apart, are often used " in Church and opera ".

[1] Old German spelling of Kammerton, i.e., the pitch used for instrumental or chamber music, as distinguished from Chorton, the pitch used for vocal or church music. (See Riemann, Musical Dictionary.)

[2] The small alto might refer to the treble trombone. Compare Prætorius' list of four trombones on p. 18.

On the whole, Matteson's descriptions and remarks agree very well with the evidence of contemporary scores and confirm much that has been said in these pages concerning orchestral instruments and their use in the latter part of the seventeenth and beginning of the eighteenth centuries. Usage undoubtedly varied to some extent in different countries, and the slow diffusion of new ideas and improvements in the construction of musical instruments under the conditions prevailing at the time easily accounts for the slight differences and omissions that may be observed.

A study of orchestration covering the first half of the eighteenth century and overlapping with the early years of the work of Haydn and Mozart must embrace not only the work of the two most prominent composers, Bach and Handel, but also that of a number of German, Italian, and French composers whose music has little but historical significance at the present time. Amongst the Germans the Hamburg group—Keiser, Matteson, and Telemann—such as Stölzel, Graupner, Schürmann, the two Grauns (Berlin), Hasse, J. C. Bach, and C. P. E. Bach will be sufficiently representative.

A group associated with Vienna includes Fux, Conti, and Caldara, with their successors Reutter, Monn, and Wagenseil; while Campra, Desmarets, Destouches, successors of Lulli in Paris, and finally Rameau, stand for French orchestration. Italian composers whose work and influence extended outside their own country, notably to England and Germany, may be adequately represented by such as Vinci, Pergolese, Lotti, Leo, Bononcini, Porpora, and rather later, Galuppi and Jomelli. The earlier of these were born before the end of the seventeenth century, and with few exceptions died before or soon after the mid-century, thus, in their working lives were contemporaneous with Bach and Handel ; the others, born in the first quarter of the eighteenth century, must be reckoned amongst the composers who with Gluck form a transition period bridging and connecting the time of Bach and Handel with that of Haydn and Mozart.

An examination of the orchestral work of all these composers serves to align them roughly in two classes, neither of which can be rigidly circumscribed, but which have for their significant features respectively the conservative and the progressive element in orchestration. Both Bach and Handel belong in varying degree to the conservative class, also the earlier composers of the Italian and Viennese groups, while most of the other Germans mentioned must be counted as progressives. All the French, except Rameau, show not only conservative but ultra-conservative tendencies, and even Rameau cannot be reckoned whole-heartedly progressive. The above rough classification concerns *orchestration only,* and takes no account of Gluck, whose life evenly spans the two halves of the century, but whose significant work belongs to the second half of the century.

The composers of the conservative class were content to orchestrate on lines which had become practically stereotyped during the first quarter of the eighteenth century. In their music the principal consideration is centred in the part and not in the instrument. For orchestration on this basis there seemed to be no possibility of further development, and indeed there was none. It worked itself to a standstill. The string part already had its individuality, the wind part had little but that which was borrowed from the string part and which when forced on brass instruments became, if anything, more and more unsatisfactory.

To the Germans of the progressive class, all of them (as time has shown) second-rate composers whose music was to suffer complete and permanent eclipse, belongs the credit of having first found the true outlet which was to lead orchestration in a direction which has not even yet come to an end. An entirely different function for string and wind instruments, a different style of part for wood-wind and brass instruments, choice by technique and colour, accompaniment instead of perpetual polyphony, these were the main avenues which led from the old contrapuntally conceived orchestration to the beginnings of modern orchestration, and prominent amongst the pioneers must be counted the now forgotten Keiser, Telemann, Graun, Hasse, and others of the so-called " Zopf[1]" composers.

Famous in Germany as an executant, Johann Sebastian Bach (1685-1750) was hardly recognised as a prominent composer during his lifetime. His orchestral works were written for performance under his own guidance in the various towns where he was employed, for variable and often insufficient resources, reaching at best a limited circle which was more local than national in extent. His orchestration follows in direct succession the beginning made by Gabrieli in Italy at the end of the sixteenth century, introduced into Germany by Schütz, further developed by succeeding German organist-composers, and finally handed on

[1] " Pig-tail ". See *Oxford History of Music*, Vol. iv, p. 62.

to Bach and his generation by the Church composers immediately preceding him, the generation of which perhaps the best remembered is Buxtehude. Confined within the radius of a few German churches and provincial courts, Bach's orchestration neither contributed to nor acquired any of the freedom and progress which marked the contemporary work of German composers in the theatre or concert-room.

Bach's resources at Leipzig are known to have been an orchestra of from eighteen to twenty, of which wind instruments would account for nine or ten players, leaving only two or three string instruments to each part. The wind players were obviously double-handed in the sense that the oboe-players, for example, would have to play on alto and tenor instruments of the same type when required, and it is not at all improbable that the players on brass instruments were similarly obliged to change from one instrument to another. Whereas a four-part string orchestra is employed in almost every work, the specific wind parts vary in a manner which suggests that Bach wrote for whatever wind instruments happened to be at his disposal and that the combination and supply varied considerably from time to time. His " memorials " complaining of the lack of necessary instrumental players bear out the impression that he was obliged to cut his coat according to his cloth, and that his orchestral " cloth " was frequently insufficient in quantity if not in quality.

Two flute parts appear in most of the scores and are often specifically for transverse flutes. Two or three oboe parts occur in practically every score. These are for either the treble instrument in C, the alto (*Oboe d'amore*) in A, or for the tenor (*Oboe da caccia*) in F. The limits of the downward compass, respectively to C, A and F are strictly observed whenever the parts are specifically for oboes, though it is sometimes exceeded—probably by accident—when oboes double the string parts for any length of time. In modern reprints the parts are usually non-transposing, and are noted respectively in the treble, treble or soprano, and alto clefs. Parts of the same range as those for *oboe da caccia* sometimes appear with the heading " *taille* " (tenor) and were evidently intended for the same instrument. Independent parts for one or two bassoons occur, but as a rule the bassoons, when specified, share a part with the string basses and *continuo*. Parts for *taille de basson* were presumably intended for tenor bassoon (tenoroon). There is no evidence to support the assertion made in Grove's *Dictionary*[1] that the tenoroon and *Oboe da caccia* were one and the same instrument, indeed, surviving specimens of old tenor oboes and the limits of the downward compass of Bach's parts seem to prove the contrary.

Bach's parts for trumpet (*tromba*) and horn (*corno da caccia*) are usually for the instruments in D. Parts for C and F trumpets occur more rarely. The only printed scores of Bach's works are those of comparatively modern times, and in these the horns and trumpets appear as transposing instruments. Three trumpets are normally demanded, and the parts, like those for horns, are strictly confined to open notes, the eleventh open note being used alternately as either F or F sharp. Certain non-transposing parts marked *clarino* and *corno*, which occur in some of the Cantatas, could not be played on natural trumpets or horns. The instruments of the time had no valves, but the treble trombone, which is evidently the same instrument as Bach's *tromba da tirarsi*[2], had the trombone slide by means of which the gaps between the open notes could be filled in, and may have been used to play those parts. The naming of the brass instruments in some of Bach's scores is inconsistent and rather puzzling, though it is always quite clear when he is writing for natural horns or trumpets. *Cornetti* and trombones—alto, tenor, and bass—are frequently used to double the vocal parts in chorales, and more rarely are given independent parts.

Fig. 11

Oboe da Caccia, eighteenth century.

An impartial distribution of interchangeable parts between string and wind instruments is the sum of Bach's method of orchestration. Whatever serves for strings, and often for voices, is either duplicated in unison or handed on in turn to wood-wind and, as far as the lack of adjacent open notes will allow, to brass instruments. The wealth of contrapuntal movement which characterizes his music hardly admits of any such thing as pure

[1] Article : " Oboe da Caccia " (1900 Edition).
[2] Slide.

accompaniment or harmonic padding. Each part is independent, melodic, and essential, and is based on figures or melodic patterns which are conceived in general, and not in individual, instrumental terms. Thus it is that flute, oboe, bassoon, string, and to a limited extent brass parts, in Bach's scores all look alike and can hardly be distinguished but for the clues which the downward compass of each instrument necessarily supplies. Under this system of orchestration balance of tone in its present-day sense is hardly considered. Almost any single wind instrument could cope with the two or three violins or voices to each part of Bach's orchestra or choir. Uniting in a common web of contrapuntal movement, the instruments sink their individuality and become the exponents of so many " parts ", each claiming and requiring equal prominence. The blend and grouping of instruments is on lines which were already common by the end of the seventeenth century. The homogeneous tone of the string orchestra, the grouping together of oboes and bassoons, of trumpets and drums, of *cornetti* and trombones is recognized as a means of supplying contrast and variety on a broadly planned scale. The greater sonority and fuller tone are simply due to multiplicity of parts. Whereas seventeenth century composers wrote two wind parts above a common bass part, Bach often wrote three, making four-part harmony with the *basso-continuo*. Tone-colour is handled on a widely-spaced plan. A fixed colour combination and set melodic figures are usually persistent throughout the course of an entire movement, and changes of colour, on the whole, are regulated by movement-lengths rather than by phrase-lengths. Nevertheless, the use of clearly distinguished instrumental groups—always a strong feature in early German Church music— is by no means neglected in Bach's works, although the gains of colour-changes are to some extent minimized by the similarity of the matter dealt with by each group.

Except in real solo parts there is little in Bach's string music which is inseparable from the nature and technique of the instruments. Strings and wood-wind share the same matter. Both *pizzicato* and *sordino* effects are used and generally continue for the length of entire movements. Wholesale duplication of parts is common. Oboes and violins ; flutes, oboes, and violins ; bassoons and string bass instruments ; voices and *cornetti* and trombones, frequently double one another in unison. The cohesive effect of sustained wind notes against activity on strings is comparatively rare. All-round activity or all-round quiescence is the rule. Horn and trumpet parts are usually melodic, often florid and conjunct, therefore necessarily written high up where conjunct open notes are available. The rhythmical characteristics of trumpets and drums are recognised, and when exploited, bring the instruments nearest to achieving individuality of style ; but the florid parts for both horns and trumpets in " clarino " style were at best unsuccessful attempts to force square pegs into round holes. This species of trumpet and horn part died with Bach and Handel, having already been rejected by the more progressive orchestrators before the middle of the century. Bach uses his *cornetti* and trombones in seventeenth century style, largely adhering to the custom of his predecessors in employing them to double choral voices.

Neglected and forgotten for a long time after his death, Bach's music eventually rose superior to all the changes of time and taste, likewise superior to a style of orchestration which already during his lifetime had become old-fashioned, a style which opened out no new paths and, finding itself in a *cul-de-sac,* actually came to a standstill.

Appealing to a wider public, with a keener sense for orchestral effect, and with a finger ever on the pulse of public taste, George Frederick Handel (1685-1759) handled his instrumental forces in a style more broadly orchestral than that of Bach, yet without discovering or following the lead of those who did discover the road which led from the old contrapuntal manner of treating orchestral instruments in the direction of modern orchestration. Handel adopted all the current conventions of early eighteenth century orchestration, amplifying and using them consistently throughout his whole career. What Purcell and Steffani did with diffidence, as though feeling their way, Handel did confidently, thoroughly and habitually.

Handel's normal full orchestra comprised a wood-wind group of oboes in two and bassoons in one or two parts, the usual four-part string orchestra, and a brass group consisting of two or three trumpets with drums. Two or three horn parts are included in many of his scores, sometimes in addition to, and sometimes in place of trumpets. One or two flute parts occur in particular movements in most of his scores, but are not usually included in the *tutti*. Parts for trombones, for piccolo or other instruments occur exceptionally, and cannot be regarded as regular members of Handel's orchestral combination. The harp parts in *Esther* (1720) and *Giulio Cesare* (1723), also those for theorbo or lute, *viola da gamba* or other unusual or obsolete instruments which occasionally crop up in eighteenth century editions of Handel's scores, are likewise exceptional and need not be taken into account except as curiosities.

The flute parts lie rather higher than the oboe parts and were sometimes specifically for transverse flutes. Oboes—always the treble instrument—cover the usual range of about two octaves from middle C upwards. Bassoons generally double the bass parts, though they are sometimes used in the tenor register, and occasionally in pairs in imitative alternation with other instruments. The standard combination of two oboes and one bassoon, the old *concerto di oubuoè* of Scarlatti, is the self-contained wood-wind group used more than any other by Handel and his contemporaries. In this connection it should be remembered that the custom of the time was to employ more than one instrument to play each oboe and bassoon part ; thus, distinction is sometimes made in the scores between *solo* and *ripieno* wood-wind parts. Handel's trumpet parts are usually for the favourite instrument in D, although sometimes for C, and more rarely for G trumpets. The parts are non-transposing in old editions of the full scores. When three parts are provided the two upper trumpets play high " clarino " parts, while the third or *principale*[1] covers only the lower or " fanfare " range. First trumpet parts ascend freely to the sixteenth open note, and both first and second use the eleventh open note alternatively as F or F-sharp for C trumpets, or as G or G-sharp for D trumpets. The flat seventh open note is also occasionally requisitioned. Timpani, tuned to tonic and dominant of the key, almost invariably play with the trumpets. Handel's horn parts are for the instruments either in D, F, or G, and appear variously as transposing or non-transposing parts[2]. The parts lie high and are in a semi-florid or melodic style which is contrived with some skill out of the available conjunct open notes. The horns are frequently used in imitative alternation with trumpets, or double the trumpet parts an octave lower ;

[1] The field or military trumpet.

[2] In the Arnold Editions of Handel's full scores (from about 1786) the parts for D horns are usually noted an octave above the actual sounds (with key-signature) but those for F and G horns are noted in C, and require transposition.

otherwise they follow the course of oboe or string parts with necessary adjustments where the supply of open notes fails.

Although scored for four-part string orchestra, much of Handel's string music is conceived in three parts, and fails to provide independent movement for violas.   The latter generally follow the rhythmical patterns of the bass part, even when playing independently.   While the two violin parts are placed close together, running in thirds or imitatively, and always melodically, the violas are obviously used more to complete the harmony than to provide melodic or contrapuntal movement.   Violoncellos and basses play the bass of the whole structure in octaves, except when a specially designed *obbligato* violoncello part gives that instrument complete independence for the time being.   The one common bass part usually serves for violoncellos, basses, and bassoons, and is always figured for organ or *cembalo*.

Broadly viewed, Handel's work shows two distinct methods of handling the orchestral body.   The first is based on a stereotyped duplication of string and wind parts, and the second on the grouping of instruments according to type and tone-colour.   By the beginning of the eighteenth century the first method had become practically standardized.   The process was simple and expeditious : First and second oboes played in unison with first and second violins, while bassoons doubled the bass part.   This was the routine orchestration which accounts for thousands of pages of full score written during the first half of the eighteenth century.   Even the most progressive of orchestrators frequently fell back on this simple recipe, and Handel as much as anyone availed himself freely of this ready-made reed and string orchestration.   The system, however, admits of three variations of tone-colour : either strings, oboes, and bassoons play all together, or strings alone, or oboes and bassoons alone, the last combination being usually disposed in three parts.   It is impossible to resist the impression that most of the music of the time apparently written for strings only was intended to be played by oboes and bassoons as well.   Specifications of instruments at the beginning of scores are often lacking, and it is frequently only during the course of a movement or work that such directions as *senza oboi, senza fagotti,* or *senza violini* reveal the fact that the music was intended for other than a string orchestra.   Most of Handel's overtures and many other of his instrumental movements are treated in this way.   The four parts are sometimes headed *Viol. I e Oboe I, Viol. II e Oboe II, viola, tutti bassi* (or *Violoncello fagotti e contra-basso*) and other similar directions indicate when either wood-wind or strings are to be silent, and when they are re-united in unison ; but the instruments are not always specified. It seems highly probable that the above was considered a standard combination for instrumental movements written in four parts, and that a detailed specification of instruments was therefore unnecessary. The directions *senza oboi* and *senza fagotti*, which occur frequently in what are obviously soft or slow movements and often when a solo voice is accompanied, lend support to the view that when four parts are provided and no instruments are named, the music was *as a matter of course* played by oboes and bassoons as well as by the string orchestra.

Handel occasionally makes some advance on the above formula by writing oboe and bassoon parts which are in substance somewhat less florid versions of the string parts. The wind thus gain a certain independence which is, however, more apparent than real. The idea is clearly based on the instinct that wind instruments are constitutionally less active than strings. This modified activity of wind parts usually accompanies rapid violin passages such as occur in the overture to *Acis and Galatea* (1721), or string passages based on the quick reiteration of the same notes. The pseudo-independence of some of Handel's oboe parts is simply due to the inability of these instruments to follow violin parts below middle C, the lowest note of oboes at the time.

Many of Handel's heavier *tutti* including horns and trumpets are also managed on the duplication system. Horn and trumpet parts are then subject to some necessary modification where the lack of open notes precludes the possibility of strict doubling. The *Water Music* (1715) and *The Music for the Royal Fireworks* (1749) provide many examples of this species of *tutti*.

Much more interesting is the type of orchestration in which Handel uses his instruments in three clearly differentiated groups of contrasted tone-colour, namely, the string group, the oboe-bassoon group, and the brass and drums group. The alternation, overlapping, or combination of these groups provide many more varied effects, and, on the whole, show Handel at his best as an orchestrator. Perhaps no better example of this treatment will be found than in the orchestral parts of the *Dettingen Te Deum* (1743). The groups are as follows :

(a)	(b)	(c)
Trumpet I	Oboe I	Viol. I
Trumpet II	Oboe II	Viol. II
Trumpet III (principale ⨏)	Bassoons	Viola
Drums		Bassi (figured)

to which are added the choral voices in a group of five parts.
Each group is used singly, and in all possible combinations. The
entries of complete groups are timed with excellent judgment and
full consciousness of effect in a broad sense. Orchestrally the
weakness lies in the similarity of the matter allotted to each group;
violin figures are handed on in turn to oboes and trumpets with
only such slight modifications as are rendered imperative by the
compass or imperfections of the wind instruments, and, except
for some occasional rhythmical and military characteristics in the
trumpet parts, the whole instrumental matter is modelled on
and dictated by violin technique. The inevitable thinness of
three-part writing for wind instruments sounds odd and unsatisfying to modern ears even if allowance is made for the filling
up of harmony by organ or *cembalo*, and the notion of balance
which regards each part and each group as being of equal power
is old-fashioned and typical; yet of the sonority and majesty
of the groups in combination, especially when united with the
rich tone of a five-part choir, their can be no question.

In the broad handling of choral and instrumental groups
Handel was most successful and abreast of his times. He
absorbed, amplified, and made thoroughly his own all the
orchestral effects known and practised at Hamburg, Hanover and
in Italy at the time of his early manhood, yet remained a conservative in orchestration all his life. His last work, *The Triumph
of Time and Truth* (1757) is orchestrated on the same lines as his
Water Music (1715).

Handel's work represents the maturity of the earlier orchestration rather than the anticipation of what was to come. All
the characteristics of early eighteenth century work persist in his
most mature scores. The frequent *obbligato* parts for solo instruments, the skeleton scoring which depends on keyboard-instruments for harmony, the " clarino " style of trumpet and horn
parts, the conventional grouping of wind instruments, the

generally contrapuntal texture of all his instrumental writing, the predominance of the violin figure in his wind parts, all these and many other features of Handel's orchestration were the culmination of seventeenth century methods on which he floated into an expansive backwater while the narrower main-stream of progress flowed past and away from him in a direction which he could hardly have followed without completely revolutionizing the very nature of his art.

Again, as in the case of Bach, the music has outlived the manner in which it was presented, and its vitality has tempted many to add to, rearrange, edit, and generally touch up the odd orchestration which hung on the contrapuntal movement of parts rather than on the colour and capabilities of instruments.

Little need be said of other non-progressive orchestrators of the Bach-Handel period. French opera composers previous to Rameau seem to have been completely hypnotized by the style of Lulli. Their scores show all the Lullian characteristics handled, it is true, rather more familiarly, yet without any signs of the advance which even the more conservative German and Italian composers had achieved in the meantime. Their conservatism went so far as to retain even the five-part organization of the string orchestra. The two flutes, two oboes, and single bassoon part, the *trompettes* and *timbales* in the more spectacular or military scenes, in fact the whole orchestral paraphernalia of Lullian opera appears practically unaltered in such works as Campra's *L'Europe Galante* and Destouches' *Issé*, both dated 1697. Some stimulus must have been given to orchestral music apart from its association with opera—by the establishment in Paris of the *Concerts Spirituels* in 1725, but it was not till the advent of Rameau that French orchestration made its first real advance on the beginning so favourably inaugurated by Lulli in the seventeenth century.

At Vienna, where orchestral music in association with the Church and stage had long been assiduously cultivated under Royal patronage, the native Johann Fux (1660-1741) and the aliens Caldara (1670-1736) and Conti (1681-1732), show in their scores a style of orchestration exemplifying all the axioms and conventions of the early eighteenth century. Four-part strings, oboes, and bassoons, run about contrapuntally, doubling one another or in alternation, just as in the works of Handel and hundreds of contemporaneous composers. Trumpet parts in

" clarino " style,*obbligati* for solo instruments, trombones handled in the old Church style, and every feature of the times, but none in anticipation of future developments, class these composers as able yet conservative and unenterprising musicians whose work just kept the ball of orchestration rolling in Vienna till the time when such as Wagenseil made some advance which helped to lift it from a well-worn rut, and bridged the gulf between the antiquated style of Fux and the achievements of Gluck in the second half of the eighteenth century.

Handel's rival Bononcini (1672–1750 ?), the famous violinist Veracini (1685-1750), Porpora (1686-1766), Vinci (1690–1730), Leo (1694–1744), and Pergolese (1710–36) are only a few of the generation of Italian composers who were contemporaries of Bach and Handel, whose works reached almost every opera-house in Europe except the exclusive institution at Paris.

Generalization or sweeping statements concerning the orchestration of these Italians may possibly prove to be unfair to some of them ; they and their works are far too numerous for exhaustive investigation ; yet, if many examples selected at random and without prejudice are at all representative of their work, it may safely be said that they contributed little if anything that was of value to the growth of orchestration. That their musical superficiality and indifferent musicianship, compared to that of Bach and Handel, were not necessarily a bar to progress in orchestration is proved by the fact that many of the lesser German composers of the same period, using the medium of a no less transient musical style, managed to guide the art aright through a critical transition stage, and succeeded in establishing the fundamental principles on which modern orchestration is based.

The Italian composers' indifference to orchestral effect as an aid to the adequate presentation of their musical matter seems surprising in view of the popularity they courted, and the success they enjoyed. The explanation probably lies in the fact that Italian opera in the first half of the eighteenth century had already come under the spell of the star-vocalist system. The singers themselves, what they sang, and how they sang, interested the public more than the actual drama, much more than dramatic truthfulness and effect, of which suitable orchestration is so important an ingredient.

To provide agreeable vocal melodies in conventional orchestral frames, and to provide them in large quantities, seems to have been the aim of those Italian opera-purveyors. Their scores indicate great fluency, facility, and readiness to do whatever was expected of them, but little interest in orchestration as such. They poured out opera after opera in astounding numbers, the manuscripts of which now repose undisturbed in libraries and museums all over Europe. Many of these scores are for nothing but a string orchestra, nominally in four parts, but which in practice shrinks down to three or even two parts. Others appear at first sight to be for strings only, but reveal a few sketchy and scanty wind parts only on closer examination. Others again are more fully and carefully scored, and show, at any rate, some desultory attempts to secure brilliance, more especially in some of the more noisy overtures. Nearly all the scores show signs of haste and anxiety to cover the ground quickly, and a corresponding degree of carelessness and inaccuracy.

Pergolese's otherwise attractive *La Serva Padrona* (1731), likewise some cantatas and the *Stabat Mater* (1736) are scored for strings only. The same composer's *Lo Frate innamorato* (Naples, 1732) is for strings with a few stray flute parts, and his *Adriano* (1734) is largely for strings with parts for either flutes or oboes and bassoons, horns or trumpets, in certain movements. Vinci's *Elipidia* (London, 1725) shows parts for oboes, trumpets, and strings in the overture, the rest of the opera being apparently for strings alone, or oboes and strings. Leo's *Demofoönte* (1735) requires only strings and horns. An opera by Bononcini entitled *Turno Aricino* demands oboes and bassoons in the overture, and later on some parts for *traversière* (flute), *chalamaux* (chalumeau)[1] and *trombe sordino* put in an appearance. Bononcini's *Griselda*, printed in score by Walsh (London, 1722), demands the typical full orchestra of the period, namely, flutes, oboes, bassoons, horns, trumpets, drums, and strings, but rarely provides more than four independent parts for the whole combination. The catalogue might be continued indefinitely, but would be of little interest.

The salient features of the orchestration are its thinness and its conventionality. More often than not the violas are given no independent part ; the common custom of writing for first and second violins in unison further reduces the score to a mere skeleton, and leaves to the *cembalo* all responsibility for filling up the harmony. Variety of colour, of pattern, figure, and rhythm,

[1] Probably clarinet parts, but written for the instrument under the name of its progenitor.

is sadly lacking in the two or three string parts which, with the
basso-continuo, supply the sole accompaniment to *aria* after *aria*.
When oboes and bassoons are specified their usual lot is to play in
unison with the strings ; flutes occasionally join the upper string
part in unison, or take it over in its entirety for a complete movement. Trumpets or horns brighten up some of the overtures
and instrumental movements, or give suitable colour when the
words of an *aria* obviously demand that their purport should be
echoed in the orchestral accompaniment. That the horn and
trumpet parts are, on the whole, less melodic and florid than those
of Bach and Handel, may conceivably be due to a right instinct
for instrumental fitness, or, on the other hand, to a lack of artistic
thoroughness and a disposition to shirk the labour necessarily
involved in devising melodic parts out of the few open notes of the
natural instruments.

If the Italians of the first half of the eighteenth century did
no pioneer work for orchestration, they were at all events in good
company, for neither of the two musical giants of their time
stepped into or over the breach which divided the reactionary
and the progressive, the antiquated and the modern, in the
history and evolution of orchestration.

The composers, or types of composers, whose orchestral work
has been summarized in this chapter have been classed as conservative orchestrators. The classification should be liberally
understood. It would frequently break down under minute
or too literal scrutiny, yet it is comprehensively sound.

Greater familiarity with the orchestra and its instruments,
the advancing technique of composition and playing, together
with the accumulated experience which came with a maturing
art, gave these eighteenth century composers a surer touch which
easily distinguishes their scores from the cruder efforts of the late
seventeenth century pioneers. Innovations had become conventions, and conventionality implies familiarity and resulting
assurance. Nevertheless, in a broad sense, the statement holds
good that the conservatives of the Bach-Handel period trod down
the path which their predecessors had opened out, making it
firm and well-defined, but without altering its direction or
exploring its byways.

CHAPTER VII

TRANSITION : GLUCK

THE period of transition from the contrapuntal manner of treating orchestral instruments, best known by the works of Bach and Handel, to the beginnings of modern orchestration as practised by Haydn and Mozart, was not confined to a few years in the middle of the eighteenth century. No one even slightly acquainted with the evolution of style in musical or other art could possibly imagine that all orchestral music composed during the first half of the century was treated in one way, and that a sudden revolution wrought such a complete change that all music dating from after 1750 was orchestrated according to new principles. Although the change of style has been placed approximately at the middle, it were more correct to state that the transition covered almost the entire century. No sudden upheaval, no calculated or designed revolution in orchestration took place in the few years which separate the last works of Bach or Handel from the early works of Haydn and Mozart. 1759 is the year of Handel's death; Haydn wrote his first symphony in 1755, and Mozart his first symphony in 1764. Judgment based only on the work of these four composers would clearly point to a sudden change. More comprehensive investigation will prove that, although some composers carried the old style of orchestration into the second half of the century, others had already given a foretaste of the new style in the first quarter of the century, and had progressed so far that by the time Haydn and Mozart were writing their early orchestral works, the transformation was practically completed. The great "classical" composers did not build on nothing ; they neither invented a new musical style nor discovered a new style of orchestration in which to clothe their music. The two roads began to separate even before Bach and Handel were fully matured composers, and were already well apart before these two masters had composed their last works. The new style of orchestration grew side by side with, and actually depended on, the changing style of musical art. It could hardly have been applied to or developed by means of contrapuntally-conceived music. Its very existence hung on the harmonic nature of the musical material which gave it birth. Thus it is that the pioneers of modern orchestration were the very same composers whose music shows the first traces of what is usually called the classical style, the style of Haydn, Mozart, and Beethoven, the chief builders, but not the inventors, of the modern symphony and of modern orchestration.

In Italy, in the first quarter of the eighteenth century, Alessandro Scarlatti had taken some of the first faltering steps which led to modern orchestration ; his Italian successors represent a period of comparative stagnation. In France a sudden advance by Rameau only partially bridged the gulf which, in Germany and Austria, was more completely spanned by a chain of composers in which such as Keiser, Telemann, the two Grauns, Hasse, Wagenseil, and Carl Philipp Emanuel Bach were strong links. Associated with both Vienna and Paris, Gluck represents an important link at the very end of the chain of progress, and in his mature works, written for the Paris Opera from about 1770 to 1780, shows the transition no longer in progress, but actually completed.

The signs to be looked for in the scores of those composers which show orchestration in the process of gradually freeing itself from the yoke of contrapuntal movement, are many. The scores of the earlier transition stage reveal only occasional departures from contemporary conventions, yet quite early in the century such features as were to become general soon after the mid-century began to creep into the scores of those whose music provided the medium for the transformation, till, in the works of the later of those composers, the old characteristics leave little more than their traces behind them. Keiser's work, for example, shows only a few infrequent but distinctive signs of progress, whereas some of the later works of K. H. Graun and C. P. E. Bach are scored in a manner which had less in common with the style of Handel than with that of the earlier works of Haydn.

All these composers had the same orchestral combination to work with as their more conservative contemporaries. The specifications in their scores show the same variability and instability in the wind section. Like all eighteenth century composers, they appear to have written parts for such wind instruments as were available at various places. Obsolescent or unusual instruments figure in many of their scores, and departures from the

EXAMPLE 37 (*a*,) (*b*,) (*c*) AND (*d*)

EXAMPLE 37 (*continued*).

EXAMPLE 37 (*continued*).

EXAMPLE 37 (*continued*).

EXAMPLE 37 (*continued*).

conventional number of parts provided for each type of instrument are frequent. The distinction between solo and *ripieno* parts occurs just as it does in Bach and in some of the early Haydn symphonies. While they did everything towards altering the course of orchestration, the constitution of the orchestra underwent little or no change. Although clarinets did not finally take their place in the orchestra till close on the end of the century, it is in the scores of the transition composers that the instrument makes its early appearance.

That their musical matter contained much of what is merely harmony or pure accompaniment contributed largely to the ease with which the change of style was accomplished. In this respect it may be questioned which was cause and which was effect, but there is no doubt that when one set of instruments began to *accompany* another, the gates of modern orchestration were opened. To supply mere harmony, colour, rhythm, or accompaniment, was a function for instruments which hardly entered into the scheme of the old style, in which every instrument joined in the prevailing contrapuntal movement of parts regardless of suitability, balance or effect. The new scheme allowed one group of instruments to provide harmony while another provided motion. Thus the most salient feature of the changing orchestration was a growing tendency to make wind instruments sustain the harmony while the strings were concerned with motion. The orchestral *tutti* then became a compound of solid harmony on the one hand, and melodic or figurative activity on the other ; the wind gave body and cohesion while the strings supplied the energy or ornament, with a resulting gain of both fullness and brilliance. A few typical bars from Bach, Handel, Rameau, and K. H. Graun will illustrate the difference in construction of the contrapuntal and the harmonic *tutti* : (Example 37).

The provision of simple harmonic string accompaniments to vocal or wood-wind solos, whether mere sustained, detached, or repeated chords, figures, or rhythmical patterns, gave a lightness and variety which was unknown in the orchestration of contrapuntally-conceived music. *Pizzicato* chords or arpeggios, and many of the devices for string accompaniment which became so hackneyed in the time of Haydn and Mozart, make their appearance in the scores of the transition composers. The solo part, undisturbed by a web of contrapuntal movement, stands out clear and distinct against a background of mere colour, harmony, and rhythm, giving birth to effects now so commonplace that it is difficult to realize that they were ever novel.

The choice and use of tone-colour for its own sake was another feature of orchestration which had its beginning when composers began to reject a purely contrapuntal texture as the only means of expressing themselves. The quality of sounds, and the effect when these were combined, began to enter into their calculations when the melodic interest of the music began to centre in one part, or when the music *was* mere harmony, rhythm, or colour. The following extracts, respectively by Schürmann and Hasse, are little else but harmony, rhythm and colour, *but they are orchestration.* The effect has been thought out ; the parts belong to the instruments, and are hardly interchangeable : (Example 38).

Although it is merely by chance, these two extracts illustrate another significant point. Schürmann's bass part is marked *senza cembalo* ; in the example by Hasse the *basso-continuo* part for the moment is blank. These are the advance signs that keyboard-instruments were about to be banished from the orchestra. The first example is from an opera, the second from an oratorio ; *cembalo* and organ are silenced in order to let orchestral colour stand alone and make its own effect, and because their harmonic support was unnecessary.

The grouping and blending of instrumental voices undergoes some slight modification in the new orchestration. The blend of string instruments was, of course, incapable of improvement, and therefore unalterable. The association of oboes and bassoons, on the whole, stands firm, but there is a distinct tendency to bring flutes into the alliance. Flutes are treated not so much as a separate and unrelated pair ; they are allowed to join the family circle of wood-wind instruments, and to add to the body of wood-wind harmony. Nor are horns handled separately or only in the *tutti*. They begin to take their place as a link between the wood-wind and the brass families ; they help to enrich the sustained harmony of wood-wind ; they blend with, and give cohesion to, the more active movement of string parts, and are no longer counted as melodists, or as belonging only to the louder and heavier voices of the orchestra. The partnership of trumpets and drums remains intact. There is as yet no sign of an harmonically self-contained brass group ; the rôle of trumpets and drums is to join in the *tutti* in their capacity as the loudest available

EXAMPLE 38 (*a*) AND (*b*)

(*a*)   Schurmann (Ludovicus Pius — 1726)

EXAMPLE 38 *(continued)*.

EXAMPLE 38 (*continued*).

voices ; trumpets, like the horns, gradually relinquish their claim to be treated as melodists.

A change in the manner of distributing tone-colour becomes evident in the transition stage of orchestration. Tone-colour, especially that of wind instruments, began to be applied for shorter periods. According to the old method, a pair of wind instruments usually played more or less continuously throughout one movement, and might be entirely silent during the next ; the colour scheme laid down at the start of each movement was maintained according to a set design till the end of that movement. The new method inclined more to break up these long stretches of wind-tone into smaller patches of less uniform duration ; the changes of colour were made at selected moments rather than at regular intervals. The visible effect is that there are more blank bars in the full-scores ; to the ear the gain is that of variety, and to some extent, of surprise.

The use of musical material which was more harmonic than contrapuntal in texture naturally had some effect on the way the parts were placed in relation to one another.   Parts which were not compelled to follow a melodic course could more easily be placed where they gave fullness or body to the harmony, where they enriched a chord, or filled up a gap.   At the same time the free crossing of parts which characterized the old instrumental part-writing, began to disappear, and with it the last trace of sixteenth century vocal polyphony vanished from orchestral music.

Some of the old features persisted, and even became accentuated in the scores of the transition composers.   The custom of writing for the string orchestra in three parts is most marked, notwithstanding the fact that four staves are used in the score. First and second violins frequently play in unison, not with the idea of adjusting balance as in a present-day score, but simply as a matter of habit when nothing else was found for second violins to do.   For the same sort of reason the violas are constantly switched on to the course of the bass part at the octave above, evidently with no great concern for either balance or effect.

The effect of the transition on individual parts may be thus briefly summarized : Flute parts incline to lie higher and, when doubling oboe parts, generally do so in the octave above.   Oboe and bassoon parts are less florid, less figurated, and more sustained than string parts. They gain in individuality, and are also liable to be used together as harmony instruments, much as clarinets and bassoons are used in nineteenth century orchestration. As the element of imitative counterpoint declines, the wood-wind are relieved of the necessity of constantly echoing string passages and figures ; concurrently they achieve some individuality of style. Thus, the features of flute technique which favour an embellished or decorative style are brought into play, while the more placid motion suited to oboes and bassoons distinguishes their parts from those of the more active flutes. Horn parts are lower in pitch, and largely lose the conjunct melodic characteristics which mark such as Handel's parts for these instruments. Their function is to give solidity and cohesion to the structure rather than to supply melodic or independent movement : (Example 39).

Gradually but decisively the transition composers abandon high *clarino* parts for trumpets. These instruments are made to play in the more manageable register lying between the third and twelfth open notes, and, instead of taking part in contrapuntal or melodic movement, fall back on rhythmical patterns of characteristic design, on the duty of marking accents, underlining rhythms, and of generally adding quantity of tone to the *tutti*.

String parts gain in variety owing to the freer use of effects which are peculiar to the nature and technique of bowed string instruments. *Pizzicato*, *tremolo*, reiteration of the same note, and figures based on the facility with which the bow can be made to alternate rapidly between two notes on adjacent strings, are used freely to give motion and brilliance to the *tutti*, and lightness and variety to accompaniments. The use of double-stopping adds richness to the inside harmony, and three or four-note chords on violins give more weight to detached chords.

The sum of the above practically amounts to a description of orchestration as it was by the time the transition had run its course, in short, the orchestral style of the second half of the eighteenth century. It should be emphasized that the transition, which began early in the century, was gradual but cumulative ; that with all the signs of change and progress in the scores are mingled characteristics which were common to all composers of the time, and that none of the composers concerned covered the whole ground of transition from contrapuntal to modern principles. It is, nevertheless, quite clear that progress was in the hands of certain composers, and that the process of transition ran its

EXAMPLE 39

course alongside, but independently of the old style of instrumental part-writing which went with contrapuntally-conceived music. It may be argued, with justice, that credit does not belong to the composers who guided orchestration along the path of progress, but to the fact that the changing style of the music made it possible, or even inevitable, that they should do so. Time has dealt harshly with most of them and their works ; yet by means of what seems a poorer art they laid the foundations on which their successors built up a new style, and in doing so gave new life to orchestration.

Reinhard Keiser (1673-1739), the first prominent figure amongst those who made Hamburg a flourishing centre of musical and operatic activity in the early years of the eighteenth century, composer of innumerable operas, cantatas, and Church works, was amongst the first of the Germans to show signs of the coming change in orchestration. His Hamburg operas cover a period of about forty years, starting with *Irene* in 1697. Allied to what now seems intolerably feeble music, much of his orchestration is of the type which knew little more variety than that which was secured by alternating or combining the string orchestra with oboes and bassoons. Keiser's scores, nevertheless, reveal many flashes of independence and well-aimed efforts to bring about more varied orchestral effects than were known to the German Church composers of his time. He was amongst the first to write parts for horns, to devise entirely *pizzicato* accompaniments for strings, and to make use of double-stopping in his violin parts ; all of which show a commendable desire to exploit what were unfamiliar, if not quite novel means of brightening up the rather monotonous colouring of contemporary orchestration. Keiser's operas *Octavia* (1705), *Croesus* (1710[1]), *Der Lächerliche Printz Jodelet* (1726) and the oratorio *Der Gekreutzigte Jesus* (1715) have been printed, and point to a certain crude enterprise and willingness to step out of the rut which confined and cramped the orchestration of many who were musically his superiors.

That they carried the development a step further is to the credit of Georg Philipp Telemann (1681-1767, Hamburg), Christoph Graupner (1683-1760, Darmstadt), Johann Georg Pisendal (1687-1755, Dresden), Georg Caspar Schürmann (1672–1751) and Gottfried Heinrich Stölzel (1690-1749), some of the German contemporaries of Bach and Handel, composers of enormous

[1] Rewritten and reorchestrated, 1730.

quantities of operas, church works, concertos, and symphony-overtures, in which the instruments of the orchestra appear to be gradually acquiring the more clearly differentiated styles and functions of their own which go to make up the composite language of the orchestra.

Orchestrally a shade more enlightened are the works of the brothers Johann Gottlieb Graun (1698-1771), Karl Heinrich Graun (1701-59) and Johann Adolf Hasse (1699-1783). To the work of the two Grauns at Berlin, and of Hasse at Dresden, is largely due the prominent position which these centres acquired as strongholds of orchestral activity in the middle of the eighteenth century. Their scores show orchestration at a stage midway between Handel and Mozart, gradually shedding the characteristics of the old style, and tentatively establishing the new principles which, in their turn, were to become conventions in the latter part of the same century. *Der Tod Jesu* (1755), probably the only work of the younger Graun known in this country, is hardly representative of his best orchestration ; it is indeed featureless and rather reactionary in style, but his *Te Deum* (1757) and the opera *Montezuma* (1755) give ample evidence of the width of the gulf already separating the orchestration of such as Graun from that of Handel. Superficial and ephemeral though they proved to be, Hasse's operas are scored more fully, with greater care and keener appreciation of instrumental effect than those of the Neapolitan composers on whose style his dramatic music was modelled. In his later operas, such as *Romolo ed Ersilia* (1765) and *Piramo e Tisbe* (1769), the instruments are clearly seen to be settling down each to its proper function in building up the more brilliant harmonic *tutti*, the combination of harmony and motion, in a manner which could never have been achieved without sacrificing the element of melodic interest in parts for wind instruments, however ingenious or involved the part-writing.

Before the middle of the century, Telemann, both the Grauns, Hasse, and several other German and Austrian composers began to write the short three-movement orchestral works which, variously named symphonies or overtures, have proved to be the immediate progenitors of the " classical " symphony. Although actually developed from the Italian form of opera overture, those embryo symphonies were expressly written for concert performance. Most of them are for four-part strings with two pairs of wind instruments—usually oboes and horns—and, judging from the large number which survive in the form of printed part-books, must have been a most popular type of orchestral piece till their vogue was completely extinguished by the superior work of Haydn and Mozart. The pre-classical symphony had little in common with the older orchestral suite, a work of many movements in dance forms. The orchestration of the newer type, on the whole, leans more to the modern than to the old contrapuntal style, and in one respect marks an important point of departure in the history of orchestration—the point at which a marked difference begins to be made between the somewhat restrained manner of handling the concert-orchestra, and the richer and more highly coloured style associated with stage works.

A generation of Germans, just a little later than the Grauns and Hasse, who helped in the early development of symphony, and cleared the way for further progress in symphony orchestration includes two sons of J. S. Bach : Carl Philipp Emanuel Bach (1714-88, Berlin and Hamburg) and Johann Christian Bach (1735-82, Milan and London), also Karl Friedrich Abel (1725-87, Dresden and London) and Johann Stamitz (1717–57, Mannheim). Of these the first was probably the finest musician, and in his orchestration may be said to represent the last stage of the transition period. C. P. E. Bach's four symphonies, written at Hamburg about 1776, are for flutes, oboes, horns, bassoon, and strings. Only a few signs of the old contrapuntal style leave their traces in the orchestration of these works. The figured bass parts for *cembalo* are lingering signs of the past, but the orchestra no longer leans for support on the keyboard-instrument. The strings give vigour, activity, and figuration, while the wind provides body, harmony, and cohesion ; the music has a composite texture which is based on string and wind technique ; the ambiguous instrumental part of the past gives way to the part which belongs to the instrument. In the light of subsequent development the orchestration of the following typical bars from C. P. E. Bach's symphony in F may seem elementary, yet in principle it has more in common with nineteenth century than with early eighteenth century work. Characteristics of the period which prevailed throughout the century and never quite lost their hold on the laying out of string parts till after the time of the great classical composers are the unison of violin parts, and the rhythmical partnership of violas and basses : (Example 40).

Georg Christoph Wagenseil (1715-77) and G. M. Monn (1717-50) were successors of Fux and the earlier Viennese group who also wrote symphonies before the middle of the century, and who just got out of the rut of contrapuntal orchestration without, however, getting much further than to suggest the lines on which the orchestration of the future was to travel.

Niccolò Jomelli (1714-74) may be singled out as one who represents progress, and the best of the transition stage amongst Italian operatic composers of the Neapolitan school. Jomelli

EXAMPLE 40

wrote opera and church music not only for Naples, Rome and
Bologna, but also for Stuttgart, where he held an appointment
for fifteen years from about 1753. Possibly the knowledge of
what northern composers were doing at the time accounts for the
better musicianship and greatly improved orchestration of this
Italian as compared with the work of many of his compatriots.
The operas *Olimpiade* (1761), *Fetonte* (1768) and his *La Passione*,
all belong to Jomelli's Stuttgart period, and are orchestrated in a
manner quite as enlightened as that of the contemporary Germans
who no doubt stimulated his interest in orchestration, and set a
higher standard than obtained in most Italian opera-houses at
that time.

The later works of Thomas Arne (1710-78) show that the
native-born English composer, though much under the spell of
Handel and the host of foreign composers who made London their

happy-hunting-ground during the eighteenth century, was able
to keep almost abreast of progress in handling the orchestra.
In the music to *Comus*, an early work of Arne's, the orchestration is
thoroughly Handelian, but his later opera *Artaxerxes* (1762)
shows more than mere traces of the transition style.   This is one
of the very first scores which contains undoubted parts for
clarinets.   Although the imitative manner of Handel's orchestration is still present, Arne's parts are more true to the nature of the
instruments, and he is obviously more ready to take advantage
of the purely instrumental effects which came with the changing
style of music than were Handel and most of the Italians whose
works would no doubt be his first models.   Arne's *Overtures*
for strings and two pairs of wind instruments, printed in 1740, are
possibly the earliest English contributions to the growth of the
independent orchestral symphony at a time when no clear
distinction was made between the two forms, symphony and
overture.

It were faint praise to say that Jean-Philippe Rameau (1683-
1764) made a great advance on the orchestration of his predecessors
in Paris.   In bringing it up-to-date,[1] Rameau quickly brushed away
an insipid style which had made no appreciable progress since
the days of Lulli, and infused fresh life into French orchestration.   His operas, ballets, and kindred stage works begin in
1733 with *Hippolyte et Aricie*, and finish with *Les Paladins* in
1760.   By uniting the two upper string parts in one, Rameau
reduced the French string orchestra from five to four parts, and
brought it into line with the contemporary custom of all other
countries, a reformation which was some fifty years overdue.

The string parts are specified as follows:

I. and II. Dessus de Violons	(1st Violins).
Hautes Contres	(2nd Violins).
Tailles	(Violas).
Basse-continue	(Basses, etc.).

The regular wood-wind parts are for flutes, oboes, and bassoons,
each in two parts.   Horns, trumpets and drums have a place in
most of the scores, but these instruments are employed only in
a few scenes in each work.   A few parts for *petites flûtes* and

---

[1] This estimate of Rameau's services to orchestration rests entirely
on the authenticity of the modern reprint of his scores, edited by Saint-
Saëns, Malherbe, etc.

musettes occur, and if some parts in *Acante and Céphise* (1751) were really intended for clarinets,[1] it is one of the very earliest instances of their use, and is quite exceptional in Rameau's work.

Like most composers of his time, Rameau was a practical violinist, and one who took more trouble than most to embody his knowledge of violin technique in his parts for string instruments. The quickly reiterated notes, arpeggios across the strings, two and three-note chords, rapid scale passages, also *pizzicato* and *sordino* effects, figure freely in his scores, and give a variety of texture to his string music which was sadly lacking in French orchestration before his time. The semi-contrapuntal structure of Rameau's music hardly favoured figurated or purely harmonic accompaniments, but for neatness, finish, and brisk movement, his string parts compare well with the best of contemporary work in other countries. Some experimentally elaborate schemes for strings are interesting and point to a standard of orchestral playing at the Paris Opera very much higher than that described by Rousseau in his *Dictionnaire de Musique* (1767).

Rameau's flutes, oboes, and bassoons are normally engaged in doubling the string parts in conventional early eighteenth century style ; otherwise they are used to sustain harmony as in the example already quoted or, more rarely, are given independent solos. When engaged in purely harmonic work the wood-wind parts are distributed with a clear notion of how to build up a substantial harmonic background of much more solid proportions than was effected by the thin conventional group of two oboe parts and one bassoon part. Rameau's additional bassoon part is obviously there for the purpose of securing a richer harmonic effect, and the frequent addition of two flutes—making, in all, six-part harmony—shows quite clearly that he was thinking independently of mere custom, and considered instrumental effect from a point of view quite foreign to that of either Bach or Handel. The flute parts are evidently for transverse flutes, and lie well up in the second octave of the instrument, or even a little higher. A certain gracefulness in the ornamental figuration of the few flute solos is quite a noteworthy feature. The oboes, although largely retaining their old duty of doubling first and second violins, are nevertheless often allowed either complete independence, or take their part in the middle of the wood-wind harmony, while bassoons figure either as harmonists, as soloists

[1] See p. 179.

in the tenor register, or merely as a reinforcement to the bass part.

Rameau's horn parts—in C, D, E, F, G, or B flat—like his trumpet parts in C, D or E—are, on the whole, melodic without being unduly florid. There is nothing like the elaboration of the true *clarino* part in these scores of Rameau. Horns are often engaged in duet-like passages in the manner of hunting calls, and are more rarely called upon to sustain long notes, or to mark rhythmical figures, while trumpets have still much of the fanfare nature to play. The brass parts in Rameau's scores lean rather towards the old-fashioned style, and reveal hardly any tendency to use the instruments in order to gain mere volume of tone in the *tutti*, or to give cohesion or emphasis at particular moments. Thus, while the future relationship of strings and wood-wind is so admirably suggested, even though not firmly established in Rameau's orchestration, he did not get so far as to build up the sound of the full orchestra with brass tone on lines which became common in Paris soon after his time.

Ushering in a period in which the orchestration of works composed for the Paris stage became a vital force in the history of the art, Rameau stands out as the first French composer who took orchestration seriously, and began to make orchestral effect part and parcel of his technique. Orchestration in Paris had to pass through many alien hands before it reached the stage at which it becames possible to discern the characteristics which, in the nineteenth century, formed a peculiarly French style, and remained quite distinct from the heavier and more closely-woven style of the Germans, yet it can hardly be pure fancy that detects in Rameau's work some of the first signs of the clearness and delicacy, the economy of means and clean colouring which have long been the great charm of French orchestration.

The classification of composers, although based mainly on their work, has so far served well enough to group them either chronologically, by nationality, or according to where their working lives were spent, and where their works first saw light. The same process of classification breaks down in more than one way when applied to Christoph Willibald Gluck (1714-87). The span of his life coincides almost exactly with that of Carl Philipp Emanuel Bach, and would place him in the last stage of the transition period. Before the death of either Bach or Handel, Gluck was already a composer of some international fame and wide operatic experience ; yet his significant work, as far as it concerns orchestration, only begins after 1760, and lasts till about 1780, by which time Haydn had written over fifty, and Mozart some thirty-four symphonies. Nationality would group Gluck with the Germans, yet, although Vienna became his headquarters in later life, the scene of his culminating triumph was Paris. His experience embraced brief or prolonged visits to Milan, Venice, Naples, Rome, Turin, London, Hamburg, Dresden, Prague, Vienna, Copenhagen and Paris, in most cases for the production of his own operas, and with only intermittent success. He would hear the works of Jomelli, Galuppi, and all the then popular Italian composers, also the works of Hasse and Graun. In London he heard Handel's music, and in Paris the operas of Rameau. Yet the orchestration of his truly representative works, his *Orfeo* (Vienna, 1762 ; Paris, 1774), *Alceste* (Vienna, 1767 ; Paris, 1775), *Iphigénie en Aulide* (Paris, 1774), *Armide* (Paris, 1777), and *Iphigénie en Tauride* (Paris, 1779) owns to the sponsorship of no particular composer, school, or national group, least of all to the native composers who were busy at Vienna when he settled down there about 1746.

Gluck's views on the function of music in opera, likewise the furious antagonism between the Gluckists and the Piccinists in Paris in the seventies, are well known and lie outside the scope of this work ; yet it is impossible to disassociate from his orchestration the principles of a composer whose artistic creed embraced such significant views as those set forth in the preface to *Alceste* : "that the instruments ought to be introduced in proportion to the degree of interest and passion in the words[1]" ; that "instruments are to be employed not according to the dexterity of the players, but according to the dramatic propriety of their tone[2]". Thus, dramatic fitness alone was to govern his use of instruments ; the effect of the orchestra was to be true to the situation on the stage. At a time when opera, and Italian opera in particular, had strayed so far from dramatic truth that almost every witty author of the time found its conventionalities a ready target for ridicule, it is hardly surprising to find that a composer who acknowledged no law but the law of dramatic truth should orchestrate his operas in a manner which broke many

[1] See Grove's *Dictionary*, Art. " Gluck ".

[2] See *Oxford History of Music*, Vol. v, p. 92.

links with the past, and established orchestral effects which inaugurated a new era in the history of the orchestration of stage works.

From all accounts, Gluck's Italian operas earlier than *Orfeo*, and several later works in which he did not embody his ideas of reform, have little to distinguish them from the current type of opera. What follows applies only to the operas mentioned above, the five works of Gluck which have never quite lost their hold on the taste of the opera-going public.

In addition to the usual parts for flutes, oboes, and bassoons, Gluck provided two parts for clarinets (in C), and occasional parts for piccolo. To the standard pairs of horns and trumpets he added three trombones. The percussion department of the orchestra was likewise enlarged for particular movements of certain works where special effects were desired ; bass-drums, cymbals, side-drum, and triangle thus make their appearance in some of Gluck's scores, probably for the first time[1]. In the same way the harp is introduced in *Orfeo* for special effects. The *basso-continuo* part practically disappears in these later scores of Gluck. Thus, as far as its constitution is concerned, his orchestra differs very slightly from the fully-grown combination of the nineteenth century. Only another pair of horns were required to make it identical with the orchestra of Weber's *Der Freischütz*, and even this addition was anticipated in one scene in the Vienna version of *Alceste*.

The printed scores of *Orfeo* and *Alceste*, representing the Vienna and Paris versions of both these operas, reveal some differences of instrumentation, and show that a certain amount of revision took place when these works were prepared for the Paris stage. The Vienna scores contain parts for *Chalumeaux*[2] ; these are replaced by clarinet parts in the Paris scores. Some parts for *Corni Inglesi* (in F), noted in modern fashion as transposing instruments, figure in the Vienna score of *Alceste* ; these, and some parts for *cornetti* in *Orfeo*, are not found in the Paris scores. Whether the change from *chalumeaux* to clarinets was merely a change of nomenclature, or actually a change of instruments, is open to question[3].

---

[1] The side-drum is said by Lavoix (Histoire de l'Instrumentation, Paris, 1878) to have been used in an opera by Marais (1656–1728).

[2] Variously spelt *chalamauz* and *chalamaux*.

[3] See p. 178.

Most readers interested in orchestration possess a copy of Berlioz's[1] treatise on *Modern Instrumentation and Orchestration*[1] in which will be found seventeen ample extracts from Gluck's five famous operas. These may serve as illustrations to many of the features now described.

The full harmony, the richer inside parts, the substantial body and solidity of Gluck's string music, are in striking contrast to the unsatisfying skeleton-harmony of so much eighteenth century work. Here is no sketchy orchestration which leaves much of the harmony to the *cembalo*, or else to the imagination. There is no yawning gap between violin and bass parts. Violas fill out the inner harmony instead of running meekly in company with the basses, and add fullness by a free use of double stopping. Four, five, six, or more notes are sounded together by the string orchestra where Handel was satisfied with two or three. For purposes of variety and " dramatic propriety " there is sustained harmony, rhythmical accompanying patterns, *tremolo* in three or four parts with or without mutes, figuration based on arpeggio or scale passages, *pizzicato* in chord or arpeggio form, and—probably one of Gluck's own discoveries—the powerful unison of the entire string orchestra, the unison which is used *for its effect*, and not simply in order to save the trouble of devising other parts. The thoroughly practicable nature of Gluck's violin parts shows that the technique of the instrument was always in his mind when writing the parts. They are not mere " parts " which might equally well be given to other instruments ; they are real violin parts ; parts of which the pattern or design arises out of violin technique ; parts in which the movement of the bow or the position of the fingers on the fingerboard, either one or both together, actually determine the design of the musical matter, and govern its very conception. Hence the straightforward effectiveness of his violin parts. To the viola, the Cinderella of the string orchestra, Gluck was the fairy-godmother who rescued the instrument from a mean position and made it not only independent and indispensable, but discovered in it an individuality which was quite its own, a peculiarity of tone-colour with which no other member of the string family was endowed. Thus, although the viola part in Gluck's scores does sometimes run with the bass part, the normal function of the instrument is either to provide essential harmony notes in the tenor register, to

[1] English translation, Novello, 1858.

balance or thicken the tone, to take part in the prevailing motion or figuration in company with first and second violins, or to create an effect by means of its own individual tone-colour. The violoncello was little more than a bass string instrument to Gluck. Its work is to play the lowest part of the harmony, usually with, but occasionally without the double-bass, and, although violoncello parts do occur which are rhythmically or melodically rather more elaborated versions of the double-bass parts, they are none the less real bass parts. Melodic parts for solo violoncello occur in Gluck's as in many other eighteenth century scores, and although tenor parts for violoncellos may be found in his scores, it cannot be said that he ever discovered the full value of violoncellos as melodists in the tenor register.

The use of wood-wind instruments in a body to supply harmonic backing to the more busy work of the strings was one of the most important of the progressive features in the orchestration of the transition composers. The principle is quite firmly established in Gluck's work. The addition of clarinets to the orchestra was, of course, a distinct gain to the substance of the wood-wind harmony, and their readiness to blend with the tone of other instruments was clearly in favour of the newcomers where only harmonic cohesion was required. Gluck treats his clarinets as another pair of rather less active oboes. They are not trusted with any real solo work. In melodic passages they double either the oboes or the violins, while as harmonists they are occasionally allowed to stand alone, but more often than not, they only duplicate the notes of the oboe parts. For solo work the flute and oboe, especially the latter, are the most favoured. A thin line of sustained oboe or bassoon tone, sounding clear and distinct through the midst of some accompanying pattern for strings, is a favourite effect of Gluck's. Another discovery in tone-colour was the peculiar charm of flutes playing in their lower octaves.

In writing for horns Gluck practically gives up any attempt to use them melodically. Their work is to sustain long notes common to the harmony, to bind together the moving fabric of the string parts, or to mark rhythms and increase the volume of tone in the *tutti*. There is likewise no trace of the old *clarino* style in Gluck's trumpet parts. These instruments are reserved for overtures, instrumental movements, and particular choruses, but are often omitted from *tutti* in which both horns and trombones appear. Although trumpets are frequently associated with horns, even to the extent of sharing their parts, there is no attempt at any harmonic alliance between trumpets and trombones. The idea that trumpets should constitute the upper voices of the heaviest brass group does not seem to have occurred to eighteenth century composers, and Gluck follows tradition in treating them as a pair apart, whose penetrating tones are not to be employed in any purely harmonic combination. Both horn and trumpet parts cover the same compass as they do in the works of Haydn and Mozart, and are noted according to the transposing system for instruments crooked in practically the same keys as those already mentioned in connection with Rameau's instrumentation. In using horns, trumpets, and drums for soft effects, Gluck probably broke new ground. The two latter especially had long been treated as the noisy element of the orchestra, only to be used when loudness or brilliancy was desired, and it cannot but have been a novel touch to hear the more weighty voices of the combination used lightly and softly, without any of the overwhelming insistence with which brass and percussion tone is apt to stand out and smother detail in the *tutti* when all are playing their loudest.

Alto, tenor and bass trombones are included only in particular movements of some of Gluck's operas, and are used harmonically, with the parts placed close together, and rather higher than is now customary. It is noteworthy that Gluck's bass trombone by no means always sounds the bass note of the chord ; also that the traditional French custom of placing trombone parts harmonically in close position seems to have its beginning in these parts of Gluck. Some passages for trombones in unison, which may also be found in Gluck's scores, would bring the part into overwhelming prominence if played with all the force of a modern *fortissimo*. There is evidence, however, that only the quieter manner of trombone-playing prevailed in the seventeenth and eighteenth centuries[1] ; it is indeed hardly possible to believe that the earlier trombone parts were played louder than what would now be considered a *mezzo-forte*.

By cutting the *cembalo* out of the orchestra Gluck got rid of not only an alien tone-colour, and a member unwilling to blend with other orchestral voices, but also a source of general weakness, due to the tendency to leave much of the inside harmony to the

---

[1] See Galpin, " The Sackbut, its evolution and history ", p. 21. Extract from the *Proceedings of the Musical Association*, 1906-7.

keyboard-instrument. This sense of dependence for harmony on an utterly inadequate support had hitherto been responsible for the thin scoring which often left the middle of the harmonic structure bare and empty. With the disappearance of the *cembalo* the duty of supplying completed harmony devolved on the real backbone of orchestral tone—the tone of the four-part string orchestra. In this capacity Gluck keeps his string instruments playing almost continuously, with the parts so disposed that normally not less than four notes are sounding at once. To this solid foundation the wood-wind add what is often an harmonically complete set of parts ; yet as a body the wood-wind are rarely allowed to be heard alone without any support from the strings. The addition of trombones had made a self-contained harmonic group of brass instruments quite feasible, and of the possible combinations, horns and trombones—such as are used in the well-known " *Divinités du Styx* " (*Alceste*)—are evidently preferred to the bolder blend of trumpets and trombones. Notwithstanding some adventitious examples which might be quoted in order to prove the contrary, Gluck did not completely emancipate the two wind groups—wood-wind and brass—from harmonic dependence on the string orchestra.

The richness of tone, harmonic solidity, and dramatic effect of Gluck's orchestration have more affinity to the work of the early nineteenth century than to that of the first half of the eighteenth century. Measured by any standard except that of time, it is more remote from the orchestration of Bach and Handel than it is from that of Weber, in spite of features which mark it clearly with the imprint of the eighteenth century. In that a set pattern of orchestration with a fixed colour scheme is usually maintained throughout an entire movement, Gluck's work belongs to his time, and to the age which preceded it, but the actual design of the patterns and colour-schemes are such as have proved to be the fundamentals of modern orchestration. Gluck's orchestral music is essentially conceived *for* the orchestra ; there is no trace of the keyboard or of vocal polyphony in its texture ; the contrapuntal, fugal, and imitative movement of parts, in which lies the main interest of early instrumental music, is replaced by a material conceived in terms of purely orchestral language, a manner of utterance which gave to the orchestra its own idioms, its own effects, and endowed it with complete and appropriate individuality of speech.

Thus, approximately in the third quarter of the eighteenth century, before Haydn or Mozart had produced their last works, the art of orchestration had turned the corner and the period of transition was over. The orchestra had acquired a language of its own which was ripe for further development along lines at once clearly defined, soundly based, and well directed.

Although such as J. G. Graun, Hasse, C. P. E. Bach, Abel, and Jomelli may be counted contemporaries of Gluck, they were hardly able to benefit by the example of his mature orchestration, which only began with *Orfeo* in 1762, and was therefore the product of his old age. In any case the work of these, and all other transition composers, places them at an earlier stage in the story of orchestration. The next generation, composers born roughly between 1725 and 1750, may be reckoned contemporaries of Gluck, and also of Haydn and Mozart. Some of the younger of this generation clearly enjoyed the advantage of having been able to reap some benefit from the example of Gluck's most advanced work, yet either died or reached the zenith of their powers just too soon to have learnt much from the maturest orchestration of Haydn and Mozart. Thomaso Traetta (1727-79) and Mattia Vento (1736–76) were typical Italian-cosmopolitan opera composers whose work merits no particular attention, but Nicola Piccini (1728-1800) and Antonio Sacchini (1734-86), at all events when in their later years they wrote opera for Paris, show a standard of work which entitles them to mention as orchestrators of merit in what may be considered the first stage in the story of modern orchestration. Sacchini's best work is hardly so rich and powerful as that of Gluck, yet is enlightened enough to bring this composer just within the circle of those whose orchestration was more than merely transitional. Decidedly more advanced is the work of Gluck's famous rival. Piccini clearly put his best foot foremost when he set to work orchestrating his *Iphigénie en Tauride* (1781) for the Paris Opera. The final test of strength between the two composers hung on their respective settings of this same libretto, and although Gluck's superior music won the day for him, it is by no means certain that he would have emerged an easy victor had the battle been fought with orchestration as the only weapon. No doubt Piccini learned from Gluck, but he learned to good purpose. *Iphigénie* is richly, dramatically, and almost brilliantly scored, with full command over the best resources of contemporary orchestral effect even when measured

by the standard of Gluck's most advanced work. Clarinet and
piccolo parts are included in Piccini's score. Some points of
interest include the real modern bow *tremolo* for strings side by side
with the effect referred to in a previous chapter and indicated by
a wavy line[1] :

EXAMPLE 41

Another point is an early instance of the harmonic combination of clarinet and bassoon tone, a successful and homogeneous blend which was soon to replace in general favour the old-
established alliance of oboes and bassoons. An example from
Piccini's *Iphigénie* will illustrate how wide was now the gulf
between the old style of instrumental part-writing, the
contrapuntal manner of Bach and Handel, and the new style in
which colour and instrumental fitness form the basis of part-
distribution, the style which laid the foundations on which
nineteenth century orchestration rests : (Example 42).
    Another composer who, though he lived till after Beethoven
had written his choral symphony, was already active in the cause
of orchestration at Paris during the time of Gluck's success, was

[1] See p. 63, chap. iv.

EXAMPLE 42

Piccini (Iphigénie _ 1781)

EXAMPLE 42 (*continued*).

EXAMPLE 42 (*continued*).

François-Joseph Gossec (1734–1829). A Belgian by birth, Gossec began his musical career at Paris in 1751, spending a long and busy life in the French capital, composing not only stage and sacred works, but also numerous orchestral symphonies, conducting at the opera, the *Concerts des Amateurs* (founded 1770), and the *Concerts Spirituels* (reorganized 1773).

During the time of the Republic Gossec became practically official composer to the new authority, and later on was identified with the founding of the *Conservatoire de Musique* (1795). Gossec claims to have written clarinet parts as early as 1757, to have added parts for these instruments to one of Rameau's operas, also to have used them in performances of symphonies[1] by J. Stamitz at the *Concerts Spirituels* in 1755. His obviously keen interest in orchestral effect on a large scale seems almost to adumbrate the schemes and projects of Berlioz some fifty years later, and clearly entitles him to a very prominent place amongst those who made Paris a home of remarkably progressive tendencies in orchestration during the time which connects Rameau—via Gluck and Piccini —with such as Cherubini, Méhul, and Spontini. One of " *citoyen* " Gossec's Republican compositions, *Le Triomphe de la République*, produced at the Paris Opera soon after the Revolution, is fully and effectively scored for piccolo, flutes, oboes, clarinets (in C, B-flat and A), bassoons, horns, trumpets, three trombones, drums, and *canon*[2], the latter surely an innovation !

The story of orchestration from the time of Gluck in Paris and Gossec, however, belongs more to the first stage in the growth of modern orchestration than to the period of transition.

---

[1] Evidently " added " parts, or else oboe parts doubled.

[2] The part is noted on the middle line of the treble staff.

CHAPTER VIII

THE PERIOD OF HAYDN AND MOZART

THE first stage in the evolution of modern orchestration, the period of Haydn's and of Mozart's activity as orchestral composers, roughly covers the last forty years of the eighteenth century. Mozart's mature and representative orchestration falls within about the last ten years of his life, from 1781 to 1791; the ten years from 1785 to 1795 similarly cover the mature works of Haydn as a composer of symphony, and if extended to 1801, would include his two oratorios *The Creation* and *The Seasons*.

The best-remembered contemporaries of Haydn and Mozart, men born while Handel was yet living, and who with few exceptions out-lived Mozart, men who were more or less in their prime when Beethoven was born, and of whom only a few survived after the death of Haydn, were the following :

ITALIAN :

Treatta 1727-79 (Italy, St. Petersburg, London)
Piccini 1728-1800 (Italy, Paris)
Sacchini 1734-86 (Italy, Germany, London, Paris)
Paisiello 1741-1816 (Italy, St.Petersburg, Paris)
Cimarosa 1749-1801 (Italy, St.Petersburg, Vienna)
Salieri 1750-1825 (Italy, Vienna, Paris)

GERMAN AND AUSTRIAN :

Cannabich 1731-98 (Mannheim, Munich)
Dittersdorf 1739-99 (Vienna, South Germany)
Karl Stamitz (the younger) 1745-1801 (Mannheim, Paris, London, St Petersburg, etc.)

BELGIAN :

Gossec 1734-1829 (Paris)
Grétry 1741-1813 (Paris)

An exhaustive list, embracing the more completely forgotten composers of the time, would include an army of Italians and Germans, with rather fewer Frenchmen and Englishmen.

Famous orchestras of the period were the Electoral orchestra at Mannheim, the Royal orchestras at Dresden and at Berlin, the opera orchestras at Naples and Paris, also those of the *Concerts Spirituels* [1] and the *Concerts des Amateurs* in the French capital. The Mannheim orchestra, sometimes under the elder Stamitz and Cannabich, had made a great reputation for its *ensemble*, and is credited with being early in the field to make a feature of *crescendo* and *diminuendo* effects. This was the orchestra which so greatly impressed Burney, who heard it play when he was travelling abroad to collect material for his History of Music. The Dresden orchestra had previously reached a high state of efficiency under Hasse, and was singled out for special praise by Rousseau, who named the Dresden and Naples orchestras as the finest in Europe, but had nothing but abuse for the orchestra at the Paris Opera the "*Académie Royale de Musique*". The inauguration of the "*Gewandhaus*" concerts at Leipzig in 1781, following the earlier "*Liebhaberconcerte*" under Hiller, is worthy of mention, and other orchestral bodies which come into prominence, largely on account of their associations with the two greatest composers of the time, were the orchestras at Salzburg and Prague for which Mozart wrote symphonies, the private orchestra of Haydn's patron at Esterházy, and that of the Haydn-Salomon concerts in London. St. Petersburg figures as a new centre of operatic activity in the second half of the eighteenth century, and in addition to the places already mentioned, Vienna, Munich, Stuttgart, Rome, Venice, Florence, and Milan all had a share in providing means for the further cultivation of orchestral playing, and opportunities for progress in orchestration.

Contemporary accounts and criticisms show an increasing interest in the rendering of orchestral music, in the selection and number of instruments employed, and even in the arrangement of the players on the platform or theatre orchestra [2].

Figured bass parts had been universal in full-scores since the beginning of the seventeenth century. The disappearance of the

[1] Called "*Concerts de la Loge Olympique*" after 1780 ; the concerts for which Haydn wrote his "Paris" symphonies.

[2] Rousseau's plan of the Dresden orchestra has often been reproduced. Other writers who give particulars of the personnel of orchestras during the period in question are Forkel, *Musikalischer Almanach für Deutschland*, 1782 ; Dörffel, *Geschichte der Gewandhauskonzerte* ; Gerber, *Lexikon*, 1790 ; Fürstenau, *Zur Geschichte . . . der Musik in Dresden*, 1861 ; Cramer, *Magazine für Musik*, 1783 ; Marpurg, *Historisch-kritische Beyträge*, 1754-78 ; Pohl, *Mozart und Haydn in London*, 1867.

basso-continuo begins about 1760 : by the end of the century the system was practically obsolete.   As a foundation or support the keyboard-instrument had become unnecessary, and although the *cembalo* or pianoforte was still used for *recitativo secco,* and organ parts in sacred works were still merely figured bass parts, by the end of the eighteenth century the keyboard-instrument in the orchestra was really little more than a conductor's desk.   It had outlived its original purpose ; the main building had been erected, and scaffolding was now only a blot and a hindrance. The method of " conducting " varied in different countries.   The use of a baton was uncommon except in churches and for choral music.   The common custom of dual direction by a " conductor " seated at the piano or organ, and a violinist-leader or " *conzert-meister* " who was the actual time-giver, kept the keyboard-instrument in the orchestra long after the *basso-continuo* had disappeared from the full-score[1] [2].   Lutes or theorbos lingered in some orchestras quite as late as 1783.   The harps which figure in many orchestral lists at the same time were probably used similarly to the lutes, as specific harp parts are very uncommon. The old *cornetti* also make their last appearances in scores during the period of Haydn-Mozart ; the principle of tone-production, however, survived well into the nineteenth century in the serpent and ophicleide.   The process of grafting clarinets on to the orchestral stem begins soon after 1750, and is not completed till the end of the century.   Trombone parts are included in the full-scores of many operas, oratorios, and masses, during the same period, but these instruments still remain strangers to the concert-orchestra.   As at all other periods, certain instruments make occasional appearances in full-scores without achieving, for the time being, a firm footing in the orchestral family.   The most frequent of these were the piccolo, tenor oboe (*cor anglais, corno inglese,* or *taille*), the tenor clarinet in F (*corno di bassetto*), and the

---

[1] " The use of the *score* is indispensable in composition : to the conductor of any performance it is also highly requisite, in order to his knowing whether each performer follows his *part,* and to enable him to supply any accidental omission with the pianoforte, or organ, at which he presides." " The Leader, after the conductor, holds the most important station in the orchestra.   It is to him that the other performers look for direction in the execution of the music, and it is on his steadiness, skill, and judgment, and the attention of the band to his motion, manner, and expression, that the concinnity, truth, and force of effect, do in a great measure depend." —*A Dictionary of Music,* by Thomas Busby, Mus. Doc., London, 4th Edition, 1813.

[2] See also Appendix B.

double bassoon. Thus, each variety of wood-wind instrument had an occasional additional representative, differing principally in size from the normal type. Bass-drum, cymbals, and triangle occur sporadically in opera scores, generally with the intention of giving local colour to Turkish or barbaric scenes, and, at all events, once in a symphony, namely, Haydn's *Military Symphony*. A few other quite exceptional instruments, such as the mandoline in Mozart's *Don Giovanni* or the *glockenspiel* in *Die Zauberflöte*, are to be found in opera scores, and usually provide solitary instances of their employment in the orchestra.

The proportionate strength of wood-wind and string instruments in orchestras of the Haydn-Mozart period differed considerably from nineteenth century or present-day standards. Only the most generously provided orchestras could boast as many as eight or ten first violins, but from three to six oboes, and a like number of bassoons, likewise three or four flutes and four horns, were evidently not considered too many to balance a string orchestra averaging about twenty-six players. Wood-wind parts in the *tutti* were clearly played by more than one instrument to each part when sufficient players were available. A preponderance of oboes and bassoons, as in the orchestras of Handel's time, seems to have been common till nearly the end of the century, and would materially affect the balance of tone in favour of the wood-wind. The proportion of violas, 'cellos, and double-basses to violins was roughly the same as was recommended by Quantz, the flute-player, who left some particulars of orchestral balance as it was understood about the middle of the century[1]. Quantz allowed one viola, one violoncello, and one double-bass to four or six violins ; two each of the lower strings, also two oboes, two flutes, and two bassoons to eight violins. To balance twelve violins his specification is three violas, four violoncellos, two double basses, four flutes, four oboes, three bassoons, a second *cembalo*, and a theorbo. Quantz insists, however, that the viola players should not be worn-out violinists ! The proportionate strength of string instruments given by Koch in his *Musical Dictionary* (1802) is two violas to eight violins, or three violas to ten violins. The following list gives some idea of the varying strength of well-known orchestras between 1750 and 1800 according to the authorities given in each case : (see also Appendix A).

[1] Johann Joachim Quantz, *Versuch einer Anweisung die Flöte Traversière zu Spielen*, Berlin, 1752.

Orchestra.	Date.	Violins.	Violas.	Cellos.	Basses.	Flutes.	Oboes.	Clarinets.	Bassoons.	Horns.	Other Instruments.	Authority.
Dresden ..	1753	8-7	4	3	3	2	5	—	5	2	trumpets, drums	Rousseau.
,, ..	1756	18	4	3	2	3	6	—	6	2	?	Fürstenau.
,, ..	1783	15	4	4	3	3	4	?	4	3	? lute	Cramer.
Berlin ..	1754	12	3	4	2	4	3	—	4	2	? theorbos	Marpurg.
,, ..	1782	13	4	4	3	4	3	—	4	2	? harp	Forkel.
,, ..	1787	20	6	8	4	2	4	2	4	4	trumpets, trombones, drums, harp	Anon, 1788.
Coblenz ..	1782	13	4	2	3	3	3	2	3	4	trumpets, drums	Forkel.
Esterházy (Haydn)	1783	11	2	2	2	?	2	—	2	2	?	Forkel.
London (Salomon)	1790-95	12-16	4	3	4	?	?	?	?	?	?	Pohl.
Mannheim ..	1756	10-10	4	4	2	2	2	—	2	4	trumpets, drums	Marpurg.
,, ..	1782	18	3	4	3	4	3	3	4	4	?	Forkel.
Paris Opera	1754	16	6	4 (Cellos & Basses braced = 12)	3	4 (Flutes & Oboes braced = 9)	3	—	?	2	?	Marpurg.

Some sort of keyboard-instrument is also included in most of the above lists, but several are obviously incomplete as regards trumpets and drums. Too close reliance should not be placed on these specifications, but they are probably accurate enough to show the general conception of orchestral balance during the period in question.

A few specially large orchestras organized for particular festival performances are on record, and include the Handel Commemoration in London (1784) with an orchestra of nearly two hundred and thirty players. A similar performance in Berlin (1786) was carried out with strings numbering thirty-eight first violins, thirty-nine second violins, eighteen violas, twenty-three violoncellos, and fifteen double-basses. Mention is also made of the performance of an opera by Dittersdorf involving the services of two hundred and thirty instrumentalists.

Improvements in the construction of wood-wind instruments during the latter half of the eighteenth century were principally those which resulted from the addition of keys covering holes bored between the finger-holes, in order to secure the easier and more certain production of the chromatic notes which had hitherto depended on the device known as " cross-fingering," or on the partial stopping of holes by the fingers. The transverse flute already had its D-sharp key, and this was the instrument of Quantz and his royal pupil, the "*traversière*" or German flute of Bach and Handel. It seems to have been some time after the mid-century that the other four keys were added which gave the remaining chromatic notes to the fundamental scale, namely, the F-natural, G-sharp, B-flat, and C-natural. Credit for introducing those keys sometime between 1770 and 1780 is often given to an English flute-player named Tacet, but Wetger[1] states that Tromlitz of Leipzig and Grenser of Dresden also added chromatic keys about the same time. Further claims are made on behalf of Richard Potter and Küsder, both of London. However that may be, it is evident that the number of keys on flutes began to grow towards the end of the century, and that flutes with up to as many as eight keys were made, and were used at the beginning of the nineteenth century before the re-organization of the key-mechanism associated with the name of Böhm gave the flute its final key-system just before the middle of that century.

[1] *Die Flöte, ihre Entstehung und Entwicklung*, Schmidt, Heilbronn.

The addition of further keys to oboes and bassoons went on more or less irregularly during the course of the eighteenth century. The old two-keyed oboe is said by several writers (who are probably only copying their statements one from the other) to have gained additional G-sharp and B-flat keys as early as 1722 or 1727, for which credit is given to one Bürgermeister Gerhard Hoffmann (1690–1740) of Rastenburg; but it is obvious that these two keys cannot have been universally adopted at that early date[1]. The two keys producing the low C and D-sharp, and occasionally a third key producing low C-sharp, are found on oboes made up to near the end of the eighteenth century. Some additional chromatic notes were obtained by means of the duplicated third and fourth finger-holes which are usually provided on oboes of the period. The bassoon gained its low G-sharp key early in the same century, and may be said to have normally had four keys (low B-flat, D, F, and G-sharp) about the middle of the eighteenth century. The subsequent addition of keys went on up to the extent of about nine keys early in the nineteenth century. No doubt the various improvements devised by many makers, all working independently and out of touch with one another, would take time to become widely known and adopted, and this would easily account for the conflicting statements and evidence which confront the investigator. The general tendency was clearly to add keys, not only in order to provide for chromatic notes, but also to supply some alternative fingerings, or even to make certain shakes possible.

Although none of the wood-wind instruments acquired their completed key-mechanisms till about the middle of the nineteenth century, the activity on the part of both makers and players which eventually led to the perfected instruments, was clearly already in progress during the time of Haydn and Mozart.

Two essential characteristics of the clarinet type, the single reed and cylindrical tube, had been known long before they were embodied in the instrument which slowly found its way into the orchestra during the second half of the eighteenth century. The *chalumeau*, a rustic instrument of the Middle Ages—not to be confused with the *schalmei* or shawms to which the oboes and bassoons owe their parentage—was the prototype of the clarinet.

[1] Numerous surviving instruments, and several tutors, indicate fairly conclusively that the two-keyed oboe was the standard instrument practically throughout the eighteenth century.

It was about 1690 that Johann Christoph Denner (1655-1707), a Nürnberg maker of flutes, oboes, and bassoons, began to improve the *chalumeau*, and though it is questionable whether anyone can be said to have " invented " any musical instrument, there seems reasonable ground for giving Denner the credit for having taken the first steps towards transforming the rude *chalumeau* into a useful artistic instrument. Hawkins[1] was not sure of his ground when he wrote of J. C. Denner : " He is said to have greatly improved the *chalumeau*, an instrument resembling the Hautboy, and described by Mersennus and Kircher ; and to have been the original inventor of *another* instrument, which neither of them do so much as mention, namely, the clarinet." This is hardly surprising as, according to Hawkins' own dates, Mersennus died in 1648, while Denner was not born till 1655. The improved *chalumeau* and the clarinet were clearly one and the same thing. The third and vital characteristic of the clarinet type is the small hole near the mouthpiece which, when opened, makes it possible to overblow the instrument and produce notes a twelfth higher than those of the fundamental scale.   This particular acoustical property is peculiar to a cylindrical closed tube, and therein lies the essential difference between the fingering of the clarinet and that of the conical-bored instruments which produce an octave as their first harmonic when overblown.   Another property of a cylindrical tube with a closed end is that the sounding length of the tube is in effect doubled ; thus, middle C on the clarinet is produced with a sounding length of one foot, whereas a conical tube requires a length of two feet to produce the same note.   According to Altenburg[2] the fundamental scale of the earliest surviving clarinets bearing J. C. Denner's name is from F to B :

On these instruments two holes, opposite one another near the mouthpiece end, are covered by keys, and are said to produce the upper A and B. Two holes close together at the lower end of the instrument produce the lowest F when both are covered by

[1] *History of Music*, Vol. iv, p. 249 (1776).
[2] *Die Klarinette*, Schmidt, Heilbronn, 1904.

the little finger of the right hand, and F-sharp when only one hole is closed. The intermediate octave (G to G) is produced by the six main finger-holes, just as on other wood-wind instruments. By opening the upper B-key, which also acts as a " speaker-key ", another series of notes, a twelfth higher than the fundamental scale, starting at 1-ft. C, would be produced. This corresponds more or less to the following extracted from a book by Caspar Majer entitled *Neu eröffneter Musiksaal* (published 1741) : " The clarinet is an instrument invented at the beginning of this century by a Nürnberg maker, and is a wooden instrument not unlike a long oboe except for its broad mouthpiece (reed ?) ; it sounds from afar something like a trumpet[1] and has a compass from tenor F to A, or possibly to high C ".

(Majer's description is suspiciously like that appearing in Walther's *Musikalisches Lexikon*, 1732.)

Altenburg, however, goes on to say that J. Denner—presumably a son[2] of J. C. Denner—made clarinets with yet another hole further down towards the bell which, when closed by a long key, sounded low E through the bell ; at the same time the " speaker " or " clarinet" hole near the mouthpiece was made narrower, with the result that it sounded B-flat instead of B-natural. B-natural would, of course, be sounded as the twelfth of the low E. Altenburg surmises that this would be about 1720. That being so, the fundamental scale of these clarinets would correspond exactly to that of the later eighteenth century and nineteenth century instruments :

Several specimens of these three-keyed clarinets dating from about the mid-century are said to be extant in various

[1] *Clarino* (Italian) = trumpet, hence the name *clarinetto*, *i.e.*, small trumpet.

[2] Hawkins states that J. C. Denner left two sons who carried on their father's business after his death.

museums and collections, bearing names which show that makers other than the Denners were making clarinets during the first half of the century.

The above account of Denner's early clarinets, based on that of Altenburg, differs slightly from that given in the Catalogue of the Musical Instruments exhibited at the Royal Military Exhibition, London, 1890[1]. In the latter the two upper keys are said to produce A and B-flat when used separately, and B-natural when opened together.

The next step was to provide keys for the low F-sharp and G-sharp, sounding C-sharp and D-sharp, a twelfth higher, when overblown. For this Berthold Fritz (died 1766 at Braunschweig) gets credit[2]. It seems tolerably certain that this five-keyed instrument was the clarinet as known to Haydn and Mozart. A sixth key producing C-sharp / G-sharp, attributed to L. Xavier Lefebvre of Paris, was added about 1791; this key, however, is not usually found on clarinets of that period, nor does it figure in contemporary tutors. It was most probably for the five-keyed clarinet that Beethoven wrote. Stadler of Vienna is said to have extended the compass of the clarinet down to low C about 1790[3]; this again does not appear to have been generally adopted.

Backofen's *Anweisung zur Klarinette*[4], an English tutor evidently dating from about the end of the eighteenth century[5], and some MSS.[6] in the British Museum by Dr J. Callcott (1766-1821) give details of the keys and fingering for the five-keyed clarinet; these agree in all except the means of producing some of the chromatic notes; the following appears to have been the arrangement of keys and fingering on the standard instrument with five keys; the two long keys (E and F-sharp) were manipulated by the little finger of the left hand, and covered holes at the bell end of the instrument, the E key standing open while all the other keys stood closed. The short key at the lower end was manipulated by the little finger of the right hand. Above that key was a hole for the same little finger, then three holes for the right hand,

---

[1] London, 1891.

[2] This appears to be based on the statement of von Gontershausen, 1855.

[3] Von Gontershausen, *Musikalische Tonwerkzeuge*, Frankfurt, 1855.

[4] Leipzig, 1803.

[5] *Compleat Instructions for the Clarinet*, Henry Thompson, no date.

[6] Articles for a projected Dictionary of Music.

three for the left, and at the back of the instrument a hole for the left thumb.   Above that, on the upper side of the instrument was a short key (A) played by the first finger of the left hand, and underneath another key (B-flat, or the "speaker") played by the thumb of the same hand.   The fundamental scale was produced as follows : low E by closing the open-standing longest key, F by leaving that key untouched, F-sharp by opening the next longest key, G by opening the hole covered by the little finger of the right hand, G-sharp by leaving that hole uncovered and at the same time pressing down the short key touched by the same little finger ; after that the next six diatonic notes (A to F) are produced by successively uncovering the six finger-holes ; the upper G is produced by uncovering the left thumb-hole, A by opening the short key on the top of the instrument, and B-flat by opening the short key underneath and nearest the mouthpiece.   That same key acts as the " speaker " key, and is kept open while a repetition of the fingering for the fundamental scale produces the whole series a twelfth higher if greater wind pressure is applied.

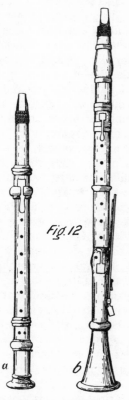

Various cross-fingerings give the intermediate semitones, which in Backofen's tutor make a complete chromatic scale from low E to C above the treble staff ; the English tutor, strangely enough, since the keys are there, does not show the low F-sharp and G-sharp, but is otherwise a complete chromatic scale up to the same high C, and extends diatonically beyond that up to F ; Callcott evidently only knew a few chromatic notes, and gives no definite upward limit.

The reed on these clarinets was tied with string on to either the upper or the lower side of the mouthpiece, evidently according to taste or custom.   From the very beginning of their history

(*a*) Clarinet by Denner (two keys), early eighteenth century ;

(*b*) Five-keyed Clarinet, late eighteenth century.

clarinets appear to have been made in several sizes. Denner's two
surviving specimens[1] are in C and high A ; other early specimens
in low A and high E-flat are mentioned by Altenburg. Soon
after the mid-century, when parts for clarinets, and so named,
begin to appear in opera scores, the instruments are in B-flat, C,
or D. Callcott mentions these three, but Gluck apparently knew
only the C clarinet. Backofen names the instruments in A,
B-flat and C, while the English tutor specifies only B-flat and C
clarinets. A Clarinet Preceptor[2]—by *an eminent Professor*—
evidently of slightly later date, mentions instruments in A, B-flat,
C, D, and E-flat. Mozart wrote for the low A, B-flat, B-natural,
and C clarinets. Parts for the B-natural instrument appear in the
original scores of *Idomeneo* and *Così fan tutte*, but are transposed
for the A clarinet in modern editions. A clarinet in low G and
the Basset horn in F, said to have been first made by Mayrhofer
at Passau in 1770 and improved by Lotz of Pressburg in 1782,
which enjoyed some popularity just towards the close of the
eighteenth century, are amongst the lower, and instruments in
high E-flat and F are the higher clarinets which, although used in
military bands, have taken no permanent place in the orchestra.
Including those of the nineteenth century, altogether quite twenty
different sizes of clarinet can be counted, some of which have
never appeared in orchestral scores. Parts for *chalumeau* appear
sporadically in a few early eighteenth century scores. Early
instances are those in Keiser's *Croesus* (1710) and in Bononcini's
Turno Aricino (c. 1710). A clarinet part of a Mass by Faber,
dated 1720, is said to be preserved in the library at Antwerp
Cathedral. It is strongly probable that the improved *chalumeau*
retained its original name for some time after the new instrument
had appeared, and that parts for *chalumeau* such as those mentioned above, Hasse's in *La Virtù appiè della Croce* (1737), and even
Gluck's in the Vienna scores of his *Orfeo* and *Alceste*, were really
played by, and were intended for clarinets. Support for this view
is found in Majer's *Neu eröffneter Musiksaal* (1741) in which both
instruments are so described that it is impossible to suppose that
they were anything but one and the same thing. Another early
clarinet part must have been one in an opera by Johann Friedrich
Agricola (1720-74) mentioned on the authority of Hiller, by Jahn.[3]

[1] In the Bavarian Museum at Munich.
[2] British Museum.
[3] *Life of Mozart* (German Edition), Vol. i. p. 385, footnote.

There is some evidence that clarinets were used in military bands during the first half of the eighteenth century.

Amongst the early clarinet parts, so named, in orchestral scores are those in Arne's *Artaxerxes* and in J. C. Bach's *Orione*, both produced in London respectively in 1762 and in 1763[1]. Arne's parts are for the C instrument but Bach's are transposing parts for B-flat and D clarinets.   Regarding some alleged clarinet parts in Rameau's *Acante and Céphise* (1751) Mennicke, in his *Hasse und die Brüder Graun als Symphoniker*[2], has pointed out that every note of the part could be played on an eight-foot natural trumpet, and concludes that the parts were written for *Clarino* (trumpet), and not for clarinet.   If it has not been quite convincingly proved that Rameau actually wrote any clarinet parts himself, it is evident that the Paris orchestra had its clarinets either shortly before or soon after his death in 1764. Gossec claims to have used them in 1757, and clarinet parts figure fairly regularly in the scores of works written for the " *Académie Royale de Musique* " from the date of Gluck's *Orfeo* (Paris 1774) onwards.   The orchestras at Mannheim and Dresden are said by some writers to have acquired clarinets respectively in 1767 and 1786, but various authorities are not quite in agreement as to the exact dates.   It is evident, however, that the instruments began to find their way into German orchestras roughly about twenty to thirty years before the end of the century. According to an anonymous author, clarinets were used in the Royal orchestra at Berlin in 1787, and were to be found—according to Forkel—in the orchestras at Koblenz, Mainz, Pressburg, Regensburg, and Ansbach in the years 1782 and 1783.   This is borne out by the statement in Koch's *Lexikon* (1802) that the instruments had become known and used during " the last thirty years ".   Clarinet parts are fairly common, but by no means universal, in scores written during the last quarter of the eighteenth century.   They occur in most of Mozart's operas, but in only five of his symphonies, also in some of Haydn's last twelve symphonies and in many operas by such as Salieri,

---

[1] Mozart, visiting London as a child, wrote a Symphony for strings, clarinets, and bassoons, in 1765. The year, taken in conjunction with the years of Arne's and Bach's operas, suggests that Mozart may have heard clarinets in London, and that when he encountered them again at Mannheim in 1777, they were not new to him. (See Jahn, Vol. i, p. 385.)

[2] Leipzig, 1906.

Bianchi, Piccini, Paisiello, and others, also in symphonies by Cannabich (Mannheim).

There was clearly some uncertainty at first whether the new-comers were to be regarded as additional to the already established group of wood-wind instruments, or as substitutes for the oboes[1]. Many composers wrote no oboe parts in the movements in which they included clarinet parts, and with others it was evidently a matter of choice whether oboes or clarinets, or both together, were to play the parts which lay between the flute and the bassoon registers. When both oboes and clarinets appear together and are given independent parts, the oboes are treated as the more active of the two.

Almost immediately after the middle of the eighteenth century the efforts of players and makers of horns and trumpets began to be directed towards producing instruments on which other than the open notes could be played. First came Anton Joseph Hampel (died 1771), a horn-player in the Dresden orchestra, with his discovery that the pitch of open notes on horns could be lowered a semitone or a whole tone by pushing the hand up the bell of the instrument. This was in 1760, and was evidently made feasible as a result of making horns with smaller, and therefore more numerous, circular windings of the tube, which brought the bell within reach of the player's right hand. The large circular horns had previously been held in hunting fashion with the bell pointing upwards, and now began to be held with the bell at the player's right side, just as at the present time. Contemporary illustrations show the horn, at all events in England, still held with the bell upwards until early in the nineteenth century, although Hampel's method of playing stopped notes is said to have been exhibited by a player named Spandau who visited England in 1773. Crooks were probably already in use at the time of Hampel's discovery, and tuning slides appear to have been added a few years earlier, also by Hampel.

Thus was the old hunting-horn transformed into the French or Hand horn such as was used in the time of Haydn and Mozart[2].

[1] Mozart's early Symphony in E-flat (Köchel 18) was written for clarinets *instead* of oboes (Jahn, *Life of Mozart*). Burney (*Present State . . . in Germany*, 1773) mentions a clarinet "which served as an hautboy", in a Brussels orchestra.

[2] According to Eichborn (*Das Alte Clarinblasen auf Trompeten*, Leipzig, 1894, p. 22-5) the "Inventions horn" was none other than the closer-wound hand horn, fitted with crooks and tuning slides.

That Hampel's device met with slow acceptance is evident from the fact that composers did not freely embody stopped notes in their horn parts until early in the nineteenth century.

It is perhaps not so well known that the same process of " stopping " was applied to trumpets. The instrument was made with more than the usual two bends in the tube, the bell being thus brought within reach of the player's hand ; or the whole instrument was made in slightly curved form with the same object. The difference in tone quality between open and stopped notes on horns is well known; Beethoven and his contemporaries clearly tolerated stopped notes just for the sake of the additional useful chromatic notes, but "stopping" on trumpets was less successful, and never gained general acceptance in the orchestra.

Fig. 13

Hand Horn with tuning slide.

The next important step is credited to one Kälbel of St.Petersburg about the year 1770. His scheme was based on the system of the old *cornetti*, on which a complete scale was obtained by shortening the sounding length of the instrument by opening finger-holes in the tube. Kälbel covered these holes with keys, and his lead was soon followed by makers in France and Germany[1]. The resulting tone of notes which did not sound through the bell of the instrument must have been even more unsatisfactory than that of the stopped notes, for neither keyed-horns nor keyed-trumpets were at any time generally adopted in the orchestra. The most successful of these instruments appears to have been the keyed bugle or Kent-horn, a short-tubed instrument of wide bore, which had some vogue in military bands before the advent of the modern cornet. Eighteenth century composers as good as ignored these and all other attempts to fill up the gaps between the open notes of horns and trumpets, and continued to write parts for the natural instruments, now provided with crooks and tuning-slides. Horns crooked in low B-flat, C, D, E-flat, E, F,

[1] Notably Weidinger of Vienna in 1801.

G, A, and high B-flat[1], and trumpets in B-flat[2], C, D, and E-flat are
commonly demanded in the scores of Haydn, Mozart and their
contemporaries.   Four horn parts is by no means an unusual
number, especially when the movement is in the minor key.   One
pair of horns in the tonic major and another in the relative major
is the usual arrangement; between them they gave a fair selection
of useful notes, but involved some awkward dodging about from
one pair to the other :

EXAMPLE 43

While the wood-wind and brass instruments were being
subjected to constant mechanical improvement, the old stringed
instruments in themselves could not be bettered, but were in the
meantime being adapted to the needs of a growing technique.
The necks were being lengthened, the bridges and fingerboards
raised, and violins were now being held with the chin on the
left side of the tail-piece.   By the end of the century the modern
bow of Tourte had replaced the heavier, shorter, and less elastic
bow of Corelli and Tartini.   A new generation of violinists, headed

[1] Horns in high C and high E-flat occur exceptionally.

[2] The 9-ft. instrument in low B-flat, double the length of the modern
B-flat trumpet.

by Viotti (1753-1824), were extending the upward compass, developing the technique of their instruments, and ever widening the breach between virtuoso and orchestral players. The principles of modern violoncello fingering[1] were being laid down by Duport (1741–1818) and even the viola had its virtuoso in Karl Stamitz, probably the first composer to write a concerto for the instrument.

Such was the state of orchestral instruments during the period which saw modern orchestration through the first stage of its growth. The same period witnessed the decline of the *concerto grosso*, and the rise of the solo concerto for violin or piano and orchestra. By the end of the century symphony and overture were clearly distinguished one from the other both in form and function.

When Franz Joseph Hâydn (1732-1809) began writing symphonies in 1755 he had only the example of the earliest symphonists before him. Like them, he wrote for a small orchestra, usually only for strings, oboes and horns, occasionally for flutes and bassoons, and more rarely for trumpets and drums. Like them, he started with giving all the essential matter to the strings, allowing the wind only to amplify the musical structure by providing harmonic backing, rhythm, colour, and volume of tone. For a long time Haydn was content to write much of his string music in three, and often only in two real parts. Either the violas duplicated the bass part an octave higher, or first and second violins played in unison or in octaves ; when both occur together the music is little else but a bare melody and bass part, sometimes with the strange result that the violas play a high version of the bass part above the melody itself. The apparent thinness of this two or three-part writing is, however, often modified by figuration in the inner or lower parts which serves in effect to complete the harmony.

The principal interest in the orchestration of Haydn's early works lies in the distribution of essential matter between strings and wind instruments. His first two symphonies are little else but string quartets in orchestral style with the addition of non-essential wind parts. Already in his third symphony (c. 1761) the oboes are required to take an indispensable part in stating the second subject of the first movement, and in the trio of the Minuet vital matter is equally distributed between oboes, horns,

[1] *Essai sur le doigter du Violoncelle.*

and strings. Quickly gaining confidence, Haydn soon goes a step further and allows all the wind instruments, either as soloists or in unison, to take responsibility for essential melodic matter on their own shoulders, thus putting them on an equal footing with the strings. In some of the works written between 1761 and 1764 may be found whole subjects entrusted to a flute or an oboe, with light string accompaniments; the horns get little melodic phrases all to themselves, or part of a subject is given entirely to a group of wind instruments.

The freedom he gained after writing a few symphonies is nowhere better exemplified than in the first movement of Haydn's Symphony No. 6 (B and H) *Le Matin*. Scored for flute, two oboes, bassoon, two horns and strings, the wind in this movement figure as indispensable soloists, or unite to form a six-part harmonic body which is freely trusted to stand quite alone. The experience of a few years was all that was necessary for Haydn to establish a satisfactory state of equilibrium between the functions of wind and string instruments. Individually and collectively the wood-wind were liberated from a state of dependence; melodically and harmonically they were emancipated; singly or in pairs, or in necessarily small groups, they might be used at any moment for almost any purpose. The old notions that wind instruments should always play in pairs, and that, once started, they should continue to play according to a set pattern throughout a whole or a considerable portion of a movement, were both abandoned.

The prevalence of elaborated solo parts for single string or wind instruments extending throughout an entire movement, is one of the old-fashioned features of orchestration which crops up periodically in Haydn's symphonies. Several movements of the early symphonies *Le Matin, Le Midi,* and *Le Soir* (1761) have two or three such *concertante* solo parts going on at once, much in the manner of the old *concerto grosso*. The Symphony No. 31 (1765) likewise contains some very elaborate horn parts and unusually ornate solos for flute, violin and violoncello. All these suggest that he was writing to show off the execution of particularly efficient players, and recall an earlier orchestral style. Apart from that feature there is no trace of the style of Bach or Handel even in the earliest orchestral works of Haydn.

Haydn's symphonies of between 1785 and 1788 show the result of rather more than twenty-five years' practical experience with the orchestra. By that time he had largely abandoned the thin two-part writing for strings which marks all his early works. The violas now get more independent tenor parts and add fulness to the sound of the string orchestra. Double-stopping on the same instrument, and occasional *divisi*, likewise help to give a more substantial inside to the harmonic structure. The difference between a lighter bass part played by violoncellos only, and the heavier bass of both violoncellos and double-basses, is more keenly appreciated in these later symphonies, and occasionally the violoncellos are allowed to move independently of the double-basses in order to provide fuller accompanying figuration in the tenor register, although for purely melodic purposes a solo violoncello is always specified. A generally more elaborate texture, more substantial body of tone, more pronounced and more frequent contrasts of tone-colour, and of dynamic light and shade, are further signs of familiarity with orchestral effect, and of progress. How much more orchestration was beginning to be appreciated for its own sake is evident by the pains Haydn now took to present recapitulated matter on its reappearance with fresh and amplified orchestration. Redistribution of parts, readjustments for the sake of balance, additional ornamentation and counterpoint give fresh interest to already familiar themes, a great advance on the older custom of repeating the original orchestration of the music, note for note. All these show clearly that Haydn's sense for orchestral effect was still continuously, although slowly, expanding even after middle age had passed. A fair example of his work at this period is the symphony in G (No. 88, B and H) which followed the six symphonies written for Paris in 1786.

Like Haydn, Wolfgang Amadeus Mozart (1756-91) scored his first symphony (1764) for strings, oboes, and horns, allowing practically no independence to the wind instruments. Making rapid and continuous progress, he soon drew level with Haydn, acquiring in a few years the same freedom in distributing his matter between the wood-wind and string instruments of the orchestra in accordance with their individual nature and technique. In laying out his string parts, Mozart, even in his very early works, secured greater fullness than Haydn did by making more independent use of the tenor instrument. Although frequently dropping into three parts, the younger composer more often wrote in four real parts for strings. A desire for yet more body shows itself in his freer use of double-stopping, in the richer figuration of his inner parts, and in his readiness to divide the

violas into two parts.   Quite a novelty was Mozart's discovery of
the pleasing effect of first violins and violas playing melodically
in octaves.   Both composers treat the violoncello as a bass
instrument, and in their earlier works rarely make any distinction
between violoncello and double-bass parts.   Like Gluck, both
seemed hardly aware of the latent possibilities which lay in the
use of *ripieno* violoncellos as melodists.   Both soon learned the
value of *pizzicato* in providing light bass parts while the upper
strings were playing with the bow, and were ready to utilize the
variety secured by making the entire string orchestra play
pizzicato, or by muting the same instruments.   Their parts show
a sound practical knowledge of violin technique within the limits
of the third position.

In 1777-8 Mozart spent some time at Mannheim, where he heard
the famous Electoral orchestra play under Cannabich.   From
that time dates the beginning of the further progress by which,
in about ten years more, Mozart's orchestration reached its apogee,
and in its turn possibly became an influence in bringing Haydn's
work to its culmination a few years later.   To the Mannheim
orchestra, to its rendering and the orchestration of the music
they played, special mention were due, had they achieved nothing
more than having furthered the cause of orchestration by
stimulating the desire of Mozart for greater orchestral effects,
for having been a contributory cause to the efforts which culminated in the orchestration of his last few symphonic works,
notably the *Prague* (1786), the G minor, the E-flat, and the
Jupiter symphonies (all 1788).

The Mannheim symphonists, including Johann Stamitz
(1717–57), Christian Cannabich (1731–98), Karl Stamitz (1745–
1801), Franz Beck (1723–1809), and Ernst Eichner (1740-77),
all of them composers, orchestral players and conductors, all of
them at some time of their lives associated with the orchestra
which during Mozart's youth was considered second to none in
Europe, were active agents in spreading the true orchestral style
and the traditions of what was virtually a school of orchestration,
a centre from which radiated a high standard of efficiency not only
all over musical Germany, but also to Paris and London.   It was
at Mannheim[1] that Mozart is said to have heard the refinements

---

[1] See Burney, *The Present State of Music in Germany*, Vol. i, p. 94,
London, 1773, for description of the playing of the Mannheim orchestra.
Also Jahn, *Life of Mozart*, Vol. I, p. 379 (English trans.).

of orchestral playing for the first time, the famous *crescendo* and *diminuendo*, the clarinets, and the *ensemble* which contemporary writers describe as being above criticism. It is probably largely due to the Mannheim influence that marks indicating loudness or softness, and the gradation of tone between loud and soft, begin to be more carefully and more freely supplied in full scores during the second half of the eighteenth century.

One thing the Mannheimers were unable to supply was the genius which was to take full advantage of, and flourish in the orchestral soil they had so richly fertilized. That Mozart's *Paris Symphony* (1778), which followed immediately after his visit to Mannheim, is scored for a larger orchestra than he employed in his earlier works is no evidence that he learned anything in the South German town, for every composer at that time varied his score according to the constitution of the particular orchestra for which he was writing ; but of the more resourceful treatment of the instruments employed, and the keener feeling for colour and effect shown in the *Paris Symphony*, as compared with the pre-Mannheim works, there can be no question. This symphony[1] is scored for flutes, oboes, clarinets, bassoons, horns, trumpets, drums and strings, the full " classical " symphony orchestra which was now taking final shape. The strings play now in unison, now in two, three, four, or five parts, relying on their own harmony, rhythm and matter, or only taking part with the wind instruments in combined colour-schemes. Melodic passages in double octaves by first violins, second violins, and violas are supplied with full harmonic backgrounds by wind instruments in four, six, or eight parts. The bass of violoncellos only is freely contrasted with the 16-ft. tone of double-basses ; violas assist now the upper, now the lower parts, or are occupied with matter which belongs to neither extreme. The wind are combined in varying partnerships—flutes and oboes, clarinets and bassoons, oboes and bassoons, oboes and horns, flutes and clarinets—are all heard melodically or harmonically combined at various times, as well as in larger six or eight-part groups. The quick alternation of full wind and string chords, and other devices difficult to describe in writing, orchestral devices only tentatively suggested in previous works, now begin to appear as part and parcel of the technique of an orchestration which is still listened to with satisfaction, and

[1] No. 31, B and H ; Köchel, 297.

requires that very little allowance be made on account of the passage of time.

A few years more, and Mozart's last symphonies, the *Prague* (1786), the E-flat, the G minor, and the *Jupiter* (all 1788), quickly followed by Haydn's *Oxford* (1788) and his twelve " Salomon " symphonies (1790-5), bring the story of orchestration on to ground which is still more familiar to the concert-goer of the present day.

The constitution of the concert-orchestra was at last settling down. A little more wavering, and the question of oboes or clarinets was to be finally settled by adopting both. The scores of Mozart's *Prague* and *Jupiter* symphonies both lack clarinet parts, the work in E-flat has clarinet but no oboe parts, and to the G minor symphony, originally scored without clarinets, the composer later on added parts for these instruments, at the same time remodelling the original oboe parts. Haydn's *Oxford* and some of the *London* symphonies likewise lack clarinet parts, but all include parts for oboes. The eight-part[1] wood-wind group was thus all but stabilized. Two horns, two trumpets, and drums[2] is the selection of brass and percussion instruments which, with the strings, constitutes the concert-orchestra as Haydn and Mozart left it, and as Beethoven found it just before the end of the eighteenth century.

There are few tangible features in the mature orchestration of Haydn and Mozart which cannot be found exemplified in some or other of their earlier works. It is more the confident handling and frequency of devices and effects already tried that distinguish the later scores of both composers from those belonging to their intermediate periods. Measured by the standard of their very earliest works the advance is enormous ; taken year by year the progress is not so easily perceptible, yet it was practically continuous and cumulative. Thus, it is hardly possible to date the steps which led to the final stage. An analysis of the orchestration of their mature symphonies will be little more than a re-statement of the features which have marked the growth of Haydn's and Mozart's work from the time of their first symphonies to the years immediately preceding their ripest periods, with the difference that the ground then being gradually conquered was now securely held, that the uncertainty of tentative experiment was succeeded

[1] Occasionally only one flute part was provided.

[2] The use of Bass drum, cymbals and triangle in Haydn's *Military Symphony* was quite exceptional, if not quite unique at the time.

by an easy confidence which only came with the familiarity of
practical and successful experience.   Greater demands on the
technique of players had increased the scope for effect in writing
both for wood-wind and string instruments.   The orchestral
compass of violins was gradually extending upwards, and it is
not unusual to find first violins required to play in the sixth
position on the E string, and second violins in the third position,
in these later symphony scores.   Violas, while sharing to a more
limited extent in the increased agility required from all string
instruments, were, however, evidently regarded as a weak spot,
for their sphere in the tenor register is frequently invaded by
violoncellos.   Though it was reserved for Beethoven and other
early nineteenth century composers finally to promote violoncellos to the rank of melodists in the orchestra, the intermediate
step was freely taken by Haydn and Mozart in their last few
symphonies.   In these works tenor parts lying well within the
compass of the viola are frequently reinforced by violoncellos ;
at times the latter completely usurp the function of the violas, and
leave the smaller instrument either to follow the bass part or to
provide harmonic padding.   More often than not, accompanying
figuration in the tenor register is given to violoncellos in preference to violas.   The richer tone of the larger instrument was
clearly beginning to be appreciated, and what was actually
a new tenor voice of characteristic tone-colour was thus added to
the string orchestra.

A catalogue of the resources used by Haydn and Mozart when
dealing with the string orchestra in their ripest symphonies
would include the unison of the entire group, two, three, or four-
part writing, and the fuller effect secured by increasing the
number of notes sounded at the same time by means of double-
stopping on violins or violas, or by dividing them into two parts.
The incursion of violoncellos into the tenor register, and the
distinction between bass parts played by violoncellos only and
by double-basses as well, have already been mentioned.   A large
variety of figurated harmonic patterns, the effects of *pizzicato*
and *sordino*, of measured *tremolo*, of sustained and repetitional
accompaniments, of completely detached chords, are only some
of the more easily classified means by which they secured variety
of treatment and effect.   Contrasts of loud and soft, of full or
thin scoring, occur freely, the thinness being now a matter of
choice for the sake of contrast, rather than of habit, as formerly.

The parts given to the wood-wind instruments completely establish their independent status as a body of harmonists or melodists. Flutes in the high register, oboes and clarinets in the medium, and bassoons in the tenor and bass registers, each are allotted duties as essential to the whole musical structure as any of the string parts. As soloists or as melodists playing in unison, in octaves or in double octaves, they freely take responsibility for any vital matter which is suitable to their compass, nature or technique. Only the clarinets are treated with some diffidence as if they had hardly yet made good their claim for admittance into the concert-orchestra. Haydn's clarinet parts, although quite indispensable, are nothing like so full or so important as his oboe parts. The new instruments were used to give additional body to the wood-wind *tutti*, to supply essential harmony, or to double melodic phrases played by one or other of the wood-wind, but all the important solo parts go to either the flute, the oboe, or the bassoon. Mozart, on the other hand, in his E-flat symphony gave over to clarinets the entire duties of the oboes in the register lying between those of the flute and bassoon, and in the *trio* of the well-known Menuet from the same work, displayed at the same time both the upper and lowest registers of the instrument in quite a novel manner. The accompanying arpeggio figure for the second clarinet, low down in the so-called " chalumeau " register, combined with the solo melody for first clarinet up in the more brilliant part of the instrument, is now familiar, but must have been a decidedly fresh effect at the time. He had already used the same effect in *Don Giovanni* (1787); that it pleased the composer is evident, for he repeated the device more than once in his opera *Così fan tutte*, written two years later. These, however, are almost isolated cases, and also appear to be the only instances in which the lowest register of the clarinet is exploited in contemporary orchestration. Mozart's addition of clarinet parts to his G minor symphony[1] involved a redistribution of the original oboe parts between clarinets and oboes. In the *tutti* clarinet parts are additional to the original scoring; they either duplicate the oboes or are given harmonic parts of similar design lying just a little lower in pitch, but for solo or melodic purposes the new instrument largely replaced the oboe, robbing it of most of its solo parts.

[1] Both old and new parts are given in the B. and H. edition of the score.

The compass required of horns in the time of Haydn's and Mozart's maturity extended from the second open note—one octave above the fundamental note—up to G, the twelfth open note. Haydn occasionally demands high A, or even high C, but Mozart avoids the upper extreme altogether, and for horns in keys above E-flat, rarely requires the eleventh and twelfth open notes. Some half-dozen notes in the *Prague*, three or four in the E-flat, two in the G minor, likewise a scattered few in Haydn's symphonies occur which could only be played as stopped notes, and seem to prove that both composers were cognizant of Hampel's device for lowering the pitch of open notes, but were either unable or unwilling to make free use of these chromatic notes. Mozart occasionally demands the sharpened eleventh open note (F-sharp), no doubt depending on stopping for the F-sharp, and also in order to correct the faulty intonation of the open note which is neither a true F nor a true F-sharp. That stopped notes were so rarely used even about thirty years after Hampel's discovery may have been due to the horn players of the time not being familiar with the working of the device, or to deliberate rejection of the idea on account of the difference in quality between stopped and open notes, or even to mere conservatism on the part of composers or players ; whatever the reason, it remains substantially true that horns were held to be diatonic instruments throughout the entire period of Haydn and Mozart. When writing in a minor key both composers either dispensed with the minor third of the key, or used a horn crooked in the key of the relative major, but neither made use of the half-stopped E-flat. So completely was the minor third avoided that Mozart would rather employ another instrument than use the stopped note, as, for example, in the first movement of the *Jupiter* symphony immediately after the first pause ; when the music is in C major the horns take a part which is given to the bassoons when, in the recapitulation, the same matter occurs again, but in the key of C minor.

The functions of horns in these well-known symphonies are familiar to every musician. They are freely allied with the wood-wind group, with the strings, or with both groups together, in order to provide cohesion, body of tone, or contrast of tone-colour, whenever the key of the music is favourable. They take part in such melodic movement as can be coaxed out of their limited range of open notes, or are used as a pair of soloists in melodic passages which actually arise out of their few available notes. The pedal-note for horns, in octaves or in fifths, is common and characteristic both in loud and soft combinations, and by means of independent rhythmical figures they add interest and variety to the orchestral fabric. In short, everything that could be done with such imperfect instruments is found exemplified in the scores of these symphonies which represent the high-water-mark of concert-orchestration in the eighteenth century. The very limitations of the natural instruments gave to the horn parts a character and individuality which fit well into the transparent beauty and simplicity of music which knew no such thing as chromatic, harmonic, or melodic progression on brass instruments.

When writing for trumpets, Haydn and Mozart were still more hedged in by the limitations of the natural instruments. Crooked only in B-flat, C, D, or E-flat, the range of available notes was necessarily smaller when the music was in other keys. For movements in G, Haydn made use of the C trumpet, which gave him tonic, dominant and sub-dominant of the key, but no third. G minor was still worse provided with trumpet notes ; may it not have been on account of that unfortunate handicap that Mozart decided to use no trumpets for his famous symphony in that key ? The working compass of the instrument was now from G (third open note) to G (twelfth open note). F, the eleventh open note,was, on the whole, avoided on account of its being rather too sharp for the key, but Haydn sometimes made it serve as F-sharp. The seventh open note (B-flat) was similarly avoided on trumpets, and was only rarely used on horns.

Although trumpets were employed largely to add brilliance and bulk of tone to the louder *tutti*, they also got an occasional part in the quieter combinations. Usually, but not invariably, playing in partnership with drums, their contribution to the orchestration is rhythmic rather than melodic. As the music wanders away from its original key the selection of available trumpet notes becomes smaller and smaller till, in remote keys, the instrument drops out of the orchestration altogether. Used under these conditions the penetrating tone of the trumpets some-times gives undue prominence to notes of the harmony which hardly bear emphasizing, and then becomes a little trying to modern ears ; but, after all, the composers were obviously often faced with the choice of either underlining undesirable notes, or of doing without trumpet-tone at times when their orchestration calls for it, and who can blame them if they preferred to put up with the first evil rather than sacrifice the brilliance which trumpets give to the orchestral *ensemble*.

Tuned always to tonic and dominant, drums join the trumpets in the loud *tutti* when the key of the music permits of their use, but occasional soft touches and more extended rolls show some slight advance in handling what had hitherto been little more than the noise-makers of the orchestra, while Haydn even ventures to let them be heard in the capacity of soloists.

With such increased freedom of choice and resource it becomes hardly possible to enumerate the various colour-combinations which figure commonly in the mature orchestration of the first two great symphonists. Broadly viewed, the grouping and combination of instruments fall into the following classes :

(a) Strings alone.   (e) Horns and strings.
(b) Wood-wind alone.   (f) Horns, wood-wind, and strings.
(c) Wood-wind and strings   (g) Wood-wind, brass, and drums.
(d) Horns and wood-wind   (h) *tutti*.

Another group consisting of only brass and drums, although theoretically possible, was hardly practicable with natural horns and trumpets, and any attempt to supply complete harmony with such inflexible material, even in the most favourable keys, always breaks down after a bar or two.

From the point of view of colour the orchestra was already a three-part body, but harmonically only the wood-wind and strings were self-contained. The concert orchestra had to wait for valves, and for trombones, before its brass group could be either melodically or harmonically emancipated.

Of the above groups (a) lacked nothing in the way of harmonic or melodic elasticity : further development lay in the direction of colour, texture and pitch. Group (b) was capable of more varied colour-combinations, but the choice of instruments with regard to blend was as yet imperfectly understood. Older characteristics which still coloured the use of the wood-wind group alone were the readiness to let them play in three part harmony, the consequent thinness of which sounds unsatisfying to modern ears, and the tendency to make each pair move in parallel thirds or sixths. Group (c) allowed still greater variety of treatment and colouring, and included all the possibilities of wood-wind solos accompanied by strings, of string melody supplied with wood-wind harmony, and the interchange of functions between two such varied and elastic groups, each able to provide its own melody or harmony. Groups (d) and (e) were subject to much the same considerations as groups (a) and (b), and were also influenced by the inflexibility of the natural horns, which often compelled the composer to write the notes he could get rather than those he would have liked. Group (f) is more of the nature of a smaller *tutti*, yet was capable of more variety of treatment and texture, and was always harmonically complete and satisfying.   Attempts to make a *wind-tutti* of group (g) were, of course, always hampered by lack of harmonic and melodic flexibility on the part of the heaviest voices, and by their limited key-range.   The full *tutti* of Haydn and Mozart are likewise largely coloured by the imperfections of the brass instruments, the handicap which gave the greatest prominence to the least vital parts by the lack of completed harmony on the instruments which carried the most tone-weight, yet were without such as the leading note and sub-mediant even of the most favourable keys.   In view of later developments it is interesting to note a difference in the way the two composers usually handled a *tutti*. Haydn took care that the string orchestra should have its own complete version of the harmony, while Mozart was more willing to entrust essential harmony notes in a *tutti* to the wind instruments ; thus, Haydn's first violins generally took entire responsibility for the melodic or florid upper part, while the second violins and violas were occupied with inside harmony.   Mozart's usual method was to concentrate both first and second violins in unison or in octaves on the upper part, in order to ensure its greater prominence, and to leave much of the inside harmony entirely to the wood-wind with the aid of such notes as could be supplied by horns and trumpets.

Mozart's later operas *Idomeneo* (Munich, 1781), *Die Entführung aus dem Serail* (Vienna, 1782), *Figaro* (Vienna, 1786), *Don Giovanni* (Prague, 1787), *Così fan tutte* (Vienna, 1790), *Die Zauberflöte* (Vienna, 1791), Haydn's oratorios *The Creation* (Vienna, 1798) and *The Seasons* (Vienna, 1801), and various Masses and sacred choral works by both composers, represent the more highly coloured orchestration associated with the stage, or the broader treatment required in combining the orchestra with choral voices. Music more illustrative and descriptive than symphony and concerto tended to draw into the orchestra instruments which

were more or less alien to the concert-orchestra. Clarinets had
as yet no definite footing in symphony orchestration, but were
included in the scores of all Mozart's later operas and in Haydn's
oratorios. Mozart occasionally replaced them with *Corni di
Bassetto* (tenor clarinets in F), generally for particular movements such as Constanze's *aria* in *Die Entführung*, the temple
scene and march of the priests in *Die Zauberflöte*, or the Requiem
Mass[1], occasions on which a sombre colouring was particularly
appropriate. Much in the same way the piccolo is introduced
into the storm scene in *Idomeneus*, and in conjunction with
triangle, bass drum and cymbals, to give a Turkish flavouring to
some scenes in *Die Entführung*[2], also in particular movements in
Die Zauberflöte, and in Haydn's *Seasons* where the husbandman
is described as whistling at his work.[3] Trombones are similarly
used for a few specially solemn or tragic scenes in some of
Mozart's operas, and in conjunction with choral voices in Haydn's
and in Mozart's sacred works, but they are not employed simply
in order to augment the volume of tone in the ordinary *tutti*.
Situations requiring instruments to be played on the stage, or
orchestral imitations of the sound of property instruments, scenes
demanding descriptive or realistic music, special effects such as
the muting of brass and percussion instruments, and similar
conditions which can hardly occur in connection with concert-
music, naturally colour dramatic music to some extent, and bring
into the scores instruments and more vivid effects, which give the
impression of greater enterprise and initiative on the part of the
composers. Thus the operas of Mozart, and even the oratorios
of Haydn, show richer effects and more pronounced colouring in
orchestration than their abstract works written for the concert
room. Haydn's naïve attempts at realism, his storms and tem-
pests, his worm with " sinuous trace " and the whole menagerie
in *The Creation*, his thunder, his quail[4] and cricket, his gun-shot

[1] The orchestration of the *Requiem* was left unfinished by Mozart.

[2] Notation in the original score is for an instrument in G, and is a
fourth above ordinary piccolo notation and a fifth lower than the actual
sounds.   Prout (*The Orchestra*, Vol. i, p. 112) calls it a Flageolet and
maintains that the notation is a twelfth lower than the actual sounds.

[3] " In furrows long he whistling works, and tunes a wonted lay ."

[4] Beethoven's quail in the slow movement of the *Pastoral Symphony*
was only a second-hand bird.

in *The Seasons*, childish though they seem to us, were all contributions towards a wider knowledge of orchestral effect which were brought about by the exigence of dramatic situations unknown to symphony or concerto.

Amongst the features which mark the orchestration of dramatic works by Haydn and Mozart are some attempts to make more extended use of the wind instruments of the orchestra without the strings. In *Idomeneus* occurs a solemn number accompanied only by trombones and horns, followed by a short *recitative* in which the harmony is sustained solely by flutes, oboes, and bassoons; more or less extended passages for wind-*tutti*, and for wood-wind, horns and string basses, occur in *Don Giovanni ;* *Così fan tutte* contains a duet and chorus accompanied entirely by wood-wind and horns, and large portions of an *aria* sung by Dorabella have similarly constituted wind accompaniments ; the slow march in *Die Zauberflöte* (Act II) is for flute, horns, trumpets, drums and trombones. These, and many passages in *The Seasons* are, at all events, evidence of a desire for more vivid colouring and bolder contrasts than were considered suitable to the more restrained handling of the orchestral voices in symphonic works, even though the means of carrying out some of these wind combinations was often unsatisfactory, and good balance was rendered almost impossible when natural horns and trumpets were employed. A few features in Mozart's opera scores demand mention if only as samples of enterprise and anticipation, even though their occurrence in contemporary orchestration is exceptional. An aria in *Idomeneo* and a Rondo in *Così fan tutte* contain florid and chromatic parts respectively for a horn in E-flat and for two horns in E, both of which involve a free use of stopped notes, and cover an unusually large compass. The performance of these different parts would be nothing less than a *tour de force* on the part of the players for whom they were designed. Some instances of carefully thought-out blending of tone-colours are also noteworthy, particularly the *aria* and chorus which occur early in the second act of *Die Zauberflöte*, in which the voices are accompanied by *corni di bassetto*, bassoons, trombones, violas in two parts, and violoncellos, a colour-combination of unusually sombre richness. Further evidence of care in blending wind instrument tone occurs in the *aria* at the beginning of Act III in *Die Entführung*, where a smooth-toned combination of flutes, clarinets, bassoons, and horns are happily united and resourcefully treated.   Other features which stand out are the *pizzicato* accompaniment to Pedrillo's Romance immediately following the above *aria*, the extraordinary variety of colour in the finale to Act I of *Die Zauberflöte*, and the dramatic handling of trombones in the last scene but one of *Don Giovanni*.

The work of Sacchini, Piccini, and Gossec, contemporaries of Gluck who lived long enough to be reckoned also contemporary with Haydn and Mozart, has been briefly noticed in the last chapter.   The solid massive style of orchestration of which Gluck was the pioneer, and of which Vienna and Paris were the homes, found in Gluck's pupil, Antonio Salieri, one who, building on the example and experience of his master, carried on the same principles with the added confidence that comes with familiarity. Salieri's Paris opera *Les Danaïdes* (1784) is fully scored on the same grand scale and with the same dramatic and broadly-coloured effects which had now become more or less standard in the serious works written for the large opera houses at Vienna and Paris, but was without the clear charm and attractive gracefulness which characterized the orchestration of Mozart.   Richness and volume of tone, rather than variety of detail or clear-cut colouring, were the salient features of the orchestration of such as Gossec and Salieri ;   this stood in strong contrast to the work of the two composers Domenico Cimarosa and Giovanni Paisiello, whose operas in lighter style had in the meantime become popular. The spirited brisk music of these two Italians, forerunners in the school which was soon to produce the brilliant Rossini, is orchestrated in a neat and pointed, but in a rather flimsy manner which, if light-hearted and not ineffective, was again in danger of becoming over-conventionalized. Like the Italian opera composers of Handel's time, it seems as if their main interest was given to the solo voices rather than to the orchestra.   A new set of accompanying figures had replaced the conventions of the first half of the eighteenth century ; accepted ways of framing their facile vocal melodies are used over and over again in the scores of these composers who by no means disdained orchestral effect as an adjunct to the presentation of their music, but were endowed with neither the fine musicianship nor the dramatic instinct of a Mozart.

The lighter side of French operatic music at this period is represented by the work of André Ernest Modeste Grétry.   So thin and colourless is the orchestration of *Richard Cœur de Lion*,

1784, said to be his best work—that it is not surprising to learn[1] that several of his operas have since been re-orchestrated by Auber, Adam, and others.

Christian Cannabich and Karl Stamitz were musicianly composers whose orchestration was no doubt an example and stimulus to the young Mozart. Their best work, and that of Karl Ditters von Dittersdorf, corresponds roughly to the standard achieved by Haydn and Mozart in their intermediate periods, but falls far short of the standard reached by the two greater composers in their ripest work.

In assessing the value and result of the influence of great composers on their contemporaries, one needs constantly to bear in mind that while they lived, the great and the second, or even third-rate composers of almost any period loomed equally large in the eyes of the public generally, and of the musical world. The work of time in sifting out the few from the mass of composers nearly always operates slowly, and true perspective in musical history is never assured till the style of any particular period has become more than merely out-of-date. In their own time the works of the composer who was destined to complete oblivion were played as often, and frequently more often, than the works of the composer who was eventually to form a landmark in musical history. After the passage of over a hundred years it is easy to pick out Haydn and Mozart from amongst the mass of composers whose work belongs to the second half of the eighteenth century, and to note how their orchestration developed till it stood head and shoulders above the work of their contemporaries. To these same contemporaries this superiority would not be so obvious. They would hear as much, or probably more, of the average orchestration of the time as they would of the best and most progressive orchestration ; the suggestiveness and stimulating effect of hearing what was in the van of progress would not be their everyday lot, nor would the selection of a model be so apparent as it would be to the next generation. Thus, if Haydn and Mozart out-distanced all their eighteenth century contemporaries, it was only the composers of the nineteenth century who could fully benefit by the example of their most advanced orchestration. Of these a few were already on the scene before the end of the century. Cherubini, Méhul, and Beethoven were already launched, and others stood at the threshold of their

[1] Grove's *Dictionary*, Art. " Grétry ".

careers ; to those composers whose working lives embrace the first twenty or thirty years of the nineteenth century one must look for signs of further growth in the art of writing for the orchestra, for the continued development which carried modern orchestration beyond the stage to which it had been brought by the first two great symphonists—Haydn and Mozart.

CHAPTER IX

THE first half of the nineteenth century barely covers most of the important developments and radical improvements in their construction which have brought the wind-instruments of the orchestra to their present state of perfection. To the wood-wind a new or reorganized key-mechanism, to the brass the invention and perfecting of the lengthening-valve, and to both better and acoustically sounder proportions, as well as better finish and greater accuracy in their manufacture, have given the facility of execution, wider key-range, better intonation, and a chromatic nature, without which the orchestra would have been hopelessly handicapped and unable to keep pace with the progress of musical art. To players, instrument makers, and musical composers belongs in varying degree the credit for having either suggested, invented, or of having actually carried out the improvements which a constantly expanding art demanded. To the mechanical skill, the inventive faculty, the enterprise and devotion of such as Böhm or Sax, to composers such as Meyerbeer or Berlioz—both ever ready to encourage and to take advantage of innovations in the construction of wind-instruments—did the composers, conductors, and players of the second half of the century owe their well-nigh perfect composite instrument, the modern orchestra. Prejudice, conservatism, and blind respect for tradition, all offered a certain amount of opposition during the periods of transition ; these factors, and that several years must always elapse before a new device can either prove its worth or become known, a not unnatural reluctance on the part of older players to acquire new instruments and possibly a new technique, all these and similar influences easily account for what may seem a certain tardiness in the rate at which parts for the improved instruments found their way into orchestras.

It is largely to Theobald Böhm (1794-1881), a famous Munich player and maker, that the flute owes its present state of perfection. If some of his innovations and improvements were based on those of Capt. W. Gordon, Tromlitz, Pottgiesser, Frederick

Nolan, and others[1], there is no question that Böhm summed up and was ultimately the sponsor of the successful improvements which gave the orchestra a reorganized flute during the second quarter of the nineteenth century. In the year 1832 Böhm produced a flute which, while retaining the conical bore of the old type, was provided with larger holes bored in acoustically correct positions, and controlled by the well-known ring-key-mechanism which has ever since borne his name. Further experiments, scientifically and patiently carried out, resulted in the finished Böhm flute of 1846. Adopting a cylindrical bore for all except the head-joint, the improved proportions, the size and position of the finger-holes, the larger mouth-hole and ingenious key-mechanism, resulted in an instrument with fuller tone, truer intonation, easier production in the third octave, and above all, with much greater facility for execution in all keys, which with other advantages required only the test of time in order almost entirely to supersede the old style of flute in the orchestra. The new key-mechanism not only provided some alternative fingerings, but also rendered practicable almost all shakes of a tone or a semitone excepting a few at the extremes of the compass. Before the time of Böhm's final improvements a slight extension in the form of the C or foot-joint, with two extra keys, had given the flute two additional semitones below its lowest D, although it seems that these two notes were by no means always available at the time when Berlioz wrote the famous book on instrumentation which was issued in 1844[2]. Modifications of his design and system have been introduced by many makers since Böhm's time without radically altering the main principles of the mechanism which soon after its invention lent some of its advantages to both the oboe and the clarinet. The later addition of a low B, or even B-flat, to the compass of the flute has not been generally adopted; thus, the three octaves from 2-ft. C. upwards have been the recognized range of the orchestral or concert flute since about the middle of last century.

[1] See Böhm, *An essay on the construction of flutes*, London, 1882; (Day), *Descriptive Catalogue of the Musical Instruments . . . Royal Military Exhibition, London, 1890*, London, 1891, p. 26; Welch, *History of the Boehm Flute*, London, 1896.
[2] Quantz mentions a similar extension as early as 1722, but Berlioz writes of it as if it were a quite recent improvement. (See *Berlioz, Modern Instrumentation*, English edition of 1858, p. 116.) Tromlitz's eight-keyed flute of 1800 had no low C or C-sharp, yet Majer (1741) describes the flute reaching down to C without, however, a C-sharp.

It need hardly be added that the piccolo or octave flute immediately shared most of the advantages of the reorganized key-mechanism of the flute, but has remained without the foot-joint, and consequently the low C and C-sharp. Other flutes, larger and smaller than the concert flute, have been made, and have at various times been specified in scores without ever becoming permanently attached to the orchestra. The choice of material, formerly ranging through various hard woods, also ivory and glass, has now settled down to either cocus-wood, ebonite, or metal, for each of which certain advantages are claimed.

The oboe had to wait very little longer than the flute for its final key-mechanism. Starting the century with anything from two to five or six keys, before the mid-century oboes had as many as from eight to fourteen keys, including the octave key. The lowest note at the beginning of the nineteenth century was 2-ft. C., but before the mid-century the B-natural, a semitone lower, was sometimes available. Yet another semitone lower (B-flat) seems to have been provided on some instruments, for Berlioz mentions this note, and Mendelssohn in the " Intermezzo " of his *Midsummer Night's Dream* music (1843) wrote one solitary low B-flat for the oboe[1]. Oboes with as many as thirteen keys arranged on the old system are mentioned by von Gontershausen as being up-to-date instruments in Germany about the middle of last century[2]. Several makers and players were busy improving the key-mechanism, bore, and positions of the holes, just before the mid-century, when Frédéric Triébert, and later on Apollon Marié-Rose Barret, borrowing certain features from the Böhm ring-key system, introducing automatic octave-keys, and making possible some alternative fingerings which facilitated the bridging-over of awkward intervals, brought the oboe mechanically and technically level with the re-organized flute just about or soon after 1850. Modern instruments have from fifteen to seventeen keys and usually include the low B-natural and B-flat. During the course of the nineteenth century the old broad reeds were replaced by the narrower reeds such as are now in use, which as a consequence modified and refined the tone of the instrument

[1] Curiously enough, low B-natural is required of the flute in the very next bar.

[2] Gassner, *Lexikon*, 1849, gives B as the lowest note. Koch-Dommer *Lexikon*, 1865, states that new oboes have thirteen keys and go down to B-flat. Kastner, *Manuel général de Musique Militaire*, Paris, 1848, shows oboes with eleven keys.

very considerably. A little difference in the reeds, and consequently in the tone, still survives ; French and English players favour the narrow, and German players a slightly broader reed.

Of the various other oboes which, from time to time, have been demanded in orchestral scores, only the tenor instrument, a perfect fifth lower than the ordinary oboe, now known as the *Cor Anglais*, has come into anything approaching general use. Under that name the instrument had made sporadic appearances in scores before the end of the eighteenth century, but became a fairly frequent visitor to the orchestra in the works of several composers who wrote opera for the Paris stage towards the middle of the nineteenth century. From the time of Wagner the *Cor Anglais* has become quite common in operatic, and later on in symphonic and other scores written for concert use. There seems to have been no sort of agreement amongst composers regarding the notation of *Cor Anglais* parts till the second half of the century. The following shows some of the varieties of notation which will confront the student who consults the first prints of the many opera full-scores published in Paris before 1850, though it is highly probable that the notation is brought into line with present-day usage in later prints :

Meyerbeer, *Le Prophète*. Treble clef, modern notation a fifth above actual sounds.
Donizetti, *La Favorita*. Bass clef, an octave lower than actual sounds[1].
Rossini, *La Gazza Ladra*. Treble clef, no transposition.
Spontini, *Olimpie*. Mezzo-soprano clef (actual sounds) ; but the player reads the part in the treble clef and gets a correct transposition, excepting in the case of certain accidentals.

Recent attempts have been made to revive the " *oboe d'amore* " (in A, a third below the oboe) and to introduce a bass oboe (octave lower) under the name of Heckelphon.

A new epoch in the history of the clarinet was opened when Iwan Müller (1786-1854) produced his improved type in Paris about the year 1810. By readjusting the positions of the holes, Müller's clarinets gained in true intonation, and in technical facility by an amplified key-mechanism requiring thirteen keys,

---

[1] This corresponds with the notation of the well-known part marked " Cor Anglais " in the score of the Overture to Rossini's *Guillaume Tell*. W. H. Stone (in Grove's *Dictionary*, art. " *Oboe da Caccia* ") maintains that this part was intended for the tenoroon.

including one which covered the F-C hole, and a special shake key. Müller's system then became subject to numerous minor improvements, and formed the basis of many other key-systems evolved by players and makers, including the two famous instrument makers of Brussels and Paris, the elder and the younger Sax. It might almost be said that every distinguished player or maker had his own system, or modification of Müller's system, during the years that followed this important landmark in the history of the clarinet[1]. The next important step was accomplished about 1843, just when the key-mechanisms of the flute and oboe were also being reorganized by means of the advantages gained by the adoption of Böhm's system. The name of Hyacinthe Eléonore Klosé (1808-80), a well-known clarinet player, is associated with that of the Paris instrument maker, Buffet, in making use of the Böhm system to benefit the key-mechanism of the clarinet. Under the advantages gained by Klosé's adaptation of the Böhm system almost all shakes became feasible on the instrument and many difficulties in playing *legato* from note to note disappeared. In spite of its advantages the adapted Böhm mechanism has never completely supplanted the old key-system inaugurated by Müller early in the nineteenth century; both are still in use, the simpler system particularly in military bands. The number of minor improvements on, or modifications of, these two main key-systems offered by modern makers is almost inexhaustible. Independent systems and freak-clarinets have come and gone. Efforts to extend the compass downwards below E, and to combine the A and B flat clarinets in one instrument have been made, but the ground-work of the Müller or the Klosé-Böhm clarinets still holds good.

Modern clarinets have from thirteen to twenty keys and are made in four pieces, of either ebonite or cocus-wood, having a compass from (written) E—a third above 4-ft. C—for about three-and-a-half octaves upwards. The substitution of metal ligatures[2] in place of string to attach the reed to the mouthpiece, and the custom of placing the reed underneath the mouthpiece so that it is pressed against the lower lip of the player, are

[1] Clarinets with keys as follows are described by (*a*) Gassner (1849), five keys only, (*b*) Kastner (1848) six, nine and thirteen keys, (*c*) von Gontershausen (1855) thirteen keys.

[2] Possibly introduced by H. J. Ziegler, of Vienna, (see von Gontershausen).

improvements which probably fall within the early part of the nineteenth century.

The three sizes of clarinet in C, B-flat, and A, remained standard during the greater part of the nineteenth century, but the once favourite instrument in C is now all but obsolete. Some players would use only the B-flat clarinet, trusting to their technical skill and powers of transposition to deal with parts written for the A instrument. It is interesting to note that even in Berlioz's time the same tendency existed amongst clarinet players; Berlioz paints a harrowing picture of the dilemma in which the all-B-flat clarinet player would find himself were he suddenly faced with the low E in a part written for the A instrument[1].

The notation of parts for ordinary clarinets during the nineteenth century has been fairly consistent, but a few fancy notations may be encountered in scores printed before the mid-century. For example, the score of Rossini's *Tancredi*, published in Paris soon after the production of the opera, shows clarinet parts for the A instruments so contrived that the player reads in the treble clef, but the score-reader uses the soprano clef as directed by means of a small soprano clef and staff placed at the beginning of the clarinet part in the full-score.

Many other clarinets besides those in C, B-flat, and A, have appeared from time to time in orchestral scores. Of these all but the bass-clarinet in B-flat (or more rarely in A) have enjoyed only a very precarious footing in the orchestra. The alto in low E-flat may be reckoned the successor of the old *Corno di bassetto* in F; the low E-flat and the high E-flat or D instruments have been specified in a few modern scores, but really belong to the military band. The bass-clarinet, said to have been " invented " just before the close of the eighteenth century[2], first came into prominence when Meyerbeer introduced it into some of his operas written for Paris in the second quarter of the nineteenth century. The younger Sax made it his special care to develop the instrument which from the time of Wagner has been freely used in grand opera, and rather later, in symphony. Meyerbeer's notation, in the treble clef a major ninth above the actual sounds,

[1] " What then would the player of the clarinet in B-flat do, whose low E only gives D ?—He would transpose the note in the octave ! and thus destroy the effect intended by the author !—which is intolerable ! " Berlioz's advice on this matter is sounder than his translator's English.

[2] Heinrich Grenser of Dresden is usually credited with having first made the bass-clarinet in 1793.

has been generally adopted in spite of Wagner's bass-clef notation. The shape of all the lower clarinets has varied considerably at different times according to the ideas of different makers. The various clarinets which are now used may usually be procured with either the simpler or the Böhm key-mechanism.

At no time has the mechanism of the bassoon undergone such drastic reorganization as befell the other wood-wind instruments just before the middle of the nineteenth century. Its lowest note (B-flat, a tone below 8-ft. C) was already fixed before the eighteenth century, and all efforts made to enlarge the compass of the instrument were directed towards extending it upwards. Late eighteenth century bassoons appear to have had eight finger-and-thumb holes, and up to as many as eight or nine keys, most of the latter being used only to produce the lowest notes. At the beginning of the nineteenth century the chromatic scale was complete but for the lowest B-natural and C-sharp. By the mid-century the compass extended from the low B-flat for three-and-a-half octaves to E-flat or even to F, and the two missing low notes were now supplied. Of the many makers or players who had a hand in adding keys to, and in generally improving the instrument during the first half of the century, one of the most prominent appears to have been Karl Almenräder (1786–1843), in his time a famous player, and sometime head of a bassoon-making business in Cologne. According to Vollbach[1], Almenräder added the low B-natural and C-sharp keys, readjusted the positions of the holes, extended the upward compass, and generally improved the purity and quality of the tone. From ten to fourteen keys, six finger-holes and two thumb-holes were provided on bassoons made in Germany about the middle of the century[2]; the instruments by Savary (Paris) with fifteen keys are said to be much prized by players, and quite modern instruments have from sixteen to twenty-two keys. Though some of the keys on modern bassoons are ring-keys, the instrument seems to have gained less from the benefits of the Böhm mechanism than other wood-wind instruments. Attempts to apply the complete Böhm system to the bassoon appear to have been unsuccessful in spite of Berlioz's wish[3]. Tenor bassoons in F or E-flat were only very

[1] Volbach, *Die Instrumente des Orchesters* (Leipzig, 1913).
[2] Von Gontershausen, Kastner, twelve keys; Koch-Dommer sixteen keys.
[3] Berlioz, *Modern Instrumentation*.

occasionally demanded in scores towards the end of the eighteenth century and early in the nineteenth century, but practically disappeared from the orchestra during the course of last century. Some intermediate sizes between the ordinary and the double-bassoon were made, but the latter is the only other representative of the type which has survived. The present double-bassoon, pitched an octave lower than the ordinary instrument, is made of either wood or metal, and lacks the extreme low notes below 16-ft. C.

Amongst the features of modern key-action on wood-wind instruments, roller keys and the Buffet needle-spring deserve mention.

In spite of a bewildering variety of models, of differences in details of key-arrangement, action and design, the makers of modern wood-wind instruments retain a broad distinction between the key-systems which owe their salient features to the Böhm system, and the simpler systems of the pre-Böhm period. With the advantages of modern machinery, tools, methods, and scientific knowledge, present-day makers of the best class are efficient and enterprising, accurate in workmanship and jealous of their reputations. Although modern conditions and needs have created the second and third-grade instrument, the best class of player demands a first-class instrument, and it may safely be said that his requirements are met and his suggestions are carried out now as carefully and willingly as in the days when the individual maker fashioned each instrument with his own hands.

Whatever the beauty of tone-quality on the natural horn and trumpet, there is no doubt that the chromatic instrument was bound to come sooner or later. The skill and ingenuity which overcame much more intricate mechanical problems in an age of inventive genius could hardly fail to devise means for making a tube quickly and easily longer or shorter at will. The instrument which could only sound some ten or twelve notes in one particular key was clearly becoming more and more inadequate as music grew more chromatic and restlesss in its tonality. Hence the stopping, the crooks, slides, and side-holes, all of them makeshifts which vainly attempted to supply satisfactorily the missing notes in the harmonic series of the open tube of horns and trumpets just before the end of the eighteenth century.

The solution of the problem began early in the nineteenth century when the idea of the lengthening-valve was conceived, but many years had to pass before a mechanical action was devised which worked well and reliably, and yet more years before composers and players accepted without reserve the gift of chromatic freedom for horns and trumpets.

Briefly stated, the history of the valve and its relation to the orchestra falls into the following four chapters, each corresponding roughly with the four quarters of the nineteenth century : (a) conception and first efforts to make it mechanically workable ; (b) experimental period, and the exceptional use of valved brass instruments in the orchestra ; (c) the rejection of all but two forms of mechanism for operating the valve, gradual disappearance of the natural instruments and success of the valve instruments ; (d) the valve instrument in universal use.

An Irishman named Charles Clagget (died about 1820) was probably the first to hit upon the idea which eventually developed into the lengthening-valve system. In 1788 Clagget produced a chromatic trumpet which was really two trumpets, one in D and the other in E-flat, joined together and blown through a mouthpiece common to both. A valve was provided by means of which the player could play on either of the two trumpets at will, and means were also provided for lowering the pitch of either instrument to the extent of one tone.[1] The second of these two ideas embodied rather more than the mere germ of the lengthening valve system, involving, as it did, the use of additional lengths of tubing controlled by a mechanism by means of which the main tubes of the two instruments could be instantly lengthened and the pitch lowered, or conversely restored to their original length and pitch. It seems that Clagget did not carry his idea any further than the experimental stage[2].

No further progress can be traced till about 1813, when a Silesian, Blühmel by name, conceived a similar idea of instantaneously lowering the pitch of a brass instrument by means of an extra length of tube which could be added to the main tube, and was controlled by a mechanism consisting of a piston working in a cylinder. When the piston was pressed down the air passage was diverted through the extra tubing, and when released, a spring restored the piston to its original position,

---

[1] See Galpin, *Old English Instruments of Music*, London, 1910.

[2] Busby writes of Clagget : " the misfortune of whose life it was, to have ideas theoretically sublime, but deficient in practical utility."—. *Concert Room and Orchestra Anecdotes*, London, 1825.

and the passage through the extra bit of tube was shut off. It appears that Blümel sold his invention to Heinrich Stölzel (1780-1844), a horn player and maker of Breslau and Berlin[1]. Stölzel applied it to the horn and provided two extra bits of tube—each controlled by a piston-valve—the one sufficiently long to lower the pitch of the instrument by a semitone, the other by a whole tone. Thus, using the valves singly or in combination, each open note could be lowered to the extent of either a semitone, a tone, or a tone-and-a-half. With that the ball was set rolling, and once launched the idea soon began to be exploited in Germany, France, Belgium and England. Many are the names which occur in connection with early valve instruments, and many the mechanical devices for operating the valves which were put forward during the first half of the nineteenth century. Of the latter only two patterns have survived, namely, the piston and the rotary action. France and England have always favoured the piston-valve ; but in Germany, where it is said to have been originated about 1820, the rotary-valve was more generally accepted[2]. It would be unjust to omit the names of Charles Joseph Sax (1791-1865) and his son Adolphe (Antoine) Sax (1814-94), the great Franco-Belgian instrument makers of Brussels and Paris, from even the briefest history of the valve. To the younger Sax valve-mechanism probably owes as much as to any of its originators.

The tone and semitone valve, used singly or in combination, had filled in all the gaps in the harmonic series of the open tube from the fourth open-note upwards. Between the third and fourth open notes a semitone was still missing, and between the second and third open notes a gap of three semitones remained. Credit for the addition in 1830 of a third valve, controlling a length of tubing equivalent to three semitones in pitch, is often given to one C. A. Müller of Mainz. With the addition of a third valve the system was complete, and a chromatic scale extending upwards from a diminished fifth below the second open note was available, the valves being employed either separately or together as follows :

[1] See Kastner, *Manuel général de Musique Militaire*, Paris, 1848.

[2] German writers—also Berlioz's translator—use the term " cylinder " for what is known in England as the rotary-valve. There is some confusion in articles and books dealing with the valve owing to an ambiguous use of the terms " piston " and " cylinder ".

[3] Gassner and Koch-Dommer.

EXAMPLE 44

8 ft. tube, actual sounds ─

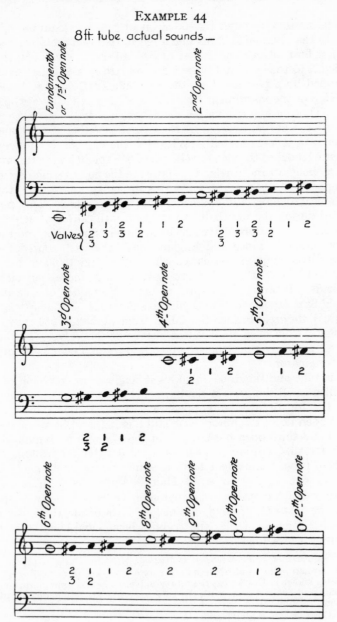

The arrangement of the valves has always been such that
the second or middle valve controls the semitone tubing, the
first valve the tone tubing, and the third valve the tubing equal
to one-and-a-half tones. The above does not, of course, represent
the compass of all valved instruments, nor the customary notation.
As before, the lowest open or valve notes were unpracticable on
the horn or trumpet, while, on the newer instruments—the
cornet, modern trumpet, or tubas, the higher part of the harmonic
series was out of reach, and of these only the tubas could sound
their fundamental note.

Particulars of the various makers, players, or others who
have been concerned in devising valve mechanisms, the merits
or defects of their systems, or anything like an exhaustive survey
of the evolution of the valve would fill a volume. For fuller
particulars, for the details and imperfections of the valve-system
the reader is referred to works dealing with the history and
construction of wind instruments, and to text books on orchestration. Forgotten and out-of-date musical dictionaries often supply
interesting information, contemporary views and facts, which
have sometimes been overlooked in later works. Conflicting
statements will be encountered in many such works, both new
and old. Prejudice or bias colours several of the older, and
ignorance of what was going on in other countries disqualifies
much that was written in the first half of the nineteenth century
concerning the progress of brass instrument making and playing
in that critical period. The sifting of such tangled matter,
however, lies outside the scope of this work[1].

[1] See Galpin, *Old English Instruments of Music*, London, 1910.
Daubeny, *Orchestral Wind Instruments*, London, 1920.
Rose, *Talks with Bandsmen*, London.
Clappé, *The Wind-band and its Instruments*, London, 1912.
(Day), *Descriptive Catalogue of the Musical Instruments . . .
Royal Military Exhibition, London, 1890*, London, 1891.
Books on Orchestration in English by Berlioz, Prout, Widor.
Corder, Forsyth.
von Gontershausen, *Neu Eröffnetes Magazin Musikalischer
Tonwerkzeuge*, Frankfurt, 1855.
Hofmann, *Musikinstrumente*, Leipzig, 1890.
Volbach, *Die Instrumente des Orchesters*, Leipzig, 1913.
Eichborn, *Die Trompete in alter und neuer Zeit*, Leipzig, 1881.
Eichborn, *Die Dämpfung beim Horn*, Leipzig, 1897.
Kastner, *Manuel général de Musique Militaire*, Paris, 1848.
Mahillon, *Les Instruments de Musique*, Bruxelles, 1907.
Musical Dictionaries by Busby (1813), Koch (1802), Gassner
(1849), Riemann, Grove, etc.

More relevant is the entry of valve-instruments into the orchestra. Nearly twenty years passed after the invention of the Blümel-Stölzel valve before valve-horns and trumpets began to be specified in full-scores. Composers whose work covers the first quarter of the nineteenth century wrote horn parts for the natural instruments, crooked in much the same keys as were used in the time of Haydn and Mozart. Horns in low A and low A-flat began to appear occasionally, in addition to the older keys, namely low B-flat, C, D, E-flat, E, F, G, high A, and high B-flat. Stopped notes were employed rather more frequently and were usually the half-stopped notes a semitone below open notes. Beethoven, Weber, Cherubini, Spontini, and Boieldieu used them more or less freely to carry out melodic phrases rather than to complete harmonies in the *tutti*. Schubert and Rossini made still more free use of stopped notes, the latter (himself a horn player) especially used them quite lavishly, as for example, in the familiar passages for four horns alone in his *Semiramide* overture (1823).

The generation which followed the above composers all used stopped notes more or less familiarly, and increased the number of keys in which the horn might be crooked by means of semitone lengthening-shanks added to the existing crooks, till every semitone from low A-flat to high B-natural, or even high C, was represented by a crook. The medium crooks, C, D, E-flat, E, and F remained, as before, the favourites, and it is for horns in one or other of these keys that most of the melodic solos in Mendelssohn's, Schumann's, and several French and Italian opera composers' works are written. The valve-horn begins to be specified in a few scores from about 1835; they were at first always associated with a pair of natural horns crooked in the same or sometimes in other keys. Halévy and· Meyerbeer are amongst the first to write for valve-horns in operas written for the Paris stage; it is not unreasonable to suppose that the appearance of the new instruments in the scores was in some measure due to the proximity of the great maker of wind-instruments, Adolphe Sax[1]. Just before the mid-century Donizetti, Berlioz, Schumann, and Wagner all helped to bring the valve instruments into the orchestra, but it was not till the third quarter of the century that the valve-horn really began to dispute the

---

[1] The elder Sax worked in Brussels, and Adolphe Sax settled in Paris in 1842.

ground with the older type. The period of Wagner and Liszt, of Verdi, and the earlier years of Tschaikovsky and Dvořák, served to settle the matter, and to establish the use of the valve-horn in the orchestra, also to undermine seriously the notion that horn parts must needs be fashioned on lines which owed their characteristics to the limited series of notes available on the natural instrument. During the last twenty or thirty years of the century the matter was no longer in the balance. The valve-horn was so completely accepted that it was not necessary to use the words " valve ", " pistons ", or " ventile " in scores or parts. The word " horn " implied valve-horn, and although conservative composers and musicians clung to the faith that the horn was essentially a diatonic instrument, its nature was now as chromatic as any other of the wind-instruments, its capabilities and functions as freely melodic as harmonic.

For a long time after the valve-instrument had come into general use composers continued to write for the horn crooked in many different keys. It was the horn players who first realized that the valve had rendered any change of crook all but redundant, and not till long after the players had settled that matter in their own practice did composers, towards the end of the century, take the practical advice of the players and begin to write in their scores for the horn on which their parts were sure to be played. With the free range of chromatic notes provided by the valves, in whatever key the horn was crooked, it is not surprising that players rebelled against playing on an instrument which might consist of anything from about nine to eighteen feet of tube. Their choice fell on the twelve-foot tube, the horn in F, which is now used, to the exclusion of almost all others.

The valve-trumpet found its way into the orchestra in much the same way, and practically at the same time as the valve-horn, except in England, where its appearance was delayed by the popularity of the slide-trumpet. Beethoven and his contemporaries wrote for the natural trumpet, and ignored the keyed-instrument which, however, had some vogue in Italian orchestras just about that time. Stopped notes were avoided, but the seventh open note (B-flat) was used fairly freely. A few isolated instances of other than open notes can be found in trumpet parts of Beethoven's period, and can only have been negotiated by means of stopping, or by the keyed-instrument[1], but these occur

[1] Two solitary D-flats occur in Rossini's *Semiramide* Overture.

very rarely before 1830. The E crook became more common, and one in low A makes its appearance during the same period. Rather later the G crook occurs, and lengthening shanks equal to a semitone in pitch were sometimes added to the more ordinary shanks or crooks, thus giving the trumpet the additional keys of low A, low B-natural, D-flat, and G-flat. Berlioz also mentions a trumpet in high A-flat. Mendelssohn's trumpet parts occasionally demand some notes which could only have been produced by means of stopping, or by keyed, slide, or valve-trumpets. As the latter were apparently always particularly specified when they were required during Mendelssohn's time, it seems as if he must have been writing either for keyed-trumpets, or that stopping was employed to produce these notes, the slide-trumpet being hardly known anywhere but in England at the time. Specific cases occur in *Melusine* overture (1833), in the *Scottish Symphony* (1842), and in the *Midsummer Night's Dream* music (1843).

A letter of one Neukom in the British Museum[1] alludes to the use of valve-trumpets in Paris in 1829[2]. Very soon after that year the instrument begins to be definitely specified in occasional opera scores. Bellini's *La Sonnambula* (1831), Meyerbeer's *Les Huguenots* (1836) and *Le Prophète* (1849), Donizetti's *La Favorita* and *La Fille du Régiment* (both Paris, 1840), and Halévy's *La Juive* (1835) are amongst the scores in which parts for valve-trumpets (*trompettes à pistons*), crooked in various keys, make an early appearance. Progress from the mid-century onwards is more or less parallel to that of the valve-horns, except that players have never been quite so unanimous in deciding to use only one size of trumpet. Parts crooked in various keys were written till close on the end of the century, although players were using either the F trumpet or the small modern instruments in high B-flat or A to play the parts. Like horn players, they have preferred to transpose the parts rather than change the crooks. Latterly the F trumpet has given way to the smaller instruments, and a still smaller trumpet in high C (4-ft.) has come into use. Modern composers generally write for one or other of these high trumpets.

[1] Add. MSS. 33965.

[2] Lavoix, *Histoire de L'instrumentation*, Paris, 1878, states that valve trumpets were used for the first time at Paris in Chelard's *Macbeth*, 1827.

From just before the close of the eighteenth century, for a period not far short of a hundred years, the foremost English players used the slide-trumpet. The *tromba da tirarsi* specified in some of Bach's scores was no doubt nothing but a treble trombone made in the same form as the larger trombones ; the English nineteenth century slide-trumpet, however, was a true trumpet provided with a shorter slide, which was drawn by the fingers towards the player, and returned to its original position by means of a spring. This U-shaped sliding tube was just long enough to lower the pitch of any open note to the extent of a whole tone when it was fully drawn out, thus, the C-sharp just above the fourth open note, also the lower A and A-flat, and several notes between the second and third open notes, were missing from the chromatic scale. The slide, however, was also used to correct the faulty intonation of the seventh and eleventh open notes. This form of trumpet appears to have been hardly recognized out of England, yet was the standard trumpet in this country till towards the end of the nineteenth century, when it began to give way to the valve-trumpet in F and the high B-flat and A instruments. The slide-trumpet was apparently rather a novelty when the last edition of Busby's *Dictionary of Music* was issued in 1813 ; the worthy doctor devotes only a few words to the new instrument after describing the capabilities of the natural trumpet : " by the aid of a newly invented *slide* many other notes, which the common trumpet cannot sound, are now produced ".

The introduction of the lengthening-valve had other effects on the orchestra and on orchestration than that of giving chromatic notes of practically equal tone-quality to horns and trumpets ; the new mechanism may also be said to have brought into being several new brass instruments, of which the cornet and the tuba were destined to join the family of orchestral instruments, and, with others of the same type, almost revolutionized the constitution of military bands, and virtually created a new organization, namely, the brass band.

Few authors venture to give the cornet either an inventor or a definite birth-year. Eichborn, however, states that the modern cornet owes its origin to the French maker Halary, who is said to have adapted piston-valves to the short tube and wide conical bore of the bugle, early in the nineteenth century. First known in this country as the cornopean, and originally supplied with only two valves, this instrument of very mixed parentage soon asserted itself as essentially *the* upper melodist of the brass group in wind bands, and, having practically driven the keyed-bugle out of existence, began to appear in French opera scores during the second quarter of the century. According to Berlioz the cornet was available " crooked " in nearly all keys from 4-ft. C down to D.   Of these all but the B-flat and A shanks have gone out of use, if, indeed, they were ever in general use. French composers usually wrote cornet parts in addition to trumpet parts, but the more usual rôle of this much-abused instrument in the orchestra has always been to take the place of trumpets in second-rate orchestras when the finer instruments are not forthcoming.   The gulf formerly existing between the cornet and trumpet has been considerably lessened since the advent of the small modern trumpets in B-flat and A.   The latter are pitched in unison with their more plebeian cousins, and differ from them only slightly in proportions of bore, bending, and mouthpiece.

Almost since Handel's time the want of a bass wind instrument which should be more powerful than the bassoon, and more flexible than the bass-trombone, seems to have been felt in the orchestra.   The first to supply this want was the serpent ; then came the keyed-serpents and " bass-horns", finally the ophicleide, a conical-bored metal instrument with cup-shaped mouthpiece and side-holes covered by enormous keys, which is said to have been " invented " by at least four men, respectively in 1780, 1790, 1805, and 1815.   Made in C (8-ft.). B-flat, and A-flat, with as many as eleven keys, this, probably the last survivor of the type which was derived from the medieval *cornetto*, had a run of barely fifty years as an occasional orchestral instrument in the middle of the nineteenth century, particularly in grand opera and in choral works.   Berlioz, aided by his translator, manages a quite entertaining description of the tone of this fearsome instrument in the English version of his famous book on Instrumentation[1].

Many years before the ophicleide had bellowed its last, its status as an orchestral instrument was being undermined by another instrument which, like the cornet, came into being as a result of the invention of the lengthening-valve.   This was the

---

[1] See 1st English Edition (1858), p. 175.

bass-tuba or bombardon[1]. The name of Wilhelm Frederick
Wieprecht (1802-72), a great reorganizer of Prussian military
bands in the first half of the nineteenth century, is sometimes
coupled with that of one Moritz as inventors of the bass-tuba.
At least three dates are offered as the birthday of this instrument :
1828[2], 1835[3], and 1858[4] [5]. The latter is certainly too late, for
Sax had already produced his low Saxhorns in 1845, and anybody
who made a bass-tuba after that year could hardly claim to
have invented it. Whoever originated those wide-bored
valve-instruments of low pitch, Adolphe Sax went a step further
when he produced his whole family of Saxhorns. These might
almost be described as a set of valve-bugles or cornets made in
all sizes ranging from high E-flat—corresponding to the high
E-flat cornet of the present-day brass bands—down to the
B-flat monster such as plays the part of a brass double-bass in
our military bands to-day[6]. The terms " tuba ", " bass-tuba ",
and " bombardon " have been rather indiscriminately applied
to all the bass instruments of Saxhorn type. Often given a
fourth, or even a fifth, valve in order to take an unbroken
chromatic scale right down to the fundamental note, or provided
with extra valves or "compensating" devices in order to correct
the faulty intonation which becomes serious when several valves
are used in combination on low-pitched instruments, it is usually
either the tuba in E-flat or in F, or even the B-flat instrument
known in England as the Euphonium, that has played the brass
bass parts which, from the time of Wagner, have become a regular
feature in scores of all sorts written for full orchestra.

For rather over fifty years the tuba has figured in orchestral
scores as the faithful companion of the trombone trio[7]. The
latter instruments underwent no fundamental change in
construction during the nineteenth century. The principle of

[1] Berlioz makes a distinction between the two, and state that Wieprecht " improved " the mechanism of the bass-tuba.

[2] Daubeny.

[3] Riemann.

[4] Volbach.

[5] Eichborn says : " Welches Wieprecht erfunden hat ", but gives
no date.

[6] Sax's original Saxhorns are depicted in Kastner's *Manuel général
de Musique Militaire*, Paris, 1848.

[7] A part for tuba appears in Wallace's *Love's Triumph*, 1862,.also in
an Overture by Otto Bach, 1858.

the slide has always remained the chief characteristic of the trombone, and only minor improvements, such as the tuning-slide and a few non-essential features added during the past century, distinguish the modern instrument from the old trombone described by sixteenth and seventeenth century writers. The particular size of trombones used in the orchestra has, however, been subject to some variation since the time when the alto (E-flat), tenor (B-flat), and Bass-trombone (E-flat or F) were regarded as the standard trio, and were used largely to play in unison with the corresponding choral voice parts. During the nineteenth century French and Italian composers have usually written only for tenor trombones, while Germans kept to the original trio with the bass instrument in F. In the course of the second half of the century the alto and bass-trombones in E-flat became practically obsolete, and in England the bass instrument in F largely gave way to the less unwieldy bass-trombone in G. The standard trio then became two tenors and one bass, instead of alto, tenor and bass, and remains so at the present time. Even before the mid-century valve-trombones had been made[1]; although they have been adopted by military bands—more especially by cavalry bands—in most countries the slide-trombone has generally been preferred for orchestral use.

Water-keys are amongst the non-essential improvements which have been generally adopted for trombones, trumpets, cornets and tubas.

Some pages might be filled merely with the names of various other brass instruments which have been made during the past century. Such as the intermediate sizes of Saxhorns, the Saxotromba, the "Wagner-tubas", the bass-trumpet, the "Bach-trumpet" and the contra-bass-trombone will readily occur to readers. All of these, and many others, have appeared in orchestral scores, or have been used in orchestras at some time or other, but without at any time effecting any real change in the constitution of the orchestral brass group.

To the list of unsuccessful aspirants for a place in the orchestra might be added the Saxophones and Sarrusophones, metal instruments of conical bore with side-holes covered by keys and, respectively, clarinet and oboe reeds.

Of percussion instruments only the timpani, bass-drum, cymbals, triangle, and side-drum can claim to be regular

[1] Kastner and von Gontershausen.

orchestral instruments. All these remain substantially as they were early in the nineteenth century, but for unimportant details in construction and finish. Several mechanical devices for tuning timpani in one operation have been offered by various makers, some of them dating from before the mid-century, yet the old system of hand-screws remains in general use. Six to eight, or even more, screws serve to tune the three sizes of timpani which began to replace the original pair just before the middle of the century.

Any attempt to supply an exhaustive list of the many other percussion instruments, the so-called " effects," which have been demanded in orchestral scores from time to time during the nineteenth century would be futile ; nor can it be said that the various types of bells, the *glockenspiel*, xylophone, *celesta*, or any other instrument not already mentioned in this chapter, except the harp, have become part and parcel of the orchestral composer's regular equipment.

Originally a diatonic instrument, early attempts to render the harp chromatic by means of additional strings, or by mechanism worked by hand, appear to have been more or less unsuccessful. The first pedal-harp is generally credited to a Bavarian named Hochbrucker, whose device for instantaneously shortening the C, D, F, G, and A strings to the extent of one semitone in pitch, by means of mechanism controlled by five pedals, dates from as early as 1720. A Frenchman named Cousineau is said to have further improved on this device in 1782 with a double-action mechanism, but it was not till about 1808, when Sébastien Erard of Paris and London (1752-1831) produced a quite satisfactory double-action harp with an enlarged compass of six-and-a-half octaves, that the instrument acquired its final and present mechanism[1]. Handel and Gluck had both written specific harp parts which must be counted as exceptional for their time, but not till the second quarter of the nineteenth century do harp parts begin to appear fairly frequently in operatic scores, and then generally in works written for the Paris stage.

---

[1] Eighteenth century harps were based on the diatonic scale of E-flat, with a compass of five octaves ; these are what Berlioz, *Instrumentation*, 1844, calls the " ancient harp ". Erard's harp is based on the tuning of C-flat major. Mahillon offers some evidence which shows that Cousineau had forestalled Erard in making a double-action pedal harp tuned in C-flat as early as 1782.

CHAPTER X

NOT until about the beginning of the nineteenth century was the constitution of the wood-wind group of the orchestra finally stabilized. From that time onwards practically all scores designed for concert use embodied parts for two flutes, two oboes, two clarinets, and two bassoons ; while dramatic scores more frequently included a piccolo part, and rather more rarely, parts for *cor anglais*, bass-clarinet or double-bassoon, in addition to the above four pairs. By that time the eighteenth century custom of employing more than one oboe or bassoon to play each of the parts provided had given way to the present arrangement by which, under ordinary circumstances, only a single wood-wind instrument is used to play each written part.

The brass group remained for some time longer in a rather more fluid state. From two to four horns, two trumpets and three trombones[1] was the usual selection for large operatic or choral works, but for symphony and concert-works generally, trombone parts were rather the exception than the rule. The above specification held good till about the mid-century, when trombones began to be more freely used in symphony, and soon after, the tuba began to take a place as a regular member of the orchestral family.

The string orchestra remained as it had been ever since just before the end of the seventeenth century. Timpani were the only regular and indispensable percussion instruments used in the orchestra, although such as the bass-drum, cymbals, side-drum and triangle were very occasionally specified in concert-works, but frequently figured in operatic scores. Harp parts were likewise almost exclusively confined to the scores of works designed for the operatic stage.

The more lavish demands made in the scores of such as Spontini, Meyerbeer and Berlioz, also in the early works of Wagner, fall within the first half of the nineteenth century, and did not,

---

[1] French and Italian opera composers sometimes wrote only one trombone part.

however, radically alter or permanently enlarge the constitution of the standard orchestral combination.

Balance of tone in the orchestra was materially affected not only by a loss of oboe and bassoon tone, but also by an increase in the number of players allotted to each string part ; this gave to the string orchestra a relatively greater tone-weight than it had previously enjoyed. As the following suggests, some of the larger and more famous orchestras of the time were provided with numbers of string players which do not materially differ from the best of present-day standards (see also Appendix A) :

	1st Vln.	2nd Vln.	Viola.	'Cello.	D-bass.	Authority.
1815 Munich (Spohr)	12	12	8	10	6	Spohr.
1820–30 Berlin (Spontini) ..	12	12	8	9	7	Dorn.
1828 Paris (Habeneck)	15	16	8	12	8	Schünemann.
c.1848 Paris Opera	12	11	8	10	8	Berlioz.

The permanently engaged orchestras at many opera houses in Germany, however, would appear to have been less fortunate in the matter of personnel, if the following particulars, given by Gassner[1] in 1844, are to be relied on :

	1st Vln.	2nd Vln.	Viola	'Cello.	D-bass.
Dresden	8	8	4	4	4
Cassel	8	8	4	5	3
Berlin	8	8	6	8–10	4–5
Vienna	8	8	4	4	4
Darmstadt	8	8	6	4	4

This would be the type of orchestra about which Wagner wrote in his essay *Uber das Dirigieren* (1869) : " I am not aware that the number of permanent members of an orchestra, in any German town, has been rectified according to the requirements of modern orchestration." If Beethoven's letter[2] to the Archduke Rudolf, asking for not less than four first and four second violins for a performance of his seventh and eighth symphonies, is any guide, concert orchestras in and about Vienna were even less well provided with string players than were the more important German opera orchestras.

[1] F. S. Gassner, " Dirigent und Ripienist " (Karlsruhe, 1844).

[2] Thayer, " Ludwig van Beethovens Leben ", Vol. iii (1879).

It was roughly during the first thirty years of the nineteenth century that the practice of conducting orchestral and operatic performances with a baton superseded the old style of joint-direction by means of a " conductor " seated at the piano and a violinist leader whose duty it was to set the orchestra going, and to guide and steady it when a change of *tempo* occurred. .Pioneers amongst the baton-conductors were such as Reichardt, Anselm Weber and Spontini at Berlin, Carl Maria von Weber at Dresden, Spohr at Frankfurt, and Mendelssohn at Leipzig. The story of how Spohr introduced baton-conducting at the concerts of the Philharmonic Society (London) in 1820 is well-known and hardly needs repetition[1]. Notwithstanding some opposition, the new style of conducting spread rapidly all over musical Europe, and soon brought into being a new type of musician who was not necessarily either a composer or an expert executant, namely, the specialist-conductor. The attention given to conducting as an art in musical literature dating from about the mid-century bears witness to the importance with which this branch of musical activity was regarded[2], and points to an increasingly high standard of efficiency in the rendering of orchestral music, which was connascent with the introduction of the new style of conducting. (See Appendix B.)

Important amongst the concert-giving institutions founded during the first half of the nineteenth century for the purpose of presenting orchestral music were the *Concerts du Conservatoire* (Paris, 1828), under François Antoine Habeneck (1781-1849), the violinist-conductor who introduced Beethoven's symphonies to the Paris public, and the Philharmonic Society (London),` founded in 1813. As far as they concern the orchestra, Paris, Berlin, Leipzig (*Gewandhaus* Concerts under Mendelssohn), Milan, Naples, Vienna, Brussels and London represent the most important centres of activity during the same period ; of these, activity in France and England centred almost entirely in their respective capitals, while in Italy, Germany and Austria it was more widely diffused. It need hardly be pointed out that

---

[1] Louis Spohr, " Selbstbiographie," II, p. 86 (1860). English trans. (London, 1878) II, p. 81.

[2] Gassner, " Dirigent und Ripienist " (1844) ; Berlioz, " Instrumenta-tion " (1844) ; Wagner, " Uber das Dirigieren " (1869) ; see also, Schüne-mann, " Geschichte des Dirigierens," Chap. vi. (Leipzig, 1913) ; Deldevez, " L'art du chef d'orchestre " (1878). Also similar modern books by Weingartner, Lasser and Speyer.

symphony and concert-music generally were more particularly
cultivated, in addition to opera, in Germany and around Vienna,
while French and Italian effort was more or less confined to
opera.

The period now under survey is also notable for the increased
facilities for the musical education of composers and orchestral
players offered by the establishment of several important
schools of music, amongst which the most prominent were :

Paris (*Conservatoire*), founded 1795, reorganised 1800, 1812,
1816.

Milan (*Conservatorium*), founded 1808.

Naples (*Collegio*), founded 1808.

Prague (*Conservatorium*), founded 1811.

Vienna (*Conservatorium*), founded 1821.

London (Royal Academy of Music), founded 1822.

Brussels (*Conservatoire*), founded 1832.

Leipzig (*Conservatorium*), founded 1843.

The printing and publishing of orchestral scores and parts,
centred more or less at Leipzig (Breitkopf and Härtel), Mainz
(Schott), Bonn (Simrock), Vienna (Artaria) and Paris, began to
increase with the greater demand and a better organized
international trade, providing a much more ready means of
diffusing orchestral music than was possible under the old
conditions which so largely depended on manuscript copies.

Another feature of nineteenth century conditions which must
be counted as having exerted some influence on the spread of
knowledge appertaining to the subject was the issue of text books
dealing exclusively with instrumentation and the technique of
orchestral instruments.   The works of Virdung, Prætorius,
Mattheson, and others, may be reckoned the prototypes of modern
text books on instrumentation, of which the first well-known
example is the famous book by Berlioz published in 1844.   Similar
works, most of which preceded Berlioz's successful effort, were
by Francœur[1], Vandenbroeck (1800), Sundelin[2], Fröhlich[3],
Catrufso (1832), Kastner[4] and Gassner[5], and, like most modern

---

[1] Francœur, *Diapason général de tous les instruments à vent* (1792).

[2] Sundelin, *Die Instrumentierung für das Orchester* (Berlin, 1828).

[3] Fröhlich, *Systematischen Unterricht . . . Orchesterinstru-
mente* (Würzburg, 1829).

[4] Kastner, *Traité général d'instrumentation* (Paris, 1837).

[5] { Gassner, *Partiturkenntniss* (Karlsruhe, 1838).
   { Gassner, *Traité de la partition* (1851).

treatises, appear to have been devoted more to the compass and
technique of orchestral instruments than to true orchestration,
namely, the art of combining, balancing, blending and distributing
the tone-colours of the orchestra.

With instruments such as were described in the last chapter,
and under conditions such as have just been outlined, orchestration entered on another phase of its history more favourably
conditioned than at any previous time.   The progress from early
Beethoven to early Wagner covers the work of composers whose
names still figure freely in the orchestral programmes of to-day,
and marks a period of expansion quite as significant as the period
which began with Wagner, and may, or may not, have ended
early in the present century.

Some sort of classification of composers must be made in order
to follow clearly the course of orchestration, and to pass in review
the work of the most significant orchestral composers of the first
half of the nineteenth century.   The most feasible scheme appears
to be a rough division of composers into two groups, namely,
those whose work falls respectively more or less within the first
and the second quarters of the century.   Subdivision of the first
of these two groups according to nationality will provide a list of
two French and three Italian-born opera composers, all of whose
work, however, centred largely in Paris :

Méhul, 1763-1817 (Paris).
Boieldieu, 1775-1834 (Paris).
*   *   *

Cherubini, 1760-1842 (Paris).
Spontini, 1774-1851 (Paris and Berlin).
Rossini, 1792-1868 (Italy and Paris).

while Germany and Austria claim two outstanding composers
of symphony, and one of opera :

Beethoven, 1770-1827 (Vienna).
Schubert, 1797-1828 (Vienna).
*   *   *

Weber, 1786-1826 (Dresden, London).

The entire output of none of these composers can be rigidly
confined to the twenty-five years, 1800 to 1825 ; the two earliest,
Cherubini and Méhul, were already matured composers when
the youngest, Rossini[1], was still a boy ; but in spite of such

[1] Rossini's operatic work ended in 1829.

differences in their birth-years, and in the span of their lives, much of their work was contemporary, and the grouping serves well enough for purposes of classification.

As in the latter part of the eighteenth century, there continued to be a marked difference between the orchestration of works designed for the concert-room, and that of works for the theatre during the greater part of the nineteenth century. The orchestration of a Rossini opera and that of a Schubert symphony, for example, seem poles asunder ; yet the work of these two composers was strictly contemporary, and in their use of orchestral raw material their scores have much more in common than might appear from casual observation. Again, the musical matter and equipment of some of the above composers differ greatly; there is a yawning gap between the matter and musicianship of a Beethoven and those of a Boieldieu, yet the radii of their orchestral horizons were not really widely divergent.

Before treating of their individual styles, idiosyncracies, and contributions to the growth of orchestration, an attempt will be made to summarise the gains which accrued to the art of writing for the orchestra from the work of these seven composers, and of their lesser-known contemporaries, during the period which extends from a few years before, to a few years after, the first quarter of the nineteenth century.

The close of the eighteenth century saw the last of what may be called threadbare or skeleton orchestration. Even the poorest orchestrator in the early nineteenth century provided sufficient harmonic body in the " inside " of his musical structure to ensure sonority and solidity of effect. The habitual duplication or doubling of parts, which left its traces in the scores of Italian opera composers until even late in the eighteenth century, practically disappeared during the maturity of Haydn and Mozart. Such doubling of parts as appears in nineteenth century scores is provided more in order to adjust the balance of tone, and to secure the adequate prominence of certain parts, than as the result of habit or indifference, as was undoubtedly the case during the greater part of the eighteenth century.

A very important feature in the growth of orchestration at this period was due to the increased use of the violoncello as an independent voice. From being at first only a bass instrument, the violoncello had become an occasional tenor instrument towards the close of the eighteenth century, and now early in the

nineteenth century it took a new place in the orchestra as a
full-blown melodist which, in addition to its former functions,
was ready and able to take over the responsibility of presenting
entirely melodic matter, either with or without the aid of other
instruments. Such as the second subject for violoncellos in
Schubert's Unfinished Symphony, or the melody for violas and
violoncellos in unison which begins the slow movement of
Beethoven's C minor symphony, are only very well-known
instances of what became a familiar way of using violoncellos
during the first twenty or thirty years of the nineteenth century,
and was a feature of orchestration unknown to eighteenth century
composers.

The upward compass of violin parts began to reach high
enough to require the seventh or eighth position for first violins,
and the fifth position for second violins. Viola parts were usually
kept within the limits of the first position, and only occasionally
strayed beyond the upper E which lies within reach of the fourth
finger on the A string, while the melodic use of violoncellos, and
a tendency to let them sometimes join in the passage-work of the
upper strings, freely took the parts for these instruments up to as
high as an octave above the sound of their highest string. The
brilliancy of higher pitch on violins, and the richness of violoncello
tone on the A string, must be reckoned gains in the treatment of
the instruments of the string orchestra which accrued during the
period of Beethoven and his contemporaries. The above
observations regarding the upward range of the string parts, of
course, take no account of special solo parts, which were always
more of the *virtuoso* type, and in consequence frequently exceeded
the usual range of *ripieno* orchestral parts.

Although the richer and more penetrating quality of
violoncello-tone on the A string was used to give special prominence
to melodic tenor parts, the viola continued to fulfil its function
as the normal tenor instrument when the music was merely
harmonic or polyphonic in design. Apart from the imitative
phrases which occur in the course of ordinary four-part polyphony
for string instruments, the violas as a group, and without reinforcement, were as yet hardly recognised as melodists, nor is there
reason to suppose that the peculiarly attractive and individual
timbre of viola-tone was really appreciated at this period, in spite
of Gluck's suggestive lead, and of Weber's readiness to exploit
the dramatic possibilities of this neglected instrument. Both

Berlioz[1] and Wagner[2] have testified to the inferior skill and status
of orchestral viola players even at a later date, and it is not
difficult to see how the prevailing conditions are reflected in the
viola parts written earlier in the century. Viola parts, however,
tended to lean more and more towards the active and florid
nature of violin parts, and to take their patterns from the
figures and passages of the upper string voices rather than
from the bass parts on which their matter was formerly so
largely modelled.

A feature of orchestration which became common in the
operatic scores of the period is the occurrence of genuine bow-
tremolo, the repetition of notes at such great and irregular
speed that the effect is that of a continuous buzz, without any
suggestion of rhythmical reiteration.   It is by no means always
quite clear whether a measured or an unmeasured *tremolo* is
required in eighteenth century scores. The use of semiquavers
or demisemiquavers, even though taken in conjunction with the
tempo of the music, is very often inclined to be ambiguous, and
shows no clear distinction between these two entirely different
effects. An early instance of undoubted *tremolo* from Piccini's
Iphigénie has already been quoted, but for the most part it
seems that eighteenth century composers required exactly four
semiquavers to the crochet when the usual abbreviated notation

(𝅘𝅥) was employed. Operatic composers of the early

nineteenth century often made it quite clear when they wanted
an unmeasured *tremolo*, either putting the matter beyond doubt
by a more careful choice of note-value, or by the use of such terms
as *tremolo, tremando,* or *tremolando.* It is open to question whether
the real finger-tremolo was used at that time. The score of
Spontini's *Olimpie* (1819) contains some demisemiquavers

written thus : 𝅘𝅥𝅘𝅥 , but here, again, the question of measured

or unmeasured alternation, each producing such a very different

---

[1] "Viola players were always taken from among the refuse of violinists."
Berlioz, *Instrumentation*, p. 25.

[2] " The viola is commonly played by infirm violinists," etc. Wagner,
Uber das Dirigiren, English translation, p. 4 (Reeves, London).

effect, cannot be definitely answered. Some instances of a *legato* interchange of notes, thus :

occur in a few scores, and may be counted as a novelty, but were certainly no finger-tremolo effect.

String parts were freely sub-divided into two parts (*divisi*), generally simply in order to provide that more notes should be sounded simultaneously, rather than for the sake of securing varied or particular shades of tone-colour. Occasional instances of divided string parts so grouped as to produce colour effects, for example, harmony on violins alone, or only on the lower string voices, are rather more exceptional than common, and occur particularly in Weber's dramatic scores. A few instances of divided violoncellos predated Rossini's well-known effect at the beginning of the overture to *Guillaume Tell*.

Harmony notes in detached or repeated chords multiplied over and over again by means of double-stopping[1], the further exploitation of *pizzicato* effects, and the muting of the string instruments, are features which occur constantly in early nineteenth century orchestration, but were not in any case innovations. A general advance in the standard of technique demanded of string players, however, may be added to the list of elements which must certainly be counted as progressive in the string work of the period.

The recent acquisition of clarinets was responsible for some of the most significant developments in the handling of the wood-wind section of the orchestra during the first two or three decades of the nineteenth century. As a solo instrument the clarinet began to assert itself only very gradually in spite of Mozart's example, and not till nearly the end of the first quarter of the century did it stand on an equality with the other wood-wind instruments in this particular capacity. The readiness with which

[1] The term " double-stopping " is generally understood to embrace either two, three or four-note chords on string instruments.

clarinet-tone blends with the tone of bassoons, horns, and with string-tone, had an even more far-reaching influence on orchestration as a whole than the gain of a new solo voice. The smooth-toned combinations of clarinets and bassoons, or clarinets, bassoons and horns, began to replace the wood-wind combinations in which the more incisive-toned oboe had previously always had a place when, early in the nineteenth century, the new-comers had at last secured an assured place in all orchestras. A distinct preference for the warmer and round-toned blends, in which clarinet-tone largely replaced the hitherto predominant oboe-tone, is a feature of orchestration which became very marked during the maturity of Beethoven, Weber and Schubert, and marks the end of the long reign of the oboe as chief and leader of the wood-wind group. Other blends which excluded oboes, and became more common during the same period, were horns and bassoons, and flutes and clarinets. The natural capacity of the clarinet for playing arpeggio passages, and appreciation of the peculiar tone-colour of clarinets and of flutes in their lowest registers, the latter apparently both due to Weber, must be reckoned gains or rediscoveries which considerably enlarged the palette of the orchestral tone-painter of the generation which followed immediately after Beethoven and his contemporaries.

The occasional use of stopped notes gave early nineteenth century horn parts some more melodic and harmonic flexibility than was possible when only open notes were used. Though retaining the same general style as the Mozartian horn parts, there are more frequent attempts to give the instrument such thematic matter as could be squeezed out of the open and a few stopped notes. The latter also began to be used to supply the minor third of the key in which the horn was crooked, and with the half-stopped leading-note, helped to give a little more fullness to the brass harmony, especially when no trombones were employed. The same object was achieved to a rather more limited extent by making use of four horns crooked in two or more different keys.

Trumpet parts remained much as they were at the end of the eighteenth century, but began to be used, as far as the very limited selection of open notes would allow, for the upper parts in association with the trombone trio. The latter were treated almost entirely as harmonists, except occasionally when suitable matter in the bass part offered opportunity for some thematic interest. More novel was the use of trombones for very soft harmony, such as occurs in some of Schubert's later symphonies, and in Weber's operas. The use of trombones at selected moments simply in order to give more volume to particular chords, or to build up and emphasize a climax, shows some advance on the older style which kept these instruments playing more continuously in the movements in which they took part. As a body the brass group still suffered greatly from the want of more flexible upper voices than could be supplied by either natural horns or trumpets ; thus, the effect of unmixed brass-tone was one which was largely denied to early nineteenth century composers.

Timpani parts gained in interest and importance by being more freely used for solo passages in soft rhythmical patterns, by the increasing use of soft and *crescendo* rolls, and enjoyed some further expansion of their usefulness by being occasionally tuned at intervals other than the tonic and dominant of the key, also by the use of two drum notes played simultaneously. The early nineteenth century composers seemed to have no idea of using the remaining percussion instruments except to let them hammer away consistently on the accented beats of the bar in loud, and more rarely, in soft *tutti*. The harp parts of the period present no features of particular interest ; Boieldieu may possibly register a claim to have been the first to make use of harmonics on the harp as early as 1825 in his opera *La Dame Blanche*.

Orchestration by early nineteenth century composers shows thorough appreciation of the value of clearness in dealing with the colours of the orchestra. The tone of each instrument is allowed to be heard in its native state as well as with the admixture of alien tone-colour ; solo parts are judiciously accompanied by others whose tone-colour does not detract from or smother the individuality of the solo instrument, and the various groups consisting of instruments of related tone-colour are freely contrasted, as well as combined, one with the other. Monochromatic or neutral-tinted orchestration, the result of too constantly combining strings, wood-wind and horns, was a later growth for which certain German composers were largely responsible. The blank staves in the scores of the earlier composers are more significant than the well-filled staves of Schumann and Brahms, the silence of their parts as telling as the sounds. Over-wrought textures, over-weighted accompaniments, and the use of prolonged composite blends of uniform density, were the products of a later generation, an over-sophistication in the art of blending orchestral tone-colours which cannot be charged against either the Italian, French or German composers who followed Haydn and Mozart not only chronologically, but also in their conception of the use of an orchestral body which was to them essentially a three-part organization in groups of tone-colour which should be heard separately as well as in combination.

It was the early nineteenth century composers who first began to understand how to build up an extended *crescendo* by adding part after part till all the instruments of the orchestra were engaged. The sense of growing power in these cumulative *crescendi* was a sensation in orchestration hardly understood by Haydn and Mozart, or even by the Mannheimers whose *crescendo* was the admiration of eighteenth century critics. The more careful gradation of tone between *ppp* and *fff* is a noticeable feature in the scores of the period, also more exact indications of phrasing and directions concerning *tempo*, rendering, and effect. More or less novel features were the frequent occurrence of soft *tutti*, and a greater sensitiveness for balance of tone shown by the varying marks of expression and dynamics supplied in the parts. The management of loud *tutti* varied very much according to the texture and content of each individual composer's musical matter. Balance of tone in the loud *tutti* is often defective when measured by present-day performing standards, and can only partially be accounted for by the fact that rather smaller string orchestras were general at the time, and possibly by the prevalence of a less strident manner of tone-production on brass instruments.

The above generalisations, covering the entire first quarter of the nineteenth century, must be modified to some extent when turning to review the work of individual composers.

Étienne Nicolas Méhul (1763-1817) and Maria Luigi Cherubini (1760-1842), both on the scene rather earlier than Beethoven, may be considered connecting links between Gluck-Piccini-Salieri and Boieldieu-Spontini-Meyerbeer, in that their lives and work were largely associated with the French capital.

Méhul's orchestration is full-bodied and sound, but a little colourless when compared to the work of Mozart on the one hand, and Spontini on the other. *Le Trésor Supposé* (1802), *Uthal* (1806) and his best work *Joseph* (1807), show much that is sufficiently solid and rich in tone, yet is lacking in

brilliancy, bright colouring, and neatness of finish.   His idea of
scoring *Uthal* for a string orchestra without violins, namely,
for first violas, second violas, violoncellos and basses, may have
been novel, but only succeeded in emphasizing the tendency to
dullness of colouring which pervades his orchestration generally.

Not only a better orchestrator, but a finer musician, was
Cherubini, the composer of operas, masses, etc., who won the
respect of all musicians during the long period of his musical
activity in Paris.   Cherubini's best operatic works fall between the
years 1791 and 1813, after which time his output was almost
entirely devoted to the service of the Church.

Médée (1797) and *Les deux Journées* (1800) are richly,
if a little heavily scored, and are fairly well abreast of the times
with regard to orchestral effect, throughout musicianly in
conception, carefully and well finished.   *Anacreon* (1803),
Faniska (1806) and *Les Abencérages* (1813) show rather
brighter colour-contrasts, more variety and resource in a full and
grand manner, without revealing any great invention or daring
in devising purely orchestral effects.

The career of Ludwig van Beethoven (1770-1827) as an
orchestral composer began with the first two piano concertos, the
Prometheus ballet-music, and the first Symphony in C (1800),
and is adequately represented by the chain of symphonies which
culminated in the Choral Symphony (No. 9) of 1823.

Beethoven's first symphony shows him handling the orchestra
with complete confidence, and alive to the resources of orchestration as far as they were developed by the end of the eighteenth
century.   The handling of the wood-wind shows clearly that
the clarinet was hardly yet reckoned the equal of either the flute,
oboe, or the bassoon.   Beethoven's clarinets at that time were
harmony or *tutti* instruments only ; all the solo work goes to one
or other of the remaining wood-wind.   Only the clarinet is
excluded from taking a share in the little answering melodic
phrases of the second and subsidiary subjects, and oboes take
much of the harmonic work which in his later orchestration falls
to clarinets.   Already in the second symphony (1802) the
clarinets are united with bassoons in stating important and
essential matter, and in the *Eroica* (No. 3, 1804), a solo
clarinet is allowed to take a share in the melodic phrases and
essential harmonies of some of the principal themes.   After that
time clarinets get more extended solo parts, and in smoother-toned

blends with bassoons and horns to some extent exclude the hitherto ubiquitous oboe.

Beethoven's earliest horn parts are practically Mozartian in style and scope. The first symphony contains no stopped notes, No. 2 has a solitary B-natural, but several more occur in the *Eroica* and succeeding symphonies, most of them being the half-stopped E-flat and F-sharp. The melodic development of his horn parts is well illustrated by the progress from the style of the earliest symphonies to that of the elaborate parts for three horns in *Fidelio*[1] (1805, re-written 1814) and the solo part for fourth horn in the slow movement of the Choral Symphony. The horn parts in the latter work involve a free use of the half-stopped minor third of the key for harmonic purposes in the *tutti*.

Beethoven's trumpet parts show no very marked or progressive characteristics, nor did he advance much on the path of progress in handling trombones. A few dramatic touches in *Fidelio* show more enlightenment in using these instruments than the parts in the *Pastoral*, C Minor, and Choral Symphonies. The possibilities of the brass group as a body are very little exploited in Beethoven's orchestration, but to the timpani he gave a prominence and a thematic importance which they had never previously enjoyed.

The earliest symphonies contain much of the three-part writing for the string orchestra which, as in Haydn's work, gave the viola part a constant tendency to run in octaves with the bass part. Before long, however, the viola seems to transfer its allegiance, and becomes, so to speak, a large violin rather than a small violoncello. The emancipation of the violoncello begins in earnest with the *Eroica* symphony. For that work the part soars far beyond the confines of the bass part, and in the fourth, fifth, and later symphonies, joins now the first violins, now the violas, in octaves or in unison, in enriching what the uninitiated would call the " tune " of the music.

When for wind instruments alone, Beethoven's orchestration is mostly for wood-wind and horns in combination, or for any of the wood-wind pairs combined with one another, or with the horns. To the second bassoon alone usually falls the duty of sustaining the sole bass part in such combinations, a function which it is often hardly strong enough to undertake quite

[1] Leonore's Aria, No. 9, Act. I.

satisfactorily when horns and all the remaining wood-wind are placed above it.

The accompanying of solo wind parts is generally carried out by strings, without the interference of other wind parts which would clog the clear utterance or distinct colouring of the solo part. Wood-wind, horns and strings are not only often combined, but are also contrasted and opposed to one another in groups antiphonally, answering, echoing, and taking over melodic and harmonic matter, one from the other, sometimes at regular intervals, but at other times quite unexpectedly.

Beethoven's orchestral *tutti* grew from those of the simple Mozartian construction in the early symphonies, to the complex texture of the mighty *tutti* in the first movement of the Choral Symphony. It is in the soft *tutti* of that wonderful movement that Beethoven touched a type of orchestration well ahead of his time, and achieved effects more impressive than any which are brought about by mere noisy brilliance.

The sudden and unexpected *fortes* and *pianos* are characteristic of Beethoven's scores, also the sudden silences, the humorous touches and freakish turns given to the music and orchestration by the master when in his " unbuttoned " mood. Some cases of bad balance occur in several of his symphonies, and are all the result of strings, or strings and brass, overpowering essential matter played by the wood-wind in loud passages. These may possibly be accounted for by the smaller number of string players which were undoubtedly provided in the Vienna orchestras of his time, or there may be something in the suggestion that the great composer's deafness was responsible for these lapses. Neither explanation is wholly satisfactory, nor is it worth while probing deeper into the matter ; the fact remains that the balance is unsatisfactory. Modern conductors usually take upon themselves to " touch up " the orchestration in these places, and by a little readjustment of the parts and the dynamic marks, succeed in letting the hearers hear what the composer undoubtedly meant them to hear.

The above are the hard facts, the tangible features of Beethoven's orchestration which lend themselves to verbal analysis. Others there are, in which orchestration can hardly be separated from musical matter, where nothing ostensibly novel appears on the printed page, yet where the ear finds a something that leaves its trace on the memory, an imprint of instrumental colour, simple enough yet indelible, something which is of Beethoven and of no other composer. The thirty or so bars immediately preceding the recapitulation of the first subject in the first movement of the *Eroica*, the alternating wind and string chords just before the recapitulation in the first movement of the fifth symphony, the long passage leading up to the beginning of the *finale*, and the approach to the final *presto* in the same evergreen work; passages such as these, and others there are sprinkled about the scores of Beethoven which linger in the memory of every concert-goer; passages which cannot be considered to be the result of calculation or of skill in the management of orchestral effect; these make the orchestra speak in terms quite unknown to the predecessors or even to the contemporaries of the great master. To some modern ears the scream of undesirably prominent trumpet notes, or the wobble of a horn over an awkward passage in his orchestration, may be distressing. They are but the marks of the time in which Beethoven lived, and have survived with his works the passage of about an hundred years. So let them remain for another hundred![1]

It is difficult to recognize the same hand in the orchestration of the early, and of the later symphonies of Franz Peter Schubert (1797-1828). His first symphony dates from 1813, by which year Beethoven had completed all but his Choral Symphony, and shows tedious string parts made up of little else than crochets and repeated quavers, wood-wind parts indifferently blended and distributed, with stiff conventional horn and trumpet parts. By 1822, the year of the now well-known Unfinished Symphony (No. 8), this boyish orchestration had grown into the rich colouration, the warm blends and clear contrasts of the familiar work by which Schubert is best known to concert-goers of the present day.

Always an indifferent contrapuntist, Schubert's musical matter is made up of little else but melody and accompaniment. Thus it is that much of his string work takes the form of accompanying block-harmony, and is weak in figuration, passage-work, and polyphony. What his music lacked in quality of texture, however, is amply compensated by a warmth of melody and harmony which lent itself particularly well to orchestration in which colour and blend play the most important parts. The

---

[1] Suggestions are periodically put forward that Beethoven's orchestration should be brought thoroughly " up-to-date."

distinction between a melodic and an harmonic function is always a well-understood feature in Schubert's mature orchestration. His appealing string melodies are accompanied by full-bodied blends of wind-tone, his wind melodies by quiet unobtrusive string tone. Melodic violin parts are doubled in octaves or in unison in order to secure intensity of tone and due prominence ; violoncellos are led upwards into the tenor register, or take entire charge of melodic matter, or conversely, the string orchestra is made to supply accompanying matter for clear-cut melodies on single or doubled wood-wind instruments. Horns are used to give richness and body to the wind harmonies, or to blend in smooth-toned co-operation with the bassoons. Clarinets and bassoons, or flutes and clarinets, are united to form a homogeneous accompanying harmony where the razor-edged tone of oboes would prove too assertive. In his use of the heavier brass voices Schubert was in advance of Beethoven. He used trumpets and trombones to give wealth of tone at any moment, rather than in the older conventional manner which made a more formal distinction between what was and what was not a *tutti*. In Schubert's works we find the trumpet allying itself more thoroughly with the trombones than with its older associates, the horns.

Alas that Schubert's mature orchestration could exert little or no influence on contemporary work till it was almost too late to be of material service, for it was not till about the mid-century that his orchestral music began to be known and played.

Much more immediate and powerful was the stimulus given to orchestration by the work of Carl Maria von Weber (1786-1826). *Der Freischütz* (1820), *Euryanthe* (1823) and *Oberon* (1826) alone contain more novel colour-effects, effects which had their being in the particular texture of musical matter allied to particular instrumental tone-colours, than are to be found in all the more soberly scored works of Méhul and Cherubini. Weber's orchestration for strings is more brilliant in passage-work and more varied in texture and colour than that of Beethoven. The irresistible rush of his violin parts in the loud *tutti*, the pointed rhythmical accompanying figures, the clear appreciation of the individual tone-colours of the higher and of the lower string voices, are features of Weber's work which, allied to a less complex musical matter, produce a type of orchestration more highly coloured, more showy, and generally more transparently effective than that of the greater master of symphonic development. The divided and muted violins (*Euryanthe*), divided violins and violas (*Freischütz*), divided violas and violoncellos (*Oberon*), each used as a separate colour-combination, each distinctive in effect and character, served to point out the way which led to the infinite variety of string-colouration found in the orchestration of Wagner. Weber's use of the dramatic characteristics of viola-tone, his melodic violoncello parts, and grouping of the instruments, show progress far beyond the eighteenth century conception which regarded the string orchestra as a body capable of producing only one uniform tone-colour.

Weber's treatment of the wood-wind instruments shows the clarinet more thoroughly appreciated and better understood, in all its capacities as melodist, harmonist, and colourist, than it is in the work of any earlier or contemporary composer. His clarinet solos, ranging over the entire compass of the instrument, exploit the individuality, the technical features, and the tone-colour of each different register to the best advantage. The dramatic effect of the low sustained notes in *Der Freischütz* is very familiar, and was probably exhibited for the first time in that favourite opera, while the readiness with which clarinet-tone blends unobtrusively with other wind, or with string-tone, made it, in Weber's hands, a much more useful and accommodating instrument for use in quiet harmonic backgrounds than the assertive oboe ever was or ever could be. The low flute notes heard in *Der Freischütz*, the two piccolo parts in Caspar's song from the same opera, and the fluttering passages for flutes and clarinets in *Oberon*, are samples of effective writing for wood-wind instruments which bore fruit very soon after they were first heard. The same two operas abound in happily conceived melodic phrases for the open notes of natural horns, eked out by a few stopped notes, also several skilfully managed hunting tunes for horns alone.

The overtures to *Rübezahl*[1] (1804), *Preciosa* (1821), *Euryanthe*, and the *Jubel-overture* (1818), show valiant attempts to make use of either the entire wind group or the brass group alone, and also illustrate how the tendency to regard trumpets as the proper treble voices to the trombones, was steadily growing, but was still severely handicapped by the limitations of the natural instrument. The soft harmonies for trombones which occur in several of Weber's scores register an expansion

---

[1] Rewritten later as *Beherrscher der Geister*.

of the functions of these instruments in the orchestra for the
purpose of dramatic effect.

Weber's loud *tutti* usually consist of two extreme parts for
strings, doubled in the octave or in unison, and supplied with
inside harmony by all the wind instruments. A florid upper
part is given to both first and second violins, frequently also to
violas or even to violoncellos, clearly with a view to ensuring
sufficient prominence for the most important melodic part, and
showing a good perception of how much tone was necessary to
balance the heavy harmony of horns, trumpets and trombones.
The vigour and clearness of his florid *tutti* gained much by this
system of part-distribution, and achieved a much better balance
of tone than the system which gave the upper melody to first
violins and flutes, allotting to all the other instruments a rather
overpowering mass of harmony.

For variety of colouring the Adagio at the beginning of the
overture to *Oberon*, and the *Wolfschlucht* scene in *Der
Freischütz*, may be cited as well-known examples of a resource
and invention which did not require the extraneous aid of
additional wind and percussion instruments in order to produce
telling and dramatically coloured effects.

The immediate and extraordinary success of *Der
Freischütz*[1] could not but have provided a potent means of
stimulating further effort, and of suggesting the lines along which
progress in orchestration was to travel, during the two or three
decades which followed the production of this epoch-making
opera. Mendelssohn, Berlioz and Wagner, not to mention
numerous lesser composers, all owed something to the orchestration
of *Der Freischütz* ; this marks it as a work which has
probably exercised more influence on the growth of orchestration
than can be ascribed to any other single work. Just as Beethoven's
orchestration appears to represent a further growth of the style
of Haydn and Mozart, so Weber's mature work stands for the
birth of a more advanced style, a style in which sonority, brilliance,
and effects dependent on the more sensuous beauty of actual
instrumental tone-colour, took increasingly important parts.

The work of François Adrien Boieldieu (1775-1834) is
adequately represented by his early success *Le Calife de Bagdad*
(Paris, 1800) and by his more noteworthy opera *La Dame*

---

[1] Within a few years of its production in Berlin, " Der Freischütz "
was played in all German towns, in Vienna, Prague, Paris and London.

Blanche (1825). Both are light-hearted works, showing a much more brightly coloured orchestration than is to be found in the scores of either Méhul or Cherubini, but are not without a trace of cheap noisiness in the loud *tutti*. These orchestral *tutti* marked the beginning of a tendency on the part of many Italian and French opera composers to be content with a noisy bustling type of *tutti* in which rather thinly represented florid first violin and flute parts struggle against a heavy harmony of the rest of the orchestra. Even if a piccolo part sometimes rescued the melodic part from being completely swamped by a torrent of harmonic padding, it cannot be said that the type of *tutti*, so frequently encountered in the operatic overtures of such as Boieldieu, Rossini, Herold and Auber, degenerating as they often did into a more or less exhilarating noise, is anything like so well-balanced as that of Weber. Apart from the *tutti*, Boieldieu's orchestration is well-balanced, full of bright contrasts and well-devised effects, much superior in its brilliance to the work of Méhul and Cherubini, yet falling short in that respect of the standard achieved by Rossini.

To Gasparo Luigi Pacifico Spontini (1774-1851) belongs a share of the credit due for further developing dramatic orchestration during the first quarter of the nineteenth century, which is perhaps only eclipsed by that due to Weber and Rossini. *La Vestale* (Paris, 1807) shows him already equipped with up-to-date ideas in the matter of blend and colour, able to present his rather pretentious music in suitably effective and practicable orchestral clothing. Spontini's *Olimpie* (Paris, 1819, Berlin 1821) is orchestrated on a still grander scale. Employing a full orchestra including piccolo, *Cor Anglais*, ophicleide, bass-drum, cymbals and triangle, in addition to a full brass group, his work in this opera ranks him not very far below Weber as a colourist, and stamps him a composer whose orchestration did more than justice to his musical matter.

Gioachino Antonio Rossini (1792-1868), although he lived till after the dates of Wagner's *Die Walküre* and *Tristan*, was by his work, nevertheless, a contemporary of Beethoven, Schubert and Weber. His operatic career, beginning in 1810, embracing *Tancredi* (1813), *Il Barbiere di Siviglia* (1816), *Otello* (1816), *La Gazza Ladra* (1817), *Mosè in Egitto* (1818), *Semiramide* (1823) and *Le Siège de Corinthe* (1826), ended with his masterpiece *Guillaume Tell* (Paris) in 1829.

Surpassing all his contemporaries in sheer brilliance, there are
however two sides to the account presented by Rossini's orchestration. On the credit side stand his clear and well-contrasted
colouring, the brilliance and piquancy of his effects ; on the debit
side are the somewhat ill-balanced noisiness of his loud *tutti*, and
what is more than a trace of vulgarity in his handling of the heavy
brass voices. The blare of *fortissimo* brass harmony, reiterated
semiquavers, and empty but showy passage-work on the strings,
the clash and rattle of percussion instruments, with an occasional
shriek from the piccolo ; all these combine to make Rossini's
loud *tutti* more exhilarating than impressive. A more or less
routine method of distributing the parts sufficed to produce the
necessary body and brilliance, but took little account of a proper
balance of tone. In inaugurating, or at all events in conven-
tionalising, the use of repeated chords for heavy brass instruments
on the unaccented beats of the bar in the manner of a vamped
piano accompaniment, Rossini did no good service to the cause of
orchestration, for his example in this respect was only too readily
followed by the succeeding generation of Italian and light French
opera composers who took their cue from his methods, and
emphasized the vulgar tinge always given to music so
orchestrated.

Apart from the above influence in establishing a none too high
grade of showy sonority and brilliance, Rossini's contributions
to the growth of orchestration were all to the good. He took the
lead in keeping the pure and elementary colours of the orchestra
clearly differentiated, and to some extent counteracted a tendency
towards monotony which was caused by too constantly employing
various types of tone-colour in neutral-tinted and non-character-
istic combinations. Rossini's solo parts stand out in strong relief
against the harmonic backgrounds of his accompaniments ; the
clear utterance of melodic wind-parts is not blurred by sustained
harmonic padding on voices of too closely related tone-colour ;
contrapuntal decoration interferes with the functions of neither
melodic nor accompanying parts, and neither lose their
individuality as the result of over-blending or intermixing the
colours. These were features of part-distribution misunderstood
by many a more profound German composer of a later period ;
features which remained excellent characteristics of French
orchestration almost throughout the nineteenth century. Almost
any of Rossini's opera overtures will provide examples of

judiciously accompanied wood-wind solos, and of clearly contrasted decorative counterpoint on the part of either string or wood-wind instruments.

As a practical horn-player Rossini enjoyed some advantage over other composers when writing for natural horns with a free use of stopped notes.   His chromatic melodic and harmonic horn parts are managed more successfully and more effectively than in the case of Beethoven's elaborate parts such as those in *Fidelio* and in the Ninth Symphony ; this was largely due to Rossini's good sense in keeping each part within a more limited compass, and more conjunct in motion.

Another successful feature of his orchestration was Rossini's treatment of the instruments in the case of an extended *crescendo*. The gradual building up of tone-power by a judicious and cumulative addition of parts was only partially understood by composers before the Rossinian *crescendo* became at first a model, and finally a mannerism.   To such a colourist as the composer of the ever-popular overture to *Guillaume Tell*, orchestration indeed owes more than to those who, after his time, were so intent on securing an evenly rich tone that they neglected to let the primary tone-colours of the orchestra speak for themselves, who were for ever doubling melodic parts on wind and string instruments, and thickening accompaniments by over-prolonged sustained harmony on strings, wood-wind, and horns.   Rossini, so to speak, let fresh air and light penetrate into the heart of the orchestra, showing clearly what was there, and what was known to be there, but what was in danger of becoming unappreciated and under-valued owing to over-sophistication.

Few decades in the history of orchestration can show such a remarkable array of works as the years 1820 to 1830.   The ten years which gave birth to Beethoven's Choral Symphony, Weber's *Der Freischütz, Euryanthe,* and *Oberon,* Schubert's Unfinished Symphony, Rossini's *Semiramide* and *Guillaume Tell,* also, as representing the work of a younger generation, Mendelssohn's *Midsummer Night's Dream* overture and Berlioz's *Symphonie Fantastique,* must be counted a time of expansion and fulfilment in orchestration difficult to match at any other period.   The growth of the romantic element was being clearly reflected in the warmer colouring and more sensuous beauty of the orchestration in which music was being clothed ; the more formal and less flexible ways of applying and combining instrumental colour were being rapidly superceded by methods into which beauty of effect and dramatic fitness entered more thoroughly than at any previous period ; thus, the path along which such as Meyerbeer, Berlioz, and Wagner were to proceed was being clearly marked out, even though it was not firmly trodden down.

CHAPTER XI

NINETEENTH CENTURY, SECOND QUARTER. MEYERBEER—
BERLIOZ—MENDELSSOHN—GLINKA

OF orchestral composers the greater part of whose work falls within the second quarter of the nineteenth century, the following are prominent and representative ; their work provides material for the continuation of the history of orchestration after the time of Beethoven and Weber, and bridges the gap between the period of these composers and the advent of Wagner :

Italian.	*German.*
Donizetti, 1797-1848.	Kreutzer, 1780-1849.
Bellini, 1801-1835.	Spohr, 1784-1859.

French.

Auber, 1782-1871.
Hérold, 1791-1833.
Meyerbeer, 1791-1864 (Paris and
Halévy, 1799-1862.   Berlin).
Berlioz, 1803-1869.

Marschner, 1795-1861.
Lortzing, 1801-1851.
Mendelssohn, 1809-1847.
Nicolai, 1810-1849.
Schumann, 1810-1856.

Less significant names are such as Adam (1803-1856) and Reissiger (1798-1859), also those of the two British composers Balfe (1808–1870) and Wallace (1812–1865), both of whose most successful operas date from before the mid-century. Search amongst the composers of other countries produces the names of the Russians Glinka (1803–1857) and Dargomyzhsky (1813–1869), their advent marking the entry of fresh nationality into the story of orchestration.

Of the above composers some were already active and well-known during the lifetime of Beethoven, notably Spohr, whose greatest operatic success (*Jessonda*) dates from as early as 1823, but whose Ninth Symphony was composed as late as 1849. Others again—such as Auber, Meyerbeer and Berlioz—although their work largely falls within the years 1825-1850, continued to produce representative works after the mid-century, thus chronologically overlapping the limits of the period now to be reviewed.

Before most of these composers had completed their careers, the earlier works of Wagner and Verdi had already been produced, but the historical significance of the work of these two composers, as well as their influence and span of their lives, belongs to a later period which classes them with the generation whose main work is covered by the third quarter of the century. In dealing with names so familiar to the present-day reader as the above are, it is hardly necessary to point out which of these composers devoted most of their energies to the composition of opera, and which were most active in composing symphony, concert, and church music, or again, which of them embraced all these spheres of creative activity.

Broadly classified according to the general style of their orchestration, the Italians Donizetti and Bellini, the composers of lighter French opera, Auber and Herold, also Balfe and Wallace, might be grouped together in that their orchestration was theatrical, showy and effective, but rather superficial, and not without a tinge of vulgarity. More dignified and pretentious, carried out with more care and finish, albeit theatrical and highly coloured, was the work of Halévy and Meyerbeer, while Berlioz, whose orchestration towers high above that of all his contemporaries, can only be satisfactorily placed in a class by himself. The Germans, whether writing symphony or opera, or both, together form a class the distinguishing feature of which was a more sober, a more restrained and musicianly style, one which was free from sensationalism or superficiality and, in some cases, leaned rather towards dullness than otherwise. The work of Glinka places him in a category by himself, and is highly interesting in that it is difficult to trace its parentage, or to find in it the influence of either a German, a French or an Italian style.

Whatever their styles, whatever their merits or demerits as orchestrators or as musicians, nearly all of the above composers wrote naturally and suitably for the orchestra. The orchestral clothing they provided was well fitted to their musical matter. Schumann alone seemed to be struggling with a language in which he could not express himself with any ease, nor without going through a process somewhat akin to adaptation or translation. Blatant or trivial music was quite naturally and fitly presented by means of noisy and brightly coloured orchestration. Music of more refined character was equally naturally associated with a more delicate and soberly coloured setting. Music composed by

Auber, but orchestrated in the manner of Spohr, would form an incongruous union, as much so as rouged cheeks and a Quakeress' garb. Thus it would be a questionable judgment to assert that Meyerbeer's orchestration was better than Mendelssohn's, or that Mendelssohn handled his orchestra better than did Bellini. Each had the same colours on his palette, and each produced a different type of picture. If the one was too rough, then the other was perhaps too highly polished. A more sensible view is that each was painting as best befitted his own particular art ; that interchange of clothing would not have effectually disguised the man.

Classification based on the distinction between composers of opera and of concert music would show that, on the whole, the former were more ready to use their colours boldly, and to employ instruments additional to the now almost standardized orchestral combination ; also that composers of opera showed more enterprise in taking advantage of the benefits conferred on brass-instrument-playing by the adoption of the lengthening-valve. Thus, it is in the opera scores of this period that parts specifically written for valve horns, valve trumpets and cornets make their earliest appearances.

Practically all opera scores of this period include parts for piccolo, for trombones, very often for serpent or ophicleide, for extra percussion instruments, and not infrequently for one or two harps, *cor anglais* or bass clarinet. The occurrence of four bassoon parts is a characteristic of nineteenth century French instrumentation which makes its appearance during the second quarter of the century. The use of trumpets or other brass instruments playing *on* the stage is also quite common in these opera scores, more particularly in works written for the ample resources of the Paris and Berlin opera houses. For concert works, piccolo, trombones, and occasionally ophicleide, bass drum, cymbals, and triangle, were beginning to be more frequently demanded, although most composers were content with the smaller orchestra such as was used by Haydn and Mozart, but with the addition of another pair of horns. The " classical " orchestra also sufficed for all *concerti* and kindred works. This generalization regarding the constitution of the orchestra takes no account of the scores of Berlioz, who, in this as in almost all other respects, stands quite apart from the rest of his contemporaries, and must be considered separately.

Taken in the aggregate, orchestration during the second quarter of the nineteenth century shows that most of the composers had a clear idea of the value of treating the orchestra according to its natural constitution in three distinct families of instruments, representing three main types of tone-colour, viz., strings, wood-wind and brass. The three-group principle was a firmly established basis of part-distribution, and was recognized as the most valuable means of securing contrast, or of guarding against monotony. The group which enjoyed the greatest homogeneity of tone-colour, which tired the ear least, and which offered the most perfect blend, namely, the string orchestra, was allowed to speak for itself and to display its own particular tone-colour without constant adulteration. The wood-wind group, less cohesive but very distinctive, was likewise allowed to have its say as an independent group, in spite of a tendency to rather frequently amalgamate with it the tone of horns. The brass, now enjoying the great benefit of at least three completely chromatic members, namely, the trombones, had become harmonically more or less self-contained, and could be trusted to speak alone without the co-operation of unrelated types of instruments. The combination of wood-wind and brass groups made yet another broadly distinguished type of composite tone-colour which was freely employed as a wind-tutti, as distinguished from the *tutti* of the whole orchestra. Just according to how much composers neglected to let the three main groups of the orchestra be heard separately, so did their orchestration become colourless and dull. The least distinctive of the larger composite groups available in orchestration, that is, the combination of wood-wind, horns, and strings, was the blend most favoured by Schumann, and the one which, when used in excess, gave a respectable dullness to so much German orchestration in the second half of the nineteenth century.

The immediate successors of Beethoven, Weber, and Rossini, found the string orchestra in a state of technical flexibility which was greatly in advance of the standard prevailing at the very beginning of the century. Further upward extension of the compass of violin and violoncello parts, passage-work and figuration more varied in pattern and more chromatic in nature, the now common unmeasured *tremolo*, the effects of playing *sul ponticello* and *col legno*, the effects of high divided violins, or of the lower string voices used as separate colour-groups, all these are

features in the scores which show the growing resources of the
string orchestra after the stimulation and example of the more
progressive works which had appeared during the significant
decade 1820 to 1830. The *legato* alternation of harmony notes
by means of the finger, thus :

became almost a commonplace during the second quarter of the
century, and provided a smoother and lighter alternative to the
older manner of reiterating harmony notes by means of the bow :

Increased agility and a much wider key-range are amongst
the greater technical demands made on the capabilities of the
wood-wind instruments. Blend was well understood, and the
value of clarinets as unobtrusive harmonists was now fully
appreciated. The necessity for strengthening independent
melodic parts on the wood-wind by means of more and more
doubling in unison or in octaves, in order to balance the greater
richness and sonority of the strings, is noticeable only in the scores
of the more practically-minded composers of this period.

In handling brass instruments, both harmonically and
melodically, quite pronounced progress was made in the
orchestration of the second quarter of the century. More flexible
and expressive horn melodies, such as, for example, those which
occur in the slow movements of Schumann's First Symphony
(1841) and of Mendelssohn's Third Symphony (1842), show that,
even though these parts were not written for valve instruments,
the horn was beginning to be given melodies which retained not
the slightest trace of the old hunting-call style, the hall-mark of
the earlier melodic or solo horn parts. A bright and novel
feature in several operatic scores of the period is the melodic

trumpet solo which, while of necessity retaining the military flavour inseparable from the use of only open notes in quick succession, was nevertheless distinctly a solo part of melodic character, and at the same time quite distinct from the older *clarino* type of trumpet part with its high-pitched florid passages in conjunct intervals. Familiar instances are those in Auber's *Fra Diavolo* (1830) and in the same composer's *Masaniello* (1828).

That the brass group was now beginning to be capable of supplying its own harmony, and could therefore be used alone without the help of either wood-wind or strings, was really due to the fact that trombones were commonly included in all well-found opera orchestras, and were just beginning to find their way into the concert orchestra. These chromatic brass instruments were able to supply the harmony notes which were so largely lacking on natural horns and trumpets, and, now that the old traditional way of treating trombones merely as supporters of choral harmony was rapidly dying out, composers found a self-contained body of pure brass-tone at their disposal, and in varying degree made use of that ready means of securing broad and strong contrasts of tone colour.

The composers who in this period began to write for valve horns and valve trumpets were able to make still more free use of these instruments as melodists, and when bold enough to ignore the traditions associated with melodies for the natural instruments, found themselves in possession of what was practically a new set of brass voices, namely, horns and trumpets which were harmonically and melodically flexible, and could be used for melodic parts either expressive or gay, parts which were completely free from the characteristics of the hunting call or the military trumpet call. Freely melodic parts of this sort for valve instruments are found in the scores of such as Halévy, Meyerbeer, Donizetti, Bellini and Nicolai, and mark a new departure in orchestration, one which, however, had still to fight against tradition for well-nigh half a century. Respect for the old instruments, and for their characteristic type of part, continued for a long time even amongst composers who were the most ready to adopt the new instruments ; thus, parts for natural horns and trumpets occur in most of the scores which also specify valve instruments, the usual arrangement being to write one pair of parts for the natural, and another pair for valve instruments.

The use of valve horns and trumpets for harmonic purposes naturally began to be exploited at the same time. The chromatic instruments gave the composer a practically free choice of notes, and resulted in a much richer and more flexible brass-voiced harmony, a feature of orchestration which is at once noticeable in the greater harmonic fulness of the *tutti* written by those composers who were able and willing to take advantage of the new type of instrument. Meyerbeer, in particular, showed no hesitation in displaying unmixed brass-tone of a hitherto unknown richness which was due simply to the free choice of notes at his disposal in the upper brass parts.

Quite a new feature in the operatic orchestration of the time was the introduction of cornet parts, especially in French scores. Those instruments were at first commonly used in addition to trumpets, and not, as latterly in smaller orchestras, in place of trumpets. Not having to contend with the tradition which clung to horn and trumpet parts even for long after these instruments had been rendered chromatic, composers of early cornet parts had no scruples in writing frankly melodic parts for the new-comers, often, it is true, trivial or sentimental in character, but quite free from the limitations imposed on parts written for instruments which could only sound their open notes. A free choice of harmony notes on cornets likewise helped to give greater fullness and body to the brass harmony of the *tutti* in scores where these instruments were included.

Though still somewhat limited, the functions of trombones in orchestration show some expansion during the second quarter of the nineteenth century. Normally their work was confined to supplying harmonic body for the brass group, or for the *tutti* of the full orchestral combination. French and Italian composers wrote largely for three tenor trombones, and continued to place the harmony in close position ; the Germans remained true to the old group of alto, tenor, and bass, spreading the parts over a rather wider compass. That trombones should add the weight of their tone to any loud chord or *tutti* was now more or less a convention ; it was, however, a distinct advance that they were no longer considered to be fit only for loud effects. The value of the effect of soft harmony on trombones was appreciated by, and exploited by, practically all composers during the period immediately following the time of Weber, and probably owes that appreciation largely to his example. The idea of giving trombones independent thematic matter, although by no means unknown, was as yet undeveloped, nor was it always successfully or confidently carried out when attempted, yet it was in this period that composers began to treat the trombone as an independent voice, and took the first steps to promote the instrument to a proper and worthy position in the organization of the orchestral body. Great strides in this direction were made by Berlioz and Wagner before the mid-century has passed, but the most substantial advance was still to come, and belongs to the time after Mendelssohn and Schumann, to the third quarter of the nineteenth century.

Further development in the use of timpani is shown in the occasional demand for three drums. Instances of a double roll (on two drums simultaneously) also occur, likewise, more variety of tuning, and a generally rather more artistic treatment of the instruments which by now had quite outgrown their original function of playing only when loudness was required, point to enlightenment and progress in dealing with percussion instruments.

In turning to the work of the individual composers selected as representative of orchestration during the second quarter of the nineteenth century, it is at once apparent how the widely different musical matter and the artistic sincerity of each composer, or type of composer, reacted on their style of orchestration. Some attempt must now be made to follow the course of orchestration through the various and deviating channels of individual achievement, and of national tendencies, and to note how much or how little the work of particular composers influenced the general progress and development of the art. The short career of Vincenzo Bellini (1801-1835) covered only about ten years of activity as an operatic composer, during which time he gave to the world some eleven operas, including *La Sonnambula* and *Norma* (both 1831), and *I Puritani* (1835). Like that of Rossini, Bellini's orchestration is brilliant and clearly coloured. The loud *tutti* are noisy; heavy harmony for the brass accompanies active string work, and shows little but conventional methods of handling the full orchestra. The accompaniments to vocal solos are suitably and commendably light, not overweighted with sustained wood-wind and horn harmony as often occurs in the work of Bellini's German contemporaries. If not quite so neat

and finished as is Rossini's best work, Bellini's colouring is, nevertheless, clear and distinct, providing well-defined contrasts between
melodic and accompanying parts. The general features are
up-to-date, but suggest that Bellini was satisfied to repeat certain
effects regularly as certain situations arose. The effect of *sul
ponticello* appears in some of the scores of Bellini, Donizetti,
Hérold, and Meyerbeer, soon after 1830.

Very much of the same type was the orchestration of Gaetano
Donizetti (1797-1848), the composer of nearly seventy operas
dating from between 1818 and 1844, notably *Lucrezia Borgia*
(1833), *Lucia di Lammermoor* (1835), *La Fille du Régiment*
and *La Favorita* (both 1840). The same brassy *tutti* as in
Rossini's and Bellini's scores show his lack of resource or invention
in handling the full orchestra, also a similar want of good balance
in distributing parts in *fortissimo*. Otherwise Donizetti shared
with these two composers the ability to present even their
shallowest melodies in attractive orchestral clothing, with clear
colouring, and bright, piquant effect. Both Bellini and Donizetti
were ready to seize on the melodic and harmonic advantages of the
valve horns and trumpets, and made good use of the wind-band
unmixed with string tone. Both avoided the inevitable monotony
of too constantly combining strings, wood-wind, and horns, and
fully understood the value of allowing the primary tone-colours
of the orchestra to be heard separately as foils one to the other.

To Italian composers of this school belongs the great merit of
having avoided dull or obscure colouring, and an over-thick
texture in their orchestration. Brilliance and brightness of effect
were their aims, which, when combined with their hasty methods,
and the lack of polish resulting from over-production, often caused
them to rely on the repetition of well-tried effects and conventional methods of distributing the parts. The manuscript score
of some forgotten opera by these Italians, showing all the signs
of hot haste in composition, contrasts strangely with a highly
polished and much-revised score by their contemporary
Mendelssohn. It is as if the Italians were writing for the moment,
for immediate success and effect, and the German with close
investigation and his future reputation ever in mind.

The two Irishmen, Michael William Balfe (1808-1870) and
William Vincent Wallace (1812–1865) adopted the orchestral
style of the Italian opera composers of their own time. The same
noisy and rather blatant *tutti* alternate with agreeably light and

well-balanced accompaniments to vocal melodies, or effective, though conventional handling of orchestral voices generally. The first-named produced his numerous operas between 1826 and 1863, while Wallace's work as an opera composer only began with *Maritana* in 1845, and ended about 1863. In their hastily written manuscript scores are found melodic parts for cornets, and more rarely for valve trumpets, also for piccolo, *cor anglais*, serpent or ophicleide, but in Wallace's *Love's Triumph* (1862) is found a part for bass tuba in place of the ophicleide.

The orchestral style of Rossini, Bellini, and Donizetti found its continuation and further development in the work of Verdi and other Italian opera composers whose work falls largely within the third quarter of the nineteenth century.

Two composers associated with a brilliant period in the history of French *opéra comique* were Louis Joseph Ferdinand Hérold (1791-1833) and Daniel François Esprit Auber (1782-1871). The first of these enjoyed only a very brief career, his successes beginning with *Marie* in 1826 and ending with *Zampa* (1831) and *Le Pré aux Clercs* in 1832. Essentially bright and effective, well contrasted and clearly coloured, Hérold's orchestration followed the style of Boieldieu to some extent, but is rather more varied and more brilliant. A tendency to a too blatant use of the brass instruments gives a rather vulgar tinge to much of his work for full orchestra, a weakness which he shared with Auber and contemporary Italians. The exhilarating effect of his loud *tutti* owes not a little to a mere brisk movement of parts in conjunction with a free use of full brass harmony and the noisy rattle of percussion instruments. An excellent sense for colour and clear-cut contrasts, however, goes far to counterbalance his over-exuberant handling of the full force of the orchestra, and is typical of the general crisp effectiveness which characterized the best French orchestration of the time. Practically the same may be said of Auber, whose best operas range from about 1825 to 1869. There is no denying the brightness and exhilaration of these French composers' orchestration, in spite of the noisy *tutti*, and their habit of treating the heaviest brass voices in the manner of a commonplace piano accompaniment. Like Rossini, they were always at their best when separating and contrasting the colours of the orchestra, or when devising suitable harmonic backgrounds or accompaniments to their lively melodies. The brightness of the piccolo and crispness of the side drum were important items in their stock-in-trade of orchestral effect, and with the new trumpet or cornet melodies, served to produce a brightness which was an excellent foil to the more sombre orchestral colouring of some of their German contemporaries.

More dignified and serious were the music and orchestration of Jacques François Fromental Elias Halévy (1799-1862), whose operas, of which *La Juive* (1835) is the best remembered, cover the period from about 1827 to 1858. Avoiding the noisy triviality of Hérold and Auber, Halévy's orchestration is full of strong contrasts, and shows some advance on previous models in his management of brass instruments alone in harmonic combination. He was also amongst the first to specify valve horns and valve trumpets in his scores.

On his own ground, however, Halévy was easily beaten by the German-born Giacomo Meyerbeer (1791–1864), whose series of important operas, following a string of conventional efforts in the Italian manner, began with *Robert le Diable* in 1831, and ended with *Dinorah* in 1859 and *L'Africaine*, produced posthumously in 1865.

His demands for a lavishly constituted orchestra render Meyerbeer's scores imposing in appearance, even when compared to the large French operatic scores of the period. Piccolo, *cor anglais*, bass clarinet, and sometimes four bassoons, are specified, while in the brass section four trumpets are frequently demanded in addition to the usual four horns, three trombones and ophicleide. Wind-bands on the stage, bells, organ behind the scenes, three timpani and two harps are amongst the additional forces which at times further increase the size of Meyerbeer's scores, and help to satisfy his desire for increased resources and wealth of tone.

The obvious signs of a composer who took orchestration seriously—the finish and careful attention to detail in his scores, the directions as to rendering, his habit of constant revision and alternative versions—all testify to Meyerbeer's keen interest and concern for orchestral effect and orchestration which is, indeed, too often worthy of better musical matter. A keen colourist, and one who loved rich and showy effects, Meyerbeer painted with a broad brush, yet with carefully blended, carefully selected colours, and with constant attention to detail. He handled his orchestra with more independence and enterprise than any of his Parisian or German contemporaries, Berlioz alone excepted. Meyerbeer's brass section is both melodically and harmonically self-contained, full in volume and well balanced. To horns, trumpets or trombones, he entrusted absolutely essential thematic matter in broad and bold melodic lines in a way which must surely have proved suggestive to Wagner, whose earlier works coincide with the period of Meyerbeer's successes at Paris and Berlin. His unison themes for brass instruments, accompanied by a network of string figuration, seem to foreshadow Wagner's similar handling of the same combination in many of his now familiar works. The low-pitched blends of clarinets and bassoons, or of bassoons, trombones and ophicleide, the high-pitched groups of divided violin parts, and many other effects to be found in Meyerbeer's scores, all appear to stand as parents to many of Wagner's well-known colour-devices ; nor need Wagner's poor opinion of Meyerbeer as a composer mislead one in tracing some of the former's most characteristic effects to their source. The unison of the entire string orchestra was used by Meyerbeer with full consciousness of its intense power. The division of each string part into two sections, the one playing *pizzicato* and the other *coll'arco* (overture to *Les Huguenots*, 1836) and the *col legno* effect in *L'Africaine* were possibly innovations at that time, and, like the *obbligato* solo part for *viola d'amore* in *Les Huguenots*, serve to indicate Meyerbeer's independence and disregard for convention. In view of those qualities shown in all his scores, and his desire for a rich and flexible body of brass tone, it is not surprising to find that Meyerbeer readily availed himself of the advantages of writing for valve horns and valve trumpets as soon as the new instruments were made practicable and reliable, and came into the hands of progressive players.

Perhaps the most remarkable figure in the whole history of orchestration is that of Hector Berlioz (1803-1869) ; remarkable in that, although he was by far the most progressive, original, independent, and daring orchestrator of his time, his music has never at any time become popular enough to generally influence or colour the orchestration of either his contemporaries or his successors.

It is difficult to find very precise dates for many of the various concert, dramatic, and sacred works by which Berlioz is even now inadequately known to the musical public. The period of actual work on many of them was spread over several years ; revision, re-writing, alterations or additions after performance, also conflicting statements, all add to the difficulty, nor does his own autobiography[1] help the enquirer in this respect. Nevertheless, there is no question that the *Francs-Juges* and *Waverley* overtures and the *Symphonie Fantastique* were written before Berlioz proceeded to Italy as winner of the *prix de Rome* in 1830. The *King Lear* overture, *Lélio*, *Harold in Italy*, *Benvenuto Cellini*, the *Requiem*, and *Romeo and Juliet* cover the period between 1830 and the beginning of his German tour in 1841 or 1842, while *Faust* and his famous *Instrumentation* can safely be dated, respectively, 1846 and 1844. *L'Enfance du Christ*, *Beatrice and Benedict*, and finally *Les Troyens* (1858), belong to his last period and were composed after 1850.

To Berlioz the orchestral setting of his music was no mere secondary matter. In his musical organism, strange, independent and unconventional as it was, instrumental effect occupied a position of great importance ; so much so, that it is almost impossible to avoid the impression that he sometimes built up music in order to show off a particular pre-conceived orchestral effect. Approaching the subject with little regard for usage or tradition, Berlioz, so to speak, spread out before him the entire material of orchestration, and then proceeded to build his own edifice ; what he evolved included much old as well as much new matter, but each design was considered independently of previous experience or custom. The possible uses of each instrument, of each tone-colour, and of all possible combinations and blends, seem to have been judged solely on their merits ; everything was investigated afresh and without prejudice. Even the most unpromising and insignificant corners in the range of orchestral effect were probed and brought into the light ; a chance was given to anything new, experimentally it might be, and not necessarily successfully, but always fairly, and even generously. It did not matter to Berlioz, for example, that drums had long been used in a few particular ways ; if a drum could sound a note of definite pitch, why should not three or more drums be played together and produce a definite chord ? If the upper string parts could be sub-divided so as to provide separate groups of particular tone-colours, why should not double-basses be treated similarly ? If string instruments could play harmonics, why not make harmony of nothing but harmonics ? and so on,

[1] English translation (London, 1884).

through all the numerous unexplored by-paths of orchestral effect, Berlioz carried out his investigations, never failing to make use of each new idea that presented itself to his enquiring and original mind.

That so enterprising an orchestrator would not be content with any ordinary means of expression is hardly surprising. Thus, even apart from his monster works such as the *Requiem* and the *Te Deum*, Berlioz's scores demand orchestras which would be counted large even at the present time. Not less than fifteen first violins, and other strings in proportion, are demanded in several scores. Third flute, one or two piccolos, one or two *cors anglais*, bass clarinet, third and fourth bassoons, third and fourth trumpets, two cornets, ophicleide and tuba, three or more timpani, other percussion instruments and two or more harps, are amongst the extra instruments specified in some of his ordinary concert works ; while for certain occasions or special effects he demanded additional brass bands, choirs and orchestras, means far beyond the resources of even the most richly provided concert-giving institutions of his own time or of the present day. That Berlioz's ideas, his demands and technical requirements, frequently brought against him the opposition of authorities, conductors, and orchestral players, almost goes without saying. How he found the orchestras which he encountered in the course of his tours and musical ventures generally inadequate, crops up constantly in his own literary works. In his autobiography Berlioz laments that *cors anglais*, ophicleides, and harps were hardly to be found in German orchestras ; that the drummer in the Berlin orchestra was " only acquainted with one sort of drumstick," and that the cymbals were generally " cracked or chipped," are typical, but significant minor complaints. His views on the necessity for sectional rehearsals, on the careful placing of instrumentalists on the platform, and on an hundred details connected with orchestral performance and rendering, personnel and organization, reveal ideals and dreams of an exceptionally high standard of performance which must surely have been difficult or impossible to reach during his time, and which must have helped to make more bitter the life-long struggle of an ever stormy and strenuous career. Berlioz's scores, his literary works, and his book on instrumentation all call out for perfection in orchestral execution, for the best of everything, for performance, conditions and circumstances which are all but impossible to attain, and point to a mentality which regarded orchestral effect as a matter of supreme importance, and orchestration with almost religious fervour.

The period of Berlioz's activity as a composer, roughly 1825 to 1862, coincides with the period in which the wood-wind instruments gained their perfected key-mechanism, and horns and trumpets a workable valve-system, also with the introduction of cornets, and finally the tuba, into the orchestra. However, like all other composers of his time, Berlioz was not able to take full advantage of these benefits, for it was only very gradually, and not without opposition, that the new types of instruments came into use, and then only in some orchestras[1], so that their presence could not generally be relied on. Berlioz's scores show him still juggling with the open and stopped notes of natural horns crooked in many different keys, and using a pair of cornets in addition to two or four natural trumpets.

To do full justice to Berlioz's orchestration, to enumerate the innovations, to catalogue the effects and blends, the patterns and designs which go to make up his orchestral fabric would require a volume. His knowledge of the instruments and his thorough investigation of their technique, capabilities, and the possible uses to which they might be put, are set forth in his well-known text-book, and are put into practical form in his own works. Only some of the most general features of his work can be noticed here ; their full significance can only be gauged when compared to the work of his predecessors and contemporaries, and when it is remembered that even the major early works of Wagner were not begun till after Berlioz had written his *Symphonie Fantastique*, *Harold in Italy* and *Romeo and Juliet*, and that the former did not become popular till some time after Berlioz's death.

In the string orchestra Berlioz recognized not only one large group of cohesive tone-colour, but also many smaller groups, each perfect in blend and distinctive in tone-colour. The smaller choirs of violins, or of violas, of violoncellos, or even of double basses, are so many colours, distinct from one another,

---

[1] According to Berlioz's autobiography (Vol. II) valve horns and valve trumpets were used at Dresden about 1841-42, but not at the famous *Gewandhaus* concerts at Leipzig. Valve trumpets appear to have been fairly common in German orchestras at that time, but not in Paris where, however, cornets were becoming common. Berlioz found the tuba in use at Braunschweig and at Berlin.

forming yet more composite colours when mixed. As melodists all his string parts share an equal responsibility and enjoy equal importance, each type with its own colour, individuality and character, and when desirable, its own function. Even the difference of tone-quality on each string of the same instrument is appreciated and exploited. To Berlioz the viola was as distinctive and as important a voice as that of any other string instrument ; it was no mere harmonic drudge destined to do nothing but fill up the harmony in the tenor register. The different textures of string music, bow or finger *tremolo*, scale or arpeggio figuration ; the variety of high or low pitch, of *legato* or detached bowing, of single notes or double-stopping ; the varying colours of *pizzicato, con sordino* or *col legno ;* all these serve in their turn, in all dynamic shades, as colours or textures, separately or in combination, to make up the changing and vivid tints of Berlioz's string music.

Berlioz wrote for wood-wind with clear perception of the distinctive tone-colour, tone-weight, and natural character of each type. The individual technique of each instrument is recognized ; as soloists, melodically, decoratively, or as accompanists, their individuality, blending capabilities, and powers of penetration are ever kept in view. The accessory members of the wood-wind section are given a proper status ; piccolo, *cor anglais*, and bass clarinet stand out as individuals possessed of features which distinguish them from the normal group of instruments.

Berlioz's struggles to make natural horns act as chromatic instruments led him to crook the instruments in many and various keys ; frequently each of the four horns is crooked in a different key. Melodic phrases made up of open and stopped notes in haphazard alternation evidently did not please him, for his horn parts are generally more harmonic and rhythmical than melodic. The same applies to Berlioz's trumpet parts, but, writing, as he did, in the first place for Parisian orchestras, he made free use of a pair of cornets in addition to trumpets, and these are made to supply the missing notes in his upper brass harmony. In spite of his affection for the old instruments, Berlioz fully realized that valve instruments were the horns and trumpets of the future, and he readily welcomed the improved instruments which were being made in Paris by the younger Sax shortly before the mid-century.   By means of cornets, trombones and ophicleide, aided by ingenious management of the crooking and open notes of horns and trumpets, Berlioz managed to produce a thoroughly sonorous, full-voiced brass harmony ; this he employed with the utmost freedom, both as an independent body, and in conjunction with the rest of the orchestra. Possibly with Meyerbeer, Berlioz may share the credit of having been the first to fully realize the immense power and effect of trombones playing thematic matter in unison. In his hands the brass parts move independently on a course of their own ; their status is musically on an equality with the two other main groups of the orchestra, and their functions are more varied and more essential to the musical structure than they are in the works of any of his contemporaries, with the possible exception of Meyerbeer.

Despite his strange and unbalanced temperament, Berlioz was clear-headed and practical enough wherever orchestration was concerned. His scores and his book show that, although he gave constant attention to detail, the larger and more important matters, contrast, blend and balance of tone, were always in the forefront of his mind, and that a broad view of the subject was not obscured by the infinite care which he lavished on the most insignificant details. Berlioz kept the three main groups of the orchestra well separated ; their functions are not allowed to rob one another of their distinctive features, to cancel their individualities by being too constantly combined, or to develop into neutrality of tone-colour by over-blending. Thus, his contrasts are strong, clearly coloured and well spaced. No one realized better the value of allowing the elementary colours of the orchestra to make their own effect in their native state, or how to keep changes of colour in reserve, and under due restraint. Berlioz's blends are carefully thought out and are not used in routine-like manner. The conventional management of the loud *tutti* was a weak spot in the orchestration of nearly all his contemporaries, a weakness due partly to indifferent or bad balance of tone, and partly to monotony of treatment. Berlioz fully realized how necessary it was to duplicate a melodic or florid string part to the utmost extent in order that it should assert itself against heavy accompanying brass harmony. In this respect he forestalled Tschaikovsky and those of the later nineteenth century composers who were not content that their loud *tutti* should present to the ear nothing but a massive harmonic progression, although to the eye the written page showed plenty of movement. Again, Berlioz had no illusions as to the power of the wood-wind against sonorous, full matter on the strings.   If necessary he concentrated the full wood-wind section in octaves on one part, so that independent or essential matter should stand out clearly, and cut its way through the thick wall of string tone.   Nor did he make the common mistake of wasting precious wood-wind tone on unnecessary harmonic padding which only obscured the clearness of more important parts when there was any question of balance between the tone of wood-wind and strings.

It seems almost tragic that Berlioz's excellent orchestration was allied to music which did not, either in his own time or subsequently, go straight to the heart of either musicians or the public, and that, consequently, the influence of his wonderful example should have been so largely lost at a time when it would have been most valuable. If his ideas on orchestras were sometimes Utopian ; if his dreams of monster combinations were over–pretentious and a trifle inartistic ; and if there was apparently no satisfying his craving for immense resources, there is no question but that Berlioz delved deeper, and with more success, into the art of orchestration than did anyone before him and many after him.

The works of Louis Spohr (1784-1859), the violinist, composer and conductor, whose long period of activity covered the entire first half of the nineteenth century, and who was therefore a contemporary of both Beethoven and Berlioz, embrace every type of orchestral music, concerto and symphony, oratorio and opera.   Although Spohr's third opera (the first to be produced) was performed in 1810 and his first symphony the following year, his orchestration will be more fairly judged by his maturer works such as the opera *Jessonda* (1823), the oratorio *The Last Judgment* (1826), the Fourth Symphony, *The Consecration of Sounds* (1832), and the later works which he continued to produce until about 1850.

As would be expected from so earnest and thorough a musician, Spohr's handling of the orchestra is sound and practical, but it lacks the brilliance and bright colouring of the best contemporary French and Italian models.   Somewhat soberly coloured, smooth in blend and safe in effect, without being old-fashioned for its period, his work shows no great independence, nor any tendency to break away from the quite pleasing and satisfactory, but somewhat dull respectability of the lesser Germans whose time falls between those of Beethoven and Wagner.   That Spohr wrote of Berlioz's work[1] " I have a special hatred of this eternal speculating upon extraordinary instrumental effect ", gives sufficient clue to his attitude towards progressive orchestration.

As in the case of Spohr, the works of Jakob Ludwig Felix Mendelssohn-Bartholdy (1809–1847) met with immediate acceptance the moment they were produced. The great popularity of Mendelssohn's music, both during and after his lifetime, acted so as to set up his orchestration as a model for most German, and for many other composers, during the period which had to elapse before the works of Liszt and Wagner became sufficiently popular to exert a noticeable and general influence on the orchestration of other composers. The Mecca of Mendelssohn's followers was the *Gewandhaus* at Leipzig, the spiritual home of many lesser Germans, such as David, Hiller, Rietz, Reinecke, and not a few foreigners, of whom the best remembered are probably William Sterndale Bennett (1816–1875) and Niels Gade (1817–1890).

Mendelssohn's environment and opportunities during boyhood favoured the cultivation of a practical knowledge of the orchestra even before he had written any of the works by which he is now known to us. These may be said to have begun with the first Symphony in C Minor (1824), and to have ended with *Elijah* in 1846. There is no sign of inexperience or want of confidence in the orchestration of either the first Symphony or the " Trumpet " overture (1825), while with the *Midsummer Night's Dream* overture (1826) the young composer at once proved himself not only merely competent, but adept at presenting his music in most attractive orchestral clothing. There is little doubt that the production of Weber's *Der Freischütz* at Berlin in 1821 proved stimulating to the youthful Mendelssohn, but even allowing for that, it must be granted that the orchestration of his popular overture is remarkable for its fanciful and delicate colouring, and for an originality which places it amongst some of the most historically significant works. In making an estimate of the value of Mendelssohn's early orchestration, it should be remembered that he always continued to revise and polish his scores for a long time after their first production, and that, therefore, the details of his orchestration as we know them now from the printed scores are possibly to some extent the result of his maturer experience.

[1] Spohr, Autobiography, English translation, p. 311 (London, 1878).

In his string work Mendelssohn made use of a rather thicker harmonic texture than did his predecessors Beethoven and Weber, and was something of a pioneer in introducing the effect of low-lying harmonic figuration, mostly achieved by dividing the violoncellos, so as to pack the harmony notes close together in the lower register. This did not prevent him from treating the strings lightly, gracefully or brilliantly, as occasion required. Melodic violoncello parts are also a feature which he carried a stage further than his great predecessors.

The neatness and clean finish of Mendelssohn's wood-wind parts, and their importance in his scheme of orchestration, are well exemplified in the quick movements of his " Scottish " and " Italian " symphonies, and particularly in the *scherzo* from the *Midsummer Night's Dream* music (1843). While there is much that is mere harmonic padding in his wood-wind parts, especially in the *tutti*, he accompanied solo wood-wind parts, on the whole, clearly and effectively.

It seems as if a certain reverence for the classical model had proved a slight check on the development of freedom and flexibility in Mendelssohn's use of the brass instruments. The lack of trombones in most of the symphonies and concert-overtures certainly left his brass section harmonically more or less helpless, and although the horns are often allowed expressive melody, and the trumpet parts do occasionally include notes other than the open notes of the natural instrument, he seems to shrink from allowing the brass group to develop the fuller use of its melodic and harmonic capabilities in the way which is found in the scores of the French opera composers of the same period. One wonders why, if he could write a few chromatic notes for trumpets, he did not make much more free use of them to secure a more full-bodied brass harmony. Love of refinement, and dread of anything approaching vulgarity, no doubt proved the drag on the wheel of progress in this particular respect. In making frequent use of brass tone played very softly, Mendelssohn helped considerably to diffuse knowledge of that valuable effect.

The maintenance of a clear distinction between the colours of the three main groups of orchestral instruments is a sound feature of Mendelssohn's orchestration which keeps his contrasts of tone-colour clear and decided, in spite of his readiness to give the horns prolonged periods of holding sustained harmony notes against the movement of wood-wind and string parts. The balance and blending of tone, too, are carried out on sound, if somewhat set lines, and without ever showing signs of an independent investigation of the problems of balance of tone which was already in progress in quarters where reverence for classical models was not allowed to obscure practical considerations.

Some few effects in orchestration may possibly be Mendelssohn's invention, such as, for example, the rich tenor unison melody for both clarinets, both bassoons, and violoncellos in the *Ruy Blas* overture (1839), and some touches of colouring in the incidental music to *Midsummer Night's Dream* (1843) ; indeed, the orchestration of the latter work, with its fanciful colouring and effects, both picturesque and to the point, has served as a model for much fairy-orchestration ever since, and remains a tribute to Mendelssohn's imagination and originality when he was dealing with situations which required delicate and refined handling.

The work of Robert Alexander Schumann (1810-1856) as an orchestral composer falls almost entirely within the ten years 1841-1851, and provides one of the few instances in which a composer of the first rank, whose music has amply proved its worth, was unable to handle the orchestra even moderately well. It may be justly said of Schumann's orchestral music that it survives *in spite of its orchestration.*

Unlike many whose weak orchestration was obviously due to indifference, haste, or an easy satisfaction with the conventions of a particular period, Schumann's scores show no signs of lack of care or lack of interest in orchestration ; on the contrary, while there is no evidence of such weakness, there is every indication of considerable effort, of independence, and even of enterprise, in some of the very pages of his scores which are the despair of those conductors who would spare no amount of trouble in order to make Schumann's orchestral misfits sound reasonably clear and worthy, rather than that his music should be unheard. The gift of conceiving music in true orchestral language seems to have been denied this composer, and, what is perhaps rather more remarkable, he did not succeed in learning how to adapt his musical matter to the medium of the orchestra, even after some considerable experience and some excellent opportunities.

That much of his musical matter was of the neutral nature which was equally suitable, or equally unsuitable, to the character and technique of the various types of orchestral instruments,

and that he did not conceive themes and passages, patterns
and textures, which owe their very being to particular instruments
or groups of instruments, would not alone suffice to condemn
Schumann's orchestration, for a process of selection and translation could have been made to cloak neutrality or unsuitability
of matter, as they have often done in the hands of more skilful
workers ; it was rather that he seems to have lacked the instinct
which enables even moderately good orchestrators to place the
right matter in the right quarter, to distribute the parts where
they can take the most useful share in contributing to the effect
of the whole.   That his string passages should sometimes prove
awkward, ineffective, or lacking in variety, is not altogether
surprising, for Schumann's musical matter was largely based on
keyboard technique.   When movement was imperative, his only
resource was the quicker repetition of notes by means of the
bow.   Less excusable were his frequent failure to secure a satisfactory balance of tone between melodic and harmonic parts, and
least of all, his consistent neglect to let the primary colours of the
orchestra be heard in their native state, and in clear contrast
one with the other.   The continuously even tone quality, the full-
bodied but monotonously rich tint of his colouring, is due to the
employment of strings, wood-wind, and horns in constant combination.   It is difficult to credit the fact that any composer
could   score   not   only   complete   movements, but   a   whole
symphony and an overture, in which string tone is not allowed
to be heard in a pure unmixed state for a single bar ; yet
Schumann achieved that feat in his D minor symphony (1851)[1]
and in his overture *Hermann und Dorothea*.   The almost continuous *tutti* which persists, for example, throughout the greater
part of the E-flat symphony (1850), the constant thickening of
tone by the almost unbroken use of horns and wood-wind in
conjunction with the string orchestra, and his readiness to thicken
the tone of the lower register of the string orchestra by frequent
divisis or double-stopping ;   all these characteristics rob his
orchestration of clearness of colouring, and obscure the prominence of melodic parts or thematic matter in a way which renders
well-balanced performances of most of his works practically
impossible without recourse to troublesome and tireless readjustments of dynamics, and sometimes even actual rescoring or
redistribution of parts in order to secure some sort of satisfactory

[1] Originally composed in 1841, but rewritten and issued in 1851.

balance.[1] A typical instance of Schumann's seeming inability to let the strings play without thickening interference by the wood-wind occurs at the beginning of the slow movement of the D minor symphony. Here is a pleasing melody for violoncellos and oboe, fitted with a perfectly well-chosen simple harmonic *pizzicato* accompaniment for strings, but blurred and spoilt by absolutely redundant duplication of the harmony on clarinets and bassoons. The otherwise clearly differentiated colour of melodic and harmonic parts, thus welded together by the cloying medium of clarinet and bassoon tone, is reckoned by some conductors to be an error of judgment sufficiently grave to justify their cutting out these wind parts altogether when the opening of the movement is played. This is only one of many instances where the same drastic treatment would—and sometimes does—clarify and let air and daylight into the stuffy interior of Schumann's orchestral combinations.

To his credit may be placed Schumann's enterprise in readily adopting valve horns and valve trumpets at a fairly early stage of their development,[2] his more freely melodic use of these same instruments, and a certain disregard for some of the conventional effects which, amongst his German contemporaries, were becoming rather dulled by repetition. These virtues, however, can hardly be said to have atoned for Schumann's responsibility in having inaugurated a style of orchestration which, by its heavy neutral-tinted example, unfortunately influenced the work of many of his German successors, and justly earned for itself such epithets as " turgid " and " muddy."

Of the German opera composers of this period, the best of whose works still hold the stage, Konradin Kreutzer (1780-1849), Heinrich August Marschner (1795-1861), Gustav Albert Lortzing (1801-1851), and Otto Nicolai (1810-1849) may be said to have upheld in slightly varying degree the standard and style of orchestration set in Germany as a pattern by the successes of Weber and Spohr. Kreutzer's *Nachtlager in Granada* (1834), Marschner's *Hans Heiling* (1833), Lortzing's *Der Waffenschmied* (1846) and Nicolai's *Die Lustigen Weiber von Windsor* (1849) stand as representative of the apt, dramatic, and clearly

---

[1] See Weingartner, Ratschläge für aufführungen Klassischer Symphonien, Band II (Leipzig, 1919).

[2] Valve instruments are specified in the first editions of the full scores of Schumann's 3rd and 4th symphonies, also in *Manfred* overture (1849).

coloured work of typical composers whose handling of the
orchestra was free from the noisy brilliance of contemporary
Italians, which lacked the rich colouring and pretentious style
of Meyerbeer, and was quite uninfluenced by the remarkable
advance made by Berlioz. If Kreutzer, Marschner, and Lortzing
did not venture far off the safe and beaten track, Nicolai did
show distinct signs of fanciful invention, and a tendency to import
a not unwelcome lightness into German orchestration, which
promise, unfortunately, was barely fulfilled owing to his early
death almost at the moment of his greatest success. The orchestration of the music to the ballet and fairy scenes of *Die Lustigen
Weiber*, particularly in the scene in Windsor forest when all
manner of insects are called upon to torment Falstaff, is quite
on a level with the best of Mendelssohn's fairy-orchestration,
and shows Nicolai in a most favourable light as an orchestrator.

More individual and, as it proved, more significant than the
work of these lesser Germans, was the beginning of an independent
school of orchestration in Russia in the hands of Michael
Ivanovitch Glinka (1803–1857), the first of a chain of nationalist
composers whose influence only began to take effect outside their
own country towards the close of last century.

Associated with music of markedly national character, and a
certain rough independence of technique, Glinka treated the
orchestra in a manner which apparently owed very little either to
his training or to the prevailing style of any other composer or
school of composers.[1]   The three main instrumental groups of the
orchestra were to Glinka so many distinct and self-contained
bodies whose functions should be clearly separated, and whose
colours should be used in sharp contrast with one another, rather
than as three parts of a whole whose individual characteristics
should be modified and toned down as far as possible by means of
combination, by intermixing and blending of tone-colours.

The use of elementary colours in their native state, separated
one from the other by clean lines of demarkation ;   clearly differentiated colours for the duties of defining the melodic line, the
harmonic background, or the decorative figure ;   opposition
rather than amalgamation ;   crudeness rather than subtlety ;

---

[1] Glinka's studies in orchestration are said to have been the scores of
overtures by Méhul, Cherubini, Mozart, Beethoven, and symphonies by
Haydn, Mozart and Beethoven.—From *A Short History of Russian Music*
by Pougin (London, 1915).

these were the articles of Glinka's orchestral faith, as against the more mixed colouring, the smoother transitions and more elaborate or congested textures of his German contemporaries. The simplicity of his colour-schemes left no room for ambiguity of intention, no doubt as to the easy distinction of melodic and accompanying parts, no question as to what he intended to stand out prominently, nor was there much chance of faulty or doubtful balance of tone in his straightforward manner of distributing the parts. While most of the Germans were inclined to over-blend their colours, Glinka kept his colours in clearly labelled separate compartments ; and thus began the divergence of the two lines which still distinguishes German from Russian characteristics in orchestration.

In Glinka's representative national opera *A Life for the Tsar* (1836), in his music to the tragedy *Prince Khomlsky* (1840), in his *Karaminskaya* and other orchestral works, will be found abundant examples of this transparently clear grouping of instrumental tone-colours, and the obvious beginning of the principle which required that each melodic line, harmonic group or figurated pattern, in his musical matter, should be allotted to and concentrated on widely different and opposing types of tone-colour, the principle which eventually proved to be the basis, and at the same time the strongest feature of Tschaikovsky's mature orchestration.[1]

---

[1] Berlioz on Glinka's orchestration : " the gift of a beautifully free, clear, and coloured orchestration."—*A Short History of Russian Music.*

CHAPTER XII

THE PERIOD OF WAGNER

By " the period of Wagner " must be understood that period during which Wagner wrote his mature and fully representative music dramas, that is, roughly, from about the middle of last century till the year of his death (1883). Although the beginning of Wagner's creative work as a composer may be placed as far back as 1833, and although *Rienzi, Der Fliegende Holländer, Tannhäuser* and *Lohengrin* were all composed and produced before the end of the year 1850, the most significant part of his output, that embracing *Tristan, Die Meistersinger, Der Ring des Nibelungen* and *Parsifal*, falls within the limits of the period defined above, as the following list of his works, and the years in which they were first produced, will show :

1834	*Die Feen*[1]	1865	*Tristan und Isolde*
1836	*Das Liebesverbot*	1868	*Die Meistersinger*
1842	*Rienzi*	1869	*Das Rheingold*
1843	*Der Fliegende Holländer*	1870	*Die Walküre*
1845	*Tannhäuser*	1876	*Siegfried, Götterdämmerung*
1850	*Lohengrin*	1882	*Parsifal*

In view of the great significance of his work, and of the powerful influence of his example on the history and development of orchestration, it is important to realize that it was not till his career was almost at an end that Wagner's works began to be universally accepted, admired and performed frequently enough to exert any pronounced and wide-spread influence on the orchestration of composers generally. This throws the period of his influence and its effects so far forward, that it may be said that the result of Wagner's work did not become apparent till the last quarter of last century.

Grouped not so much according to the span of their lives, but more according to the period in which their most important works were written, the following composers may be counted contemporaries of Wagner, yet they were, excepting Liszt,

---

[1] First performed in its entirety in 1888.

Cornelius, and Verdi in his last phase, practically pre-Wagnerian
orchestrators :

	Wagner, 1813-1883.		
Liszt,	Thomas,	Verdi,	Macfarren,
1811-1886.	1811-1896.	1813-1901.	1813-1887.
Flotow,	Gounod,	Rubinstein,	Sterndale Bennett,
1812-1883.	1818-1893.	1829-1894.	1816-1875.
Raff,	Bizet,	Smetana,	
1822-1882.	1838-1875.	1824-1884.	
Cornelius,		Gade,	
1824-1874.		1817-1890.	

It will be seen that while the main stream of progress in orchestration was flowing evenly onwards, more or less divided into
channels governed by national style, a radical change of direction
in the course of the art, although clearly laid down by Wagner,
was not generally followed by composers during his lifetime, nor
can it be said that his influence, although destined to become
very little short of all-powerful, was ever completely and absolutely
universal in its effect.

It was stated that the growth of the orchestra was practically
complete by about the middle of the nineteenth century. The
statement is correct as far as the constituent elements of the
orchestra are concerned. Four types of wood-wind instrument,
the flute type, the oboe type, the clarinet and bassoon types,
including in all cases both normal and abnormal sizes, together
with three types of brass instrument, horns, trumpets and trombones, also strings, percussion and harps, all these were either
regular or occasional constituents of the orchestra before the mid-
century ; it only remained for the tuba to finally oust the
ophicleide or serpent, these last lingering representatives of the
mediæval *cornetto* type, from their places. To this day the
orchestra has retained practically its mid-nineteenth-century
constitution, and, as far as its primary colours are concerned,
has ceased to grow. Growth of another sort, however, growth in
bulk, in number of instruments, growth involving additional
quantities of the already established primary tone-colours, was still
to come. Foreshadowed in the scores of Berlioz and Meyerbeer,
this bulk-expansion of the orchestra developed further during the
period of Wagner, and, largely owing to his lead, the expanded
orchestra became more or less standardized, during the last two
or three decades of the century, for works of large scale. When

Wagner demanded three or four of each type of wood-wind instrument, when he wrote for eight horns, for three or four trumpets, for a bass trumpet, for contra-bass trombone, for contra-bass tuba, for more drums and extra harps, he was not adding to the constituent elements of the orchestra ; he was really only asking for an increased number of instruments, or greater volume of tone from each of the already established groups. It was not so much new colour as increased quantity, or greater display of surface of the old colours, that he demanded. But when Wagner asked for a quartet of so-called Wagner-tubas, instruments of tuba-like proportions fitted with conical mouth-pieces of the horn pattern, he certainly attempted to add a new element to the orchestral body, and, as has since been proved, failed to do so. Wagner's service to the orchestra, as far as its constitution is concerned, and quite apart from his service to the cause of orchestration, was to inflate the old body rather than to add any new element to it.

The resources of orchestration gained much during the period of Wagner from the gradually increasing use of wood-wind instruments provided with the radically improved key mechanism for which Böhm was so largely responsible. As the new instruments found their way into the hands of orchestral players, the greater technical facilities, the truer intonation, and wider key-range of the new patterns naturally contributed towards creating a higher standard of quality in wood-wind instrument playing, which, with the growing use of valved brass instruments, rendered the wind section of the orchestra more and more flexible and independent. It was during this period that the contest between the valved and the natural horns and trumpets began in real earnest. The question then became not so much whether valved instruments were a desirable *addition* to the orchestra, but whether they were desirable as *substitutes* for the natural instruments. At the same time the early conception of the use of the valve, namely, that its purpose was simply to effect an instantaneous change of crook, gave way to the modern conception that the real use of the valve was to render the scale of the instrument completely chromatic. In spite of unanswerable argument and practical demonstration in favour of the valve, the old instruments and their characteristic technique died hard, and can hardly be said to have become obsolete during Wagner's lifetime. It is evident that even after that time the old horn technique had left a lasting impression on the style of part associated with the instrument, an impression which still lingers. In the course of its victorious career the valve to a large extent conduced to the gradual disuse of the crook, but it was not till some considerable time after the players had decided that it was once more practicable to play with as little change of crook as possible, that composers, realizing that their specified changes of crook were doomed to be ignored, finally fell into line with the actual practice of the players.

The progress and development of orchestration from about the middle of last century up to the end of Wagner's time may be conveniently followed along the following channels :

1. The advanced German group, summed up in Wagner and Liszt.

2. Other Germans who placidly followed the lines of Mendelssohn and other composers of the " Gewandhaus " school, connecting with a later group represented by Brahms and his imitators.

3. The French operatic group, with well-marked national characteristics.

4. Italians, notably Verdi, in continuation of the typical work of the former Italian generation.

In addition to these, there are other channels which, although for the time being they produced no very marked result, were destined to become influential just at the close of the century. Of these the Russian school inaugurated by Glinka, in spite of the western tendency of some of its prominent members, may be counted as the most important.   English composers of the period, largely following the paths of the mid-century Germans, and showing no marked individuality or enterprise in their orchestration, served as a link to connect up with the more significant work of later generations ; and finally the appearance on the scene of fresh nationality, such as the Bohemian Smetana and the Scandinavian Gade, should not be altogether overlooked in view of the subsequent popular success of such strongly national composers as Dvořák and Grieg.

Without touching on the very early works of Wilhelm Richard Wagner (1813-1883), the few operas and overtures composed before 1840, his orchestration may be considered as exemplified in two groups of music dramas : those which appeared between 1840 and 1850, and the works of his maturity, ranging from *Tristan* to *Parsifal*.

The operas Wagner would hear in his early manhood, which in his capacity of conductor he would direct and become familiar with, no doubt provided him with a foundation on which to base his own earlier efforts in orchestration. If it can be said that he took any composers' works as models, or that his early orchestration was influenced and his efforts stimulated by example, the operas of Weber, Marschner, Halévy and Meyerbeer may be cited as most likely to appeal to his taste for dramatic force and colouring in orchestration. Whether he owed most to the example of others, or to his own early experiences as conductor and composer, is a problem which can hardly be solved with any certainty ; the fact remains that in the score of *Rienzi*, Wagner showed himself not only fully equipped as an orchestrator, but already well abreast of the most advanced tendencies up to date, having nothing to learn even from Meyerbeer. The overtures to *Rienzi, Der Fliegende Holländer, Tannhäuser* and *Lohengrin* alone suffice to illustrate his mastery over all hitherto known orchestral effects, and how he used, with the ease of familiarity, and had even amplified, all the most recent and daring developments of orchestration before they had become absorbed in the current language of progressive contemporary composers' work.

The vertical structure of his harmony is at once on a large scale, rich in tone by the sheer number of different notes sounded at the same time, the parts placed so as to produce a full and sonorous volume of tone, whether in loud or in soft effects. This ample and widely spread harmonic structure is applied to all sections of the orchestra, and gives the rich quality of tone, now so familiar, which distinguishes a Wagner chord in the orchestra from a chord as placed by Beethoven or Mendelssohn.

Amongst the features of the string work are, the frequent use of melodic parts doubled in unison or in octaves, and the occurrence of the short figures in quick notes so often used to provide the web of movement which frequently accompanies bolder thematic matter on the brass voices. When eighteenth century composers used the string-unison it was because it was not their habit to trouble much about writing inner parts ; with Wagner it was a matter of balance and intensity of tone ; it was the modern unison used consciously of its effect, as against the old-fashioned casual unison of the older masters. The characteristic " turning " demi-semiquaver figures in *Rienzi*, the groups of six quavers in the *Holländer* and *Tannhäuser*, the familiar semi-quaver figure in the overture of the latter opera, are well-known instances of what Wagner did with his strings in the *tutti* when the brass in unison took entire charge of thematic matter. For brilliance and fullness Wagner took his first and second violins high up, and in that sense extended their upward compass for orchestral purposes. Like Berlioz, he made his violas either soprano, tenor or bass instruments, as dictated by questions of balance of tone, or used them for the sake of their own individual tone-colour. Wagner's violoncellos are, more than ever before, melodists, and as such frequently invade the old preserves of the upper strings, either alone or in order to act as a reinforcement of tone for the purposes of intensity or balance. The high-pitched harmonic groups of divided violins, disposed in either solo or *ripieno* groups, or in both together, the sombre combinations of divided violas or violoncellos, all used less for the sake of their pitch than for their particular tone-colours, are no rarities in these earlier Wagner scores, but are employed freely and familiarly, also without any hesitation in taking the pitch to either extreme. Finger-tremolo becomes in Wagner's hands a resource as common as was bow-tremolo to his forbears.

With his groups of three of each type of wood-wind instrument, and his tendency to treat bassoons harmonically as tenor instruments, to be used for inside parts rather than merely as the bass voices of the group, Wagner, even in these earlier works, secured an opulence of harmonic tone on the wood-wind alone which the earlier nineteenth century composers often failed to achieve when they called up the services of their brass voices as well. As melodists the wood-wind figure as soloists pure and simple, well selected from the point of view of their character and technique, and when handled as melodists in a body receive the necessary duplication which alone can help them to cope with the greater tone-weight of the other sections of the orchestra.

Starting as he did by writing for one pair of valve-horns and one pair of hand-horns, Wagner made the best of an awkward situation by causing his third and fourth hand-horns to dodge about, giving useful harmonic and melodic help to the first and second valve-horns whenever it was possible (much in the same manner as Berlioz did with his natural trumpets and cornets) stretching the hand-horn technique to its utmost limits in the process. With *Lohengrin*, however, he seems to have finished with the compromise, and, in spite of the strange vagaries

of his notation for horns in that opera, had evidently decided once
and for all that the valve-horn was the instrument of the future.
If the nature of the third and fourth horns in Wagner's earlier
works may be disputed, there can be no possible doubt that his
trumpets were valve instruments, although it is true, parts for
natural third and fourth trumpets are specified in *Rienzi*. With
trombones, ophicleide or tuba, valve-horns and valve-trumpets,
Wagner's brass group was virtually a completely chromatic brass
band, and any concessions made to natural instruments are
clearly nothing more than rather annoying necessities.

Practically unhampered by the want of notes in any part of
his brass group, Wagner's parts for these instruments appear
disposed either in complete and satisfying harmony, or the instruments speak as frankly unrestricted melodists. When in
harmony the parts are judiciously grouped, and the whole is amply
filled up with inner parts, care being taken that all the essential
notes of a chord are well represented. The awkward gaps in the
brass harmony of his predecessors finally disappeared when valve
instruments began to be freely employed ; this gave to the heavy
harmony of the orchestra a substantial " inside " such as it had
never known before. When using his brass voices as melodists,
in octaves or in unison, Wagner at once brushed away the last
remnant of any such restraint as still lingered even in the scores
of Berlioz and Meyerbeer. The loud unison parts for three trumpets and three trombones, so well exemplified in the close of
Tannhäuser overture, the various brass-unison themes in the
Holländer and in *Lohengrin*, to mention only familiar examples,
show how well Wagner appreciated the telling power of the
heavier brass instruments when playing in unison, how fearlessly he made use of the device, and also his sound sense in
not allowing the clearness of their utterance to be clogged by
harmonic accompaniments played by other brass voices of equal
power and penetration. It would have been not only possible,
but also much more conventional, to have given the main theme
at the close of *Tannhäuser* overture to trumpets and trombones in *harmony* instead of in *unison* ; the difference of effect
can easily be imagined.

That Wagner was fully alive to the advantages of treating the
orchestra as a compound of so many instrumental choirs is well
illustrated in the prelude to *Lohengrin*. The constitution of
each group, and the order of their entry, is well worth careful

examination : bar 5, violins only ; bar 20, all the wood-wind ; bar 36, horns and lower strings ; bar 45, trombones and tuba ; bar 50, trumpets and drums. Again, it is easy to imagine the effect of this piece scored in groups of mixed types, or in groups based on the difference of pitch rather than on their tone-colour and tone-weight.

In spite of the blatant brass work in the *Rienzi* overture, Wagner knew well how to keep his effects and colours in reserve, and how to contrive that a climax should be unmistakable ; witness the reserve of the trumpets and extra percussion instruments in *Tannhäuser* overture. Many other features of Wagner's earlier orchestration might be noticed ; the strong reinforcement of inner melodic parts when they are required to be prominent ; the avoidance of conventional formulæ for the orchestration of *tutti*, and so on.

Although it can hardly be said of any of the devices employed in those of Wagner's scores which appeared before 1850 that he actually created them, or that no suggestion or lead had been given him by other composers' works of somewhat earlier or of contemporary date, there is no question but that he seized on every suggestive device and, without apparent experiment, at once produced the consummative result at which others had more or less tentatively aimed. The finished production shows no signs of hesitation, timidity, or reluctance to embark on an unfamiliar path ; on the contrary, he planted his feet firmly wherever he wished to tread, and fearlessly and wholeheartedly embarked on " neck or nothing " adventures with a faith attended by no doubts, with no scruples, and achieved his ends without using any half-measures. If an effect was to be produced, Wagner depended on it absolutely ; he burned his boats and left open no means of retreat. The passages embodying unconventional orchestration are by no means short, nor did he employ an effect only once in case it should not " come off " well.

Fifteen years after the production of *Lohengrin* at Weimar, *Tristan und Isolde* was produced under von Bülow at Munich. *Die Meistersinger, Rheingold*, and the other operas comprising *Der Ring des Nibelungen*, followed at comparatively short intervals, the *Ring* in its entirety being first performed at Bayreuth in 1876.[1]

---

[1] It is hardly necessary to point out that *Das Rheingold* and *Die Walküre* were composed before *Tristan* and *Die Meistersinger*.

For *Tristan* and *Die Meistersinger* Wagner used approximately the same instruments as for *Lohengrin*, but for the vaster undertaking, which comprised four full-sized operas conceived and staged on a scale never attempted before, the orchestra specified demands still further additions to the already enlarged groups, also a group of tubas organized so as to provide self-contained harmony amongst themselves. Four each of the flute, oboe and clarinet types, and three bassoons are required in the scores of the *Ring* ; eight horns, four of which were at times to be replaced by two tenor and two bass tubas, a contrabass tuba, three trumpets and a bass trumpet, four trombones, including a contrabass trombone, two pairs of timpani with sundry other percussion instruments, six harps and some stage instruments, in addition to strings specified as sixteen first violins, sixteen second violins, twelve violas, twelve violoncellos and eight double basses, make up the huge palette of orchestral colours that Wagner employed to paint the colossal picture of which the dramatic basis was no personal, local or historical affair, but the great universal story of northern mythology. All horns, trumpets, and tubas were to be valve instruments ; piccolos carried the range of sound higher, and *cor anglais*, bass clarinet, and if necessary a double bassoon, extended the range of the various wood-wind lower ; harps were fully chromatic, and strings were there in sufficient numbers to sub-divide into smaller orchestras, groups or sections.

Not only the musical matter and the technique at his command, but also the orchestration of all Wagner's operas composed after *Lohengrin*[1], show a maturity of style which can hardly have developed suddenly during the two or three years which passed between the production of *Lohengrin* and the composition of *Das Rheingold*. The experience of orchestrating, and of hearing what he did hear of his earlier operas, must have been working on his mind during the years of struggle, and finally banishment, which followed the production of *Tannhäuser* in 1845. Nevertheless, whatever the process, if the printed scores as we now have them of *Das Rheingold* and *Die Walküre* are what Wagner actually wrote in 1854-56, the sum of the development must indeed be counted remarkable. Remarkable also is the reflection that *Tristan* and

---

[1] Wagner did not actually hear *Lohengrin* till 1861.

Die Meistersinger were composed before Wagner had had the experience of hearing *Das Rheingold* and *Die Walküre* performed.

In association with a finer-wrought musical matter, the orchestration of *Tristan* and *Die Meistersinger* seems wonderfully mellowed and ripe when compared with that of the composer's earlier works. All the rather blatant noisiness, the brass-band effects, the more tawdry brilliance and sharp-edged contrasts of *Rienzi,* are softened down into more plastic and less crude changes of colour. The sensuous yearnings of the lovers in *Tristan* are accompanied by sounds and blends which melt into one another over less easily perceptible boundaries. The string parts in the same opera are more complex, less easy to separate into either melodic or accompanying matter, often made up of tiny phrases whose function it is to unite in forming a tissue of movement in which every part cannot be, and is not intended to be distinctly heard, a moving texture of sound, the constituents of which act co-operatively rather than individually. Wood-wind and horn parts weave themselves into the fabric without proclaiming their entries, and may be discovered when their presence was unsuspected. Brass voices grow into the music rather than plunge into it ; the subtleties of *crescendo* and *diminuendo* in individual parts, and the gradual addition of parts, replace the well-marked group-entries of *Lohengrin* and the earlier works. In *Die Meistersinger* the string-work is likewise finely worked, more contrapuntal and more refined in conception, the blends of wind-instruments more intense, and welded together by less obvious means.

For all the subtle and more involved management of his tone-colours in the orchestration of these two operas, Wagner did not lose sight of the fact that there were three main groups of instrumental colour in the orchestra, and that over-prolonged blending of mixed groups must in the end conduce to monotony. Pure string-tone is given its opportunity, and may be heard unmixed ; the brass group is a rich-voiced body, but not an open-air band. With *Tristan* and *Die Meistersinger* Wagner seems to have completely finished with whatever he may have learned from the orchestration of Meyerbeer and others ; after using them, he had discarded their moulds and patterns, and worked with what he himself had evolved. His very musical conception no longer fitted the setting of the spectacular, the showy and gaudy orchestration, which may have served a purpose in giving him a sure hand and an ear for sumptuous effect.

In *Der Ring des Nibelungen* Wagner painted with a broader brush. The colours of his choice were not only provided in greater quantity, but were spread more boldly over vaster surfaces than in the two operas with which he interrupted his work on the *Ring*. The wood-wind group was capable of sounding fifteen notes at the same time, and could provide four smaller but complete instrumental choirs of quite homogeneous tone-colour. The horns and wood-wind combined placed at his disposal twenty-three parts. Brass instruments could be made to sound in four complete and independent choirs, or to unite in a body of seventeen parts ; the wind-band alone could be displayed over a range of about seven octaves, sounding in thirty-two parts. The string orchestra, with a similar range, could play in almost any number of parts, or in numerous smaller groups. To carry on the reckoning *ad extremum*, Wagner could have written for this orchestra in over one hundred parts, or, without mixing tone-colours, for about seventeen complete instrumental choirs. If the possibilities of blending or mixing these tone-colours or groups of tone-colours, and all the variety that technique, texture and dynamics could provide were to be taken into account, the services of a professional computator would be necessary in order to enumerate the shades, tints and colour-schemes at the disposal of the sound-painter who was equipped as was Wagner when he decided on the constitution of the orchestra with which he wished to present *Der Ring des Nibelungen*.

While most of the distinctive and characteristic features of the orchestration met with in *Tristan* and *Die Meistersinger* are also to be found in the *Ring*, there is a certain largeness of manner in the handling of the instrumental masses which distinguishes the scores of the cyclical operas from those of the two separate works. The changes of colour are more broadly spaced, and the treatment of instruments in groups of the same tone-colour is much more pronounced. The association of particular dramatic situations, characters, and even scenes, with particular instrumental combinations, is carried out more consistently and on a grander scale.

Group orchestration in the *Ring* is a prominent feature which can hardly escape even casual observation. The complete groups made up of each type of wood-wind tone are not so

thoroughly exploited as are those made up of pure brass tone ;
yet the clarinet group often figures alone in harmonic combination,
and the three bassoons are frequently called on to provide
unobtrusive harmonic backgrounds. Taking the wood-wind as a
body, Wagner's tendency was to group the flutes, oboes, and
clarinets in their various sizes together, but to ally bassoons with
horns. In the larger sustained harmonic combinations the
horns are generally associated with the entire wood-wind group.

The grouping of the brass instruments is much more distinctive
and less mixed. The following occur frequently and consistently :
four horns ; four tubas and contrabass tuba ; trumpets (or bass
trumpet) and trombones ; four trombones ; four trombones and
contrabass tuba. All these are used in not less than four, and
often in five, six, or seven parts, alternating one with the other,
each in its native state, or overlapping or combining to form mixed
groups. Of the various string groups the following are common :
violins alone (divided) ; violins and violas ; violas and
violoncellos ; a very distinctive group comprising a solo violoncello,
four violoncello parts and a double-bass part, the desks being
reduced in number in the case of the *ripieno* parts.

Of prolonged colour-schemes compounded of more or less
mixed tone-colours, and with instruments playing parts of set
patterns, many examples will readily occur. The prelude to
Das Rheingold shows a bold experiment both as regards
musical matter and orchestration : a chord of E-flat represents
the sole harmony, and there is no actual melody ; above a pedal
bass-note played by bassoons and string basses, the eight horns
intertwine their tones round the chord of E-flat in ceaseless movement ; the whole prelude is simply a matter of movement and
tone-colour. Again, the last scene of the same opera shows a
design, complex in pattern yet simple in harmony, in which no
less than twenty string parts mingle their arpeggio figures in one
composite mass of pure movement, joined later on by six harps
all playing in different arpeggios. The string texture made up of
legato arpeggios across the four strings of each instrument, which
occurs just before the end of Act I of *Die Walküre*, must have
been something novel at the time, although the same idea in
elementary form was not an uncommon feature of orchestral
string-technique in the time of Bach and Handel. The patterns
which make up the moving backgrounds to the main melodic
matter in the music which accompanies most of the *Ride of the*

Valkyries, and in the *Fire-music* at the end of the same opera, afford well-known examples of those set patterns, compounded of figurative movement and tone-colour, which form the accompanying matter to brass-unison themes, a type of orchestration which Wagner made quite his own.

In the orchestration of the *Ring* the brass-unison (or octaves) again plays an important part. The heroic nature of so many of the themes called for treatment by brass-unison in frequency such as does not occur in either *Tristan* or *Die Meistersinger*. Trumpets, bass trumpet and trombones, also horns and tubas, even contrabass tuba and trombone, in two, three or more duplications, and in various grades of force, all take part in the significant unison themes which stand out with such overwhelming clearness above the moving masses of accompanying matter. The secret of their irresistible power of penetration lies in the fact that they are unhampered by the presence of harmonic matter on other instruments of equal tone-weight. For the handling of large masses of tone-colour, for brass harmony of gorgeous intensity, for bigness of effect and majesty of movement, *Götterdämmerung* sums up the matter and the manner of Wagner's mature orchestration when he was occupied with the destinies of creatures elemental and non-human. Gods and goddesses, heroes and heroines, gnomes of the underworld, Rhinemaidens, valkyries, giants, dragons, magic swords, shields, and all the rest, demanded accompanying sounds on a more colossal scale, more vivid and massive, than the ecstasies of human lovers or the humours of mediæval pedantry ; and they got it in orchestration in Wagner's *Der Ring des Nibelungen*.

When contemplating the opulence and massiveness of Wagner's mature orchestration in the *Ring*, it is not inopportune to recollect that the same hand which painted with such broad sweeps of the brush in the cyclic operas, also designed the delicate line-drawing of the *Siegfried Idyll*.

For his last work, *Parsifal* (1882), Wagner reduced the number of brass instruments in his orchestra to more ordinary dimensions, but retained the groups of four of all the wood-wind, except the flutes ; the demand for extra trumpets, trombones, and bells on the stage, however, brings the total instrumental forces required quite up to the strength of the huge orchestra of the *Ring*.

The nature of the drama in *Parsifal* called for orchestration less stirring or vivid than the story of the *Ring* ; thus it is that the fiery energy of so many characteristic scenes in the *Ring* finds no counterpart in the more smooth and solemn handling of the orchestra in the semi-religious music-drama. When solo voices are concerned, the orchestration in *Parsifal* largely presents the same features as that of Wagner's other mature works ; but when in association with scenic action or choral effects, the orchestration of *Parsifal* has a massive and dignified character of its own, in which group-orchestration takes a most important part. The nature of the themes, their harmonic conception and association with religious feeling, bring into great prominence the antiphonal treatment of instrumental groups, all rich in tone but varied in tone-colour, yet clearly separated, and distinct in their entries. The brass-unison is again exploited to the full ; the differences in pitch and colour of string and wood-wind groups or sub-groups, the weaving of figurated harmonic backgrounds, and all the features of the *Ring*, except its ruggedness and fiery brilliance, make their appearance in *Parsifal*, with the same wealth of tone and confidence in their effect, but with an added atmosphere of calmer solemnity.

Allowing for all that Meyerbeer, or even Berlioz, had done and were doing for orchestration just when Wagner was beginning his career, it cannot be disputed that, when he died in 1883, Wagner left to all succeeding composers a legacy in the form of an orchestral language made much more rich by his own expansion of its vocabulary, than by that which he owed to either his own immediate predecessors or his contemporaries. In providing a satisfying wealth of tone and judicious distribution of parts in every section or sub-section of the orchestra, in weaving figurated textures of mere movement, in fully developing the melodic capacities of each brass instrument, in successfully blending and grouping the instruments, and in balancing tone-power, Wagner gave more than he owed. It is impossible to suppose that without the example of his work, orchestration could have reached the stage of development at which composers found it towards the close of the nineteenth century.

Foremost amongst the sympathizers with and advocates of Wagnerian principles must be counted Franz Liszt (1811-1886). Not only by his enthusiasm and practical propagandism, but also as a composer who met with considerable popular success, did Liszt help to spread the tenets of advancing orchestration at a time when its path was by no means unobstructed.

Liszt's most important orchestral works, the symphonic poems, fall roughly within the period of his activity at Weimar (1848-1859) ; to the end of this period belong his *Faust* and *Dante* symphonies, the oratorios *The Legend of St. Elisabeth* and *Christus*, and similar choral-orchestral works.

Liszt's principles in orchestration followed those of Wagner in that they were progressive, richly coloured and sonorous ; to these he added a showy brilliance of his own, and a somewhat perilous dependence on purely superficial orchestral effect. The grouping of his tone-colours is well-contrasted, excellently clear, yet obvious in design ; his readiness to exploit all new devices is patent in all his scores, and it is more in the different texture of his musical matter, than in intention, that his orchestral effects differ from those of Wagner. Strings, wood-wind, and brass are given clearly differentiated functions ; groups are harmonically satisfying and well blended, and the free use and power of the brass-unison against string figuration is thoroughly appreciated. The lack of continuous symphonic development—this in spite of his " transformation of themes "—brings about changes of colour or design in the orchestration which are always well devised, but are inclined to be rather regular or square-cut in their incidence, while his lack of contrapuntal skill induces much obvious harmonic padding in the parts. Certain elaborate designs, such as, for example, the divided string parts about the middle of *Mazeppa* (1858), suggest that Liszt sometimes allowed musical matter to grow out of orchestral effect, rather than orchestral effect out of musical matter.

For all his evident desire to dazzle and please by means of brilliant colouring, to Liszt cannot be denied the credit of having very considerably helped to impart a glow of warmth and colour into orchestration at a time when so many German and Austrian composers were content to follow a path of undistinguished dullness.

Of the other Germans of the period whose work shows any clear signs of their having profited by the forward impulse given to orchestration by Wagner and Liszt, it must suffice to mention Peter Cornelius (1824-1874), a composer whose *Der Barbier von Bagdad* (1858) and *Der Cid* (1865) show more enterprise in orchestration than is found in the average work of contemporary Germans, but less than is shown in the scores of the greater man who so largely overshadowed Cornelius' fame. The brass group in Cornelius' scores is full-toned and chromatic, but is not granted the duty of uttering thematic matter to the extent one would expect from a disciple of the advanced Weimar school. Orchestrally, Cornelius may be placed at a point midway between the two representative German types of the period—Wagner and Raff.

The other side of the story of orchestration in Germany and Austria during the period of Wagner's activity brings up a large number of composers' names whose works have by now suffered almost complete, and possibly permanent eclipse. The names of Raff, Hiller, Volkmann and Reinecke must act as a representative few at the top of a list of composers who, in descending scale, gradually reach down to the level of what are sometimes described as composers of *kapellmeister-musik*.

Joseph Joachim Raff (1822-1882) may be taken as adequately representative of this brand of German composer whose orchestration was based on what has already been dubbed the " Gewandhaus school ", but was harmonically rather fuller in tone. This was the standard style of orchestration in Germany and Austria before the influence of Wagner began to take effect. It was a style safe and quite agreeable ; it was orchestration which cannot fairly be described as bad or even poor. The brass tone is richer than in Mendelssohn's work, for valve instruments were then beginning to assert their harmonic superiority, and trombones were more freely used in concert works ; there is much doubling of string and wood-wind parts, and monotony is aggravated by a constant thickening by dull horn parts in the middle of the structure. The wood-wind too frequently supply only harmonic versions of more active string parts, and the prolonged use of string, wood-wind and horn-tone together, gives a smooth but tedious tone-quality to long stretches of the music. The clearness of wood-wind solo and melodic parts is often blurred by unnecessary harmonic padding on other wood-wind instruments, while brass parts are usually featureless and weak in thematic interest. The treatment generally is unenterprising and lacks clear colouring. The music itself usually lacks the contrapuntal interest of Mendelssohn's musical matter, also his lightness of touch. Conventional treatment of *tutti* is another concomitant of this worthy but uninteresting school of orchestration, which apparently borrowed some of the least attractive features from Schumann's, and lost some of the most attractive features of Mendelssohn's example.

Another German composer, although in lighter style, whose span of life almost exactly corresponds with that of Wagner, was Friedrich von Flotow (1812–1883). His earlier and most successful operas, *Alessandro Stradella* (1844) and *Martha* (1847), show orchestration more French than German in style, admirable in its clearness, and not without the briskness and brilliance of the best Italian models.

In contrast to the work of the lesser Germans of the same time, French composers' orchestration during the period of Wagner became more than ever strongly nationalized in style ; it shows its most attractive features consolidated, and will be well exemplified,in the work of a generation of French composers which will be readily recognized by the mention of three names : Charles Louis Ambroise Thomas (1811-1896), Charles François Gounod (1818-1893), and Alexandre César Léopold Georges Bizet (1838-1875).

The work of their progressive predecessor Berlioz was practically without effect on the orchestration of this group. The process by means of which this French style of orchestration grew into maturity can be traced from the days of Rameau, or even of Lulli, not, it is true, without vicissitudes, nor without admitting the help and influence of alien hands at various times, but nevertheless as a continuous history which, by the third quarter of the nineteenth century, had crystallized into a manner of treating the orchestra which is typically French, or, it might quite justly be said, which is typically Parisian. At this time French orchestration discarded some of the noisy brilliance associated with the work of the earlier nineteenth century Italians whose work to some extent had centred in Paris ; it now flourished entirely on its own root, having owed a certain amount of its earlier nourishment to Italian,. possibly a little to Viennese, but least of all to German sources. The sum of the process was a graceful and attractive style in which clear, transparent colouring is the main feature which distinguishes it from the heavier and more thick-toned work of the lesser Germans of the same period.

The German tendency to continually combine tone-colours, to mix or blend instrumental voices or groups, finds its antithesis in the work of these French opera composers. The clearness of their colouring comes from the use of orchestral voices in their native state, without constant admixture of allied or alien tone-colours. Whether as individuals or in groups, the instruments show their own particular tone-colours in clear-cut contrast to accompanying or contextual matter. The boundaries between melodic and accompanying parts, also between contiguous phrases or subjects, are clearly defined, and unambiguous in choice of tone-colour. To that readiness to trust to the elementary colours of the orchestra, rather than to tone-blending schemes or overwrought textures, do these French composers owe the chief charm of their orchestration. Where the German would combine strings, wood-wind and horns at the same moment, and on the same musical matter, the Frenchman would rather let each be heard one after the other, or if together, he would clearly segregate their functions. A simple musical structure, together with the native grace and rather lighter charm of their musical material, emphasizes this tendency in favour of segregation rather than of combination. Thus, while the contemporary German score is apt to be evenly and only too well filled with notes, the French score shows more uneven distribution of notes, more empty bars, more clearly defined entries, and the harmony, although quite full, is not so often supplied in duplicate by different groups of instruments.

Certain characteristics of this French school deserve particular, although not necessarily in every case favourable, mention. Their piquant treatment of the wood-wind instruments melodically, their light, but quite adequate, string accompanying figures and designs, are certainly entries on the credit side. The horn parts show that, on the whole, hand-horn technique still held good amongst French players at the time, and indeed, had still to endure for some time before valve-technique was to be fully recognized. In their scores we find cornets taking a more definite place in the orchestra, not so much as additions to the trumpets, but rather as substitutes for trumpets. In writing for cornets these French composers largely abandoned the old-style trumpet type of part, and treated the instrument quite light-heartedly as a melodist ; it was, no doubt, to some extent, their rather flippant treatment of the cornet as a melodist which led to the abuse of that instrument in the last half of last century, rather than the actual tone of the instrument itself. As upper parts in conjunction with trombones, cornets gave the French opera composers an harmonically flexible and full-voiced brass group which was quite satisfactory in blend and balance, even if it lacked somewhat the quality and nobility of the trumpet-trombone combination favoured by the more advanced of their German contemporaries. The custom of using three tenor trombones, instead of two tenors and one bass, still prevailed in France, and accounts for the distribution of trombone parts harmonically in close position, resulting in a certain brilliance of tone, not without loss of some dignity of effect. While the tuba was still a stranger to these French scores, all other accessories, such as piccolo, *cor anglais*, harps and extra percussion instruments, figure quite freely. Lack of variety and invention in the treatment of their *tutti* is a sin of omission in their orchestration which these French composers shared with most of their German contemporaries. The combination of solid and complete harmony by each section of the orchestra, the quite satisfactory but featureless standard *tutti* of nineteenth century orchestration, generally served their purpose when employing all instruments together. The resourcefulness of Berlioz, Wagner, and Liszt, in this respect, had yet to leave its impress on orchestration.

Occupying a position well-poised between the dull soberness of the lesser Germans and the highly-coloured brilliance, amounting sometimes to blatant noisiness, of their Italian contemporaries, the Frenchmen Thomas, Gounod and Bizet established a style of orchestration which is characterized by its clearness and economy of colour, as well as by its fitness and delicacy ; and, although some of their successors were destined to be affected by the onrush of Wagnerian influence, it may be said that, on the whole, French orchestration of to-day owes to them the best of the features which still keep its national individuality of style intact.

Italian orchestration after the time of Donizetti and Bellini is represented at its very best by the work of Giuseppe Verdi (1813-1901), the most prominent of his native group, moreover a composer who lived long enough to be an active contemporary of both Wagner and of Wagner's successors, and was able not only to witness the advance of orchestration practically throughout the nineteenth century, but was also able and competent to benefit by its progress almost up to the last. If in his earlier works his orchestration was modelled on that of his successful forebears, Verdi eclipsed their best work in his popular successes just after the mid-century (*Rigoletto* 1851, *Il Trovatore* 1853), and developed still further in his full maturity (*Aïda* 1871, *Requiem* 1874, *Otello* 1887, *Falstaff* 1893), even to the extent of showing the influence of Wagner, at the same time, however, remaining true to national style. The main characteristics of the orchestration of the earlier nineteenth century Italians, the noisy brilliance, clear colouring, strong contrasts, variety and showiness of Rossini, Donizetti, and Bellini, is combined, in the case of Verdi's later works, with a superior musicianship, some considerable inventiveness, and a fine sense for effect which continued to develop at an age when most composers' powers show signs of stagnation or of decline. Verdi's work shows implicit faith in the value of displaying the primary tone-colours of the orchestra in unmixed condition. Plenty of pure string-tone is used, and the Italian's usual considerateness in accompanying vocal solos is combined with his love of dynamic force and high colour, the latter to an extent bordering on exaggeration. The parts are harmonically wide-spread and full in body, rich and voluptuous in tone, without being thick or smudgy. The colouring has the clarity of contemporary French work, with less of its delicacy and restraint. In this way a somewhat too lavish use of full brass harmony gives Verdi's work an occasional noisiness which seems unnecessary, a blatant forcefulness not unlike that of Meyerbeer in his spectacular vein. The use of three tenor trombones in close harmony is again characteristic of French and Italian orchestration in the mid-nineteenth century.

During the course of his long career, Verdi not only kept alive what was typically Italian in nineteenth century orchestration, but also added to its resources, improved its musical qualities, and set a standard which, but for his successful example, might easily have degenerated, or might have exaggerated the weaknesses of Italian operatic orchestration at a time when progress was by no means the outstanding feature of his compatriots' work.

Of orchestration in the hands of Russian and Polish composers during the period of Wagner's activity, it may be said, that although the school of which Glinka is usually described as being the founder was in active growth, music by Glinka's native successors had yet to find its way outside of Russia. The work of such as Borodin and Moussorgsky was actually in the making at that time, but had to wait till even after that of Tschaikovsky for any sort of general recognition in musical

Europe. The only composer of Slavonic birth whose work reached the concert rooms and opera houses outside of Russia during the period in question was Anton Gregor Rubinstein (1829-1894), who, like Liszt, combined a large output in composition with the rôle of virtuoso pianist of international fame. By training and musical sympathy more German than Russian, Rubinstein's orchestration followed, on the whole, the German model, without showing any Wagnerian influence, yet with a shade better colouring than that of the lesser and duller Germans of his day. Lacking the clearness and delicacy of the French, the vividness of the best Italian and the crude effectiveness of the as yet unrecognized Russian style, Rubinstein's work may be cited as typical of a cosmopolitan variety which has served countless composers of varied nationality at any time within the last forty years of last century.

In the meantime, working out their own salvation according to their own principles, several younger Russians were producing works which did not penetrate outside of their own country, and consequently could not for the time being exercise any influence in the wider musical world. The eventual effects of the popularity of Tschaikovsky's work, and the belated recognition in European circles of works by such as Borodin, Moussorgsky and Rimsky-Korsakov, belong more properly to a period after that of Wagner.

If it is impossible to find any marked individuality or national characteristics in the orchestration of British composers in the earlier part of the second half of the nineteenth century, it is possible to point to the competence with which the best of them handled the orchestra, and to note how they kept the art on a safe but unadventurous course, till the time when the prevailing Mendelssohnian model was to give way to more progressive influences.

George Alexander Macfarren (1813-1887) and William Sterndale Bennett (1816-1875), both in their time students and principals of the Royal Academy of Music, followed the placid path of the " Gewandhaus " school, the standard style of German orchestration before the potence of Wagner's example took effect. Sterndale Bennett's work is unusually neat and polished, but never without a certain sleekness which, however well it suits his musical matter, lacks variety and force of character. The same unenterprising treatment of their *tutti*, the same readiness to fall back on melodic doubling or harmonic padding on the wood-wind, and their old-style horn and trumpet parts combine to emphasize their kinship to those of the German composers of their own generation whose orchestration shows all the negative virtues of smoothness and safety.

Almost the same might be said of the Dane, Niels Wilhelm Gade (1817-1890), who added some of Schumann's harmonic thickness to a Mendelssohnian type of orchestration, but lost some of the lightness of touch which was one of the most attractive features in the work of his exemplar.

To the Bohemian, Friedrich Smetana (1824–1884), must be credited a progressive spirit in his orchestration which, added to individuality in his music, raises him well above the mass of composers of his time who failed to reach the first rank. Something of the independence and enterprise of Wagner and Liszt appear in the orchestration of Smetana's set of six symphonic tone poems *Má Vlast*. Broad, clear colouring, clear-cut contrasts and distinct grouping of his orchestral voices are combined with some inventive fertility and imagination. The brass voices are fully chromatic, vigorous and thematic in their incidence, while the weaving of figured string textures and patterns shows affinity to the newer growth of orchestration which would allot separate functions to each orchestral group when all are playing together, rather than spread one function over the whole body with but very little modification.

CHAPTER XIII

THE PERIOD OF BRAHMS—TSCHAIKOVSKY

THE last thirty years of Wagner's life saw the rise of another generation of composers, most of them born between 1830 and 1850, composers whose mature works appeared approximately during the last thirty years of last century, and of which the most prominent names are Brahms and Tschaikovsky. The following is a list grouped according to nationality, far from complete, but adequately representative, and sufficiently typical of the composers who lived late enough to hear and to know Wagner's works, yet who did not all necessarily show the influence of his example in their orchestration :

German, Austrian, Hungarian.	French, Belgian.	Russian.
Bruckner, 1824-1896.	Franck, 1822-1890.	Borodin, 1834-1887.
Goldmark, 1830–1915.	Lalo, 1823-1892.	Moussorgsky, 1835-1881.
Brahms, 1833-1897.	Saint-Saëns, 1835-1921.	
Bruch, 1838-1920.		Cui, 1835–1918.
Gernsheim, 1839-1916.	Delibes, 1836-1891.	Balakirev, 1837-1910.
Götz, 1840–1876.	Chabrier, 1841-1894.	
Brüll, 1846-1907.	Massenet, 1842-1912.	Tschaikovsky, 1840-1893.
Nicodé, 1853-1919.	Fauré, 1845-1924.	
Humperdinck, 1854-1921.	Duparc, 1848–1933.	Rimsky-Korsakov, 1844-1908.
	d'Indy, 1851–1931.	

Various.

Ponchielli, 1834-1886, Italian.   Mackenzie, 1847–1935, British.
Boito, 1842-1918, Italian.   Parry, 1848-1918, British.
Dvořák, 1841-1904, Bohemian.   Stanford, 1852-1924, British.
Grieg, 1843-1907, Norwegian.   Cowen, 1852–1935, British.
Sullivan, 1842-1900, British.

What resistance was offered to Wagnerian influence in orchestration during his period arose from either lack of sympathy with his music and ideals, from conservatism (Wagner was still largely regarded as a revolutionary), from strong individuality, or from strongly marked national style.

Broadly regarded, the constitution of the orchestra remained as before, except that the tuba had by then almost entirely superseded the ophicleide. The enlarged orchestra used by Wagner for his later works was often employed by composers who were able to command, or who hoped to command, such rich resources for the presentation of their large-scale works ; yet the majority of works, both symphonic and operatic, were scored for the standard mid-nineteenth-century combination, viz., the usual strings, pairs of wood-wind with the frequent addition of such as the piccolo, *cor anglais*, bass clarinet and double-bassoon; four horns, two trumpets, three trombones and tuba, with occasional extras of the same types ; timpani, etc. ; harps. Slight deviations from the above were governed more or less by local or national custom, for example, the French tendency to employ three or four bassoons, and a pair of cornets. It should not be understood that no other instruments were ever used in orchestras during the last thirty years of last century ; on the contrary, it were hardly exaggeration to assert that there is no European musical instrument of any sort which has not made either isolated or occasional appearances in some full score or other during that period. The bowed string group was least of all susceptible to the attentions of would-be innovators, and, in spite of a few attempts by such as the viola-alta[1] and others,[2] retained its late seventeenth-century constitution intact. The following, no doubt incomplete, will give some idea of the variety of other instruments which have appeared in sundry full scores towards the end of the nineteenth century or soon after. They constitute that shifting fringe of the orchestra which never is, and never has been quite stable, and is always open to extension at the whim of any composer, however insignificant[3] :

Flutes of various sizes, other than the concert flute and piccolo.

Oboes of various sizes, other than the ordinary oboe and *cor anglais*.

Clarinets of various sizes, other than the ordinary clarinet and bass clarinet.

Saxophones and Sarrusophones (particularly in French scores).

[1] A viola of larger build with an additional fifth (E) string.

[2] The Violotta and Cellone (see Berlioz-Strauss, *Instrumentationslehre*, vol. i., p. 81).

[3] See list of instruments in Forsyth's *Orchestration*.

High-pitched cornets.

Tubas and Saxhorns of various sizes.

Drums of all sorts, and other percussion instruments of infinite variety.

Celesta and sundry bell-instruments.

Guitar, Mandoline, Banjo.

Piano.

Organ.

Concertina.

Bagpipes.

Of the individual instruments, the strings underwent no change beyond that a double-bass with a fifth string tuned to low C was tried, and eventually abandoned.   Another device was rather more successful, and although used in certain orchestras, has not been generally adopted.   In this case a mechanical contrivance effects an instantaneous change of the lowest string to any note from E to C.[1]   A change from the old-fashioned double-bass bow to that of the modern violoncello type, also the decline of the three-stringed instrument, came more or less within the period now being considered.

Wood-wind instruments provided with the reorganized key-mechanisms of mid-century came into general use in high-class orchestras, while the older types still survived in small orchestras and military bands.   The gains in key-facility, in ease in reaching the extreme high notes, and in facilitating the rendering of shakes and *tremoli* which were formerly either difficult or impossible, were combined with some variability of the downward compass in the case of particular makes and instruments.   Various makers added to the low notes on their clarinets, and the lowest B-flat on the oboe was by no means always available ; yet, on the whole, the compass down to written E for the clarinet, and to B-flat for the oboe, may be said to have remained standard.   The C clarinet suffered more and more neglect, and has since been finally abandoned by orchestral players.

Valve-horns and valve-trumpets completed their triumph over the natural instruments, and although composers largely continued to write for them variously crooked, players tended more and more to settle down to the use of one crook, transposing the written parts at sight.   Their selection was the F crook for the horn and trumpet, or the B-flat and A shanks for the smaller trumpet,

---

[1] Two devices, by Bruno Keyl and Max Poike, are extant.

according to their own convenience. The natural horn, abandoned everywhere else, still lingered in France. In England the slide trumpet gave place to the valve instrument. The use of horns and trumpets fitted with either the piston or the rotary mechanism varied in different countries, and to some extent locally, likewise the use of either slide or valve-trombones. The organization of the trombone trio—two tenors and one bass— was practically stabilized, with, however, some continued vacillation between the claims of a bass trombone built in either F or G. The size of the tuba actually used by players also varied locally to some extent, the commonest instruments being those in either B-flat, F or E-flat. Following the issue in 1844 of Berlioz's famous treatise on orchestration, several other books designed more or less on the same plan appeared during the course of the second half of last century. Those by Lobe (1850 German), Buszler, Hofmann, Jadassohn (German, 1889 English), Riemann (German, English) and the more famous treatise by Gevaert—*Traité Général d'Instrumentation* (French), revised as *Nouveau Traité d'Instrumentation* (1885 French, 1887 German)— gave in convenient form much useful information to students and others, while two native musicians, Corder (*The Orchestra, and how to write for it*, 1895) and Prout (*The Orchestra*, 2 vols. 1897), provided similar help for English readers. Further works on the same subject published since 1900 are :

Widor. *The Technique of the Modern Orchestra* (French, German, 1904-5 English).

Berlioz-Strauss. *Instrumentationslehre* (2 vols. 1906 German).

Rimsky-Korsakov. *Foundations of Orchestration* (1912 French, 1922 English).

Forsyth. *Orchestration* (1914 English).

Ricci. *L'orchestrazione* (1920 Italian).

All these, as well as numerous smaller text-books, have made the path of the embryo orchestrator somewhat easier, if only by providing a means of learning about the compass and technique of orchestral instruments, and by giving extracts from scores which might otherwise prove inaccessible; but all necessarily suffer from a complaint common to dictionaries and cyclopædias, namely, that they begin to be out-of-date from the moment they are written ; furthermore, the learning of orchestration is really only acquired by the practical experience which neither text-book nor teacher can supply.

The technical difficulty of Wagner's orchestral parts was probably largely instrumental in raising the standard of execution amongst orchestral players towards the end of last century. All composers after Wagner benefited by this, as well as by the advantages of having their orchestration rendered by orchestras established, trained and organized by a race of conductors, many of whom were the product of conditions set up by the demand of Wagner's works for interpretive conducting of exceeding high standard and high ideals, both technically and æsthetically. Headed by Bülow, this race of Wagner-conductors, comprising such as Levi, Richter, Schuch, Seidl, Nikisch, Mottl and Mahler, raised their art to a level which could not but directly influence for good, orchestration by composers whose works passed through their hands, and orchestral playing by bodies committed to their charge. A similar advance was due to such as Lamoureux, Colonne and Chevillard in France, and Mancinelli in Italy, most of whom, with the Wagner-conductors, shed the benefits of their enlightened conducting far beyond the confines of their own countries. Academical training in orchestration and orchestral playing, conducted more thoroughly and systematically than ever before, must also be given credit for having helped to spread knowledge and experience of orchestration during the epoch which coincided with the growing familiarity and more regular production of Wagner's works.

The personnel of important orchestras during this period shows an ample and usually well-balanced body of strings, supplemented by such additions to the regular wind body as were rendered imperative by the demands of influential composers. The following[1] suggests that Wagner's remarks in his essay " Uber das Dirigieren " (1869) on the personnel of orchestras hardly held good about the time of his death :

	1st Violins.	2nd Violins.	Violas.	'Celli.	Basses.
London, Philharmonic (1880)	14	12	10	10	8
Paris, Conservatoire (1880)	15	14	10	12	9
Leipzig, Gewandhaus (1880)	14	14	9	9	9
Vienna Philharmonic (1880)	20	20	6(sic)	12	9
Bayreuth (1876)	16	16	12	12	8

[1] From Grove's *Dictionary of Music and Musicians*, 1878–1889.

Orchestration by composers of Teutonic origin during the period of Brahms and Tschaikovsky falls roughly into two classes : that which did, and that which did not show the influence of Wagner.   In the last class the work of Johannes Brahms (1833-1897) stands out, purely by reason of the lasting value of his music, and not at all by virtue of his manner of presenting it orchestrally.   Unsympathetic to the colour and warmth of Wagner's example, disdaining the glitter and brilliance of Liszt, Brahms refused to learn from them the possibilities of the modern orchestra, or to profit by their suggestiveness and their experiments in orchestral colouring, even if he could have used such methods in conjunction with his own particular musical matter. Looking backward rather than forward, Brahms built directly on the foundation of Beethoven and Schumann, adding to theirs his own individual technique, a more extensive and richer harmonic scheme, and, without altering their general style of treatment, took some, but far from full advantage of such mechanical improvements as had given greater melodic flexibility and harmonic resource to the brass instruments of the orchestra.

Brahms' string parts are spread over a large vertical compass, the middle being closely filled up with double-stopping, subdivided parts, or by a busy figurated polyphony.   Low-lying parts for violas and violoncellos, active or sustained, and both frequently sub-divided, are largely responsible for a Schumannesque thickness of tone, which, combined with the ever-present horn parts covering the lower tenor register, has caused Brahms' orchestration to be described as " thick and muddy."   Individually, the string parts are often strangely ungrateful in effect, rather more awkward than difficult. They abound in large skips and uncomfortable intervals across the strings.   Ranging over the entire compass of each instrument, the parts doggedly pursue their own course, freely crossing one another, often syncopated or rhythmically at cross-purposes, and are rarely left to display their own particular tone-quality without the partnership of some other instrument of equal range, but dissimilar tone-colour.   The violoncellos wander about the string texture expansively, independently, and often very expressively, but are usually hedged around with much detailed motion by other parts.

The wood-wind as a body take a very generous share of the musical matter, doubling one another each in its respective register, or, rather less frequently, acting as an independent group, but rarely as unencumbered soloists. As a group they work mostly in conjunction with horns. A noticeable feature of Brahms' orchestral technique is a reactionary tendency to distribute the wood-wind parts in four well-defined pairs, often running in consecutive thirds or sixths, rather than to treat them as soloists, or to use them together as a self-contained group. The two bodies, strings and wood-wind, are treated as being of practically equal power, and, except for the more active figuration and passage-work of the strings, carry out functions which are similar in character and range. Matter which at one moment is string work is transferred bodily to the wood-wind at another, or *vice versa*. This interchangeability of medium is often carried out in an unyielding manner, subject to the limitations of compass more than to any difference in the character of the individual instruments. The horns act as a binding material, and are. almost continuously employed as such, providing a somewhat monotonous cohesion by means of parts which are not exactly melodic, yet are more than mere harmonic padding.

The brass section in Brahms' work enjoys only comparatively little standing as a self-contained group. The horns, although relying much on valve-produced notes, are often crooked in two different keys at the same moment, as if to secure as many open notes as possible. Short melodic phrases sometimes fall to the horns, but for the most part they are occupied with matter which is rather more chromatic, yet not more melodic than the horn parts in the later Beethoven symphonies. Trumpets occasionally get a chromatic note, and have but little real melodic movement. They are similarly crooked in various keys, as if for natural trumpets.

In the matter of grouping and contrasting the main sections of the orchestra, Brahms seems to have adopted one of the least attractive features from Schumann's orchestration. A sort of semi-tutti, comprised of strings, wood-wind and horns, is his favourite and almost constant combination. The groups rarely appear in unmixed form. Brahms' first symphony in C minor (1876) does not contain a single complete bar of music for wood-wind alone, and, if he did not quite achieve Schumann's feat of orchestrating an entire symphony without letting pure string-tone be heard for a single bar, Brahms certainly came very near to it in more than one of his works. Such clearer grouping as occurs in the third movement of the second symphony in D (1877) is more the exception than the rule.

A general view of Brahms' orchestration suggests that he deliberately isolated himself, taking no part in the development which was in progress all around him. He apparently disdained purely orchestral effect, and never relied solely on the mere attractiveness of instrumental colour. His love for a full, dense harmony led him to constantly duplicate parts and combine instrumental voices, thus preventing the possibility of instruments and groups acting in clear contrast to one another. While always dignified and sonorous, his orchestration lacked the lighter touch and charm so often found in the work of many an inferior composer. But Brahms carried his own musical technique into the orchestra itself, creating situations arising out of that very technique, making, in a sense, an orchestral language peculiar to himself, and not without considerable influence on the work of many composers, Teutonic and otherwise, who at the end of last century carried their admiration for his music so far as to let his orchestral manner influence theirs.

A famous conductor aptly said, apropos of Brahms' orchestration : " The sun never shines in it."

A large number of what might be called the rank and file of German, Austrian and Austro-Hungarian composers, during the last thirty years of last century, followed a path which brought them to a practically stationary position. This was really the ultimate development of the Mendelssohnian school of orchestration, the type which by that time had come to be regarded as normal, and which might justly be described as scholastic or text-book orchestration. Of these Max Bruch (1838-1920) will serve as a typical and quite influential representative. His work typifies the sound, unoffending, conventional Teutonic orchestration of the period ; orchestration which took no risks, which is not quite so heavy and unbending as that of Brahms, yet which lacks enterprise, lightness and vigour. If it never offends or shocks, it may at times tire the ear. In it there are more of the sombre low-pitched blends than are found in the work of the generation from which these composers inherited their style, groupings of instrumental tone which are rather fuller in quantity of tone, yet a trifle dull in effect. Pervaded by a certain monotony arising from the very common combination of string, wood-wind and horn tone, all being occupied with similar matter which is only slightly modified to suit the individualities of particular instruments, the typical weaknesses are : conventional handling of the *tutti*, the large amount of sustained harmonic padding for wind instruments, and the lack of bolder thematic treatment of the brass voices.

Associated with Bruch in style of orchestration may be named such as Jadassohn, Gernsheim, Hofmann, Goldmark, Götz, Brüll, and a great number of others who have in their time earned a respectful hearing and some varying measure of success. Nor should late nineteenth century orchestration of this type be associated only with Teutonic composers, for it served many others of varying nationality, but of no very great individual gifts, before, and even after the time when Wagnerian influence was becoming dominating. Very many such, it is true, owed their training to Germany. The sense for instrumental colour shown in the orchestration of such composers as have been named naturally varied to some extent with the individual. Few were so shy of clear colouring as was Brahms, yet few showed any very pronounced feeling for bold colouring or telling effects. The Hungarian composer, Goldmark, for example, was more of a colourist than most of that school, yet his work hardly entitles him to be grouped with any but those of the Germans and Austrians whose work did not embody the advances accruing to orchestration due to Wagner's influence.

Of those who did clearly take Wagner as their model, it will suffice to mention Anton Bruckner (1824-1896), and, although born thirty years later, Engelbert Humperdinck (1854-1921), the first a composer who developed unusually late in life, and the second fairly early.

If Bruckner's influence outside of Germany and Austria has been of the slightest, there can be no question that, especially in Vienna, where his work stood as a species of opposition to the cult of Brahms, his nine symphonic works, produced roughly between 1868 and 1896, have been taken very seriously. The enlarged orchestras of Wagner are required in Bruckner's later symphonies, even to the extent of demanding eight horns (four of which are to be interchangeable with four tubas) in the ninth symphony[1]. Bold work for the brass instruments, good grouping and contrasts of tone-colour, elaborate weaving of textures, and all the outward signs of the Wagnerian manner, with its bigness of style and freedom from convention, show themselves in the mature scores of

---

[1] Two five-stringed double-basses are specified in the score of this symphony.

this composer, whose orchestration seems to be almost too good for the musical matter which it clothes. In Humperdinck's orchestration the echo of Wagner is again distinctly heard, strangely combined with a charm, a modesty of means and simplicity of idea, that have brought success to the one opera by which he is universally known.

A composer typical of a few who occupied a position, so to speak, on the border-line between the duller German and the Wagnerian schools of orchestration, was Jean Louis Nicodé (1853-1919). His symphonic works, *Maria Stuart* and *Das Meer* (1889), have much massiveness of tone, one of several indications that the composer had absorbed the spirit of Wagner's orchestration without carrying the practice of his methods beyond a stage which can only be described as half-hearted. The score of the latter work is one of a few in which four tubas and a contra-bass tuba are demanded.

Brought up in the same school and according to the same principles as Thomas, Gounod and Bizet, the French composers Charles Camille Saint-Saëns (1835-1921), Léo Delibes (1836-1891) and Jules Frédéric Massenet (1842-1912), inherited unimpaired the style of orchestration described in the last chapter as being typically Parisian. Practically contemporaneous with the former group, the latter link up with a slightly later group comprising such as Chabrier, Fauré, Duparc and d'Indy, whose work again preluded the more recent developments associated with the names of Debussy and some of his contemporaries. Rather apart from any of the above in his orchestration, stands César Auguste Franck (1822-1890), the Belgian-born musician whose development as a composer came rather late in life[1].

Any analysis of the orchestration of Delibes and Massenet would amount to little more than a recapitulation of what has already been written about that of Thomas, Gounod and Bizet. With some added richness of tone, both upheld the traditions and characteristics of Parisian theatrical orchestration, with its transparent design, clearness of colouring and sensuous charm. Saint-Saëns comprehensively handled every class of music in which the orchestra figures as a medium. His work is associated with a more cultivated musicianship, and this reflects itself in his orchestration which, however, rests on precisely the same

[1] Franck's important works nearly all appeared between 1880 and 1890.

fundamentals as that of the French composers named in the last chapter. The segregation of the function of each instrument or group of instruments at any particular moment, the clear distinction between the tone-colour of instruments employed for melodic and for accompanying purposes, the judgment which governs the choice of the moment of entry and cessation for a particular tone-colour, the spacing of change of colour, the knack of using very few notes effectively, and of avoiding combinations in which one tone-colour cancels the individuality of another ; all these give variety, clearness, and balance to the work of Saint-Saëns, and place his work at the extreme opposite pole to that of Brahms and many of his German contemporaries. His light touch and restraint served Saint-Saëns particularly well when orchestrally accompanying solo instruments or solo voices ; almost the only quite satisfactorily scored violoncello concerto by a nineteenth century composer is his well-known work in A minor. In enterprise and invention Saint-Saëns must be credited with having made some advance on the orchestration of his immediate forbears, and on that of some of his French contemporaries.

While the orchestration of Saint-Saëns, Delibes and Massenet remained essentially French, showing unmistakably its close kinship to that of the generation of Gounod, their younger contemporaries have shown tendencies which, it cannot be denied, owe something to the example of Wagner. A more intense tone, fuller harmony and a rather more complex texture are combined with native characteristics which avoid obscurity and monotony. More subtle blends replace the simple transparency of their immediate forbears, and not infrequently they go further in pointing the way in a direction which was destined to be more fully exploited by Debussy and his followers. While showing individually somewhat varied characteristics, such as, for example, Chabrier's reliance on brilliance of effect, or d'Indy's more pretentious impressiveness, the broad distinction between a French and a German style was still clearly maintained. If they lost a little in clearness, and sacrificed some of the charm of simplicity, the French composers of the late nineteenth century added some forcefulness and power to the orchestration of their older contemporaries, and at the same time showed a readiness to experiment in creating new composite tone-colours of rather elusive nature. Their scores show much regard for detail,

and some considerable elaboration, while certain peculiarities in
the constitution of their orchestras persist, of which the following
are noticeable : the use of an additional pair of bassoons, a pair
of cornets in addition to the usual two trumpets, a pair of natural
horns in conjunction with two valve horns, a generous array of
percussion instruments, and two usually elaborated harp parts.

In César Franck's orchestration, a German richness and full
volume of tone are combined with the French clear colouring and
distinctive grouping of instrumental voices. By concentrating
melodic lines each on a different type of tone-colour, and by
providing sufficient tone-quantity by means of doubling in
unison or in octaves, Franck preserved an excellent balance and
an intensity of tone not unlike that of Tschaikovsky in his
maturity, although it is probable that this was the outcome of
experience, possibly aided by the example of Wagner, rather than
the result of having learned from the methods of the Russian
composer. The brass parts are freely melodic, effectively so
when concentrated in unison on the melodic lines of the canonic
imitation which so frequently figures in Franck's musical matter.
Short chords for the heavy brass voices in the *tutti*, instead of the
more conventional sustained harmony, give further evidence
of a strong instinct for good balance of tone.   Somewhat peculiar
is the consistent use of cornets for harmonic, and trumpets for
melodic purposes, in the composer's well-known *Symphony in D*
(1889).   If Franck's musical matter involved some sacrifice of the
characteristic lightness and charm of truly French orchestration,
his more opulent and intense tone, combined with a fine musicianship, makes ample amends.

A contemporary of Franck, Édouard Victor Antoine Lalo
(1823-1892), combined the native clearness of French orchestration with some enterprise and lively freshness of outlook.

Whatever his position with regard to nationalism in the
development of Russian music, the popular success of the
orchestral works of Peter Ilich Tschaikovsky (1840-1893) in all
music-loving countries from shortly before the close of last
century, together with the consequent effect of that popularity
on the work of his immediate successors, has made his example
one of the most powerful influences in orchestration during the
last forty years, indeed, probably the most far-reaching since that
of Wagner. The combination of music and orchestration, both
of which make a direct appeal, appearing at a favourable moment,

not unnaturally finds a quick and clear reflection in the work of composers who are at the time young enough to be susceptible to its influence. There can be no denying that Tschaikovsky's work has acted beneficially towards orchestration on the whole, from the time when his music began to be widely diffused and generally admired, or that the power of his influence is still vital.

Purely as regards their orchestration, Tschaikovsky's works may be roughly divided into two groups, representing an immature and a mature period. The dividing line falls somewhere soon after 1875, the year of the third symphony and the popular piano concerto in B-flat minor. As several of his earlier works were subjected to revision or re-writing subsequent to their first production and publication, it is hardly possible to follow the actual development of his growth as an orchestrator with any great certainty from the published scores of Tschaikovsky's works as we now have them. Both the first and the second *Symphonies* (circa 1868 and 1873) appear to have been revised or re-written after the dates given, likewise *Romeo and Juliet* (1870, revised 1881) and the piano concerto, the latter being re-issued in its present form as late as 1889. It is not unreasonable to suppose that the orchestration of these works would be amended to some extent under conditions of added experience. All that can be done under the circumstances is to consider the scores as they are, but at the same time to make some allowance for the possible effects of revision.

From the very beginning Tschaikovsky pinned his faith to orchestration which embodied the essential characteristics of Glinka's work, and that of the prevailing French school. He amalgamated the rougher, but quite clear orchestration of the former with some of the equally clear lightness and delicacy of the latter, avoiding, on the one hand, the thickness and monotony of the German, and on the other, the exaggerated dynamics of the Italian schools. Clear grouping of allied tone-colours in opposition to one another, rather than combinations of mixed tone-colours in co-operation with one another, was the fundamental principle on which both Russian and French orchestration was based ; from his earliest to his most mature phase, Tschaikovsky remained a firm adherent to the former of these two opposing principles.

In his first symphony—*Rêveries d'hiver* (1866–68)—much of the orchestration can hardly be identified with Tschaikovsky's late individuality. The first movement might well have been scored by, say, Saint-Saëns or some other French composer. Melodic matter on the wood-wind, whether solo, in unison or in octaves, is accompanied rather lightly by string harmony or figuration ; conversely, string melodies are harmonically supported by wood-wind or horns. When all are combined the function of each group usually differs. Horn parts are sustained and fairly conventional, but by no means always associated with the wood-wind group. A prominent subject is given to the four horns *soli*, with a light bass part for the bass string instruments. Some antiphonal use of the wood-wind and string groups is characteristic of Tschaikovsky's mature style, likewise his readiness to double the string parts in unison or in octaves. The slow movement shows much pure string-tone, some solo work for single wood-wind, and a quite characteristic melodic part for horns in unison (*forte*) against a very soft string accompaniment. An occasional lapse shows some semi-tutti less clearly handled, and might have been planned by some lesser German composer. In the *Scherzo* the wood-wind and strings are often in contrasted opposition, but at other times are more conventionally combined. In the last movement the piccolo, trombones, tuba, bass drum and cymbals are introduced, and the treatment is alternately full and robust, or thinner and contrapuntal. Some bold treatment of brass, string, and wood-wind groups, each section concentrated on one melodic part, is more characteristic of the later Tschaikovsky. The orchestration of the symphony as a whole, while being clear and well contrasted, does not display the sumptuous tone now associated with the composer's work ; some of the methods which he employed so freely later on are certainly present in embryo, but are not presented with such complete confidence, nor are they carried out quite thoroughly and whole-heartedly. Means are not at hand for ascertaining how the present score[1] compares with the original version.

The third *Symphony in D*, dated 1875, exhibits the same clear grouping, together with some of Tschaikovsky's mature characteristics rather more fully developed, yet far from being completely matured or confidently offered. The much more mature work in the piano concerto of the same date suggests that the revision of 1889 affected the orchestration as well as the solo part of that popular work.

[1] *Nouvelle édition, revue et corrigée par l'auteur.*

From the fourth *Symphony* (1877) onwards, Tschaikovsky's
orchestration appears to be matured and settled.

One of the most individual features of his work centres largely
round a method of part-distribution which is contrary to the
advice of all text-books, and to the example of countless full scores.
That each of the parts which make up his musical matter should
be concentrated on *one* particular type of tone-colour, that each
part therefore stands out in relief to the others rather than blends
with them, is the cardinal principle which governs Tschaikovsky's
system of part-distribution when several different types of
instrument are sounding together, and is in direct opposition to
the text-book axiom that harmony should be complete or self-
contained in each section of the orchestra. The process can be
seen carried out again and again in the last three symphonies and
other mature works. It is commonly used when, as frequently
happens in Tschaikovsky's orchestral music, two melodic parts, one
harmonic or figurated part, and a bass part make up the musical
whole. The following from the last three symphonies are typical :

Work.	First melodic part.	Second melodic part.	Harmonic part or third melodic part.	Bass part.
Symphony No. 4, Second movement at letter D.[1]	All wood-wind (except bass-oons)	All strings (except d-basses)	Four horns	D-basses and bassoons
Symphony No. 5, Second movement, 5 bars after letter H.	All wood-wind	Four horns	Violins and violas	Violoncellos and d-basses
Symphony No. 5, last mov. Mod. assai after letter Y.	All strings (except d-basses)	Horns and trumpets	All wood-wind	D-basses, bass trombone and tuba
Symphony No. 6, last mov. 5 bars after letter D.	Upper strings	All wood-wind	Four horns	Bass strings
Ditto, at letter E.	All strings (except d-basses)	Two trumpets and two trombones	All wood-wind	D-basses and bass trombone

[1] Miniature scores.

The same principle, sometimes more or less modified in order to ensure good balance, is employed as a standard method in Tschaikovsky's mature works, and is the key to the wonderful clearness of part-movement, combined with intensity of tone, which so admirably fits the composer's musical conceptions.

The use of self-contained instrumental groups antiphonally is another feature which is frequently in use, and is carried out with as little mixing of alien tone-colours as is possible.   Probably no example of pure group-work in the whole range of orchestral music is more remarkable for its thoroughness in this respect than that of the third movement of Tschaikovsky's fourth *Symphony*. The three groups (*a*) strings *pizzicato*, (*b*) wood-wind, and (*c*) brass, from first to last never lose their identity or mix their functions.   The same sort of treatment by contrasted groups occupies much of the third movement of the sixth *Symphony*, and is, indeed, in constant requisition throughout Tschaikovsky's works.

When dealing with a single melodic line against an harmonic or figurated accompaniment, Tschaikovsky draws a very distinct line between the tone-colour of the melodic part and that of the accompanying parts.   His aim is always to provide as complete a blend as possible amongst the accompanying instruments, but to ensure that the melodic part shall be sharply distinctive in colour.   Many such solo parts for single wood-wind instruments, or for a horn, accompanied by nothing but pure string-tone, can hardly fail to occur to anyone who is the least bit familiar with his work.   The same process of differentiation of tone-colour between melody and accompaniment, or between primary and secondary matter, is carried out with equal thoroughness when presented with fuller orchestration.   When the dimensions of a full *tutti* are reached, every possible ounce of tone-weight is piled on to the melodic part in the effort to secure a satisfactory balance of tone ; hence the many *tutti* in which an active melodic part is in the hands of all the strings excepting double-basses, plus the entire wood-wind group, while the harmony is supplied solely by the brass group.

Other features of Tschaikovsky's work are too many to deal with fully, yet some merit particular mention.   Such are : the spacing of changes of tone-colour and of treatment ; the reserve of tone-colour and effect for climactic purposes ; consciousness of the value of thin part-writing as a contrast to full-bodied

orchestration ; care in adequately providing for the representation
of essential harmony notes in purely harmonic work ; cohesion
of tone-quality in selecting harmonic groups. All these features,
which Tschaikovsky shared with many another good orchestrator,
are overshadowed by the cardinal principle of his creed, which
provides that the clear utterance of no melodic part shall be
clogged by the presence of other or secondary matter on instruments of the same tone-colour or of similar tone-weight. It is
to his consistent adherence to this principle that Tschaikovsky
owed the good balance, the clearness, and, indeed, the general
success of his orchestral combinations.

It is worth while noting that Tschaikovsky did not require a
number of extra instruments, nor in fact anything larger than
the ordinary concert orchestra, in order to achieve a full and
adequate quantity of tone.

That his principles were the outcome of calculated effort and
thought, aided by the accumulation of practical experience,
cannot be doubted. That no blind instinct guided him, and that
his admiration for a composer's music was not coloured by
his views on the same man's orchestration, is demonstrated
very clearly by his acknowledged love of Schumann's music,
side by side with his expressed opinion on the same composer's
orchestration : " but it is an undisputed fact that this composer
(Schumann) is the brightest star among recent musicians "—
" his creative power is proportionate to his wonderful productive-
ness "—" that great fault which prevails in all the works of
Schumann, considered especially as a symphonic writer. This fault
would be called by painters a lack of colour, it is a pallor, a dryness—
I may almost say harshness—of orchestration. Without entering
into technical details, I may explain to my readers that the art
of instrumentation (i.e., the distribution of a work amongst
the various instruments) consists in understanding how to employ
alternately the individual groups of instruments ; how to blend
them appropriately ; how to economize strong effects—that is
to say, the application of *timbre* (tone-colour) to musical ideas.
This knowledge Schumann has not acquired. His orchestra
works continuously ; all the instruments take part in the
exposition and development of his ideas. They are not used in
detachments ; there is no contrast between them (and contrasting
effects are inexhaustible in orchestration) ; most of the time
they mingle in a continuous roar, often spoiling the best parts of

a work. As regards instrumentation, Schumann not only stands on a lower level than such masters as Berlioz, Mendelssohn, Meyerbeer, and Wagner, but he cannot even be compared with many second-rate composers who have borrowed his best inspirations."—" Schumann had not the art of clothing his wealth of ideas in beautiful sounds ; his orchestration is always opaque and heavy, and lacks brilliance and transparency."[1]

These are the words of one of the very best, on one of the worst orchestrators amongst the prominent composers of the nineteenth century.

A descent for Tschaikovsky's orchestration can most easily be found in the work of Glinka. His use of grouped instruments in alternation for purposes of contrast, and his method of distributing parts so as to secure clear part-contrast, are both clearly foreshadowed in the scores of the older Russian composer ; to Berlioz, Tschaikovsky may have owed some of his enlightenment and courage in carrying the development of his orchestral creed to its logical conclusion ; but the most powerful impulse most probably came as the result of his own practical experience and keen observation.

Following on the great popularity of Tschaikovsky's music came the inevitable signs that many younger composers of many nationalities had begun to assimilate some of his methods of orchestration, although it remains doubtful whether his methods have as yet been assessed at their full value by either composers or teachers of orchestration.

While the diffusion of Tschaikovsky's music proceeded rapidly, that of most of his Russian contemporaries emerged only rather slowly and incompletely from its state of comparative obscurity. Judging from the fact that most of the important of the rather few accessible scores of Borodin and Moussorgsky appear to have been amended or reorchestrated by such as Rimsky-Korsakov, Liadov and Glazounov, it would seem as if their orchestration was regarded, rightly or wrongly, as being technically crude by the more westernised of their surviving contemporaries. The work of Cui shows no particular characteristics, except a certain amateurish simplicity, but that of Balakirev, notably *Tamara* (1881), contains certain of the elements which have since become familiar through the medium of Tschaikovsky's scores. Rimsky-Korsakov added to the elements identified with the earlier

[1] Newmarch, *Tschaikovsky, His Life and Works* (London, 1900).

Russian orchestration a super-brilliance and splendour of colouring, also a sophistication which almost hides the foundations on which his style rests.   Exploring every corner of the orchestra for variety of colour and novel treatment, he surpassed Tschaikovsky in sheer brilliance and enterprise, but at the cost of losing to some extent in clearness and good balance.

Of Italian orchestration during the last thirty years of last century there is little to record beyond what was said in the last chapter, except to note the beginning of a gradual infiltration of the Wagnerian influence, which, however, did not subjugate the native characteristics of nineteenth century Italian opera orchestration.   The best of the work still came from the veteran Verdi, and just during the last decade a sudden rise into popular fame of three young opera composers—Mascagni, Leoncavallo and Puccini—provided for a continuation of all that was congenitally Italian in orchestration.   The limited Wagnerianism of the Italians at that time is well exemplified in the orchestration of such as Boito's *Mefistofele* (1868).   Here are all the elements of Italian operatic orchestration treated with a pretentiousness and tone-quantity of something approaching Wagnerian proportions.

British composers during the same period, in particular Sullivan, Mackenzie, Parry, Stanford and Cowen, showed some considerable variety of attainment in their orchestration, and an eclecticism which has served them well in suiting the orchestral presentation of their works to their musical matter.   A variety of styles, ranging from that of a Mendelssohnian simplicity to that of a Wagnerian breadth and vivid colouring, can be found in the scores of these composers, whose music has characteristics more strongly individual and more strongly national than their orchestration.   On the whole, the German model maintained its position as a standard for British composers, and especially for those who progressed in sympathy with the advance of orchestration as it developed under the now potent and growing influence of Wagner's example.   While avoiding the dull neutral colouring of many Germans, they have also avoided eccentricity and reliance on superficially conceived orchestral effects ; nor have some of them disdained to treat the orchestra briskly and with engaging lightness in works where heavy and pretentious orchestration would have been out of place.   The happy scoring in Sullivan's comic operas remains a model of fit orchestration which has not been surpassed by even the best of foreign composers in that particular *genre*.

The national and musical kinship of Smetana and Anton Dvořák (1841-1904) might suggest a stronger affinity in their orchestration than is actually discernable. Both were excellent colourists, and neither can be said to have been a very marked adherent of any particular national school of orchestration. If a theory of succession and its resulting influence were to be applied to the orchestration of these two Bohemian composers, it would seem to be almost more feasible were they placed in chronologically reversed positions ; whereas Smetana's work does show some dependence on the example of Wagner and Liszt, that of Dvořák might easily have been evolved without owing anything to the advanced German school.

Pursuing a course of happy moderation between the neutral-tinted thickness of Brahms' and the more voluptuous intensity of Tschaikovsky's work, Dvořák's orchestration might well stand as representative of what would have been the normal development of the art towards the close of the nineteenth century, had no such composers as Berlioz, Wagner and Liszt appeared on the scene. His melodic and harmonic treatment of the brass instruments is just what might have been expected to ensue as the result of the common use of valve instruments, and of the introduction of trombones into the concert-orchestra.

In distributing his musical matter amongst the available tone-colours, whether intuitively or by the exercise of reason, Dvořák followed what was more a French, or a Russian, than a German proclivity, as is manifested by his choice of unrelated tone-colours for the various functions, melodic lines and harmonic matter, which generally holds good throughout his mature work. In this respect he did not go anything like so far as did Tschaikovsky, but he went far enough to ensure clearness of outline and, on the whole, to maintain good balance of tone. Thus, the concentration of one part in unison on one entire section of the orchestra is comparatively uncommon in Dvořák's scores, and the resulting tone-quality not so intense as it is in the mature work of his Russian contemporary. In using self-contained groups of instruments by way of contrast, Dvořák again stood at a point midway between the two contemporary extremes as represented by Brahms and Tschaikovsky, but showed sufficient instinct for variety and contrast to entitle him to be classed as a pronounced colourist. While following a classical model generally, Dvořák's *tutti* are relieved from the charge of conventionality by his ready use of the brass voices for thematic matter of primary importance, and have all the brilliance and full tone which were concomitant with the extended upward range of orchestral violin parts, and the more generously provided brass harmony of late nineteenth century orchestration. The variety given by strong dynamic contrasts, by the alternation of thin or full part-writing, of high and low pitch, and by alternative treatment of themes, all helps to impart to Dvořák's orchestration an attractiveness which aids so well the orchestral presentation of his strongly metrical and picturesque musical matter. Some particular features of his orchestration are the effects of his somewhat individual type of figuration, and of his free use of shakes and mordents in the wood-wind parts.

The orchestration of Edvard Hagerup Grieg (1843-1907) shows a certain peculiarity owing to the composer's method of conceiving his music, in the first place, in terms of the keyboard, and then, as a separate operation, of translating it into orchestral language. So thinly disguised is the pianistic origin of his matter that the " hand on the keyboard " can often be easily detected in the deployment of his orchestral parts. The above consideration, combined with the rhythmical squareness of his melodic matter, and the absence of the contrapuntal element in the texture of his music, renders Grieg's orchestration very simple of construction and easy to dissect.

For Grieg, to transcribe his music for orchestra meant simply to select suitable tone-colours for melodic and for accompanying parts, and to provide changes of colour and treatment at obviously suitable moments. The element of selection is often betrayed very clearly by the ingenuousness with which it is carried out, a process not unlike that of a child selecting colours from a paint box when colouring a given outline drawing. A preference for natural unmixed tone-colours, and an instinct for picturesque effect, usually assured the choice of quite appropriate instruments, or groups of instruments, for both melodic and harmonic purposes ; allied with the individual qualities of his music, Grieg's orchestration thus presents an attractive succession of clearly differentiated colour, agreeably varied, well-defined in outline, and quite free from any ambiguity of intention. In spite of occasional miscalculations affecting the balance of tone, an amateurish weakness for dividing his string parts, and a certain theatrical tawdriness in his effects, Grieg generally managed to hit the mark when devising orchestral equivalents for his pianistically-conceived music, and, by the transparency and unsophisticated freshness of his methods, probably made more of his strongly individual musical matter than would have been possible had he employed the more sophisticated formulæ of the German school to which he owed what he had of academical training.

CHAPTER XIV

STRAUSS—DEBUSSY—ELGAR

A PERIOD covering roughly the last ten years of last century and the first few years of the present century, will act as a link connecting what is really nineteenth century orchestration with the art of the present day. With the end of that period any attempt to deal with the historical aspect of this or of any other subject must necessarily be suspended, for the evolution which is in progress at the moment is not history to us, nor will it become history until sufficient time has passed to enable the historian to see in its proper perspective the true course of what to-day is quite undetermined, uncertain in its course, or at best a matter for speculation. The line, therefore, which has to be drawn somewhere, will be drawn at those of modern composers who were born after 1865, or in other words, at those whose maturity comes entirely within the present century.

The programmes of orchestral concerts and the repertoires of opera houses during the period first defined show a large preponderance of the names of what are frequently termed "classical" and "romantic" composers, together with a substantial proportion of such names as Wagner, Tschaikovsky, and their contemporaries. To these a leavening of fresh names began to be added shortly before the close of last century, largely the names of composers born between 1855 and 1865. These were composers who were practically in the student stage, and therefore susceptible to the influence of the work of the successful and mature composers of the moment, just when the music of Wagner began to be widely diffused, and who, before their own maturity was reached, would also be more or less subject to any such influences as arose from the frequent performance of works by composers of the Brahms-Tschaikovsky period.

Of those younger men the most prominent and influential appear to have been : Strauss—representing the continuance of what was called in the last chapter the advanced German or Wagnerian school ; Debussy—as far as orchestration is concerned,

a successor only in part to the previous generation of French
composers, and otherwise the inaugurator of a distinctive
style which has shed certain of the earlier French characteristics ;
Elgar—an individualist orchestrator whose influence has, so far,
been almost entirely confined to Great Britain ; and an Italian
operatic group comprising Mascagni, Leoncavallo and Puccini,
inheritors of an unbroken Italian tradition. With Strauss may
be grouped Mahler ; with Debussy, such contemporaries as
Dukas, Chausson and Charpentier ; with Elgar, such widely
different composers as German and Delius. The corresponding
Russian generation may be represented by Glazounov, but it
should be remembered that the music of Rimsky-Korsakov and
his contemporaries, in fact, Russian music in general apart from
that of Tschaikovsky, had hardly gained any footing outside
of Russia before a younger generation of composers were already
taking possession of the international ear. Contemporaneous
names such as Sibelius (Finnish) and MacDowell (American)
serve to show the widening of the circle of nationality from which
influences in musical art or orchestration might have been
expected during the period which will be made to close this
survey.

If orchestration still flowed in channels distinguishable one
from the other and characterized by national style, it must be
granted that the influence of a few prominent and successful
composers' work, at the end of last century, soon after took effect
in producing a large amount of work which can only be classed
as cosmopolitan or non-stylistic. The modern circumstances and
conditions, under which orchestral music may be very quickly
diffused, have operated so as to ensure the immediate imitation or
emulation of any particular effect or suggestive device almost as
soon as it is heard, the only essential being success, and as a
corollary, frequent performance. As a consequence, the numerous
second and third-rank composers, who now abound in almost every
civilized country, by no means always betray their nationality
by their orchestration, but, on the contrary, may be trusted to
pick here and there from the most diverse and divergent types
of orchestration as practised by a few prominent composers of
the time, of whatever nationality.

The end of last century found the influence of Wagner and
Tschaikovsky predominant in orchestration. Wagner's effects
had become the common property of every student, theatrical

conductor, arranger or adaptor. On that foundation have been super-imposed the varying influences of Strauss and Debussy, of the recently emerged Russians, and, to a lesser extent, those of the Italians, and of Elgar.

When the great bulk of the music produced about the end of last century meets with its ultimate fate, the surviving remainder will probably show that national style in orchestration was still clearly distinguishable, and that a German, a French, a Russian, and an Italian style still continued to exist in the midst of a great variety of cross-styles. Time may yet prove that a British style has been, or is being formed. Whatever the eventual verdict of Time, credit in the meantime seems to be due to Strauss, Debussy, and Elgar, as individual and representative composers, for carrying on the development of the art which followed chronologically on that of Brahms and Tschaikovsky, and in their works may be sought the advanced orchestration, and presumably the vital orchestration, of a period in musical history which still lies almost too near the present day to ensure a perfectly clear and balanced judgment.

Full scores from round about twenty-five years ago show that the tendency to increase the size of orchestras still continued as hitherto. By adding more to the number of instruments already represented, and by adding still more representatives of the same types, but of either higher or lower pitch, the volume of available sound was increased, but without corresponding gain of variety of effect. Time will probably show that the culmination of the growth of the orchestra, that is, merely as regards its bulk or numbers, was reached by about the beginning of the present century, and that orchestration at that time did not owe its further advancement to any increased volume of sound, but rather to increased variety of treatment of the instruments, or the groups of instruments, which were already long and firmly established members of the combination. Quite apart from non-musical considerations, the constant addition to the volume of the tone-colours already well represented in the orchestra has since apparently met with a check; it would now seem as if he who would add permanently a new instrument to the orchestral family must necessarily at the same time invent a new method of setting air into vibration.

Of the instruments themselves there is nothing of importance to add to what has already been written; minor mechanical improvements in key-action and other facilities still appear from time to time, and give added convenience to the wind-player, but little if anything to the orchestrator.

A ready response to the increased demands for executive skill required by the orchestral parts of Strauss, and for sensitive playing by the scores of Debussy, Elgar and others, was forthcoming from orchestral players as the works of those composers became more and more frequently played ; likewise, the interpretive powers of conductors kept pace with the exacting demands of full scores which by no means " played themselves," but left more than ever to the technical skill and musical insight of the generation of conductors which succeeded the famous race of Wagner-conductors of the late nineteenth century.

The benefits accruing to students of orchestration by the issue by many publishers of miniature full scores should not be overlooked when surveying the progress of orchestration just at the junction of the nineteenth with the present century.

As a preliminary to the series of symphonic poems, by means of which Richard Strauss (1864–1949) has made such contributions to progress in orchestration as have been equalled by few, if any, of his generation, the early symphony in F minor (1884) will serve, if only as an interesting yet immature starting point from which to begin to trace the growth of his remarkable power in handling the orchestra.

Although written at the age of nineteen, the score shows no signs of inexperience. The music is polyphonic, rather in the manner of Brahms, and unmistakably German in its orchestration, especially in the tendency to employ rich, thick-toned but smooth, combinations in the lower register of the orchestra. Contrasted grouping of wood-wind, brass and strings, is frequent, yet quite conventional, and when used together, the three main instrumental choirs preserve their own identity and carry out their allocated functions clearly and independently. Even at that early age Strauss shows a clearer conception of the diverse functions of the three main groups than did Brahms in his most mature period. The brass parts in his symphony, moving over a wide range of compass, are freely melodic. The whole shows the hand of one thoroughly versed in the German tradition, fond of sonority, yet alive to the value of clearness and contrast of tone-colour. The style is that of the concert-room, not of the theatre, and provides the fullness of the Wagnerian manner with neither its picturesqueness nor the pattern-weaving of moving harmonic backgrounds which fits a theatrical, more readily than a symphonic, style. The normal full orchestra of Brahms and Tschaikovsky is employed. In view of his later achievements this first symphony has little more than historical interest, but it shows the composer able to express himself in orchestral language with complete assurance, and, from the point of view of orchestration, competent to do more than justice to his musical matter.

Thus equipped at such an early stage in his career, it is not surprising to find Strauss developing independence and individuality in the orchestration of his next group of works, comprising the symphonic poems *Macbeth* (1887), *Don Juan* (1888) and *Tod und Verklärung* (1889).

Not content with the standard symphony orchestra, Strauss adds the usual third representative to each of the wood-wind types, a third trumpet (also a bass trumpet in *Macbeth*) and some extra percussion instruments and harps.

Effects producing special tone-qualities and colours, few of them new, yet hardly everyday sounds in the orchestras of the time, are drawn on with frequency, albeit in moderation ; such are, in the string orchestra : *sul ponticello*, four-note arpeggios across the strings, solo string parts ; in the wind, muting of brass voices, stopped horn passages played *fortissimo*, and directions to reinforce brass tone by directing the bells of the instruments towards the audience ; also the use of wooden-headed drumsticks (à la Berlioz), cymbals and tam-tam struck with hard sticks or triangle beater, side drum played " off " and so on ; harp *glissando*, harmonics and *tremolo* for harps, *tremolo* for *glockenspiel*, and such-like devices, show an increasing search for sounds which were not then part and parcel of the ordinary routine of orchestration.

With larger forces, and no doubt, a riper judgment, Strauss soon found out the necessity for concentrating instruments of one type on parts for which he required special prominence and intensity of tone ; thus the octave-unison treatment of wood-wind, of all the upper strings, and of the various brass instruments, figures more and more frequently in these scores. Melodic parts for brass instruments of unusually wide compass, chromatic, *legato* and string-like in character, and very free in movement, adumbrate what was to prove a strong characteristic of Strauss' later work, and, combined with a fearlessness in carrying parts

to the extremes of the instruments' compass, produce that force-
ful type of tone-intensity which, especially in a contrapuntal
texture, has since become a familiar feature in orchestration.

The grouping of instrumental voices, carried out, sometimes
for the sake of contrast or variety of tone-colour, sometimes for
the sake of balance, and at other times merely as the result of a
desire for more volume of tone, appears as a further growth of
what was at that time the accepted practice amongst those
composers whose musical matter demanded sonorous and vigorous
treatment. A rich, yet clear, deployment of parts, in spite of a
growing tendency towards elaboration of texture, kept the
orchestration of these three symphonic poems still recognizably
in the direct line of succession to Wagner's use of similar means
for his own dramatic purposes, and marked a stage in the
development of an orchestrator whose invention and resource
were still quickly growing, yet who had already left the
impression of his own individuality on the art.

After an essay at opera—*Guntram* (1894)—Strauss again
turned his attention to the symphonic poem, and produced a
series of four such works during the last few years of the century :
Till Eulenspiegel (1894), *Also sprach Zarathustra* (1895), *Don
Quixote* (1897) and *Ein Heldenleben* (1898).

In these works the composer emerged free from any restraining
influence, and, throwing aside any such hesitation as was based
merely on respect for conventional methods, appeared as an
orchestrator standing quite independently on his own ground,
as an innovator who had done with the models of others, and
complete master of his own gigantic instrument.

The craving for more, and yet more, volume of sound is again
evident. Four of each type of wood-wind (including high clarinets
in either D or E-flat), from six to eight horns, four, five or six
trumpets, three trombones and two tubas, organ, all manner of
drums, harps, bells, and such contrivances as a wind-machine
and a big rattle, in addition to a string orchestra on a large scale,
are demanded in one or other of these immense full scores. In
technical difficulty the parts easily outdid anything that had been
expected of orchestral players hitherto, while, for certain solo
string parts, nothing but execution and musicianship of the
highest order would suffice.

Devices which had formerly been regarded as exceptional,
or to be kept in reserve for special dramatic moments, were now

handled as commonplaces, while others were invented ; the sub-division of string parts was sometimes carried so far that each desk had its own part ; in *Also sprach Zarathustra* six desks of violas are occupied each with its own *tremolo* on artificial harmonics ; five solo violins play independently in *Till Eulenspiegel :* a pronounced use of the *portamento* effect is specified in the same work ; three or four-part chords for divided double-basses are common ; the wood-wind have to render not only *legato tremolo* alternating between two notes, but are also required to execute repetitional *tremolo* by means of tonguing, on one note ; a novel method of articulation—*flatterzunge*—for flutes, is requisitioned in *Don Quixote;* strong *portamento* for wood-wind is also indicated ; the muting of brass instruments, even down to the tubas, appears without the air of self-conscious novelty ; two trumpets or four horns are given simultaneous shakes to play ; the brass group are made to create a repetitional *tongue-tremolo :* rapid chromatic passages of almost pianistic appearance occur freely in the brass parts ; the organ is used as an orchestral instrument for the sake of its own tone-quality, and so on.

The above reads almost like orchestral sounds in a state of anarchy ; but these are only the unaccustomed effects which Strauss gradually accumulated during the last years of the century, and let loose, possibly sometimes in the spirit of *tours de force,* at ears which still regarded the orchestra as a composite instrument to be used only to produce sounds in which the smooth beauty of euphony was the result aimed at. Disregarding such special efforts, and the many unusual effects which arise from the adventitious juxtaposition of unaccustomed notes and tone-colours when the resources of a large orchestra are used un-conventionally, the orchestration of these four symphonic poems presents other features which bear strongly on the present state of orchestration.

The growing contrapuntal complexity of Strauss' musical matter had by this time largely dissipated any possibility of treating the *tutti* according to the old axiom that each main group of the orchestra should in itself provide a substantially complete harmonic version of the music being played ; indeed, the hard and fast distinction between what was, and what was not *tutti,* had practically disappeared. When the full, or nearly full, forces of the large modern orchestra are employed, the problem of securing adequate tonal force for each melodic part in a contrapuntal texture threatens to become, except in soft orchestration, more a question of balance than one of tone-colour, and the only way to secure due prominence for parts is to resort to an extensive doubling of parts in unison or octaves. The unison-octave treatment of from six to eight horns, of from twelve to sixteen wood-wind instruments, of three trombones and two tubas, or of the entire string orchestra, in these mature works of Strauss, amply supports the practice of Tschaikovsky in giving each part as far as possible to instruments of one type or family ; yet Strauss is often driven to more mixing of tone-colours, in his efforts to secure balance and intensity of tone, than is compatible with absolute clearness of part-outline, and frequently reinforces his parts by the addition of tone which is apparently selected for the sake of its weight rather than only for the sake of its tone-colour. His horns thus frequently find themselves playing in unison with the various string parts, intensifying parts which are string-like both in conception and in compass. Trumpets, tubas, and even trombones, are also asked to duplicate active *legato* string parts when nothing else would give these parts sufficient weight and penetrating power. This tendency grew on Strauss as his development proceeded, reaching its full growth in *Ein Heldenleben* and in subsequent works, and has actually exerted a noticeable influence on brass instrument-playing in orchestras since the appearance of these mature works.

The orchestration of *Till Eulenspiegel* is actually clearer than that of *Ein Heldenleben* : this is not only due to the above considerations, but also to the fact that Strauss' musical matter became more and more crowded with opposing interests as time went on. The weaving of harmonic backgrounds which owe their texture to mere *movement* of parts, was a successful feature of Wagner's dramatic tone-painting ; Strauss, as he progressed, almost excluded the element of harmonic padding from his music, and instead, added a multiplication of contrapuntal interests which, when combined with the daring and freedom of his harmonic schemes, produced textures in which the jostling of opposing interests often comes dangerously near to mere confusion. The process became intensified after *Till Eulenspiegel*; both *Also sprach Zarathustra* and *Don Quixote* show it maturing, and in *Ein Heldenleben*, and in the *Symphonia Domestica*, are found moments when the actual musical outlines become completely obscured, and are indistinguishable, simply because there are too many of them going on at the same time. Parts interfere with the clearness of one another till they merge into a din which the ear is unable to disentangle. Whether Strauss actually intended to produce the confused sounds that sometimes proceed from the orchestra, or whether he did not, is a question the answer to which lies hidden in the composer's conscience.

The deliberately designed cacophony which also makes its appearance in *Ein Heldenleben* is quite another matter ; here the intention of the composer cannot be misunderstood. The part labelled " critics " sounds, and is intended to sound, ridiculous. The effect to the unhardened ear of twenty-five years ago was simply that of a lot of parts, having no connection with each other, being played at the same time. It has since been found that nothing is easier than to make the orchestra emit odd sounds. Recklessness and audacity are the only necessities in the equipment of composers who would act " the funny man " with the orchestra.

Apart from moments of confusion, designed or fortuitous, and moments when the composer was frankly fooling with the orchestra, Strauss' work in his four symphonic poems, as in the opera *Feuersnot* (1901), shows him at his best, standing one amongst few at that time as an orchestrator whose power to present his music in orchestral clothing was completely on a level with the advanced state of his development as a composer. The force and virility of his music found its counterpart in his orchestration, and as a super-orchestrator his model was at once accepted for imitation by many who found his example irresistible.

When considering the constitution of the orchestra for his *Symphonia Domestica* (1904), it seems as if Strauss was looking around for more instruments to add to the already rather unwieldy bulk of the symphony orchestra, and as if it occurred to him that he had not yet broached the Saxophone family. Four saxophones were accordingly included in a score which also demands some eighteen wood-wind and sixteen brass instruments, two harps, sundry percussion, and the usual string orchestra. Little need be said of this comparative failure of Strauss to add another storey to a building which seemed already high enough. The same masterful control of his material, the same bold sweep of his orchestral brush, and the same tendency to sometimes

present more than the ear can accommodate, suggest a development at a stage just beyond its ripest, unable to grow further
without becoming distorted, and now only waiting to run to seed.
No further variety could be extracted even from this huge orchestra
as long as the same course of development was pursued. No
fresh colours could be created by a mere increase in tone-volume ;
Strauss had got so much colour on his orchestral palette that
continued mixing of them produced no novel tints.

Salome (1905) showed the composer skilled as ever, but
inclined to seek novelty by over-loading his score, by aiming at
mere oddity, and by straining after effects by means of elaboration.
The rest of Strauss' work abuts too closely on the orchestration
of the present day for any just appraisement of its ultimate
value.   In the meantime a younger generation of composers has
appeared in the arena ; to some of them has probably been
entrusted the responsibility of shaping the course which can only
be described when it can be clearly seen, that is, when Time has
brushed away much that at the moment seems important, yet
which may easily prove to be of little consequence in the
long run.

Whatever their tendencies, styles or tastes, for orchestration
purely as such, the present generation of composers owe to Strauss
as great a debt as that which he owed to Wagner.   Without the
Strauss of 1895-1905, orchestration at this day would have been
appreciably the poorer, and the vanguard of progress some steps
in arrear of its present position.

Less influential than Strauss, because less successful, Gustav
Mahler (1860-1911) must nevertheless be counted as important
amongst those composers who made very definite efforts to bring
orchestration some steps forward on the path which had been
opened up and surveyed by Wagner.   Mahler's symphonies
began to appear during the same period which has marked Strauss'
greatest activity, namely from 1888 onwards, for about two
decades.

Like those of Strauss, his ideas of an adequate symphony
orchestra grew continuously, till the proportions of the body
rendered his works playable only under conditions which could
afford to disregard any ordinary economy, either of means, time
or concert-room space.   The fifth symphony (published 1904)
requires only thirteen wood-wind, six horns, four trumpets, three
trombones, tuba, drums, etc., harp and strings, but the *finale* of

his sixth symphony specifies piccolo, four flutes, four oboes, *cor anglais*, D clarinet, three ordinary clarinets, bass clarinet, four bassoons and double-bassoon (twenty wood-wind), eight horns, six trumpets, four trombones, tuba, numerous percussion, bells, harps, celesta, etc., and strings in due proportion. These significant signs of a Teutonic tendency towards excess in the early years of this century were not confined only to the size of the orchestra, but also affected the length of time occupied by the performance of a work, in the case of this sixth symphony, no less than seventy-seven minutes.

Such an overwhelming quantity of tone, such a wealth of colour, combined, in the hands of a thoroughly practical man, with a serious aim and a progressive spirit, could hardly fail to produce orchestration which is striking and impressive, whatever the intrinsic value of the music it clothes. All the latest devices of Strauss, such as the frequent muting of brass voices, directions for wind instruments to be played with their bells raised, *tremolo* for wood-wind, rapid chromatic scales for brass instruments, harp *glissando*, and so on, accompanied by numerous and minute written directions as to the manner of rendering, are to be found in Mahler's full scores. These, with the same growing elaboration of texture, and the increasingly harsh clash of interests in the music itself, must suffice to convey to the mind a picture of these full scores by a composer whose music has never been taken quite as seriously in this country as it has been in certain others. Mahler's work is not only amply, but is clearly coloured, and that he was no mere glutton for sound is sometimes shown in his works when, as in the fourth movement of the fifth symphony, scored only for strings and harp, the ear is allowed a prolonged period of quiet and restful tone-colouring. Both Strauss and Mahler have by their inventiveness, skill and boldness, also by the massiveness of their conceptions, given much to orchestration ; but, if the lessons of Teutonic orchestration in the early years of this century have been properly learned, they will surely prove to have shown that orchestration has nothing more to gain from a mere increase in volume of sound ; that variety of colour, of treatment and texture, have more to offer ; that the ear will find continued stress and complexity of construction in the long run as monotonous as continued dullness, and that periods of restfulness alone can serve to give contiguous periods of excitement and energy their due effect.

Apart from the work of Debussy, and of several rather younger composers who have followed closely on his heels, French orchestration at the close of last century retained only some of that clearness, transparency, and characteristic fitness which marks the work of Saint-Saëns and others who were not only the forbears, but at the same time, the contemporaries, of their younger successors. Of three representative examples Paul Dukas (1865-1935), if only by virtue of his attractive *L'Apprenti Sorcier*, stands out as a composer whose orchestration has in it that directness of aim, well-balanced clearness, and at the same time that brilliance, which kept French orchestration in a channel of its own during the last half of last century. The resources of a large orchestra, the French custom of writing for three or four bassoons, and for a pair of cornets in addition to two trumpets, the ready play with harps, *glockenspiel*, and sundry percussion instruments, together with many of the orchestral devices which at the time were more or less unfamiliar, were used by Dukas without obscuring the clear definition of his tone-colouring, and without any of the more crowded intensity of the contemporary German manner. Less characteristically French, less clear, and more tainted with a somewhat half-hearted Wagnerism, is the work of some composers for whom Ernest Chausson (1855-1899) may stand as a representative of type. A third name, Gustave Charpentier (1860-1956), typifies those French composers of the period whose rather more sentimental semi-impressionism has been attractively presented by means of orchestration treated in truly Parisian theatrical style ; rich, yet not ponderous, clear and to the point, the orchestration shows them modernized upholders of the native tradition, tinctured with the impressionism which was permeating French art towards the end of last century.

It would be difficult to find a parallel in the whole history of music for two contemporary composers the tenets of whose artistic creeds were so completely divergent as were those of Strauss and Claude Debussy (1862-1918). Like their music, their orchestration shows each handling the same raw material, using many of the same technical devices and the same instrumental tone-colours, yet producing completely different final impressions. The one so largely depending on the arguments of force and volume, the other on quality ; the one exuberant and animal, the other reticent and spiritual ; both were logical and consistent, yet mutually discrepant—the one a true German, the other a true Frenchman. Debussy's orchestras are often small, sometimes fairly large, but never large for the purpose of producing a big volume of tone. *L'Après-midi d'un faune* (1892) is scored for three flutes, two oboes, *cor anglais*, two clarinets, bassoons, four horns, two harps, strings and *cymbals antiques*: *Gigues* requires two piccolos, two flutes, two oboes, *oboe d'amore*, *cor anglais*, three clarinets, bass clarinet, three bassoons and double-bassoon, four horns, four trumpets, three trombones, drums, cymbals, side-drum, xylophone, celesta, harps and strings; in the latter piece—some 235 bars of music— the trombones play only in fourteen bars, and quite softly in eight of these. Such a word as *tutti* is hardly usable in connection with orchestration which, like Debussy's, speaks with a hushed voice in delicately varied and subtly blended tone-colours, and often with intentionally blurred outlines.

In such delicately constituted orchestration the string group is not unnaturally often sensitively sub-divided, each part into two or more parts, by desks, solo parts, muted and unmuted groups, into sections playing harmonics, *pizzicato*, *sur le chevalet* or *sur la touche*, with bow or finger *tremolo*, into varieties of texture, sometimes thinly disposed and widespread, at other times more fully and congested; there are often many notes, but there is rarely much volume of sound.

The wood-wind speak sometimes in thin melodic lines for solo voices, sometimes in blended groups, both overlapping and picking up the threads of melody or harmony, one from the other, with carefully concealed joints. Much is made of the peculiar tone-quality of low flute notes, or of the veiled quality of high bassoon notes; anything approaching wholesale harmonic or wholesale unison-octave treatment of the entire wood-wind group is rare.

The brass voices are often muted, sometimes holding soft sustained sounds of great duration, sometimes strangely active like wood-wind, but rarely do they speak out or proclaim their message. Trumpets in particular are frequently required to be chromatically active, throwing in little squirts of muted tone-colour at odd moments. The brass as a group just occasionally flare up into brilliance for a moment, perhaps only for a second or two in a whole piece, and then subside. Like most French composers, Debussy wrote for three tenor trombones, and placed the parts close together. These instruments are not allowed any rhetorical swagger ; they may be menacing for a moment, they may angrily bark or spit, but pompousness and eloquence are denied them. Whatever their function, they are never allowed to overdo it.

In some of his scores Debussy makes much subtle play with the sounds of percussion instruments. Such as hardly audible rolls on a cymbal, or light elusive touches on a side-drum, put in an appearance, and then vanish as if they had lost themselves. Quite a curiosity is the timpani part in *Gigues* with its *acciaccaturas*, the three instruments being tuned to low F-sharp, G-sharp and A. The importance and careful elaboration of Debussy's harp parts, and indeed his dependence on the harp generally, are typically French. Harmonics for harps abound, and *glissando* scales carried out on a whole-tone-scale tuning are, of course, in constant requisition.   To the delicate sound-combinations are often added such as a note here and there from the xylophone, or a gentle touch from the celesta.

In Debussy's hands the orchestra became a super-sensitive instrument.   In *Pelléas and Mélisande* (score 1902) it murmurs dreamily to itself, speaks or suggests in veiled tones, swells up for a moment and again subsides or dwindles down almost to disappearance. The outspoken clearness, the well-defined outlines and transparent intentions of his native predecessors were of less use to Debussy than their delicacy and their tentative experiments in impressionistic tone-painting. These latter characteristics he developed and made so much his own, that Debussy may be said to have created his own manner of orchestral speech, a manner which was readily adopted by many sympathetic composers, both French and otherwise, as soon as his works found recognition.

As a foil to any tendency of orchestration to become blatant, gross, and overladen with tone at the close of last century, Debussy's work has acted admirably, but it is not orchestration for every composer's music ; not for music that speaks with virile or heroic accents, not for the pompous, not for the theatrical, nor for the composers who build on a foundation of folk-song. Paradoxically, Strauss and Debussy, although pulling in opposite directions at the same time, have both pulled orchestration onwards on the path of progress.

The mature works of Edward Elgar (1857–1934) began to appear rather later than those of Strauss and Debussy, in fact largely in the present century. Excluding fairly recent works, his important output is as follows : *Enigma Variations* (1899) ; *The Dream of Gerontius* (1900) ; *Cockaigne* overture (1901) ; *The Apostles* (1903) ; *In the South* overture (1904) ; *The Kingdom* (1906) ; *Symphony No. 1* (1908) ; *Violin Concerto* (1910) ; *Symphony No. 2* (1911).

Like most of his contemporaries, Elgar began satisfied with the moderate dimensions of the standard symphony orchestra plus a very few additional instruments, but demanded greater resources in his later works. A double-bassoon, a third trumpet, and a few percussion instruments are specified in the score of the Variations ; the Oratorios demand third representatives of the wood-wind types, occasional extra brass, percussion, bells, harps, and organ ; the two symphonies are alike in their demand for three of each wood-wind type, except that a high clarinet is required for the second of these works, both specify the usual four horns, three trumpets, three trombones, tuba, timpani and harps, and some extra percussion for the later work. There is in these specifications no desire for an overgrown amount of brass tone, nor for any superficial or realistic percussion effects.

The orchestration of the Variations shows a modern fullness of tone, rich, yet not overwhelming, contrasted with many lighter and very delicately handled sections. The clearness is due to the choice of distinctive tone-colours for each function, to the absence of harmonic padding in the more lightly treated sections, and to a carefully considered balance of tone when a more full and intense volume of sound is produced. Very sharp contrasts are, on the whole, avoided by smoothing down the colour-outlines by a process of overlapping the tone-colours, a characteristic of Elgar's which grew as the development of his orchestral style proceeded. Individual features of the score are : the extraordinary edge given to the bass figure by three timpani in the seventh variation, and the peculiar texture—divided violas, solo violoncello and a timpani roll played with side-drum sticks— accompanying the " quotation " in the thirteenth variation.

Coming nine years after the Variations, the orchestration of the first symphony shows a more mature and settled policy, more individuality, and some invention. The music itself is more highly organized, yet there is little of it that could not be reduced to a satisfactory framework of four-part writing ; the actual melodic shape of the parts may be disguised by their moving in inverted intervals, by undulatory figuration, by their joining one part for a note or two and then following the course of another, or by their reinforcing only particular portions of a phrase. All these contribute to a complexity which is more apparent than real, a texture more involved on paper than it is in performance, yet obviously written with full intention, and producing modifications of tone-colour which are subtly and carefully thought out.

Elgar's individuality in his orchestration lies in his highly developed faculty for blending tone-colours ; the primary colours of the orchestra are rarely employed in an unmixed state ; in the first movement of the first symphony there are not twenty bars left entirely to the strings, and hardly any to either wood-wind or brass groups alone. The parts are distributed in a manner which provides plenty of colour-contrasts, but these merge one into the other without exposing clearly defined boundaries. This elaborate process of blending is carried out, sometimes with the object of creating particular qualities of sound, and at other times with a view to adjusting the balance of tone. Elgar's colouring is never very obvious, nor is his method of arriving at the various tints transparent or easy to reconstruct without seeing the full score. The minutely graded inflections of tone-colour often require careful attention if they are to be heard and appreciated, and the more delicate textures especially are more highly organized than might be expected from simply hearing the result. In fuller orchestration the parts are reinforced from all over the orchestra with such tone-weight as will ensure pro-portionate prominence and adequate penetration. The details of the process are interesting, the more so as they reveal methods the very reverse of those employed by Tschaikovsky. While Tschaikovsky aimed at very clear definition of each part by concentrating instruments of allied tone-colour on any one part, Elgar selects from various types of tone-colour and secures equal richness and sonority, yet less clearly defined part-outlines.

In the second symphony a rather more complex musical texture is treated with the same full compounds of mixed tone-colours, each blend merging into the next by stages sometimes so finely graduated as to be practically unnoticeable. Rarely does any group act alone and in sharp contrast with another group, yet the blends themselves are contrasted, not only by virtue of their tone-colour, but also on account of their texture.

Of some completely new orchestral devices which stand to Elgar's credit, the *pizzicato tremolando* in the last movement of the Violin Concerto merits special mention.

Relying less on elementary colour-contrasts, and more on smooth blend and gradual transformation, Elgar's full orchestration has all the richness of Strauss' without its brute force ; the element of the surprising, the rash or eccentric, in the German's scores find their counterpart only in a more suave humour in those of the English composer. In its quieter moments Elgar's orchestration has some of the delicacy and elusiveness of Debussy's, without the Frenchman's vagueness and frail construction. All three composers have advanced the technique of orchestration by their inventiveness and resource, yet each, using the same raw material, has developed on lines which show as clearly as ever how a composer's orchestration is indefinably bound up with his own musical individuality.

Other British composers of the same generation as Elgar provide a continued example of the eclecticism which has for so long prevailed in orchestration in this country. The pleasing and unpretentious complacency in the work of Edward German (1862–1936) contrasts strangely with the precursive spirit which has always pervaded the orchestration of Frederick Delius (1863–1934), even before the latter's works had won any sort of recognition in England. Delius' works are usually scored for a large orchestra, including three or four of each wood-wind type, six horns, three trumpets, three tenor trombones, tuba, harps, drums, etc., and up to recent times have shown a variety of tendencies, ranging from the rich intensity of the German model to the delicately shaded sensitivity of modern French impressionism ; his opera *Koanga* (1895–97) and the orchestral piece *Paris* (1899) led the way to more distinctive work in *Brigg Fair* (1907), *In a Summer Garden* (1908) and *A Dance Rhapsody* (1908), in the last of which are used two organizations of the string orchestra[1], also the bass oboe and low sarrusophone. Delius' work, however, really belongs more to the story of orchestration in quite recent years than to that of a quarter of a century ago.

The work of three Italian composers of opera whose initial successes were scored in the last few years of last century show that, in spite of a limited infiltration of Wagnerian influences,

[1] A full group of 16, 16, 12, 12, 12, and a smaller group of 8, 8, 6, 4, 4 players.

Italian operatic orchestration was still securely contained within bounds which were indigenous to the country where opera had its birth. A series of popular successes was opened by Pietro Mascagni (1863–1945) with *Cavalleria rusticana* (1890), closely followed by Ruggiero Leoncavallo (1858–1919) with *Pagliacci* (1892) ; more consistently successful has been the output of Giacomo Puccini (1858–1924), whose first successes, *Manon Lescaut* (1893) and *La Bohème* (1896), have been repeated in his subsequent operas, *Tosca* (1900) and *Madame Butterfly* (1904).

Like that of their forbears, the orchestration of these Italians has the great merit that it usually produces exactly the effect the composers intended. Their aim is sure, and rarely fails in its effect. The desired effects may be bald and obvious, theatrical, showy and transparently devised, they may sometimes be a trifle vulgar, but they cannot be said to be inconsistent with the dramatic feeling which the composers sought to express. The straightforward use of the primary tone-colours of the orchestra, and of the main and subsidiary groups of instruments, both without any great elaboration of texture, ensures clear colour-definition and contrast, the latter, it may be, often dynamically exaggerated or over-emphasised, but generally distinctly, if theatrically, presented.

The superior musicianship of Puccini, compared with that of either Mascagni or Leoncavallo, is reflected in the orchestration of the four operas mentioned above. The attractive clearness of his work is partly due to the fact that he never puts more into the texture of the music than the instruments can express without one part interfering with another. A frankly straightforward use of the instrumental groups of the orchestra, keeping each group to a particular function whenever it is involved, emphasizes this clearness, and ensures effectiveness, even though the means employed are simple enough. Puccini's *tutti* are based on quite conventional formulæ, but in other respects he uses the more recent devices of orchestration freely and quite successfully. Like many Italian opera composers he incorporates a certain amount of obvious keyboard-idiom in his orchestral music. The orchestras employed are moderate in size and quite normal in constitution, except that three tenor and one bass trombone are specified, but no tuba.

Without making any attempt to bring it completely up-to-date, the story of orchestration in the hands of Russian composers may be rounded off by reference to the work of Alexander Glazounov (1865–1936), the youngest of that chain of composers which reaches back to Glinka, but whose music only became influential outside of Russia during a period lying well within living memory.

Equipped with a musicianship and a technique much sounder than those of several of the previous generation of Russians, Glazounov—if judged solely by his orchestration—can hardly be reckoned one of the true breed of Russian nationalists. His fifth, sixth and seventh symphonies (1895-1901) show good sound orchestration in a manner as much German as it is Russian, with neither the individuality of Tschaikovsky nor the inventiveness of Rimsky-Korsakov, and quite free from that unsophisticated roughness which marks the work of several Russians whose aim was the consolidation of a strongly national school. Well coloured though it is, the brilliance and clearness of Glazounov's work are slightly dulled by his readiness to duplicate the same part by instruments of different tone-colour, and to generally smooth over the sharp contrasts between distinctive groups of instruments. It seems almost as if the native element in orchestration had been distilled out of him by education and musicianship, leaving behind a residue of diluted brilliance.

Altogether, the story of Russian orchestration during the nineteenth century seems to point to the conclusion that sophistication tended to act so as to rob the orchestration of what was its strongest native characteristic, while, on the other hand, unsophistication generally produced the crudeness which usually goes hand in hand with inefficient technique. Exceptionally, Tschaikovsky combined a good technique with his own individual and successful methods, and so retained the clearness of colouring which properly belongs to Russian orchestration.

The popularity of a few of his pieces brought the name of Jean Sibelius (1865–1957) repeatedly into orchestral programmes in the early years of this century. The Finnish composer's orchestration has all the simple methods of the early Russians. A string band, a wood-wind band, and a brass band appear in alternation or in combination, each retaining its own status, and carrying out its allotted function without the slightest ambiguity of intention. The same happens when instruments are employed as melodists; they speak quite distinctly against their accompanying matter. Like an *écorché*, the whole construction always stands revealed at first sight. Modern tone-qualities, of course, are used often enough, but the effect is never in doubt, for the tone-colours or instrumental groups are not allowed to stray outside of what is for the moment their own particular preserve. These straightforward methods are exemplified in *Finlandia* and in Sibelius' less familiar works—the Symphony No. 1 (1899), Symphony No. 2 (1901), and *En Saga* (published 1903). Another piece, *Der Schwan von Tuonela* (1893) is scored for an orchestra without either flutes or trumpets, a commendable, if rare example of a composer omitting to write for instruments which he did not actually require.

No notice can be taken of the orchestration of hundreds of composers of the same generation as Strauss, Debussy and Elgar, whose work was either neutral in style, unrepresentative, un-individual, or of those whose works have not secured popularity enough to become influential. Of these there always has been a seemingly unlimited supply, as there is now, and presumably always will be. Plenty of clever craftsmen began to reproduce the orchestral effects of Strauss and Debussy soon after these were heard ; what was new and stimulating to the ear of 1900 has already been absorbed into the everyday language of the orchestra.

Even as the composers whose work bridges the end of the nineteenth and the beginning of the twentieth century were reaching their maturity, another generation was already in training, and part of their training was the assimilation of what they could learn from those who were saying the last word in orchestration from about twenty to twenty-five years ago. Already some of these have by now (1924) taken the reins out of the hands of their older contemporaries, and have driven orchestration along roads which will eventually turn out to have been either precarious, dead-ends, circular, or good roads laid on secure foundations, and which lead definitely onwards. Some bubbles will have to be pricked, and some froth must be blown away before the story of orchestration in the first quarter of the twentieth century can be told without fear of contradiction by the cruel but sound action of the passage of Time.

With the works of Strauss, Debussy and their contemporaries, a chapter in the history of orchestration has probably been definitely concluded. The gains accruing to orchestration after Wagner and after Tschaikovsky can be seen fairly clearly, and their value can be assessed with reasonable assurance. The number of the primary colours on the orchestral palette has not been increased, but their quantity, the ways of mixing them, of applying them, and the ways of shading and graduating them, have been multiplied and amplified. New sounds have been produced, not by new instruments, but by new parts for the old instruments, by new combinations of instrumental tone-colour, by further development of the technique of instrumental playing, by new textures in the music, by the modification of freely muting wind-instruments, also, it should be observed, by making instruments simultaneously sound notes which would not have been tolerated fifty years ago ; for some of the unfamiliar sounds in modern orchestration are not due to orchestration proper, but to the incidence of notes to which the ear is not yet quite accustomed.

One of the most significant developments in orchestration after Wagner and Tschaikovsky is that which relates to the spacing of colour-changes. The first half of the eighteenth century saw colour-schemes formally fixed, and lasting usually for the duration of a whole movement. The second half of the same century developed changes of tone-colour coinciding more often with change of theme or treatment. In the nineteenth century changes of tone-colour were drawn still closer together, often synchronizing with the phrase-length. The tendency generally has been to change tone-colour at ever shorter intervals of time. Yet the greatest masters of orchestration in the second half of last century did not bring changes of colour unduly close together ; they have all known the value of allowing the ear to dwell on a particular variety of sound, not till it became satiated, but long enough for a change to be welcome and significant when it did come. It may be that the ideal spacing of colour-changes was that current in the last half of last century. Composers writing at the very end of that century have often run the risk of tiring the ear by too frequent changes of tone-colour, or in other words, by too closely packed variety. That there is a risk can be proved by carrying the process to extremes. If one could produce sixty different varieties of tone-colour in succession during the course of a minute, and could then continue to provide them in infinite variety for a quarter of an hour, the ear would not be conscious of having heard any of them ; they would simply merge into one continuous roll of sound, and one of the most deadly monotony.

Therefore, by providing the utmost variety of tone-colour at too short intervals, the ear, having no time to dwell on any of them, refuses to recognize any variety at all. Tone-colour in orchestration acts very similarly to visual colouring. A picture of hundreds of small areas of diverse colours would have no outlines ; the effect to the eye would be just one big neutral area. That very fact, carried out on a larger scale, was made use of during the war to " camouflage " ships, guns and other objects ; a large variety of colours spread each over small areas produced indistinguishability or invisibility. Tone-colouring varied at very short intervals of time likewise discounts its own variety. A composer may spend an hour " colouring " a page of his score with a dozen successive tone-colours, but the ear may have to hear that page played in a dozen seconds, and will retain no impression of any of these varieties of colour. There are pages in the full scores of Strauss, Debussy and Elgar, and still more in those of some of their younger contemporaries, in which great varieties of diverse tone-colours are compressed into a short period of time. The ear can probably recognize each variety, yet finds that the closely packed succession does not give the impression of change ; surprise is discounted, variety overdone becomes monotony, and the very object of variety fails in its purpose. It may be that this is one of the features of modern orchestration which is destined to be subject to the effects of reaction.

Another danger had its birth about the same time, and is no less liable to defeat its own ends. The multiplication of interests in the texture of the music, even though each interest is undertaken by a quite distinctive tone-colour, if carried too far, also produces a neutrality of texture and of tone-colour which tends more or less towards one common quality ; the persistence of a common quality, even though the means of arriving at it vary, in the long run produces the effect of monotony ; thus again, apparent variety has no variety, and the ear longs for change. This danger is all the more serious because it is so easy to add interests to a full score in the process of writing.

It is tempting to speculate on the effects of progress in orchestration during the last few years, on that of the moment, and on that of the future. Musical art again appears to have been in the melting pot, and the outcome of the process has not yet had time to set. At present it is difficult to see the wood for trees. The calmer judgment of fifty years hence will be able

to deal with accomplished facts, and will be able to sift out actual
results from a mass of heterogeneous influences which loom so large
at the present time only because we are so close to them.   Time
takes no account of distorted views seen from too close a standpoint, and may pass over as of little account the very things that
seem so momentous to those who are witnessing their happening.
Whatever the verdict of Time, it cannot possibly record any want
of activity in orchestration during the first quarter of the twentieth
century ; it cannot record any lack of initiative, of innovation,
of experiment, or of the spirit which has fostered progress in the
past.   Time may record that orchestration has taken some
wrong turnings, or that it has wandered into some blind alleys ;
it may prove that the road of complexity is blind ; that the road
of eccentricity, of oddity, or of merely impertinent recklessness,
has no outlet ; that the road of reaction must, or must not, be
traversed ; it may prove that the process of marking time is
necessary so that a good road may be selected, or it may prove
that marking time only leads to staleness, and staleness to
decay.   Whatever Time proves, it surely cannot be that there
is no road open for orchestration to-day which will mean
genuine progress, and that the composers of yesterday, of to-day
and of to-morrow, whose work will in the end prove to be really
vital, have not found the road which will take them further than
those have travelled whose names head this chapter.

Unless the portents of to-day are woefully misleading, it will
surely be recorded that British composers now have a hand in
guiding the destiny and regulating the progress of orchestration
in the twentieth century.

CONCLUSION

THOSE readers who have followed throughout these pages the author's attempt to delineate the history of orchestration have seen the orchestra grow from a state of being a collection of any instruments, or groups of instruments available at any particular place, roughly thrown together around a feeble core of medieval keyboard-instruments and lutes, through the various stages of its growth in which some instruments were permanently adopted while others were rejected, to the highly organized condition of the combination which only became thoroughly stabilized about the middle of last century, and which has since attracted to itself a more or less vacillating fringe of additional instruments. They have seen orchestration develop from a state of being governed by the uncertain results obtainable from the adventitious use of instruments, from a state of being unconscious of its very existence, to the complex and very conscious art of the present day.

Of the various elements which together go to make up the technique of writing and presenting music, none can show a more remarkable expansion than can orchestration, yet the development of none appears to have been so largely dependent on the mechanical improvement of instruments. The instruments of the string orchestra were ready for exploitation almost before string technique had begun to exist ; but wind instruments have kept orchestration impatiently waiting on their mechanical improvement, delaying and hampering it for the greater part of three centuries. The delicate little axel connecting the movement of two or more keys on a wood-wind instrument, and the ingenious valve which governs the byways in the tube of a brass instrument have been great and vitalizing gifts which have made modern orchestration possible, for without modern wind instruments, modern orchestration would have been heavily shackled, and still limping.

Of all the aspects of musical history that which is the most difficult to reconstruct is the standard of performance prevailing at any period which is too remote for memory or tradition to afford enlightenment. The effect of an orchestra playing as they must have played one, two, or three hundred years ago, can only be vaguely imagined. Nevertheless, a great abundance of impeccable evidence tells a tale of a standard so poor as to be almost repugnant when associated in the mind with the master-pieces of the great composers. The absence of marks showing *tempo*, light and shade, phrasing, and all the factors which help to make for adequate rendering, in the original full scores of the seventeenth and eighteenth centuries, even the absence of the names of the instruments in most of the early scores, does not necessarily indicate a low standard of performance; for conditions were such that composers usually ·controlled performances in person, and probably gave verbal directions at rehearsals; but much more damning evidence of what orchestral performances must have been continually crops up in contemporary musical literature throughout the seventeenth, eighteenth, and part of the nineteenth centuries. Alessandro Scarlatti said of wind instruments in 1725 that " they are never in tune "; Burney wrote of them fifty years later that " it is natural to these instruments to be out of tune "; indeed, the surviving specimens of old instruments, the positions of the holes on the old wood-wind instruments, and the crude devices for producing chromatic notes given in the early instruction books, all tell a tale which makes the fastidious flesh of the present-day imagination creep. The mental pictures of seventeenth and eighteenth century orchestras playing under the direction of " conductors " seated at and playing the *clavicembalo*, of violinist-leaders struggling to control their forces with nods of the head and stamps of the foot, of Paris conductors thumping out the beats with a pole, of Gluck conduct-ing " violin in hand," of Mozart who " thought it well to sit at the piano and conduct," or " taking the violin out of the hands of M. La Houssage, and conducting myself," of the ludicrous scene between Dr. Hayes and Mr. Cramer at the first Handel Commemoration Festival[1], even of Beethoven conducting the

[1] "The overture and *Dead March* in *Saul*, and the *Gloria Patri* from the *Jubilate* composed in 1713 were next given, and received every possible advantage from such a correct and numerous band. When this great event was in contemplation, two very pompous gentlemen, Dr. Hayes of Oxford and Dr. Miller, of Doncaster, came to town to give their gratuitous assistance as conductors, by beating time. After several meetings and some bickerings, it was at length agreed that Dr. Hayes (Mus. Dr. Oxon)

Choral Symphony without being able to hear it ; these and dozens
of similar stories of the musical past more than hint at standards
of performance too harrowing for present-day composers to think
about.   The idea of each player adding ornaments and " graces "
to his written part according to his own fancy and skill, the idea
of a serpent playing " like an angry calf," of choirs of twelve
voices accompanied by orchestras of twenty-four players, of
operas composed and produced within three or four weeks ; such
ideas, taken at random from the annals of the past when
orchestration was no longer in its infancy, but was growing surely
and vigorously, make one wonder at the growth that has given
to composers an instrument so sensitive, so varied, so perfect,
and one which is capable of such manipulation by players and
conductors as is the modern orchestra.

Truly, orchestration owes much to the makers who have
gradually built up the modern wind instrument, and it also
owes much to the succession of orchestral players, and to the
conductors, who have helped to make the orchestra the wonderful
instrument it now is.

Orchestration has been many things to many composers.
It has been a servant of the great, a support to the mediocre, and
a cloak for the feeble.   Its past lives enshrined in the works of
the great dead, its present pants after the exertion of recent
progress, and its future lies as completely hidden as it lay at the
end of the sixteenth century.

---

should conduct the first act, and Dr. Miller the second.   With regard to
the third, I suppose they were to toss up for it.   When the time of
performance had arrived, and Mr. Cramer, the leader, had just tapt his
bow (the signal for being ready), and looked round to catch the eyes of the
performers, he saw, to his astonishment, a tall gigantic figure, with an
immense powdered toupee, full dressed, with a bag and sword, and a huge
roll of parchment in his hand.

> The son of Hercules he justly scorn'd
> By his broad shoulders and gigantic mien.

' Who is that gentleman ? ' said Mr. Cramer.   ' Dr. Hayes,' was the
reply.   ' What is he going to do ? '   ' To beat time.'   ' Be so kind,'
said Mr. Cramer, ' to tell the gentleman that when he has sat down I will
begin.'   The Doctor, who never anticipated such a *set down* as this, took
his seat, and Mr. Cramer did begin, and his Majesty and all present bore
witness to his masterly style of leading the band."—From Musical Memories,
by W. T. Parke, 1830.

APPENDIX A

ADDITIONAL LISTS OF ORCHESTRAS

1636. String orchestra. 6 Dessus, 4 Haute-contres, 4 Tailles, 4 Quintes, 6 Basses. *Authority*, Mersennus.

Date.	Place.	1st Violins.	2nd Violins.	Violas.	Cellos.	D-basses.	Flutes.	Oboes.	Clarinets.	Bassoons.	Horns.	Other Instruments.	Authority.
1700–50	(Bach) Leipzig	2/3	2/3	4	2	1	2	2/3	—	1/2	—	3 trumpets, timpani	Forkel.
1761	Bologna	—	—	—	—		70 performers, including 2 pianists						Dittersdorf.
1770	Milan (Church)	4	4	4	4	4	4 wind instruments						Burney.
1770	Naples (San Carlo)	18	18	?	2	5	wind not specified						Burney
1772	Stuttgart	8	8	6	3	4	2	4	—	2	3	?	Burney.
1772	Berlin (Opera)	6	5	4	5	2	4	4	—	4	2	2 harpsichord, 1 harp	Burney.
1777	Mannheim	10/11	10/11	4	4	4	2	2	2	4	2	Trumpets, timpani	Mozart (Jahn).
1781–83	Vienna (Opera)	6	6	4	3	3	2	2	2	2	4	Trumpets, timpani	Jahn.
1814	Concert at Vienna (Beethoven)	18	18	14	12	17	wind not specified					2 double-bassoons	Thayer.
1816	Milan (La Scala)	12	12	?	8	8	wind not specified						Spohr.
1841	Berlin (Opera)	14	14	8	10	8	4	4	4	4	4	4 trpts., 4 trbs., timpani, Bass drum, Cymbals, 2 harps	Berlioz.

APPENDIX B

RELATING to the various methods of conducting orchestras, from eighteenth and early nineteenth century musical literature.

DATE.

1732   TACT (time or beat)—formerly measured with the foot, now generally with the hand.
CONDUCTEUR—*der Anführer.*
Walther, *Musikalisches Lexikon.*

1741   MANADUCTEUR—*Ein Tact-führer* (a time beater).
Caspar Majer, *Neu eröffneter . . . Musiksaal.*

1753   Baron Grimm names the conductor at the Paris Opera a " wood chopper " owing to the custom of beating time audibly which, since the time of Lulli, had prevailed in French opera.
Schünemann, *Geschichte des Dirigierens* (1913).

1759   At Vienna—" on these occasions Gluck, violin in hand, appeared *à la tête* of the orchestra."
Dittersdorf, *Autobiography.*

1761   At Bologna—" With Italian orchestras of that size, two pianos are required, and Mazzoni, the well-known *Kapellmeister*, presided at the second."

1767   Articles *Baton de Mesure, Orchestre* and *Battre la Mesure*, state that audible time-beating with a big wooden stick prevailed at the Paris Opera.
Rousseau, *Dictionnaire de Musique.*

1770   At Turin—" In the chapel there is commonly a symphony played every morning . . . by the King's band, which is divided into three orchestras, and placed in three galleries ; and though far separated from each other, the performers know the business so well that there is no want of a person to beat time, as in the opera and *Concert Spirituel* at Paris."
Burney, *The Present State of Music in France and Italy.*

DATE.

1770   Choral service at the *Duomo*, Milan—" Under the direction
        of Signor Fioroni, who beat time, and now and then
        sung."
        Burney, *Present State—in Italy*.

1772   At Brussels—" The orchestra of this theatre is celebrated
        all over Europe. It is, at present, under the direction
        of M. Fitzthumb . . . who beats the time."
        Burney, *Present State of Music in Germany*.

c.1778 At Paris—The Italian opera was conducted from the
        piano only, while in the French opera time was beaten
        audibly with a stick.
        Jahn, *Life of Mozart*.

1802   " In Church music the *Kapellmeister* beats time . . .
        but in opera he plays the figured-bass from the score."
        Koch, *Musikalisches Lexikon*.

1809   At Frankenhausen Musical Festival—" Herr Spohr leading
        with a roll of paper, without the least noise, and without
        the slightest contortion of countenance."
        Spohr, *Autobiography*.

1813   MANU-DUCTOR. The name given by the ancients to the
        officiate whose province it was to beat the time with
        his hand at public performances.
        CONDUCTOR. A term applied to the person who arranges,
        orders, and directs the necessary preparations for a
        concert ; and also superintends and conducts the
        performance.
        LEADER. A performer who in a concert takes the principal
        violin, receives the time and style of the several move-
        ments from the conductor, and communicates them to
        the rest of the band. (See also page 169, Chapter VIII.)
        BEATING TIME is that motion of the hand or foot used by
        the performers themselves, or some person presiding
        over the concert.
        Busby, *A Dictionary of Music*.

DATE.

1816 At *La Scala*, Milan—" Signor Rolla   .   .   .   directed as
      first violin.   There is no other direction whether at the
      piano, or from the desk with a baton."

1817 At Frankfort—" My predecessor had led with the violin,
      and by the wish of the singers I began also in the same
      manner, indicating the time with the bow, and keeping
      the violin ready at hand, in order to assist with that
      when necessary.   .   .   .   I now laid the violin aside
      and directed in the French style, with the bâton."

1820 Philharmonic, London—" It was at that time still the
      custom then that when symphonies and overtures were
      performed, the pianist had the score before him, not
      exactly to conduct from it, but only to read after and to
      play with the orchestra at pleasure, which, when it
      was heard, had a very bad effect.   The real conductor
      was the first violin, who gave the *tempi*, and now and
      then, when the orchestra began to falter, gave the beat
      with the bow of his violin.   So numerous an orchestra,
      standing so far apart from each other as that of the
      Philharmonic, could not possibly go exactly together,
      and in spite of the excellence of the individual members,
      the *ensemble* was much worse than we are accustomed
      to in Germany.   I had, therefore, resolved when my turn
      came to direct, to make an attempt to remedy this
      defective system.   Fortunately at the morning rehearsal
      on the day when I was to conduct the concert, Mr. Ries
      took the place at the piano, and he readily assented to
      give up the score to me and to remain wholly excluded
      from all participation in the performance.   I then took
      my stand with the score at a separate music desk in front
      of the orchestra, drew my directing baton from my
      coat pocket and gave the signal to begin.   Quite alarmed
      at such a novel procedure, some of the directors would
      have protested against it ; but when I besought them
      to grant me at least one trial, they became pacified.
      The symphonies and overtures that were to be rehearsed
      were well known to me, and in Germany I had already
      directed at their performance.   I therefore could not

only give the *tempi* in a very decisive manner, but indicated also to the wind instruments and horns all their entries, which ensured to them a confidence such as hitherto they had not known there. I also took the liberty, when the execution did not satisfy me, to stop, and in a very polite but earnest manner to remark upon the manner of execution, which remarks Mr. Ries at my request interpreted to the orchestra. Incited thereby to more than usual attention, and conducted with certainty by the *visible* manner of giving the time, they played with a spirit and a correctness such as till then they had never been heard to play with. Surprised and inspired by this result, the orchestra, immediately after the first part of the symphony, expressed aloud its collective assent to the new mode of conducting, and thereby overruled all further opposition on the part of the directors. In the vocal pieces also, the conducting of which I assumed at the request of Mr. Ries, particularly in the recitative, the leading with the baton, after I had explained the meaning of my movements, was completely successful, and the singers repeatedly expressed to me their satisfaction for the precision with which the orchestra now followed them.

". . . The triumph of the baton as a time-giver was decisive, and no one was seen any more seated at the piano during the performance of symphonies and overtures."

1820   Italian Opera, Paris—"I became confirmed but the more strongly in my opinion, that a theatrical orchestra, however excellent it may be, on account of the great distance of the extreme ends, should not be conducted otherwise than by a continual beating of the time, and, that to mark the time constantly by motions of the body, and the violin, like Mr. Grasset does, is of no use."

Spohr, *Autobiography.*

INDEX

Numbers refer to pages unless otherwise stated

INDEX

345

Fantini, 45
'Fauré, 290, 299
Flatterzunge, 318
Flotow, 269, 284
Flute, 13, 14, 15, 115, 117, 120, 130, 172, 200-1, 291
—— alt-flöte, 14
—— bass-flöte, 14
—— Böhm flute, 200-1
—— discant, 14
—— flautino, Ex. 32, 39 (see also piccolo)
—— flauto dolce, 13
—— flûte-à-bec, Fig. 2, 13, 14, 93, 115, 117
—— flûte allemande, 13, 117
—— flûte douce, 13, 14, 117
—— keys added, 172
—— petites flûtes (see piccolo)
—— plockflöte, 13
—— quartet, 77
—— querflöte, 13, 117
—— recorder, 13
—— schnabelflöte, 13
—— transverse, Fig. 4, 15, 115, 117, 120, 130
Forkel, 168, 179
Forsyth, 64, 291, 293
Franck, 290, 299, 301
Francœur, 223
Fritz, 176
Fröhlich, 223
Furstenau, 168
Fux, 118, 128, 129

Gabrieli, Ex. 3, 16, 18, 25, 26, 29, 57, 119
Gade, 269, 271, 289
Gagliano, 32, 36, 51, 52
Galpin, 18, 208, 211
Galuppi, 118
Gassner, 202, 204, 211, 221, 222, 223
Gerber, 113, 168
German, 313, 328
Gernsheim, 290, 298
Gevaert, 293
Gewandhaus concerts, 168, 222
—— school, 271, 283, 288
Glazounov, 313, 330
Glinka, Chap. XI, 243, 266, 271, 307
Glissando (harp), 316, 322, 325
Glockenspiel, 170, 219, 316, 323
Gluck, Chap. VII, 17, 129, 154-60
Goldmark, 290, 298
Goldschmidt, 39

Gontershausen, 17, 176, 204, 206, 211
Gordon, 200
Gossec, 166, 167
Götz, 290, 298
Gounod, 269, 284-6
Graun, J. G., 148, 161
—— K. H., Ex. 37d, Ex. 39, 118, 119, 133, 148
Graupner, 118, 147
Grenser, 172, 205
Grétry, 167, 197
Grieg, 271, 290, 310
Grove, 38, 61, 90, 121, 155, 198, 211
Guitar, 291

Habeneck, 222
Halary, 215
Halévy, 243, 253
Hammerschmidt, 33, 59
Hampel, 180
Handel, Chap. VI, Ex. 37b, 89, 113, 123-28
Harmonics (harp), 230, 325
—— (strings), 255, 324
Harp, 22, 53, 124, 156, 219, 220, 230, 245, 279, 286, 316, 325
Hasse, Ex. 38b, 112, 118, 119, 133, 140, 148, 161, 178
Hawkins, 40, 174
Haydn, Chap. VIII, 132, 179, 183-96
Heckelphon, 203 (see also Oboe, bass)
Hérold, 243, 252
Hiller, 283
Hochbrucker, 219
Hoffmann, 173
Hofmann, 211, 293, 298
Horn, Fig. 10, Ex. 33, Ex. 34, Ex. 43, 89, 104, 112-14, 117, 121, 124, 154
—— hand, Fig. 13, 180, 182, 191, 229, 247, 273, 285, 292
—— keyed, 181
—— notation, examples of, Ex. 36
—— valve, 212, 213, 218, 248, 253, 265, 270, 273, 292
Hotteterre, 115
Humfrey, 90
Humperdinck, 290, 298, 299
Hunting horn (see Horn)

d'Indy, 290, 299, 300
Instrumentation, text books, 223, 293

Jadassohn, 293, 298
Jomelli, 118, 150-51, 161

A CATALOGUE OF SELECTED DOVER BOOKS
IN ALL FIELDS OF INTEREST

A CATALOGUE OF SELECTED DOVER
BOOKS IN ALL FIELDS OF INTEREST

RACKHAM'S COLOR ILLUSTRATIONS FOR WAGNER'S RING. Rackham's finest mature work—all 64 full-color watercolors in a faithful and lush interpretation of the *Ring*. Full-sized plates on coated stock of the paintings used by opera companies for authentic staging of Wagner. Captions aid in following complete Ring cycle. Introduction. 64 illustrations plus vignettes. 72pp. 8⅝ x 11¼.   23779-6 Pa. $6.00

CONTEMPORARY POLISH POSTERS IN FULL COLOR, edited by Joseph Czestochowski. 46 full-color examples of brilliant school of Polish graphic design, selected from world's first museum (near Warsaw) dedicated to poster art. Posters on circuses, films, plays, concerts all show cosmopolitan influences, free imagination. Introduction. 48pp. 9⅜ x 12¼.   23780-X Pa. $6.00

GRAPHIC WORKS OF EDVARD MUNCH, Edvard Munch. 90 haunting, evocative prints by first major Expressionist artist and one of the greatest graphic artists of his time: *The Scream, Anxiety, Death Chamber, The Kiss, Madonna,* etc. Introduction by Alfred Werner. 90pp. 9 x 12.   23765-6 Pa. $5.00

THE GOLDEN AGE OF THE POSTER, Hayward and Blanche Cirker. 70 extraordinary posters in full colors, from Maitres de l'Affiche, Mucha, Lautrec, Bradley, Cheret, Beardsley, many others. Total of 78pp. 9⅜ x 12¼.   22753-7 Pa. $5.95

THE NOTEBOOKS OF LEONARDO DA VINCI, edited by J. P. Richter. Extracts from manuscripts reveal great genius; on painting, sculpture, anatomy, sciences, geography, etc. Both Italian and English. 186 ms. pages reproduced, plus 500 additional drawings, including studies for *Last Supper,* Sforza monument, etc. 860pp. 7⅞ x 10¾. (Available in U.S. only)   22572-0, 22573-9 Pa., Two-vol. set $15.90

THE CODEX NUTTALL, as first edited by Zelia Nuttall. Only inexpensive edition, in full color, of a pre-Columbian Mexican (Mixtec) book. 88 color plates show kings, gods, heroes, temples, sacrifices. New explanatory, historical introduction by Arthur G. Miller. 96pp. 11⅜ x 8½. (Available in U.S. only)   23168-2 Pa. $7.50

UNE SEMAINE DE BONTÉ, A SURREALISTIC NOVEL IN COLLAGE, Max Ernst. Masterpiece created out of 19th-century periodical illustrations, explores worlds of terror and surprise. Some consider this Ernst's greatest work. 208pp. 8⅛ x 11.   23252-2 Pa. $5.00

THE DEPRESSION YEARS AS PHOTOGRAPHED BY ARTHUR ROTH-STEIN, Arthur Rothstein. First collection devoted entirely to the work of outstanding 1930s photographer: famous dust storm photo, ragged children, unemployed, etc. 120 photographs. Captions. 119pp. 9¼ x 10¾.
23590-4 Pa. $5.00

CAMERA WORK: A PICTORIAL GUIDE, Alfred Stieglitz. All 559 illustrations and plates from the most important periodical in the history of art photography, Camera Work (1903-17). Presented four to a page, reduced in size but still clear, in strict chronological order, with complete captions. Three indexes. Glossary. Bibliography. 176pp. 8⅜ x 11¼.
23591-2 Pa. $6.95

ALVIN LANGDON COBURN, PHOTOGRAPHER, Alvin L. Coburn. Revealing autobiography by one of greatest photographers of 20th century gives insider's version of Photo-Secession, plus comments on his own work. 77 photographs by Coburn. Edited by Helmut and Alison Gernsheim. 160pp. 8⅛ x 11.
23685-4 Pa. $6.00

NEW YORK IN THE FORTIES, Andreas Feininger. 162 brilliant photographs by the well-known photographer, formerly with Life magazine, show commuters, shoppers, Times Square at night, Harlem nightclub, Lower East Side, etc. Introduction and full captions by John von Hartz. 181pp. 9¼ x 10¾.
23585-8 Pa. $6.00

GREAT NEWS PHOTOS AND THE STORIES BEHIND THEM, John Faber. Dramatic volume of 140 great news photos, 1855 through 1976, and revealing stories behind them, with both historical and technical information. Hindenburg disaster, shooting of Oswald, nomination of Jimmy Carter, etc. 160pp. 8¼ x 11.
23667-6 Pa. $5.00

THE ART OF THE CINEMATOGRAPHER, Leonard Maltin. Survey of American cinematography history and anecdotal interviews with 5 masters—Arthur Miller, Hal Mohr, Hal Rosson, Lucien Ballard, and Conrad Hall. Very large selection of behind-the-scenes production photos. 105 photographs. Filmographies. Index. Originally Behind the Camera. 144pp. 8¼ x 11.
23686-2 Pa. $5.00

DESIGNS FOR THE THREE-CORNERED HAT (LE TRICORNE), Pablo Picasso. 32 fabulously rare drawings—including 31 color illustrations of costumes and accessories—for 1919 production of famous ballet. Edited by Parmenia Migel, who has written new introduction. 48pp. 9⅜ x 12¼. (Available in U.S. only)
23709-5 Pa. $5.00

NOTES OF A FILM DIRECTOR, Sergei Eisenstein. Greatest Russian filmmaker explains montage, making of Alexander Nevsky, aesthetics; comments on self, associates, great rivals (Chaplin), similar material. 78 illustrations. 240pp. 5⅜ x 8½.
22392-2 Pa. $4.50

THE AMERICAN SENATOR, Anthony Trollope. Little known, long unavailable Trollope novel on a grand scale. Here are humorous comment on American vs. English culture, and stunning portrayal of a heroine/villainess. Superb evocation of Victorian village life. 561pp. 5⅜ x 8½.
23801-6 Pa. $6.00

WAS IT MURDER? James Hilton. The author of *Lost Horizon* and *Goodbye, Mr. Chips* wrote one detective novel (under a pen-name) which was quickly forgotten and virtually lost, even at the height of Hilton's fame. This edition brings it back—a finely crafted public school puzzle resplendent with Hilton's stylish atmosphere. A thoroughly English thriller by the creator of Shangri-la. 252pp. 5⅜ x 8. (Available in U.S. only)
23774-5 Pa. $3.00

CENTRAL PARK: A PHOTOGRAPHIC GUIDE, Victor Laredo and Henry Hope Reed. 121 superb photographs show dramatic views of Central Park: Bethesda Fountain, Cleopatra's Needle, Sheep Meadow, the Blockhouse, plus people engaged in many park activities: ice skating, bike riding, etc. Captions by former Curator of Central Park, Henry Hope Reed, provide historical view, changes, etc. Also photos of N.Y. landmarks on park's periphery. 96pp. 8½ x 11. 23750-8 Pa. $4.50

NANTUCKET IN THE NINETEENTH CENTURY, Clay Lancaster. 180 rare photographs, stereographs, maps, drawings and floor plans recreate unique American island society. Authentic scenes of shipwreck, lighthouses, streets, homes are arranged in geographic sequence to provide walking-tour guide to old Nantucket existing today. Introduction, captions. 160pp. 8⅞ x 11¾. 23747-8 Pa. $6.95

STONE AND MAN: A PHOTOGRAPHIC EXPLORATION, Andreas Feininger. 106 photographs by *Life* photographer Feininger portray man's deep passion for stone through the ages. Stonehenge-like megaliths, fortified towns, sculpted marble and crumbling tenements show textures, beauties, fascination. 128pp. 9¼ x 10¾. 23756-7 Pa. $5.95

CIRCLES, A MATHEMATICAL VIEW, D. Pedoe. Fundamental aspects of college geometry, non-Euclidean geometry, and other branches of mathematics: representing circle by point. Poincare model, isoperimetric property, etc. Stimulating recreational reading. 66 figures. 96pp. 5⅝ x 8¼.
63698-4 Pa. $2.75

THE DISCOVERY OF NEPTUNE, Morton Grosser. Dramatic scientific history of the investigations leading up to the actual discovery of the eighth planet of our solar system. Lucid, well-researched book by well-known historian of science. 172pp. 5⅜ x 8½. 23726-5 Pa. $3.00

THE DEVIL'S DICTIONARY. Ambrose Bierce. Barbed, bitter, brilliant witticisms in the form of a dictionary. Best, most ferocious satire America has produced. 145pp. 5⅜ x 8½. 20487-1 Pa. $1.75

AN AUTOBIOGRAPHY, Margaret Sanger. Exciting personal account of hard-fought battle for woman's right to birth control, against prejudice, church, law. Foremost feminist document. 504pp. 5⅜ x 8½.
20470-7 Pa. $5.50

MY BONDAGE AND MY FREEDOM, Frederick Douglass. Born as a slave, Douglass became outspoken force in antislavery movement. The best of Douglass's autobiographies. Graphic description of slave life. Introduction by P. Foner. 464pp. 5⅜ x 8½.
22457-0 Pa. $5.00

LIVING MY LIFE, Emma Goldman. Candid, no holds barred account by foremost American anarchist: her own life, anarchist movement, famous contemporaries, ideas and their impact. Struggles and confrontations in America, plus deportation to U.S.S.R. Shocking inside account of persecution of anarchists under Lenin. 13 plates. Total of 944pp. 5⅜ x 8½.
22543-7, 22544-5 Pa., Two-vol. set $9.00

LETTERS AND NOTES ON THE MANNERS, CUSTOMS AND CONDITIONS OF THE NORTH AMERICAN INDIANS, George Catlin. Classic account of life among Plains Indians: ceremonies, hunt, warfare, etc. Dover edition reproduces for first time all original paintings. 312 plates. 572pp. of text. 6⅛ x 9¼.
22118-0, 22119-9 Pa.. Two-vol. set $10.00

THE MAYA AND THEIR NEIGHBORS, edited by Clarence L. Hay, others. Synoptic view of Maya civilization in broadest sense, together with Northern, Southern neighbors. Integrates much background, valuable detail not elsewhere. Prepared by greatest scholars: Kroeber, Morley, Thompson, Spinden, Vaillant, many others. Sometimes called Tozzer Memorial Volume. 60 illustrations, linguistic map. 634pp. 5⅜ x 8½.
23510-6 Pa. $7.50

HANDBOOK OF THE INDIANS OF CALIFORNIA, A. L. Kroeber. Foremost American anthropologist offers complete ethnographic study of each group. Monumental classic. 459 illustrations, maps. 995pp. 5⅜ x 8½.
23368-5 Pa. $10.00

SHAKTI AND SHAKTA, Arthur Avalon. First book to give clear, cohesive analysis of Shakta doctrine, Shakta ritual and Kundalini Shakti (yoga). Important work by one of world's foremost students of Shaktic and Tantric thought. 732pp. 5⅜ x 8½. (Available in U.S. only)
23645-5 Pa. $7.95

AN INTRODUCTION TO THE STUDY OF THE MAYA HIEROGLYPHS, Syvanus Griswold Morley. Classic study by one of the truly great figures in hieroglyph research. Still the best introduction for the student for reading Maya hieroglyphs. New introduction by J. Eric S. Thompson. 117 illustrations. 284pp. 5⅜ x 8½.
23108-9 Pa. $4.00

A STUDY OF MAYA ART, Herbert J. Spinden. Landmark classic interprets Maya symbolism, estimates styles, covers ceramics, architecture, murals, stone carvings as artforms. Still a basic book in area. New introduction by J. Eric Thompson. Over 750 illustrations. 341pp. 8⅜ x 11¼.
21235-1 Pa. $6.95

A MAYA GRAMMAR, Alfred M. Tozzer. Practical, useful English-language grammar by the Harvard anthropologist who was one of the three greatest American scholars in the area of Maya culture. Phonetics, grammatical processes, syntax, more. 301pp. 5⅜ x 8½.   23465-7 Pa. $4.00

THE JOURNAL OF HENRY D. THOREAU, edited by Bradford Torrey, F. H. Allen. Complete reprinting of 14 volumes, 1837-61, over two million words; the sourcebooks for *Walden*, etc. Definitive. All original sketches, plus 75 photographs. Introduction by Walter Harding. Total of 1804pp. 8½ x 12¼.   20312-3, 20313-1 Clothbd., Two-vol. set $50.00

CLASSIC GHOST STORIES, Charles Dickens and others. 18 wonderful stories you've wanted to reread: "The Monkey's Paw," "The House and the Brain," "The Upper Berth," "The Signalman," "Dracula's Guest," "The Tapestried Chamber," etc. Dickens, Scott, Mary Shelley, Stoker, etc. 330pp. 5⅜ x 8½.   20735-8 Pa. $3.50

SEVEN SCIENCE FICTION NOVELS, H. G. Wells. Full novels. *First Men in the Moon, Island of Dr. Moreau, War of the Worlds, Food of the Gods, Invisible Man, Time Machine, In the Days of the Comet.* A basic science-fiction library. 1015pp. 5⅜ x 8½. (Available in U.S. only)
20264-X Clothbd. $8.95

ARMADALE, Wilkie Collins. Third great mystery novel by the author of *The Woman in White* and *The Moonstone.* Ingeniously plotted narrative shows an exceptional command of character, incident and mood. Original magazine version with 40 illustrations. 597pp. 5⅜ x 8½.
23429-0 Pa. $5.00

MASTERS OF MYSTERY, H. Douglas Thomson. The first book in English (1931) devoted to history and aesthetics of detective story. Poe, Doyle, LeFanu, Dickens, many others, up to 1930. New introduction and notes by E. F. Bleiler. 288pp. 5⅜ x 8½. (Available in U.S. only)
23606-4 Pa. $4.00

FLATLAND, E. A. Abbott. Science-fiction classic explores life of 2-D being in 3-D world. Read also as introduction to thought about hyperspace. Introduction by Banesh Hoffmann. 16 illustrations. 103pp. 5⅜ x 8½.
20001-9 Pa. $1.50

THREE SUPERNATURAL NOVELS OF THE VICTORIAN PERIOD, edited, with an introduction, by E. F. Bleiler. Reprinted complete and unabridged, three great classics of the supernatural: *The Haunted Hotel* by Wilkie Collins, *The Haunted House at Latchford* by Mrs. J. H. Riddell, and *The Lost Stradivarius* by J. Meade Falkner. 325pp. 5⅜ x 8½.
22571-2 Pa. $4.00

AYESHA: THE RETURN OF "SHE," H. Rider Haggard. Virtuoso sequel featuring the great mythic creation, Ayesha, in an adventure that is fully as good as the first book, *She.* Original magazine version, with 47 original illustrations by Maurice Greiffenhagen. 189pp. 6½ x 9¼.
23649-8 Pa. $3.00

DRAWINGS OF WILLIAM BLAKE, William Blake. 92 plates from Book of Job, *Divine Comedy, Paradise Lost,* visionary heads, mythological figures, Laocoon, etc. Selection, introduction, commentary by Sir Geoffrey Keynes. 178pp. 8⅛ x 11.   22303-5 Pa. $4.00

ENGRAVINGS OF HOGARTH, William Hogarth. 101 of Hogarth's greatest works: *Rake's Progress, Harlot's Progress, Illustrations for Hudibras, Before and After, Beer Street and Gin Lane,* many more. Full commentary. 256pp. 11 x 13¾.   22479-1 Pa. $7.95

DAUMIER: 120 GREAT LITHOGRAPHS, Honore Daumier. Wide-ranging collection of lithographs by the greatest caricaturist of the 19th century. Concentrates on eternally popular series on lawyers, on married life, on liberated women, etc. Selection, introduction, and notes on plates by Charles F. Ramus. Total of 158pp. 9⅜ x 12¼.   23512-2 Pa. $5.50

DRAWINGS OF MUCHA, Alphonse Maria Mucha. Work reveals draftsman of highest caliber: studies for famous posters and paintings, renderings for book illustrations and ads, etc. 70 works, 9 in color; including 6 items not drawings. Introduction. List of illustrations. 72pp. 9⅜ x 12¼. (Available in U.S. only)   23672-2 Pa. $4.00

GIOVANNI BATTISTA PIRANESI: DRAWINGS IN THE PIERPONT MORGAN LIBRARY, Giovanni Battista Piranesi. For first time ever all of Morgan Library's collection, world's largest. 167 illustrations of rare Piranesi drawings—archeological, architectural, decorative and visionary. Essay, detailed list of drawings, chronology, captions. Edited by Felice Stampfle. 144pp. 9⅜ x 12¼.   23714-1 Pa. $7.50

NEW YORK ETCHINGS (1905-1949), John Sloan. All of important American artist's N.Y. life etchings. 67 works include some of his best art; also lively historical record—Greenwich Village, tenement scenes. Edited by Sloan's widow. Introduction and captions. 79pp. 8⅜ x 11¼.
                                23651-X Pa. $4.00

CHINESE PAINTING AND CALLIGRAPHY: A PICTORIAL SURVEY, Wan-go Weng. 69 fine examples from John M. Crawford's matchless private collection: landscapes, birds, flowers, human figures, etc., plus calligraphy. Every basic form included: hanging scrolls, handscrolls, album leaves, fans, etc. 109 illustrations. Introduction. Captions. 192pp. 8⅞ x 11¾.
                                23707-9 Pa. $7.95

DRAWINGS OF REMBRANDT, edited by Seymour Slive. Updated Lippmann, Hofstede de Groot edition, with definitive scholarly apparatus. All portraits, biblical sketches, landscapes, nudes, Oriental figures, classical studies, together with selection of work by followers. 550 illustrations. Total of 630pp. 9⅛ x 12¼.   21485-0, 21486-9 Pa., Two-vol. set $14.00

THE DISASTERS OF WAR, Francisco Goya. 83 etchings record horrors of Napoleonic wars in Spain and war in general. Reprint of 1st edition, plus 3 additional plates. Introduction by Philip Hofer. 97pp. 9⅜ x 8¼.
                                21872-4 Pa. $3.75

ART FORMS IN NATURE, Ernst Haeckel. Multitude of strangely beautiful natural forms: Radiolaria, Foraminifera, jellyfishes, fungi, turtles, bats,
etc. All 100 plates of the 19th-century evolutionist's *Kunstformen der
Natur* (1904). 100pp. 9⅜ x 12¼. 22987-4 Pa. $4.50

CHILDREN: A PICTORIAL ARCHIVE FROM NINETEENTH-CEN-
TURY SOURCES, edited by Carol Belanger Grafton. 242 rare, copyright-
free wood engravings for artists and designers. Widest such selection
available. All illustrations in line. 119pp. 8⅜ x 11¼.
23694-3 Pa. $3.50

WOMEN: A PICTORIAL ARCHIVE FROM NINETEENTH-CENTURY
SOURCES, edited by Jim Harter. 391 copyright-free wood engravings for
artists and designers selected from rare periodicals. Most extensive such
collection available. All illustrations in line. 128pp. 9 x 12.
23703-6 Pa. $4.00

ARABIC ART IN COLOR, Prisse d'Avennes. From the greatest orna-
mentalists of all time—50 plates in color, rarely seen outside the Near
East, rich in suggestion and stimulus. Includes 4 plates on covers. 46pp.
9⅜ x 12¼. 23658-7 Pa. $6.00

AUTHENTIC ALGERIAN CARPET DESIGNS AND MOTIFS, edited by
June Beveridge. Algerian carpets are world famous. Dozens of geometrical
motifs are charted on grids, color-coded, for weavers, needleworkers, craftsmen, designers. 53 illustrations plus 4 in color. 48pp. 8¼ x 11. (Available
in U.S. only) 23650-1 Pa. $1.75

DICTIONARY OF AMERICAN PORTRAITS, edited by Hayward and
Blanche Cirker. 4000 important Americans, earliest times to 1905, mostly
in clear line. Politicians, writers, soldiers, scientists, inventors, industria-
lists, Indians, Blacks, women, outlaws, etc. Identificatory information.
756pp. 9¼ x 12¾. 21823-6 Clothbd. $40.00

HOW THE OTHER HALF LIVES, Jacob A. Riis. Journalistic record of
filth, degradation, upward drive in New York immigrant slums, shops,
around 1900. New edition includes 100 original Riis photos, monuments of
early photography. 233pp. 10 x 7⅞. 22012-5 Pa. $6.00

NEW YORK IN THE THIRTIES, Berenice Abbott. Noted photographer's
fascinating study of city shows new buildings that have become famous
and old sights that have disappeared forever. Insightful commentary. 97
photographs. 97pp. 11⅜ x 10. 22967-X Pa. $4.50

MEN AT WORK, Lewis W. Hine. Famous photographic studies of construction workers, railroad men, factory workers and coal miners. New
supplement of 18 photos on Empire State building construction. New
introduction by Jonathan L. Doherty. Total of 69 photos. 63pp. 8 x 10¾.
23475-4 Pa. $3.00

CATALOGUE OF DOVER BOOKS

THE COMPLETE WOODCUTS OF ALBRECHT DURER, edited by Dr. W. Kurth. 346 in all: "Old Testament," "St. Jerome," "Passion," "Life of Virgin," Apocalypse," many others. Introduction by Campbell Dodgson. 285pp. 8½ x 12¼. 21097-9 Pa. $6.95

DRAWINGS OF ALBRECHT DURER, edited by Heinrich Wolfflin. 81 plates show development from youth to full style. Many favorites; many new. Introduction by Alfred Werner. 96pp. 8⅛ x 11. 22352-3 Pa. $4.00

THE HUMAN FIGURE, Albrecht Dürer. Experiments in various techniques—stereometric, progressive proportional, and others. Also life studies that rank among finest ever done. Complete reprinting of *Dresden Sketchbook*. 170 plates. 355pp. 8⅜ x 11¼. 21042-1 Pa. $6.95

OF THE JUST SHAPING OF LETTERS, Albrecht Dürer. Renaissance artist explains design of Roman majuscules by geometry, also Gothic lower and capitals. Grolier Club edition. 43pp. 7⅞ x 10¾ 21306-4 Pa. $2.50

TEN BOOKS ON ARCHITECTURE, Vitruvius. The most important book ever written on architecture. Early Roman aesthetics, technology, classical orders, site selection, all other aspects. Stands behind everything since. Morgan translation. 331pp. 5⅜ x 8½. 20645-9 Pa. $3.75

THE FOUR BOOKS OF ARCHITECTURE, Andrea Palladio. 16th-century classic responsible for Palladian movement and style. Covers classical architectural remains, Renaissance revivals, classical orders, etc. 1738 Ware English edition. Introduction by A. Placzek. 216 plates. 110pp. of text. 9½ x 12¾. 21308-0 Pa. $7.50

HORIZONS, Norman Bel Geddes. Great industrialist stage designer, "father of streamlining," on application of aesthetics to transportation, amusement, architecture, etc. 1932 prophetic account; function, theory, specific projects. 222 illustrations. 312pp. 7⅞ x 10¾. 23514-9 Pa. $6.95

FRANK LLOYD WRIGHT'S FALLINGWATER, Donald Hoffmann. Full, illustrated story of conception and building of Wright's masterwork at Bear Run, Pa. 100 photographs of site, construction, and details of completed structure. 112pp. 9¼ x 10. 23671-4 Pa. $5.00

THE ELEMENTS OF DRAWING, John Ruskin. Timeless classic by great Viltorian; starts with basic ideas, works through more difficult. Many practical exercises. 48 illustrations. Introduction by Lawrence Campbell. 228pp. 5⅜ x 8½. 22730-8 Pa. $2.75

GIST OF ART, John Sloan. Greatest modern American teacher, Art Students League, offers innumerable hints, instructions, guided comments to help you in painting. Not a formal course. 46 illustrations. Introduction by Helen Sloan. 200pp. 5⅜ x 8½. 23435-5 Pa. $3.50

UNCLE SILAS, J. Sheridan LeFanu. Victorian Gothic mystery novel, considered by many best of period, even better than Collins or Dickens. Wonderful psychological terror. Introduction by Frederick Shroyer. 436pp. 5⅜ x 8½.   21715-9 Pa. $4.00

JURGEN, James Branch Cabell. The great erotic fantasy of the 1920's that delighted thousands, shocked thousands more. Full final text, Lane edition with 13 plates by Frank Pape. 346pp. 5⅜ x 8½.
                                                                      23507-6 Pa. $4.00

THE CLAVERINGS, Anthony Trollope. Major novel, chronicling aspects of British Victorian society, personalities. Reprint of Cornhill serialization, 16 plates by M. Edwards; first reprint of full text. Introduction by Norman Donaldson. 412pp. 5⅜ x 8½.   23464-9 Pa. $5.00

KEPT IN THE DARK, Anthony Trollope. Unusual short novel about Victorian morality and abnormal psychology by the great English author. Probably the first American publication. Frontispiece by Sir John Millais. 92pp. 6½ x 9¼.   23609-9 Pa. $2.50

RALPH THE HEIR, Anthony Trollope. Forgotten tale of illegitimacy, inheritance. Master novel of Trollope's later years. Victorian country estates, clubs, Parliament, fox hunting, world of fully realized characters. Reprint of 1871 edition. 12 illustrations by F. A. Faser. 434pp. of text. 5⅜ x 8½.   23642-0 Pa. $4.50

YEKL and THE IMPORTED BRIDEGROOM AND OTHER STORIES OF THE NEW YORK GHETTO, Abraham Cahan. Film *Hester Street* based on *Yekl* (1896). Novel, other stories among first about Jewish immigrants of N.Y.'s East Side. Highly praised by W. D. Howells—Cahan "a new star of realism." New introduction by Bernard G. Richards. 240pp. 5⅜ x 8½.   22427-9 Pa. $3.50

THE HIGH PLACE, James Branch Cabell. Great fantasy writer's enchanting comedy of disenchantment set in 18th-century France. Considered by some critics to be even better than his famous *Jurgen*. 10 illustrations and numerous vignettes by noted fantasy artist Frank C. Pape. 320pp. 5⅜ x 8½.   23670-6 Pa. $4.00

ALICE'S ADVENTURES UNDER GROUND, Lewis Carroll. Facsimile of ms. Carroll gave Alice Liddell in 1864. Different in many ways from final Alice. Handlettered, illustrated by Carroll. Introduction by Martin Gardner. 128pp. 5⅜ x 8½.   21482-6 Pa. $2.00

FAVORITE ANDREW LANG FAIRY TALE BOOKS IN MANY COLORS, Andrew Lang. The four Lang favorites in a boxed set—the complete *Red, Green, Yellow* and *Blue* Fairy Books. 164 stories; 439 illustrations by Lancelot Speed, Henry Ford and G. P. Jacomb Hood. Total of about 1500pp. 5⅜ x 8½.   23407-X Boxed set, Pa. $14.00

HOUSEHOLD STORIES BY THE BROTHERS GRIMM. All the great Grimm stories: "Rumpelstiltskin," "Snow White," "Hansel and Gretel," etc., with 114 illustrations by Walter Crane. 269pp. 5⅜ x 8½.
21080-4 Pa. $3.00

SLEEPING BEAUTY, illustrated by Arthur Rackham. Perhaps the fullest, most delightful version ever, told by C. S. Evans. Rackham's best work. 49 illustrations. 110pp. 7⅞ x 10¾.   22756-1 Pa. $2.00

AMERICAN FAIRY TALES, L. Frank Baum. Young cowboy lassoes Father Time; dummy in Mr. Floman's department store window comes to life; and 10 other fairy tales. 41 illustrations by N. P. Hall, Harry Kennedy, Ike Morgan, and Ralph Gardner. 209pp. 5⅜ x 8½.   23643-9 Pa. $3.00

THE WONDERFUL WIZARD OF OZ, L. Frank Baum. Facsimile in full color of America's finest children's classic. Introduction by Martin Gardner. 143 illustrations by W. W. Denslow. 267pp. 5⅜ x 8½.
20691-2 Pa. $3.50

THE TALE OF PETER RABBIT, Beatrix Potter. The inimitable Peter's terrifying adventure in Mr. McGregor's garden, with all 27 wonderful, full-color Potter illustrations. 55pp. 4¼ x 5½. (Available in U.S. only)
22827-4 Pa. $1.10

THE STORY OF KING ARTHUR AND HIS KNIGHTS, Howard Pyle. Finest children's version of life of King Arthur. 48 illustrations by Pyle. 131pp. 6⅛ x 9¼.   21445-1 Pa. $4.00

CARUSO'S CARICATURES, Enrico Caruso. Great tenor's remarkable caricatures of self, fellow musicians, composers, others. Toscanini, Puccini, Farrar, etc. Impish, cutting, insightful. 473 illustrations. Preface by M. Sisca. 217pp. 8⅜ x 11¼.   23528-9 Pa. $6.00

PERSONAL NARRATIVE OF A PILGRIMAGE TO ALMADINAH AND MECCAH, Richard Burton. Great travel classic by remarkably colorful personality. Burton, disguised as a Moroccan, visited sacred shrines of Islam, narrowly escaping death. Wonderful observations of Islamic life, customs, personalities. 47 illustrations. Total of 959pp. 5⅜ x 8½.
21217-3, 21218-1 Pa., Two-vol. set $10.00

INCIDENTS OF TRAVEL IN YUCATAN, John L. Stephens. Classic (1843) exploration of jungles of Yucatan, looking for evidences of Maya civilization. Travel adventures, Mexican and Indian culture, etc. Total of 669pp. 5⅜ x 8½.   20926-1, 20927-X Pa., Two-vol. set $6.50

AMERICAN LITERARY AUTOGRAPHS FROM WASHINGTON IRVING TO HENRY JAMES, Herbert Cahoon, et al. Letters, poems, manuscripts of Hawthorne, Thoreau, Twain, Alcott, Whitman, 67 other prominent American authors. Reproductions, full transcripts and commentary. Plus checklist of all American Literary Autographs in The Pierpont Morgan Library. Printed on exceptionally high-quality paper. 136 illustrations. 212pp. 9⅛ x 12¼.   23548-3 Pa. $7.95

CATALOGUE OF DOVER BOOKS

PRINCIPLES OF ORCHESTRATION, Nikolay Rimsky-Korsakov. Great classical orchestrator provides fundamentals of tonal resonance, progression of parts, voice and orchestra, tutti effects, much else in major document. 330pp. of musical excerpts. 489pp. 6½ x 9¼. 21266-1 Pa. $6.00

TRISTAN UND ISOLDE, Richard Wagner. Full orchestral score with complete instrumentation. Do not confuse with piano reduction. Commentary by Felix Mottl, great Wagnerian conductor and scholar. Study score. 655pp. 8⅛ x 11. 22915-7 Pa. $12.50

REQUIEM IN FULL SCORE, Giuseppe Verdi. Immensely popular with choral groups and music lovers. Republication of edition published by C. F. Peters, Leipzig, n. d. German frontmaker in English translation. Glossary. Text in Latin. Study score. 204pp. 9⅜ x 12¼. 23682-X Pa. $6.00

COMPLETE CHAMBER MUSIC FOR STRINGS, Felix Mendelssohn. All of Mendelssohn's chamber music: Octet, 2 Quintets, 6 Quartets, and Four Pieces for String Quartet. (Nothing with piano is included). Complete works edition (1874-7). Study score. 283 pp. 9⅜ x 12¼. 23679-X Pa. $6.95

POPULAR SONGS OF NINETEENTH-CENTURY AMERICA, edited by Richard Jackson. 64 most important songs: "Old Oaken Bucket," "Arkansas Traveler," "Yellow Rose of Texas," etc. Authentic original sheet music, full introduction and commentaries. 290pp. 9 x 12. 23270-0 Pa. $6.00

COLLECTED PIANO WORKS, Scott Joplin. Edited by Vera Brodsky Lawrence. Practically all of Joplin's piano works—rags, two-steps, marches, waltzes, etc., 51 works in all. Extensive introduction by Rudi Blesh. Total of 345pp. 9 x 12. 23106-2 Pa. $13.50

BASIC PRINCIPLES OF CLASSICAL BALLET, Agrippina Vaganova. Great Russian theoretician, teacher explains methods for teaching classical ballet; incorporates best from French, Italian, Russian schools. 118 illustrations. 175pp. 5⅜ x 8½. 22036-2 Pa. $2.00

CHINESE CHARACTERS, L. Wieger. Rich analysis of 2300 characters according to traditional systems into primitives. Historical-semantic analysis to phonetics (Classical Mandarin) and radicals. 820pp. 6⅛ x 9¼. 21321-8 Pa. $8.95

EGYPTIAN LANGUAGE: EASY LESSONS IN EGYPTIAN HIERO-GLYPHICS, E. A. Wallis Budge. Foremost Egyptologist offers Egyptian grammar, explanation of hieroglyphics, many reading texts, dictionary of symbols. 246pp. 5 x 7½. (Available in U.S. only) 21394-3 Clothbd. $7.50

AN ETYMOLOGICAL DICTIONARY OF MODERN ENGLISH, Ernest Weekley. Richest, fullest work, by foremost British lexicographer. Detailed word histories. Inexhaustible. Do not confuse this with *Concise Etymological Dictionary,* which is abridged. Total of 856pp. 6½ x 9¼. 21873-2, 21874-0 Pa., Two-vol. set $10.00

"OSCAR" OF THE WALDORF'S COOKBOOK, Oscar Tschirky. Famous American chef reveals 3455 recipes that made Waldorf great; cream of French, German, American cooking, in all categories. Full instructions, easy home use. 1896 edition. 907pp. 6⅝ x 9⅜.   20790-0 Clothbd. $15.00

COOKING WITH BEER, Carole Fahy. Beer has as superb an effect on food as wine, and at fraction of cost. Over 250 recipes for appetizers, soups, main dishes, desserts, breads, etc. Index. 144pp. 5⅜ x 8½. (Available in U.S. only)   23661-7 Pa. $2.50

STEWS AND RAGOUTS, Kay Shaw Nelson. This international cookbook offers wide range of 108 recipes perfect for everyday, special occasions, meals-in-themselves, main dishes. Economical, nutritious, easy-to-prepare: goulash, Irish stew, boeuf bourguignon, etc. Index. 134pp. 5⅜ x 8½.
23662-5 Pa. $2.50

DELICIOUS MAIN COURSE DISHES, Marian Tracy. Main courses are the most important part of any meal. These 200 nutritious, economical recipes from around the world make every meal a delight. "I . . . have found it so useful in my own household,"—N.Y. Times. Index. 219pp. 5⅜ x 8½.   23664-1 Pa. $3.00

FIVE ACRES AND INDEPENDENCE, Maurice G. Kains. Great back-to-the-land classic explains basics of self-sufficient farming: economics, plants, crops, animals, orchards, soils, land selection, host of other necessary things. Do not confuse with skimpy faddist literature; Kains was one of America's greatest agriculturalists. 95 illustrations. 397pp. 5⅜ x 8½.
20974-1 Pa. $3.50

A PRACTICAL GUIDE FOR THE BEGINNING FARMER, Herbert Jacobs. Basic, extremely useful first book for anyone thinking about moving to the country and starting a farm. Simpler than Kains, with greater emphasis on country living in general. 246pp. 5⅜ x 8½.
23675-7 Pa. $3.50

HARDY BULBS, Louise Beebe Wilder. Fullest, most thorough book on plants grown from bulbs, corms, rhizomes and tubers. 40 genera and 335 species covered: selecting, cultivating, naturalizing; name, origins, blooming season, when to plant, special requirements. 127 illustrations. 432pp. 5⅜ x 8½.   23102-X Pa. $4.50

A GARDEN OF PLEASANT FLOWERS (PARADISI IN SOLE: PARADISUS TERRESTRIS), John Parkinson. Complete, unabridged reprint of first (1629) edition of earliest great English book on gardens and gardening. More than 1000 plants & flowers of Elizabethan, Jacobean garden fully described, most with woodcut illustrations. Botanically very reliable, a "speaking garden" of exceeding charm. 812 illustrations. 628pp. 8½ x 12¼.   23392-8 Clothbd. $25.00

HISTORY OF BACTERIOLOGY, William Bulloch. The only comprehensive history of bacteriology from the beginnings through the 19th century. Special emphasis is given to biography-Leeuwenhoek, etc. Brief accounts of 350 bacteriologists form a separate section. No clearer, fuller study, suitable to scientists and general readers, has yet been written. 52 illustrations. 448pp. 5⅝ x 8¼. 23761-3 Pa. $6.50

THE COMPLETE NONSENSE OF EDWARD LEAR, Edward Lear. All nonsense limericks, zany alphabets, Owl and Pussycat, songs, nonsense botany, etc., illustrated by Lear. Total of 321pp. 5⅜ x 8½. (Available in U.S. only) 20167-8 Pa. $3.00

INGENIOUS MATHEMATICAL PROBLEMS AND METHODS, Louis A. Graham. Sophisticated material from Graham Dial, applied and pure; stresses solution methods. Logic, number theory, networks, inversions, etc. 237pp. 5⅜ x 8½. 20545-2 Pa. $3.50

BEST MATHEMATICAL PUZZLES OF SAM LOYD, edited by Martin Gardner. Bizarre, original, whimsical puzzles by America's greatest puzzler. From fabulously rare Cyclopedia, including famous 14-15 puzzles, the Horse of a Different Color, 115 more. Elementary math. 150 illustrations. 167pp. 5⅜ x 8½. 20498-7 Pa. $2.50

THE BASIS OF COMBINATION IN CHESS, J. du Mont. Easy-to-follow, instructive book on elements of combination play, with chapters on each piece and every powerful combination team—two knights, bishop and knight, rook and bishop, etc. 250 diagrams. 218pp. 5⅜ x 8½. (Available in U.S. only) 23644-7 Pa. $3.50

MODERN CHESS STRATEGY, Ludek Pachman. The use of the queen, the active king, exchanges, pawn play, the center, weak squares, etc. Section on rook alone worth price of the book. Stress on the moderns. Often considered the most important book on strategy. 314pp. 5⅜ x 8½. 20290-9 Pa. $3.50

LASKER'S MANUAL OF CHESS, Dr. Emanuel Lasker. Great world champion offers very thorough coverage of all aspects of chess. Combinations, position play, openings, end game, aesthetics of chess, philosophy of struggle, much more. Filled with analyzed games. 390pp. 5⅜ x 8½. 20640-8 Pa. $4.00

500 MASTER GAMES OF CHESS, S. Tartakower, J. du Mont. Vast collection of great chess games from 1798-1938, with much material nowhere else readily available. Fully annotated, arranged by opening for easier study. 664pp. 5⅜ x 8½. 23208-5 Pa. $6.00

A GUIDE TO CHESS ENDINGS, Dr. Max Euwe, David Hooper. One of the finest modern works on chess endings. Thorough analysis of the most frequently encountered endings by former world champion. 331 examples, each with diagram. 248pp. 5⅜ x 8½. 23332-4 Pa. $3.50

CATALOGUE OF DOVER BOOKS

TONE POEMS, SERIES II: TILL EULENSPIEGELS LUSTIGE STREICHE, ALSO SPRACH ZARATHUSTRA, AND EIN HELDEN-LEBEN, Richard Strauss. Three important orchestral works, including very popular *Till Eulenspiegel's Marry Pranks,* reproduced in full score from original editions. Study score. 315pp. 9⅜ x 12¼. (Available in U.S. only)
23755-9 Pa. $7.50

TONE POEMS, SERIES I: DON JUAN, TOD UND VERKLARUNG AND DON QUIXOTE, Richard Strauss. Three of the most often performed and recorded works in entire orchestral repertoire, reproduced in full score from original editions. Study score. 286pp. 9⅜ x 12¼. (Available in U.S. only)
23754-0 Pa. $7.50

11 LATE STRING QUARTETS, Franz Joseph Haydn. The form which Haydn defined and "brought to perfection." *(Grove's).* 11 string quartets in complete score, his last and his best. The first in a projected series of the complete Haydn string quartets. Reliable modern Eulenberg edition, otherwise difficult to obtain. 320pp. 8⅜ x 11¼. (Available in U.S. only)
23753-2 Pa. $6.95

FOURTH, FIFTH AND SIXTH SYMPHONIES IN FULL SCORE, Peter Ilyitch Tchaikovsky. Complete orchestral scores of Symphony No. 4 in F Minor, Op. 36; Symphony No. 5 in E Minor, Op. 64; Symphony No. 6 in B Minor, "Pathetique," Op. 74. Bretikopf & Hartel eds. Study score. 480pp. 9⅜ x 12¼.
23861-X Pa. $10.95

THE MARRIAGE OF FIGARO: COMPLETE SCORE, Wolfgang A. Mozart. Finest comic opera ever written. Full score, not to be confused with piano renderings. Peters edition. Study score. 448pp. 9⅜ x 12¼. (Available in U.S. only)
23751-6 Pa. $11.95

"IMAGE" ON THE ART AND EVOLUTION OF THE FILM, edited by Marshall Deutelbaum. Pioneering book brings together for first time 38 groundbreaking articles on early silent films from *Image* and 263 illustrations newly shot from rare prints in the collection of the International Museum of Photography. A landmark work. Index. 256pp. 8¼ x 11.
23777-X Pa. $8.95

AROUND-THE-WORLD COOKY BOOK, Lois Lintner Sumption and Marguerite Lintner Ashbrook. 373 cooky and frosting recipes from 28 countries (America, Austria, China, Russia, Italy, etc.) include Viennese kisses, rice wafers, London strips, lady fingers, hony, sugar spice, maple cookies, etc. Clear instructions. All tested. 38 drawings. 182pp. 5⅜ x 8.
23802-4 Pa. $2.50

THE ART NOUVEAU STYLE, edited by Roberta Waddell. 579 rare photographs, not available elsewhere, of works in jewelry, metalwork, glass, ceramics, textiles, architecture and furniture by 175 artists—Mucha, Seguy, Lalique, Tiffany, Gaudin, Hohlwein, Saarinen, and many others. 288pp. 8⅜ x 11¼.
23515-7 Pa. $6.95

CATALOGUE OF DOVER BOOKS

THE COMPLETE BOOK OF DOLL MAKING AND COLLECTING, Catherine Christopher. Instructions, patterns for dozens of dolls, from rag doll on up to elaborate, historically accurate figures. Mould faces, sew clothing, make doll houses, etc. Also collecting information. Many illustrations. 288pp. 6 x 9. 22066-4 Pa. $4.00

THE DAGUERREOTYPE IN AMERICA, Beaumont Newhall. Wonderful portraits, 1850's townscapes, landscapes; full text plus 104 photographs. The basic book. Enlarged 1976 edition. 272pp. 8¼ x 11¼. 23322-7 Pa. $6.00

CRAFTSMAN HOMES, Gustav Stickley. 296 architectural drawings, floor plans, and photographs illustrate 40 different kinds of "Mission-style" homes from *The Craftsman* (1901-16), voice of American style of simplicity and organic harmony. Thorough coverage of Craftsman idea in text and picture, now collector's item. 224pp. 8⅛ x 11. 23791-5 Pa. $6.00

PEWTER-WORKING: INSTRUCTIONS AND PROJECTS, Burl N. Osborn. & Gordon O. Wilber. Introduction to pewter-working for amateur craftsman. History and characteristics of pewter; tools, materials, step-by-step instructions. Photos, line drawings, diagrams. Total of 160pp. 7⅞ x 10¾. 23786-9 Pa. $3.50

THE GREAT CHICAGO FIRE, edited by David Lowe. 10 dramatic, eyewitness accounts of the 1871 disaster, including one of the aftermath and rebuilding, plus 70 contemporary photographs and illustrations of the ruins—courthouse, Palmer House, Great Central Depot, etc. Introduction by David Lowe. 87pp. 8¼ x 11. 23771-0 Pa. $4.00

SILHOUETTES: A PICTORIAL ARCHIVE OF VARIED ILLUSTRATIONS, edited by Carol Belanger Grafton. Over 600 silhouettes from the 18th to 20th centuries include profiles and full figures of men and women, children, birds and animals, groups and scenes, nature, ships, an alphabet. Dozens of uses for commercial artists and craftspeople. 144pp. 8⅜ x 11¼. 23781-8 Pa. $4.00

ANIMALS: 1,419 COPYRIGHT-FREE ILLUSTRATIONS OF MAMMALS, BIRDS, FISH, INSECTS, ETC., edited by Jim Harter. Clear wood engravings present, in extremely lifelike poses, over 1,000 species of animals. One of the most extensive copyright-free pictorial sourcebooks of its kind. Captions. Index. 284pp. 9 x 12. 23766-4 Pa. $7.50

INDIAN DESIGNS FROM ANCIENT ECUADOR, Frederick W. Shaffer. 282 original designs by pre-Columbian Indians of Ecuador (500-1500 A.D.). Designs include people, mammals, birds, reptiles, fish, plants, heads, geometric designs. Use as is or alter for advertising, textiles, leathercraft, etc. Introduction. 95pp. 8¾ x 11¼. 23764-8 Pa. $3.50

SZIGETI ON THE VIOLIN, Joseph Szigeti. Genial, loosely structured tour by premier violinist, featuring a pleasant mixture of reminiscenes, insights into great music and musicians, innumerable tips for practicing violinists. 385 musical passages. 256pp. 5⅝ x 8¼. 23763-X Pa. $3.50

CATALOGUE OF DOVER BOOKS

THE PHILOSOPHY OF HISTORY, Georg W. Hegel. Great classic of Western thought develops concept that history is not chance but a rational process, the evolution of freedom. 457pp. 5⅜ x 8½. 20112-0 Pa. $4.50

LANGUAGE, TRUTH AND LOGIC, Alfred J. Ayer. Famous, clear introduction to Vienna, Cambridge schools of Logical Positivism. Role of philosophy, elimination of metaphysics, nature of analysis, etc. 160pp. 5⅜ x 8½. (Available in U.S. only) 20010-8 Pa. $1.75

A PREFACE TO LOGIC, Morris R. Cohen. Great City College teacher in renowned, easily followed exposition of formal logic, probability, values, logic and world order and similar topics; no previous background needed. 209pp. 5⅜ x 8½. 23517-3 Pa. $3.50

REASON AND NATURE, Morris R. Cohen. Brilliant analysis of reason and its multitudinous ramifications by charismatic teacher. Interdisciplinary, synthesizing work widely praised when it first appeared in 1931. Second (1953) edition. Indexes. 496pp. 5⅜ x 8½. 23633-1 Pa. $6.00

AN ESSAY CONCERNING HUMAN UNDERSTANDING, John Locke. The only complete edition of enormously important classic, with authoritative editorial material by A. C. Fraser. Total of 1176pp. 5⅜ x 8½. 20530-4, 20531-2 Pa., Two-vol. set $14.00

HANDBOOK OF MATHEMATICAL FUNCTIONS WITH FORMULAS, GRAPHS, AND MATHEMATICAL TABLES, edited by Milton Abramowitz and Irene A. Stegun. Vast compendium: 29 sets of tables, some to as high as 20 places. 1,046pp. 8 x 10½. 61272-4 Pa. $12.50

MATHEMATICS FOR THE PHYSICAL SCIENCES, Herbert S. Wilf. Highly acclaimed work offers clear presentations of vector spaces and matrices, orthogonal functions, roots of polynomial equations, conformal mapping, calculus of variations, etc. Knowledge of theory of functions of real and complex variables is assumed. Exercises and solutions. Index. 284pp. 5⅝ x 8¼. 63635-6 Pa. $4.50

THE PRINCIPLE OF RELATIVITY, Albert Einstein et al. Eleven most important original papers on special and general theories. Seven by Einstein, two by Lorentz, one each by Minkowski and Weyl. All translated, unabridged. 216pp. 5⅜ x 8½. 60081-5 Pa. $3.00

THERMODYNAMICS, Enrico Fermi. A classic of modern science. Clear, organized treatment of systems, first and second laws, entropy, thermodynamic potentials, gaseous reactions, dilute solutions, entropy constant. No math beyond calculus required. Problems. 160pp. 5⅜ x 8½. 60361-X Pa. $2.75

ELEMENTARY MECHANICS OF FLUIDS, Hunter Rouse. Classic undergraduate text widely considered to be far better than many later books. Ranges from fluid velocity and acceleration to role of compressibility in fluid motion. Numerous examples, questions, problems. 224 illustrations. 376pp. 5⅝ x 8¼. 63699-2 Pa. $5.00

CATALOGUE OF DOVER BOOKS

THE SENSE OF BEAUTY, George Santayana. Masterfully written discussion of nature of beauty, materials of beauty, form, expression; art, literature, social sciences all involved. 168pp. 5⅜ x 8½.   20238-0 Pa. $2.50

ON THE IMPROVEMENT OF THE UNDERSTANDING, Benedict Spinoza. Also contains *Ethics, Correspondence,* all in excellent R. Elwes translation. Basic works on entry to philosophy, pantheism, exchange of ideas with great contemporaries. 402pp. 5⅜ x 8½.   20250-X Pa. $3.75

THE TRAGIC SENSE OF LIFE, Miguel de Unamuno. Acknowledged masterpiece of existential literature, one of most important books of 20th century. Introduction by Madariaga. 367pp. 5⅜ x 8½.
20257-7 Pa. $3.50

THE GUIDE FOR THE PERPLEXED, Moses Maimonides. Great classic of medieval Judaism attempts to reconcile revealed religion (Pentateuch, commentaries) with Aristotelian philosophy. Important historically, still relevant in problems. Unabridged Friedlander translation. Total of 473pp. 5⅜ x 8½.   20351-4 Pa. $5.00

THE I CHING (THE BOOK OF CHANGES), translated by James Legge. Complete translation of basic text plus appendices by Confucius, and Chinese commentary of most penetrating divination manual ever prepared. Indispensable to study of early Oriental civilizations, to modern inquiring reader. 448pp. 5⅜ x 8½.   21062-6 Pa. $4.00

THE EGYPTIAN BOOK OF THE DEAD, E. A. Wallis Budge. Complete reproduction of Ani's papyrus, finest ever found. Full hieroglyphic text, interlinear transliteration, word for word translation, smooth translation. Basic work, for Egyptology, for modern study of psychic matters. Total of 533pp. 6½ x 9¼. (Available in U.S. only)   21866-X Pa. $4.95

THE GODS OF THE EGYPTIANS, E. A. Wallis Budge. Never excelled for richness, fullness: all gods, goddesses, demons, mythical figures of Ancient Egypt; their legends, rites, incarnations, variations, powers, etc. Many hieroglyphic texts cited. Over 225 illustrations, plus 6 color plates. Total of 988pp. 6⅛ x 9¼. (Available in U.S. only)
22055-9, 22056-7 Pa., Two-vol. set $12.00

THE ENGLISH AND SCOTTISH POPULAR BALLADS, Francis J. Child. Monumental, still unsuperseded; all known variants of Child ballads, commentary on origins, literary references, Continental parallels, other features. Added: papers by G. L. Kittredge, W. M. Hart. Total of 2761pp. 6½ x 9¼.
21409-5, 21410-9, 21411-7, 21412-5, 21413-3 Pa., Five-vol. set $37.50

CORAL GARDENS AND THEIR MAGIC, Bronsilaw Malinowski. Classic study of the methods of tilling the soil and of agricultural rites in the Trobriand Islands of Melanesia. Author is one of the most important figures in the field of modern social anthropology. 143 illustrations. Indexes. Total of 911pp. of text. 5⅝ x 8¼. (Available in U.S. only)
23597-1 Pa. $12.95

CATALOGUE OF DOVER BOOKS

THE STANDARD BOOK OF QUILT MAKING AND COLLECTING, Marguerite Ickis. Full information, full-sized patterns for making 46 traditional quilts, also 150 other patterns. Quilted cloths, lame, satin quilts, etc. 483 illustrations. 273pp. 6⅞ x 9⅝. 20582-7 Pa. $3.95

ENCYCLOPEDIA OF VICTORIAN NEEDLEWORK, S. Caulfield, Blanche Saward. Simply inexhaustible gigantic alphabetical coverage of every traditional needlecraft—stitches, materials, methods, tools, types of work; definitions, many projects to be made. 1200 illustrations; double-columned text. 697pp. 8⅛ x 11. 22800-2, 22801-0 Pa., Two-vol. set $12.00

MECHANICK EXERCISES ON THE WHOLE ART OF PRINTING, Joseph Moxon. First complete book (1683-4) ever written about typography, a compendium of everything known about printing at the latter part of 17th century. Reprint of 2nd (1962) Oxford Univ. Press edition. 74 illustrations. Total of 550pp. 6⅛ x 9¼. 23617-X Pa. $7.95

PAPERMAKING, Dard Hunter. Definitive book on the subject by the foremost authority in the field. Chapters dealing with every aspect of history of craft in every part of the world. Over 320 illustrations. 2nd, revised and enlarged (1947) edition. 672pp. 5⅜ x 8½. 23619-6 Pa. $7.95

THE ART DECO STYLE, edited by Theodore Menten. Furniture, jewelry, metalwork, ceramics, fabrics, lighting fixtures, interior decors, exteriors, graphics from pure French sources. Best sampling around. Over 400 photographs. 183pp. 8⅜ x 11¼. 22824-X Pa. $5.00

Prices subject to change without notice.

Available at your book dealer or write for free catalogue to Dept. GI, Dover Publications, Inc., 180 Varick St., N.Y., N.Y. 10014. Dover publishes more than 175 books each year on science, elementary and advanced mathematics, biology, music, art, literary history, social sciences and other areas.